SCANDAL

SCANDAL

THE CULTURE OF MISTRUST IN AMERICAN POLITICS

SUZANNE GARMENT

TIMES 𝕿 BOOKS

RANDOM HOUSE

Library of Congress Cataloging-in-Publication Data

Garment, Suzanne.
Scandal : the culture of mistrust in American politics / by Suzanne
Garment — 1st ed.
p.   cm.
Includes index.
ISBN 0-8129-1942-4
1. Corruption (in politics)—United States.   2. Political ethics—
United States.   I. Title
JK2249.G37   1991
320.973—dc20   91-50185

Manufactured in the United States of America
9   8   7   6   5   4   3   2

Book design by Guenet Abraham

For Len, Sara, Paul, and Annie

ACKNOWLEDGMENTS

This book is built in large part on the generosity of the hundreds of individuals who agreed to talk with me about political scandals in general and particular scandals in which they had been the pursuer, the pursued, or a ringside observer. For understandable reasons, some of these people chose to remain anonymous, but others appear by name in the text. I am grateful to them all.

While writing the book, I held the position of resident scholar at the American Enterprise Institute for Public Policy Research, where for two years I was also the DeWitt Wallace Fellow in Communications in a Free Society. I had a great advantage in my colleagues at AEI. They have among them an enormous range of knowledge about American politics and public policy, and they were unfailingly ready to share this wealth. AEI's librarian, Evelyn B. Caldwell, performed miracles of ingenuity in ferreting out background materials for me. My similarly resourceful research assistant, Elizabeth W. Fisher, stood steadfast guard against error and inconsistency. In the project's early stages I had valuable research assistance from Benjamin Frankel.

Robert L. Bartley, Susan Lee, Eugene J. McCarthy, Norman Podhoretz, and James Q. Wilson read various versions of the work in progress. It is far better for their comments and suggestions—as, given talents like these, it could hardly help being. My editors, Peter Osnos and Kenneth Gellman, not only made the manuscript into a book but did so with great skill and equally great fortitude in the face of authorial anxieties, demands, and quirks.

C O N T E N T S

INTRODUCTION
1

|

IN THE GREAT TRADITION
13

2

AN HONEST PRESIDENT
36

3

THE RESPONSIBLE MEDIA
57

4

THE ETHICS APPARAT: INDEPENDENT COUNSELS
83

5

THE ETHICS APPARAT: A CAST OF THOUSANDS
109

CONTENTS

6

PROSECUTORS ON THE HILL
142

7

SEX
169

8

THE SCANDAL OLYMPICS: IRAN-CONTRA
198

9

CONGRESS IN THE DOCK
223

10

PERSONAL EFFECTS
259

11

A CULTURE OF MISTRUST
285

NOTES
305

INDEX
317

SCANDAL

INTRODUCTION

"Nothing goes on paper." The political appointee was explaining how top managers in her federal agency make their official decisions. "Any comments we want to make to one another are made on yellow stick-on paper that later gets thrown away. And we have oral government: I've had to learn to absorb things by ear and rely on people who are good at giving oral briefings."

"It used to be," said E. Pendleton James, White House personnel director in the Reagan administration, "that if the president actually asked someone to come to Washington, the guy would agree. 'You don't say no to the president' was the saying. Well, they sure say no to the president now. I've sat in the Oval Office and watched them do it."

"Every taxpayer," writes Ellen Hume, former *Wall Street Journal* reporter, "deserves an answer to this question: Why did the well-paid, well-educated, and constitutionally protected press corps miss the savings and loan scandal, which is the most expensive public finance debacle in U.S. history?"[1]

Welcome to American politics after Watergate, in which survival counts as a victory, public servants are busily perfecting the
art of government by Post-it note, and a scandal-hunting press
corps somehow missed some of the biggest scandals of all.

These varied features of the modern political landscape have
a common source: They stem from the unprecedented numbers
of public scandals that have erupted in national politics over the
past 15 years.

Not that political scandal is a new phenomenon in America:
On the contrary, such scandal is one of the most pervasive elements of our history—or of any other country's, for that matter.
Scandal illuminates the weaknesses of the scandalizers and the
moral character of those who are scandalized, and it does so in
ways that more conventional politics never can. Beyond this
high-minded justification, scandal persists because it is, across
eras and nations, utterly irresistible. When we see the public
masks slip, we become like those laboratory rats who, when
taught to trip a switch stimulating pleasure centers in their
brains, keep doing it over and over, to the exclusion of food and
sleep. When there is scandal on the scene, it drives out the
human appetite for more mundane sorts of political news.

Still, our time is different from the decades preceding it. Political scandal has proliferated, and this proliferation reflects not
so much an increase in corruption at the federal level as it does
our growing capacity and taste for political scandal production.

The resulting culture of mistrust has made the always difficult
job of governing measurably harder. The climate of sensationalism has contributed to public cynicism and to the fact that
symbolic issues, like flag burning and public funding for offensive art, shoot more speedily than ever to the top of the public
agenda.[2]

Moreover, the habit of making large scandals out of what were
once thought of as garden-variety misdeeds has enabled us to
avoid looking into the mirror and attending to matters, like the
savings and loan problem, that spring less from individual
wrongdoing than from more widespread failures of political will.

The present scandal wave is unprecedented in size. It is hard
to make precise historical comparisons, but we have some
benchmarks.

One of them is the amount of money involved. In the Crédit Mobilier scandal of 1872, the public learned that stock of the railroad-building company of the same name had been given out to congressmen and other high officials to stave off a government investigation. The stakes consisted of some $23 million in corporate profits on railway projects paid for by the U.S. government. The corporation's illegitimate payments to congressmen were small, often only hundreds of dollars. The Teapot Dome scandal of 1922–23 grew out of $385,000 in bribes paid to Secretary of the Interior Albert B. Fall to win the lease of government oil reserves. For today's savings and loan scandal, which has revealed the squandering of federally insured deposits, the early estimates of a $150 billion cost to taxpayers now seem low. Indeed, one reputable estimate has now put the cost at $1 *trillion*.[3]

When we measure by the number of officials involved, the result is equally striking. In 1875, for instance, the American public first learned of the Whiskey Ring, a conspiracy to skim federal alcohol taxes. This scandal was the largest in the nation's history up to that date: The toll was 238 men indicted and 110 convicted. Here is another example: As a result of the huge Internal Revenue Service scandal of 1950–51, which exposed the bribery of income tax agents, 66 employees were fired and 9 went to jail. In both of these historic cases, the large numbers consisted mainly of low-level employees caught up in a single scandal net.

The number of officials involved in scandals since Watergate is much larger. A search of the record turns up more than 400 relatively senior federal officials and candidates for federal office who have been publicly accused in the national press of personal wrongdoing.[4] This number includes officials from many federal agencies spread across all branches of government.

These high figures reflect a federal government that has grown enormously since the time of the Whiskey Ring. Moreover, they accumulated over a number of years. On the other hand, the incidence of scandal has risen exponentially in recent years even though the number of federal employees has remained relatively stable over the same period of time. Also, the 400-odd officials involved in scandal over the past 15 years are all figures of substantial rank, spread throughout the government, rather than low-level employees caught up in the net of a single big scandal.

When it comes to senior appointees and politicians, past numbers have simply not been anywhere near as high as in our own day. During the 1980s, newspapers and magazines, aware of the extraordinary nature of today's numbers, began to publish long lists—sometimes with mug shots—of political figures deemed to be under an ethical cloud.

Charges of wrongdoing have filled the press, crowding other sorts of political issues off the national screen. Scandals have periodically commandeered the attention of the political community and have literally exhausted the time of the officials immediately involved in them. The imbroglios have left bad reputations and low morale in their wake and more generally undermined the legitimacy of individuals attempting to make national policy and run the government.

Our vivid scandals have also habituated us to a rich diet of symbolic politics. If issues like flag desecration and obscenity in the arts rise so readily to political prominence nowadays, it is partly because their moralistic message makes them well suited to compete with the moralistic appeal of political scandal stories. Conversely, issues that are not ready scandal fodder, like the savings and loan cancer metastasizing through most of the 1980s or the persistent problems of this country's underclass, attract little public concern or are denied prominent debate.

How did this scandal wave come about? According to political reformers—in the press, public interest advocacy groups, the Congress, and elsewhere—the answer is corruption. In their view, Watergate revealed an American political life filled with acts that are, or should be, crimes. The disease has persisted, in the reformers' analysis, and our numerous modern political scandals are a sign of it. It follows that if we reduce corruption, we will ultimately lower the number of our political scandals. We will thereby increase citizen trust in public officials and enable our government to work more efficiently and effectively.

Since the early 1970s and especially since Watergate this argument has exercised great influence over our public life, and government has enacted many new laws and regulations to deal with the problem of official corruption. We have new rules to limit campaign contributions, force more disclosure of campaign expenditures, regulate the jobs that ex-public officials may take and the government lobbying they may do, and make high government officials reveal more than ever about their personal finances.

Still other new laws and regulations have forced executive branch agencies to make many more of their internal records available to the public and press so that citizens can keep a more informed watch over government activity. Congress has also created many new investigators, largely independent of presidential control, to keep tabs on the ethics of federal officials.

During these same years, greatly expanded congressional staffs have stepped up their oversight of the executive branch. Executive agencies themselves have enlarged their internal investigative staffs. Federal prosecutors have become much more aggressive in the public corruption field, not only at the federal level but with state and local governments. Between the early 1970s and the late 1980s, federal prosecutions of public officials grew by a factor of 10.[5] Finally, the national press has become more active in publicizing official malfeasance.

Yet these efforts have had ironic results. Since Watergate, despite the growth in our anticorruption efforts, the number of our political scandals has continued to increase. The post-Watergate scandals did not simply proliferate while corruption was being exposed and then abate as politicians began complying with today's new, more rigorous standards. Instead, the scandals have continued at their high levels for more than 15 years, with the recent savings and loan debacle the biggest of all. In other words, the attack on corruption seems to have had few of the cleansing effects that such efforts are supposed to bring in their wake.

Some of those who pressed for the ethics reforms of the 1970s explain these perverse consequences by saying that the scandals remain numerous because our political life has grown even more corrupt since then. This time the critics accuse the Reagan administration of having brought low ethical standards to Washington and claim that the rising cost of political campaigning has made congressmen ever more indebted to the special interests. The deepening crisis of public corruption, in this view, is the root cause of our persisting political scandals and calls for a continuation or even an intensification of the campaign for more ethics in government.

But this crisis of public corruption almost surely does not exist.

There are crooks in the federal government, of course, and we will always need corruption fighters to ferret them out. Moreover, some kinds of corruption have grown along with the growth of government and the benefits it distributes. Some types of corruption in the Reagan era have been especially conspicuous. Yet on the whole, the federal government in recent years has been at least as clean as in the past and probably a good deal cleaner.

Certainly there is no plausible estimate of any actual rise in federal corruption since Watergate that matches the explosive increase in scandal during the same period. For one thing, the serious wrongdoing exposed by some modern scandals is simply not typical. As Stanley Sporkin, a legendary career civil servant who has been head of enforcement at the Securities and Exchange Commission and general counsel of the Central Intelligence Agency and is now a federal judge, said recently of the current rash of scandals, "I don't think it's reflective of what's going on." In general, he said of his experience, "I've been impressed with the honesty and integrity of government."

Moreover, we must judge today's politics in historical perspective. A good deal of our current scandal activity stems from heightened ethical sensitivities and a distaste for what were once accepted practices in American politics. For instance, today's political campaigns may not seem ethically attractive to the modern eye, but fund-raising methods now are far more honest than in the days when cash changed hands under the table and individuals did their buying of congressmen in secret. In the same way, when we look down the list of recent political scandals that have embroiled executive branch officials, we quickly see that many of them involved offenses that would never have become known at any other time in our political history or would not have been considered worthy of serious, sustained attention.

There is simply no persuasive evidence that the increase in scandal has taken place because of a corresponding rise in corrupt official behavior. Today's myriad scandals come in much larger part from the increased enthusiasm with which the political system now hunts evil in politics and the ever-growing efficiency with which our modern scandal production machine operates.

Today's intense focus on government corruption began with

the shock of Watergate, but the political passions that inspired the drive were in full flower years before. The energy of today's anticorruption efforts, in fact, owes less to Watergate than it does to the attitudes toward American government and society that emerged among the political elite during the early 1960s and appeared on the national scene in opposition to Lyndon Johnson's presidency and America's participation in the Vietnam war.

The spirit of that opposition, as we shall see, was no mere disagreement over policy or even ideology. Instead, as the war continued, the antagonism to it increasingly embodied the conviction that the people governing this country were fundamentally illegitimate in their claims to authority and criminal in their behavior. It followed that the job of driving out the menace posed by such officials could not be done through conventional American politics, because the old political system entailed too much ordinary electoral activity, endless negotiation, and vitiating compromise. Instead, a good number of the Vietnam-era activists trying to create a more virtuous government reached for political power through means that seemed less likely to violate their moral certainties. Such people formed new grass-roots organizations. Some of the activists organized street demonstrations. They made their appeals through the media. They changed the basic rules that governed the political parties themselves. They helped shape a political system very different from the one that flourished as late as the administration of President John F. Kennedy.

Since Kennedy's time, traditional political parties and economic interest groups have declined in power. The press and the courts have, correspondingly, grown in importance. So have new kinds of ideologically based interest groups, along with the political professionals who run them. Compromise and private agreement have declined as political strategies, while the use of publicity, litigation, and appeals to moral principle have risen. Forces like party loyalty and institutional authority, which used to protect conventional politicians from attack or unfriendly scrutiny, have weakened, while the means most easily used to challenge their authority—the component parts of the scandal production line—have grown stronger.[6] These changes have produced a new type of politician, more dependent on the media and less inclined to follow party or legislative leadership.[7] Finally, the spirit that gave rise to these changes also created a new scandal politics and a new breed of individuals who devote their careers to fighting corruption.

In some respects the corruption fighters of today, manning news desks, Hill offices, and investigating and prosecuting organizations, are very different from the antiwar protesters of the late sixties. The college-educated, politically progressive foot soldiers of today's activism are more likely to have gained their political experience with an environmental group or some Ralph Nader organization than in street demonstrations. These activists do not wear the garb of a distinctive, self-conscious counterculture but often spend their working hours in dress-for-success suits of the male or female variety, the better to gain general credibility. If these new activists had youthful experiences with recreational drugs, they do not trumpet the fact in general company. Fighting the established order has become a yuppie job.

Today's fighters for virtue are not given to talking about ideas like world peace or strategies such as capturing the government and using its huge discretionary power to improve the lot of the poor. They speak instead of the need to stand guard against government officials and political figures who are willing and eager to misuse such discretion for selfish ends. Instead of speaking, sixties-style, about reverence for individual rights, the new political avengers have sometimes been heard to talk like street cops safely out of earshot of the American Civil Liberties Union. In short, unlike their 1960s ancestors, who sometimes looked and talked like creatures from another planet, the corruption fighters of today are the very picture of the traditional, venerated American journalists, investigators, prosecutors, and public-spirited lawyers who have fought simply and doggedly for the past hundred years against crime, corruption, and fraud upon the public.

Yet despite the visible differences, the activists who form such a prominent part of today's anticorruption campaign harken back to the 1960s in fundamental attitudes. The unforgiving stance adopted by the new crusaders reflects not simply an aversion to crime but the same radical opposition to conventional authority, the same denial of its legitimacy, and the same sort of drive for political power that we saw in the streets of Chicago more than two decades ago. Moreover, today's ethics police practice scorched-earth warfare of a sort readily recognizable from Vietnam days. They are not content to throw the book at a political figure who becomes their target; instead, they spend great effort figuring out how to hit him or her with the whole library. They display impressive inventiveness in not simply catching criminals but trying to ensure that what is offensive or imprudent behavior today can be treated as scandalous or even criminal behavior tomorrow. They display the same awesome skill as the most radical antiwar activists did in ignoring the question of whether the pain they cause in individual cases is worth the good they do.

In this self-righteousness and lack of restraint, they recall the excesses of the most dangerous part of the antiwar generation rather than the temperament of most of their historical predecessors in the fight against corruption, whether in the press, in prosecutors' and investigators' offices, on the Hill, or in other bastions of the good-government effort. Indeed, the new breed works with an avariciousness that is the mirror image of the greed in the malefactors they pursue. The immoderation of some of the modern ethics enforcers threatens to give petty crime a good name.

People of this temperament have had a major impact on government because of the powerful positions they hold and the large weapons they have at their disposal, because today there are increased numbers of them on the national political scene, and because since Vietnam and Watergate the American political system has been more hospitable to their efforts and ready to help them along. Indeed, by now the enforcers have become part of a self-reinforcing scandal machine. Prosecutors use journalists to publicize criminal cases while journalists, through their news stories, put pressure on prosecutors for still more action. Investigators inside government agencies know how to advance their projects by collaborating with congressional committees, while committee staffers use the investigators to bypass agency heads and gather the material for splashy public hearings. All these players are aided immeasurably by the growing public focus on the politician as a celebrity, subject to the intense, probing attention that a celebrity commonly receives. Along the way, the hunt for bad deeds has become a business like any other, and large numbers of people have developed personal stakes in its continuing.

The new scandal politics has also spread via imitation and retaliation. The ethics laws passed after Watergate were mainly meant to empower Democrats in Congress and put Republican presidents on a short political leash. Yet it was not long before the increased vigor of federal enforcement efforts began to breathe down congressional necks as well, and the Republicans soon enough figured out how to use the Democrats' scandal techniques to get back at the Democrats themselves. The grenade came rolling back down the Hill, and another rich new vein of scandal was blown open.

Thus our present scandal politics has become not only self-reinforcing but virtually endless in its prospects. It exercises a power over government and the public agenda that is now out of proportion to the benefits it brings us. We can free ourselves of its worst effects only if we determine to keep it under control, and in order to form that determination we must first see the phenomenon for what it is.

This book begins its scrutiny of the topic in chapter 1 by taking a swift look at the history of American political scandal since the inception of the republic. Even such a brief examination shows us that in some ways American scandals have been strikingly similar to one another across the years. Yet in a few periods of our history, the politics of scandal have come to play a dominant role in public life. Our own era, largely because of the scars left by Vietnam and Watergate, has become one of those times.

Chapter 2 explains how modern scandal politics flowered in the years just after Watergate. The Carter administration, which came to office promising a higher ethical standard in politics, found itself crippled by scandals involving people close to the president. By the end of the Carter years, we had begun to see the efficient meshing of the elements of today's scandal system: a more aggressive press, tougher ethics laws, increasingly powerful congressional investigating committees, and a proliferation of prosecutors and other government sleuths.

The next four chapters, dealing mainly with the Reagan administration, look at each of these elements in more detail. There are discussions of the press, the new institution of the independent counsel, the growing aggressiveness of executive branch corruption fighters, and the congressional committees for whom scandal hunting has become an increasingly useful and common strategy. Throughout these chapters we also see the clashes of party, ideology, and culture that have played their own part in making the pursuers in this chase so avid and the quarry so bitterly resistant.

The executive branch was by no means the only part of the federal government to become enmeshed in scandal during the Reagan years. The number of scandals involving congressmen rose impressively in the years after Watergate, and two of the chapters are devoted to the great, everlasting factors—sex and money—at the base of almost all these episodes.

During the 1980s the legislative and executive branches each went through a climactic scandal—Iran-contra for the presidency and the savings and loan scandal for the legislature—that put on highly visible display the operations of the modern scandal system and its effect on the conduct of politics. Therefore the book includes separate discussions of these two major scandal upheavals.

Finally, today's scandals have devastating effects on the people involved in them. These consequences of political scandal do not usually receive much attention, so this book devotes a chapter to the topic.

The quoted material in these chapters was, unless otherwise labeled, taken from the author's interviews. The particular cases discussed in the book were chosen to illustrate the chapters' themes and arguments and to cast light on general features of the present era. These cases also had to meet several more specific requirements. They could not be greatly atypical or idiosyncratic. Where possible, they were to be recognizable episodes rather than obscure ones and were not to raise technical issues beyond the reach of general readers (or this writer). Finally, the cases had to be temporally appropriate, so that they not only illustrated the ideas in the book but also more or less followed the actual chronology of political scandal in the post-Watergate years.

This book, as it has turned out, names some 80 of the individuals who have been involved in modern political scandal. They are more or less evenly apportioned among Republicans and Democrats, executive branch officials and legislative personnel. These neat divisions required no special planning. They reflect, as the reader will soon see, the way that scandal politics has bounced from one end of Pennsylvania Avenue to the other in the years since Watergate.

My husband, attorney Leonard Garment, represented three of the individuals mentioned: Robert C. McFarlane, Edwin J. Gray, and Edwin Meese III—during Meese's 1984 confirmation hearings for the post of attorney general but not in the 1987 investigation of Meese's financial affairs. These are names not easily omitted from an account of recent political scandals. My views of these people and their scandals agree with my husband's opinions in some respects and differ in others. Perhaps more important, for better or worse I have been expressing such views, in both my unmarried and married states, for the past 20 years.

CHAPTER

IN THE GREAT TRADITION

WHEN IT COMES to political scandals, America has a great tradition, full of color and vivacity. On the whole, these scandals have not been great forces in our political history. But there are exceptions to this rule. The national political scandals of the 1850s, for example, delegitimated President James Buchanan, Congress, and existing political parties, and in this way probably contributed to the coming of the Civil War.[1] Even more dramatically, in the post–Civil War period, political scandals triggered a major political movement seeking broad change in American government and society. At that time, prominent social critics broadly condemned the American political system and its corruptions and helped generate the momentum that brought the reforms of the Progressive Era. When we look back on these periods, we find it surprisingly hard to determine how much of the scandal-filled atmosphere was due to corruption as we understand the term today, how much stemmed from corruption as our forebears defined it, and how much was caused by the fears, misperceptions, and personal interests of those who pointed to the scandals and called for dramatic political change. Our own time has become one of those shaped by political scandal, and it is already clear that future historians will find our behavior similarly ambiguous and confusing.

The first step in understanding the role that scandals have

played in our politics is to get the definitions straight. The word *scandal* has two main roots: a Latin word meaning "cause of offense or stumbling" and a Greek word meaning "trap" or "snare." Nowadays the major meaning of scandal, the *Oxford English Dictionary* tells us, is "damage to reputation" or "rumor or general comment injurious to reputation."

So scandal is not the same thing as evil or sin or corruption, though sometimes we use the word in those looser senses. Whether an act makes for scandal does not depend on the deed's intrinsic nature alone. It depends just as heavily on what happens when other people learn about the act and judge it against a set of shared values. The sin that shocks no one in its audience is like the tree that falls in the forest with no one to hear it: The tree makes no sound and the sin is no scandal. The relationship works in the opposite direction, too: An act that affronts the moral sensibilities or pretensions of its audience may cause a scandal even if it is in reality no sin.

If we want to learn about political corruption, we can do so by investigating crooked officials and the seamy acts they perpetrate. These officials create corruption on their own through their own bad deeds. By contrast, if we want to learn about political scandal we must look beyond the malefactors themselves, for their evil deeds alone do not constitute scandal. A scandal is created not only by the individual who scandalizes his community but, just as important, by the community that is scandalized when it learns what the miscreant has done. We find historical scandals that have played to tolerant audiences and scandals created by political communities with the collective temperament of Savonarola.

Because understanding a political scandal requires us to look at the political landscape surrounding the imbroglio, scandals open new windows onto the politics of the times and places in which they occur. When we look through these windows we are reminded that political morality and moral fashions can vary enormously from one country or era to another. Even countries whose sense of right and wrong is more or less like ours can have jarringly different notions of what constitutes politically scandalous behavior. Those who lived through Watergate need no further demonstration of this fact. As the event unfolded, commentators in Britain and France, our fellow heirs to the Judeo-Christian moral tradition of the West, repeatedly scratched their heads and concluded that our massive agitation over wiretaps and break-ins was just another fascinating tribal ritual in the primitive and endlessly strange politics of the New World. But, then, the French allowed François Mitterand to survive in politics even after they heard that in the mid-1960s he had actually staged an assassination attempt on himself, arranging for two gunmen to shoot at him as he sat at a sidewalk café in Paris.

Looking at American political scandals over time also reveals pronounced variations. Within the past 25 years, for instance, we have undergone a revolution—some would call it a counter-revolution—on the issue of whether a politician's private life is public property. *The Miami Herald* staked out the living quarters of presidential candidate Gary Hart in 1987 in hopes of finding evidence of sexual peccadilloes; journalists did not do the same for candidate John F. Kennedy in 1960. In the fall of 1989 the ethics committee of the House of Representatives was considering four separate cases of alleged sexual misconduct by congressmen, involving sexual harassment, prostitution, and sex with a minor. In Kennedy's time such a committee did not even exist.

Comparisons bridging a century and more reveal still broader differences in community mores. Over the years, for example, we have progressively tightened the limits on the outside income a congressman can earn. Today a congressman-lawyer is not allowed to make any money from practicing law. If some enterprising journalist finds the congressman operating a law business on the side, the journalist will report the fact and the story will cause a scandal. Yet a hundred years ago, a typical congressman simply would not believe that the only way for him to be an ethically responsible legislator was to give up all the money he made from the law; if you tried to tell him so, he would think you as daft as if you had told him that in order to be a good representative of the people he had to take a vow of celibacy.

Such differences across the years give us fascinating glimpses of the political culture of long ago. Yet they do not arrange themselves into a proper history of American political scandals, for these scandals have no real history of their own. They are not connected to one another in a coherent way over time, in either their nature or their consequences.

Some of them, for instance, have affected the politics of their times in very concrete ways. The Buchanan-era scandals helped "Honest Abe" Lincoln gain the presidency in 1860. During Harry Truman's administration, the bribery and coverup scandal that struck the Internal Revenue Service most probably helped elect Dwight D. Eisenhower president in 1952. The Chappaquiddick scandal of 1969 foreclosed the presidency from Senator Edward M. Kennedy.

Yet for every political figure brought low by scandal we can unearth one who survived it. The Republican representative James A. Garfield was one of those caught holding Crédit Mobilier stock in the 1872 scandal, but he went on to become the country's president less than a decade later. In the presidential campaign of 1884, voters learned that candidate Grover Cleveland had fathered an illegitimate son. They elected him anyway, preferring his private vices to the shiftiness that his opponent James G. Blaine had displayed in public affairs.

In 1921, scandal engulfed then-Assistant Secretary of the Navy Franklin D. Roosevelt. That year, a Senate subcommittee report revealed that in order to expose a ring of suspected homosexuals at the naval training station in Newport, Rhode Island, an investigative unit under Roosevelt's direction had sent out young enlisted men to gather evidence by engaging in homosexual acts with the suspects. A naval court, disturbed by the matter, had made an inquiry. Roosevelt, according to the congressional report, had compounded his sins by lying to the court in order to cover up his involvement. The incident cast a dark cloud on his career, but Roosevelt was president little more than 10 years later.[2]

If scandals are uncertain in their consequences, they are also hard to mine for their lode of information about the political times in which they occurred. Though they always reflect their times in some way, it can be a tricky job to figure out how. Did the many scandals in the administration of President Ulysses S. Grant, for instance, show that something in Grant's character encouraged his political associates to lie and steal? Or did some of these scandals occur only because Grant was willing to have such abuses exposed? In 1929, to take another such puzzle, ex-cabinet secretary Albert Fall was convicted of accepting the bribe that lay behind the Teapot Dome scandal. In 1931 he became the first former cabinet official to be sent to prison. Did the conviction and sentence come about because Fall's sin was egregious even by the loose standards that governed public morality during the 1920s? Or did the great stock market crash, and the Depression during which his appeal was considered, harden the country's attitude toward his type of offense?[3]

Thus a political scandal is a fragment of its historical period, like a finding at an ancient archaeological dig; the explorer must piece it together with other evidence in order to decipher an era's message.

If the variations in our political scandals are sometimes hard to interpret, their continuing themes are easier to recognize. A number of elements in our political scandals occur so often that we can fairly think of them as universal, or at least as parts of something like a national character. These recurring human personality types and their flaws, often the most vivid parts of political scandals, are as well known to us today as to their original audiences. By pointing to these foibles, scandal stories make our ancestors familiar to us and strengthen our connection to our past. This is why people who love American politics are so often to be found telling tales of political scandal.

In the recounting of these stories, the villains, like Milton's Satan, are often more strikingly and engagingly drawn than the hero who puts a halt to their evil practices. In the absence of unusually vicious crimes, we can easily come away from these stories liking the sinners at least as well as we do the righteous men and women who routed them out and administered punishment. Thus scandal stories not only tie us to our political past but allow us to embrace the upright and the fallen alike.

Take sex, for instance. In this area our scandal tradition is as old as the republic. Indeed, one of the Founding Fathers, Alexander Hamilton, was almost ruined by a sex scandal. In 1791 the new federal government was housed in Philadelphia. Treasury Secretary Hamilton spent extended periods of time there, leaving his family behind in New York. Hamilton began an affair in Philadelphia with a woman named Maria Reynolds, who turned out—along with her husband, James—to be a blackmailer. For two years Hamilton paid them money to keep the relationship quiet.

When Hamilton finally tried to break with the fun couple, Reynolds retaliated like a serious man. He sent a confederate to spill the story to members of the Democratic-Republican party, rivals of Hamilton's Federalists. In 1792 three Republican congressmen paid a surprise visit to Hamilton and confronted him with their information. Defending himself, Hamilton argued to them that he had never abused his public office in the course of his affair with Mrs. Reynolds. The congressmen believed him and decided not to make a public scandal out of his predicament.

The self-restraint was only temporary. Four years after the confrontation, one of the congressmen leaked the story to a Republican pamphleteer, who promptly published it. Hamilton was forced to counter this move by publishing his own version of the affair. His pamphlet became a best-seller, and his career stayed afloat.

A few elements of Hamilton's story will seem strange to the modern reader, especially the part about the congressmen's keeping the tale secret for four years. Yet there is a familiarity and even a timelessness to the other elements of it—the passion, the blackmail, the disappointed office seeker, the leaks to the press, the use of scandal as a tool of party warfare, and the politics of confession. The Hamilton scandal remains intelligible to us despite the centuries that separate us from it.

From this early seedling came a strain of sex scandal that has been sporadic in occurrence but unquestionably robust. When Thomas Jefferson was president, an opposition journalist revealed that the Virginian had seduced two married women, one of them the wife of a close friend. In both the 1824 and 1828 presidential campaigns, opponents of Andrew Jackson circulated the information that the first two years of his marriage had in fact been years of adultery because his wife, Rachel, had not yet been divorced by her first husband. Rachel, who had a heart condition, fell into a depression over the charge and died before Jackson took office in 1829. Jackson was convinced that her accusers had killed her. After his inauguration, part of official Washington began giving similarly cold treatment to Peggy Eaton, wife of one of Jackson's cabinet members, who was said to have enjoyed a wild youth as an innkeeper's daughter. Jackson, enraged at the behavior, dissolved his entire Cabinet in order to purge the offenders.

And if we really want robust, we can hark back to the case of

Rep. Daniel Sickles, a Democratic New York congressman of violent temper who arrived in Washington in 1857. He became friends with Captain Phillip Barton Key, U.S. attorney for the District of Columbia and son of the author of "The Star Spangled Banner," and helped Key get reappointed as U.S. attorney. Key reciprocated by starting an affair with Sickles' wife, Teresa. Key would signal to her by walking past the Sickles home on Lafayette Square, opposite the White House, and waving a white handkerchief. In 1859 Sickles found out about the affair and forced his wife to sign a lurid confession. The next day, when Key appeared at Teresa's window and waved the customary handkerchief, Sickles emerged from the house and shot the unarmed man dead.

In the scandal that followed, Teresa's confession made its way to the front pages of the newspapers, which published story after story full of speculation about the details of the case. "It is reported," said one article, "that Mrs. Sickles is *enceinte*, and has made an affidavit that she became so in consequence of her intercourse with Key."[4] "It is insinuated," reported another, "that Mr. Sickles knew of the too great intimacy between his wife and Mr. Key some months ago, and that only when he found it must become generally known did he determine to take Key's life."[5]

When Sickles went to trial later that year, his lawyers argued that their client was innocent because he had been driven insane by Teresa's monstrous betrayal. This early use of the temporary insanity defense worked, and Sickles was acquitted. Stanton, like any proper trial lawer, did a jig in the courtroom upon hearing the verdict. "Of course I intended to kill him," Sickles said of Key when talking with friends after the acquittal. "He deserved it."[6]

Seen through the window of scandal, Sickles' America is in some ways strange to us, especially in its open tolerance of violent behavior by respectable men. In other ways, though, Sickles' world makes us feel right at home. During the scandal, newspapers happily probed the most intimate corners of the congressman's life with a prurience that makes today's press look prudish. The papers were chock full of quotes from anonymous sources, typically using the phrase "it is reported" instead of today's "sources said," and Sickles clearly used leaks to manipulate this appetite. The modern press, Sickles' case makes clear, did not invent sensationalism.

We cannot expect the good luck of having every one of our sex scandals culminate in the mesmerizing drama of a murder trial. Yet later sex-related political scandals have not done badly in measuring up to the Hamilton-Sickles standard. When it comes to sex among politicians, the last years of the 19th century and the first years of this one were a veritable tabloid heaven. In 1883 former senator William Sharon (R-Nev.) was sued by a woman who claimed he had "married" her without benefit of official ceremony. For years the case raged in the courts, culminating in the brief arrest of Supreme Court Justice Stephen J. Field in connection with the murder of the woman's lawyer. In 1884 came the election of President Grover Cleveland, illegitimate child notwithstanding. Beginning in 1885, one of Florida's Senate seats stood empty for over a year because its occupant was in Michigan, in hot and obsessive pursuit of a lady love. In 1890 former Democratic representative William Taulbee of Kentucky was killed in an act of self-defense by a reporter who had exposed the congressman's affair with a secretary and thus ruined the ex-legislator's career and personal life.

In a more portentous sign of the times, the mistress of an eminent Kentucky Democrat, Rep. William Breckenridge, successfully sued him in 1893 for breach of promise. When he ran for reelection he was dogged by crowds of women protesting his immorality. The protesters were led by an emerging leader named Susan B. Anthony. Because of the controversy, Breckenridge was narrowly beaten in the primaries.

Our own era is a worthy successor to the Gay Nineties. After a period of reticence in the mid-20th century, sex has once more emerged as a prime political topic. The country has been entertained by the doings of some classic couples: stripper Fanne Foxe and her boyfriend Rep. Wilbur Mills, nontypist Elizabeth Ray and Rep. Wayne Hays, lobbyist Paula Parkinson and Rep. Tom Evans, and pharmaceutical saleswoman Donna Rice and presidential candidate Gary Hart. Certain women in our modern sex scandals hark directly back to the hopelessly appealing Peggy Eaton. We can recognize others, the complainants in our modern sexual harassment cases, as the descendants of those mad-as-hell, not-going-to-take-it-anymore women who

stormed the courts a hundred years ago and unleashed the nuclear weapon of publicity on the politicians who they thought
had abused them.

When it comes to financial scandal in our political history, we
can also identify some recurring types. The figure of the con-
niving, embezzling, exuberantly crooked politician is one of the
staples of the American scandal tradition. Somehow the administration or party with which he is associated usually manages to
survive him. If, for example, we reach down into the river of
American financial scandal at the point where it passes the rock
marked "Jacksonian Era," we encounter the classic figure of
Wiley P. Harris, receiver in the federal land office at Columbus,
Mississippi, whose behavior caused a scandal when it was discovered in 1836 that he had left office with his accounts short by
a nice, precise $109,178.08. The Jackson administration re-
placed Harris with his friend Colonel Gordon D. Boyd, who
proceeded to filch some $55,000 of the same funds in just his
first six months on the job. Lest this story make Jackson's administration seem indifferent to thievery, it should be noted that
a federal land examiner did conduct an investigation of Boyd's
discomfiting shortfall. Yet the examiner recommended that Boyd
be continued in office since, in the watchdog's resigned opinion,
"Another receiver would probably follow in the footsteps of the
two."[7]

This breed of thief has survived in a nearly unbroken line to
our own times. For instance, even across a gap of 126 years
Messrs. Harris and Boyd would recognize and salute Billy Sol
Estes. The Estes financial scandal of 1962 had it all: greed,
cunning, expansive style, complicated plots, overreaching, a
swift denouement, and limited political consequences.

In the year the scandal broke, Estes was a 37-year-old pro-
moter from Pecos, Texas, who had been named one of the country's 10 outstanding young men by the U.S. Junior Chamber of
Commerce. Estes used adept financing techniques to profit from
enterprises as diverse as cotton farming, surplus housing developments, and farm-building construction. He was, we would say
today, a master of synergy.

In one attempt to get fresh capital, Estes the alchemist tried to
turn fertilizer into cash. He started selling his Pecos neighbors
storage tanks for liquid fertilizer that he was already supplying to

them. To finance the purchases, they took out mortgages from an Estes-connected finance company. Estes then leased the tanks back from his neighbors at exactly the same monthly rate as the farmers' monthly payments on their mortgages. Next, Estes' friends at the mortgage firm sold the mortgages to finance companies at discounted prices, and the money from these sales became capital for Estes. The cooperating farmers, in return for their neighborliness, got a rake-off of 10 percent of the face value of the mortgages.

Get it?

Many of the new fertilizer tanks never actually got built. Eventually the editor of a Pecos newspaper, scrambling for stories, discovered from official records that his community boasted more fertilizer tank mortgages than it did fertilizer tanks. The paper announced its findings in January 1962, and Estes' web began to unravel. The financier was soon indicted on fraud charges, and after conviction he served time in federal prison.

The Estes case became a national political scandal because the programs he had exploited were federal subsidy programs, and Estes had engaged in a good deal of influence peddling at the Department of Agriculture. Indeed, at the time the scandal broke, the department already knew it had an Estes problem, and more than one investigative unit was on his trail. Yet even while the internal investigations were going on, the highest levels of the department treated Estes with particular respect and continued to do so until the scandal became big news. On one occasion, after Estes had been fined for shady manipulation of the department's cotton allotment subsidy program, Secretary of Agriculture Orville Freeman nevertheless renamed him to the National Cotton Advisory Committee. When Estes' dealings became public, he claimed that he had enjoyed his political pull because he was a big contributor to the Democratic party—often in cash. He said he had made large cash contributions to Texas Democratic senator Ralph W. Yarborough, for instance, and to Vice President Lyndon Johnson.

Congressional Republicans charged that Agriculture's favoritism toward Estes was massive and systematic. They demanded a thorough public investigation and Freeman's resignation. But at a May 1962 press conference President John F. Kennedy responded to the rising demands by pointing to Freeman's record as a war hero and saying unequivocally, "I have the greatest confidence in the integrity of Secretary Freeman."[8] Observers at the time said that Kennedy's strong defense of Freeman discouraged the scandalmongers from pursuing the secretary much further; this was one of the last occasions on which a president could use the "greatest confidence" gambit without his listeners beginning to snicker in anticipation of the firing that was sure to follow.

The investigations that followed in the Estes affair were another disappointment to anyone who had hoped the scandal would bag some political higher-ups, for the public never got to hear about those cash contributions Estes said he had made to Democratic politicians. Two congressmen especially close to Estes lost reelection bids, but the sanctions against executive branch officials stopped with four lower-level figures who resigned or were fired for taking gifts from Estes or hiding their relationships with him. The political dustup surrounding Estes had ended like a good, traditional scandal: shocking, entertaining, and only temporarily disruptive.

The other symbol of financial malfeasance in the early sixties was the Bobby Baker scandal, which at first seemed to pose a greater threat than Estes' to high-level politicians but ended by following the same pattern. Baker first went to the Senate as a page during World War II at the age of 14 and stayed to work his way up. He became close to then-senator Lyndon Johnson, and when Johnson became Senate majority leader in 1955, he made Baker secretary to the Senate majority. In 1961 Johnson left the Senate upon becoming vice president, but Baker kept his post as Senate secretary. He also grew close to the wealthy Senator Robert S. Kerr (D-Okla.).

Baker knew an immense amount about how the Senate worked and was a prime source for journalists in the capital. He also had a great deal of power, and he used it to build himself a tidy nest egg. Baker accumulated financial interests in real estate, an insurance agency, a credit bureau, a mortgage firm, motels, a travel agency, a cemetery, and more. He was undone, like similar hustlers before him, when he reached too far for the extra dollar. Baker used his influence to get a government contract for a man named Ralph Hill that allowed Hill to install vending machines at a defense plant. But not long after this act of generosity, Baker started trying to buy Hill's company. When Hill refused, Baker vengefully attempted to get the contract taken away from him. Hill filed suit against Baker in September 1963, the story became public, and the scandal hunt began.

It was impossible to deny that the Baker scandal reflected on the Senate as an institution, and the Senate rules committee had to organize hearings. Insiders whispered knowingly that the vice president, because of his close connection with Baker, was going to be dropped from the 1964 Democratic ticket. But the Senate's Democratic majority managed to slow the proceedings, and by the time hearings finally started in 1964, Johnson was president.

The Baker hearings were run along strict partisan lines. Witnesses provided tantalizing leads, linking Baker to congressmen and Democratic party officials and citing illegal campaign contributions from various corporations, including International Telephone and Telegraph. A flamboyant Maryland insurance agent charged that Johnson aide Walter Jenkins, in a kickback scheme, had pressed him to buy advertising at a Johnson-owned radio and TV station in return for Johnson's buying an insurance policy from him. But, judged committee chairman Everett Jordan (D-N.C.), "We're not investigating senators."[9]

The hearings were declared finished, but the Republicans dug up new leads and forced a reopening of the Baker matter. Committee member John J. Williams (R-Del.), the Republicans' designated scourge in the Baker case, offered a resolution that would have permitted the committee to investigate senators and questionable campaign contributions and would have allowed the committee minority to call witnesses. The Democratic majority killed the motion in the full Senate, noted one reporter, "following one of the angriest exchanges in its history," which is quite a tribute.[10]

In 1966 the government charged Baker with stealing almost $100,000 in cash that savings and loan executives had given him to help with Democratic party campaign expenses. Baker claimed he had given the money to Kerr in return for Kerr's dropping a tax amendment that the S&Ls opposed. But Kerr had died in 1963, so that Baker, in defending himself, was pointing his finger at a dead man. Baker was tried and convicted, and he served some 18 months in prison.

The Baker affair, like the Estes controversy before it, revealed a scandal politics much more limited than ours is today. The Baker scandal was filled with ugliness but exposed no major political figures. It put on display the awesome ingenuity of American entrepreneurial energy gone awry and produced frenetic activity in Washington while it was at its height, but it then subsided. There is little reason to think that President Johnson was able to "fix" the Baker case, as has been rumored; but if a scandal like Bobby Baker's were to occur today, it would snowball straight down Pennsylvania Avenue to the White House. Senators would almost certainly not stand together as a party and hold the line on further investigation. If today's media watchdogs were thrown bits of information about a sitting president like those spewed forth in the Baker case, the journalists would trample one another in a full-scale, round-the-clock, 40-camera rush for the presidential scalp.

Despite the Baker scandal's limits, its outbreak created a new institution: a Senate ethics committee, formally named the Senate Select Committee on Standards and Conduct, which in later years would find itself very busy.

Our scandals have not always been so contained. After the Civil War, for instance, American politics grew heavy not only with scandals but also with political and social critics who claimed that the country's political corruption threatened American democracy itself. The whole society, in this view, was suffused with a new sort of greed, personified by robber barons like Cornelius Vanderbilt and John D. Rockefeller, who were then building their industrial and financial empires. A similar greed was said to have infected Washington: Some critics, in fact, called this era the Great Barbecue because of the avariciousness with which individuals feasted on government largesse. The Crédit Mobilier and Whiskey Ring scandals became symbols of the way private wealth was misusing public power, and the latter affair ultimately implicated even President Grant's personal secretary.

Social critics such as Mark Twain and Henry Adams produced scathing indictments of the era and its ethos. In 1873 Mark Twain christened the period, probably for all time, the Gilded Age. The themes introduced by such observers persisted through the turn of the century in the work of journalists who became known as "muckrakers." These writers named the names of public officials, from city halls to the U.S. Senate, who had allegedly been bought by wealthy private interests.

The critics had great success in fueling the political reform movements of their day. Yet the views of the post–Civil War anticorruption advocates have been somewhat battered by the judgment of history. Historians and political scientists who look back at that era have increasingly argued that the critics did not understand the politics or the society around them.

As an example, historian Margaret Susan Thomas, in her book *The Spider Web*, a study of congressional lobbying during the Grant administration, writes that though some scandals of this period were "scandalous by any standard,"[11] the politics of the post–Civil War years did not consist mainly of men standing around waiting their turn to feed from the public trough. During these years the country was being transformed. It was becoming industrialized, urbanized, and settled in the West. The federal government's work load was expanding by orders of magnitude. Congress and the executive branch complained of being overwhelmed, as they were. Increased numbers of lobbyists appeared in Washington to break the logjams and get their clients' business with the government done.

Some of what these lobbyists did was corrupt. Much of it was not. But critics on the scene, struck by the novelty of so many lobbyists hovering around the national government, did not distinguish between the deeds that were crooked and those—such as writing letters, making introductions, presenting cases—that are odious only to those who hate politics itself. The critics made scandals out of legitimate politics and painted their political culture as worse than it really was.

Thomas' position is not idiosyncratic. In a history of Tammany Hall boss William Marcy Tweed and his Tweed Ring, which in its heyday stole huge amounts of money from the city of New York, Alexander B. Callow, Jr., lays out the grisly details of the ring's corrupt activities.[12] Yet Callow also shows the necessary and legitimate function that Tweed's organization performed as it transferred political power in New York City from the old governing elites to the more numerous masses, including new immigrants. Many of the reformers, it is clear, hated the immigrants at least as much as they hated corruption, and the drive against corruption was a tool with which to keep the newcomers from taking control of the city. When a reader of this book compares Tweed's type of greed with the reformers' passion to keep New York under their authority, it is not easy to say which side is the more ethically distasteful.

In a final example, if there is one man who symbolizes the scandalous nature of politics a hundred years ago it is the financier Jay Gould. He was described in his time as the man who tried to corner the gold market, took control of the railroads for the sole purpose of stripping them of assets, and put legislatures in his pocket. This judgment of Gould has come down to us today. Yet Maury Klein, author of a meticulous modern biography of Gould, says that much of what we know about the man is not so. Gould's business ethics were "probably no worse and in some respects better than those of most men" of his time.[13] He did not loot the railroads without creating value: On the contrary, he built them, extended their reach, and added to their worth. He saw the potential of telegraph transmission tied to railway operations, helped shape the modern telecommunications industry, and made undeniable and fundamental contributions to the country's economic development.

So why the near-universal assumption that Gould was merely a speculator and a scoundrel? Klein explains with massive documentation how historians who have written about Gould got their information from the same few demonstrably inaccurate and often self-interested pieces of Gould-era journalism. The historians then handed these errors, uncorrected, down to us.

After seeing this new picture of Gould, we can still disapprove of things he did, but we can no longer view him as the living scandal he became in his own time. Simple outrage or moral shock is clearly inappropriate to the complexity of his character and career. And when complexity enters the picture, the moral jolt necessary to a good scandal quickly dies away.

These historical second thoughts come from modern observers on both the right and the left of the political spectrum. Even those historians who harbor the least affection for men like Jay Gould see his actions, and those of other such entrepreneurs, as results of the great, complicated economic and structural forces driving the development of post–Civil War America rather than as failures of personal morality.[14]

It is possible, then, for a generation of critics to become so heated and expansive in defining corruption and deciding what constitutes scandalous behavior that their posture eventually loses force and becomes suspect itself. Future generations will question it and see self-interested motives in the people who embraced it. Our own era, filled with scandal and sweeping indictments, is beginning to look like a candidate for the same type of fate.

If we want to find the roots of our numerous present scandals and the generalized fear of corruption that underlies them, we must start in the early 1960s, when Billy Sol Estes flourished and fell. That decade began with almost unprecedented political optimism and turned into a nightmare of violence and bitterness. By now there are many versions of how the descent occurred, but for our purposes we should first remember how full of possibility the country seemed at the beginning of the sixties for people who considered themselves sensitive to issues of justice and compassion in politics.[15] Voluntary organizations devoted to peace and social change were gaining membership. The civil rights movement, already at work by the start of the decade, was beginning to attract mass support for the heroic struggle. On February 1, 1960, four black freshmen from North Carolina's Agricultural and Technical College were refused service at a Woolworth's lunch counter in Greensboro; within weeks 50,000 people throughout the South had joined picket lines and sit-ins in their behalf.

Three months later, in May 1960, the House Un-American Activities Committee traveled to San Francisco to hold hearings, and protesters met HUAC's arrival with mass demonstrations. In 1962 the anthem "If I Had a Hammer," first sung at meetings of left-wing and Communist-linked organizations, moved out of its marginal status and up to the top of the pop charts. Newly elected president John F. Kennedy had relatively conservative politics, yet his youthful look and charismatic presence helped give liberal activists a sense that they were buoyed by the forces of history.

Looking back on those years, we can now see that the seeds of political disillusionment were present early on. Journalism, especially television journalism, was developing in ways that would soon make it impossible for American political leaders to command admiration or exercise leadership as they had done in earlier eras. At the 1960 anti-HUAC demonstrations in San Francisco, local police gave some of the protesters their first taste of fire hoses and billy clubs. As the civil rights struggle moved on from its easy targets to more dangerous areas of the South, activists began to meet with greater hostility. In June 1964, three civil rights workers were murdered with particular brutality in Mississippi. The federal government seemed unwilling or unable to stop the violence.

During these years, restiveness increased on other fronts as well. In 1962 Rachel Carson published her book *Silent Spring*,[16] a plea for environmental awareness. Carson did not simply say that the country had specific environmental problems to clean up. Instead she argued that profound, fundamental flaws in our modern system of production led to practices, like our use of pesticides on farm crops, that threatened the essential balance of nature and would end by destroying human life. Carson's book became the founding document of the environmental movement as we know it today.

The next year a lawyer and free-lance journalist named Ralph Nader went to Washington and became a consultant on highway safety to then-Assistant Secretary of Labor Daniel P. Moynihan. In 1965 Nader published *Unsafe at Any Speed*,[17] a radical critique of U.S. automobiles and their lack of safety features. Nader focused on the Chevrolet Corvair, made by the giant General Motors. The Corvair, said Nader, was not only dangerous but dangerous in ways that GM was able to prevent. When GM hired a detective to follow Nader around and dig for dirt in his life, the plot was discovered and Nader's view of the corporation seemed confirmed. Nader's book was not merely a treatise on auto safety but an attack on the motives of corporate America, portrayed by Nader as guilty of criminal negligence. Nader's arguments and rise to prominence, like Carson's, showed a new political militancy and adversarial spirit at work.

Carson's book appeared before Kennedy's assassination in 1963, while Nader's work came afterward. There is little doubt, though, that the assassination played a large role in arranging the discontents of those years into a pattern of systematic suspicion about established institutions.

In general we should be skeptical of speculations about the effects of a blow like the assassination on an entire nation, but the case of Kennedy's death requires no great theoretical leaps. People who admired Kennedy, both those who were already active in politics by 1963 and those who became so later, readily speak of the sense of shock and loss that the murder in Dallas produced. The assassination seemed a vast betrayal. Here was Kennedy, embodiment of the best impulses of the popular will, killed by a gunman whose desires came to outweigh all the votes of the democracy. It is no accident that the possibility of a wider plot to murder Kennedy has mesmerized conspiracy theorists, who refuse to believe the Warren Commission's official findings on the assassination. Like all good conspiracy buffs, they suspect a coverup, and their attitude is shared by millions. In 1991, almost 30 years after the assassination, a major Hollywood producer was busily at work on a big movie based on an alleged coverup of the alleged fact that Lee Harvey Oswald had not acted alone.

Neither is it a surprise that by the mid-1960s we began to hear political activists expressing the same mistrustful attitude toward American political life in general. Political decisions, in this view, were being made in secret. Power was being maintained by hidden means. Government could no longer be counted on to champion moral values or protect the people. This mistrust was no passive attitude. It was accompanied by an energy that soon started to reshape national politics.

The Kennedy administration, thinking it could ride the tiger of political change in the Third World, cemented America firmly into South Vietnam, even encouraging the military coup that toppled the country's existing regime in 1963. Yet it was no surprise that soon after Johnson became president, America's Vietnam involvement became known as Johnson's war. The war attracted the same kind of hatred that was directed at Johnson himself by those who saw his presidency as the living symbol of all that had been lost with Kennedy's death. Johnson, seen as a president brought to office by the most illegitimate of means, became the object of violent vilification. Modern America did not invent the art of political attack, but the sixties definitely made a bid for the hall of fame when the play *MacBird* opened at New York City's Village Gate in 1967: The drama was based on the premise that Johnson had usurped the presidency by killing Kennedy.

America's Vietnam involvement came in for many criticisms, and some were well deserved. One group of critics argued that the war was wrong because it could not be won. Others pleaded the humanitarian case, pointing to the unspeakable suffering the conflict caused. Yet as the months wore on, with Johnson's presidency giving way to Nixon's, another strain became increasingly prominent in the antiwar criticism: that of the criminality of the war and the systematic, illegal deceit with which it was waged. The protesters sounding this theme cited a litany of criminal and quasi-criminal acts: the deception behind the Gulf of Tonkin resolution, the presidential and military lying to the press, the secret bombing of Cambodia, the illegal domestic counterintelligence activity by the FBI and the CIA, the attempted suppression of the Pentagon Papers, and more.

This type of criticism of the Vietnam war did not treat the issue as if it were a massive policy dispute or a power struggle or an ideological battle or even a moral debate. Instead, this attack treated the war as a massive scandal—both a violation of the law and an unambiguous moral shock, once the truth became known, to the American people. Moreover, the critique went, this was no mere scandal involving small vices like lust and greed. No, the Vietnam scandal stemmed from the exposure of criminal abuse of power. The presidency itself had become corrupt in the deepest sense. The corruption was so outrageous and threatening that it demanded the almost undivided attention and steady anger of the citizenry.

With this kind of moral intensity permeating the politics of Vietnam, it was not surprising that new moral standards were soon asserted in more ordinary politics as well.[18] This broader change could be seen as early as 1966 in events like the financial scandal involving Democratic senator Thomas Dodd of Connecticut.

The Dodd case was as emblematic of its day as the Estes scandal was of a time gone by. Dodd, before his election to Congress in 1953, had served as special assistant to five successive attorneys general and a member of the Justice Department's first civil rights section. He had been executive trial counsel for the United States at Nuremberg. He was a thundering anti-Communist, a friend of J. Edgar Hoover, and one of President Lyndon Johnson's closest allies in the Senate.

In 1966 columnists Drew Pearson and Jack Anderson published some 30 columns making charges of corruption against Dodd. They said that he had acted improperly to advance the interests of businessmen who had given him gifts and campaign contributions. The columnists also claimed that the senator was guilty of repeated double billing, charging both the government and private parties for expenses incurred on a single trip. They further said that Dodd had misappropriated $100,000 in political contributions, including funds from two "Tom Dodd Day" dinners at which Lyndon Johnson had been a guest and a drawing card, by diverting the sum to personal use.

The columns were bombshells because of the specificity of the accusations: Pearson and Anderson quoted extensively from Dodd's personal and office records. These records, in turn, came from disaffected employees and ex-employees of Dodd's. For more than a year these staffers had worked at putting together incriminating evidence on the senator, and they made some 4,000 documents available to Pearson and Anderson.[19]

President Johnson, asked about the charges against the senator at a press conference, promptly distanced himself from Dodd: "I have had no information about any dinners held for anyone to obtain funds for personal use. . . . I didn't know that it was for personal, or political, or local campaign, or national [purposes]."[20] Johnson said he would defer in his judgment of the matter to the new Senate ethics committee. The charges against Dodd were the committee's first major order of business.

To many political observers at the time, Dodd's was hardly an open-and-shut case. Even after the committee had held two sets of public hearings on Dodd, *Time* magazine wrote, "No one . . . was likely to call any aspect of the Dodd investigation simple." *Time* went on: "Dodd himself occasionally seemed genuinely confused about the difference between his personal and his political expenses. . . . For a man whose life is politics, the line must sometimes be easily blurred. The question is whether it was blurred just a little too often in the case of Tom Dodd. . . ."[21]

The committee had to choose whether to exonerate Dodd or punish him by means such as censure or expulsion from the chamber. In April 1967 the committee members unanimously voted to recommend censure on two counts, and on June 13 the issue went to the Senate floor. There Dodd's chief defender was the Senate majority whip, Russell Long of Louisiana. The critical issue on the floor was Dodd's personal use of his campaign funds, and Long argued to his Senate colleagues that Dodd had acted in accordance with common Senate practice. The rules Dodd was said to have violated were in fact not clear or definite rules at all. "Half the Senate," said Long to newsmen during the fight, "couldn't stand the investigation Senator Dodd went through."[22] Long may well have been right, but he was no more effective than the attorney for House speaker Jim Wright would be in making the very same argument 22 years later. The final vote on Dodd was an overwhelming 92 to 5 against him.

With the censure, Dodd joined a list of just six other senators who had been punished with censure or its equivalent over the course of the Senate's 200-year history. Almost all the other censures were for offenses of great gravity: divulging secret documents relating to France's cession of the Louisiana Territory, leaking materials pertaining to the treaty annexing Texas, engaging in physical violence on the Senate floor, and, for Senator Joseph R. McCarthy, a series of offenses such as obstruction of the legislative process. One pre-Dodd censure had covered a less serious offense: a senator's hiring, to deal with tariff legislation, a staffer who was still on the payroll of a trade association as secretary to its president. The year of that censure was 1929, another time at which outside events weakened the rule of tradition in the Senate.

If the Billy Sol Estes and Bobby Baker affairs were notable for where they did not go, the Dodd scandal is interesting—in light of the uncertain state of the rules at the time—for how far it did. Afterward, varied explanations were given for why the Senate had dealt with Dodd so dramatically. Part of the answer stemmed from the fact that Dodd was not popular in the Senate. Those senators who thought Dodd pompously self-righteous were happy to see him humbled by his scandal. Those who did not like his brand of anticommunism were just as happy to see his positions discredited.

Clearly some of Dodd's staffers did not like him either. Yet if Dodd was not a very nice man to work for, he was heir to a long and colorful line of U.S. senators who have not been nice men to work for. If he did unethical things, he had lots of company among his Senate colleagues. The main reasons for the outcome of the Dodd affair lay not in personal factors but in the systematic changes that were taking place in American politics during the mid-sixties.

For instance, the crucial filched documents in the Dodd case came from staffers not only angry at their boss but also willing to go public with their anger in an almost unprecedented way. In prior eras such employees would have been part of smaller staffs. They would have spent more time with their boss and fewer hours meeting regularly over drinks, as Dodd's staff did, to provide each other with moral reinforcement in their crusade against the senator. More important, Dodd's dissident staffers acted out of a Vietnam-era view of where their moral obligations lay. They did not think it immoral to steal Dodd's records and breach his trust: These old-fashioned ethical issues had to be subordinated to the demands of a higher political morality that put service to principles far above obligations to persons or institutions. Old-style politics—counting loyalty to leaders, allies, and parties as a cardinal virtue, while viewing most political ideas and arguments as chips to be traded and compromised—was in its death throes, and with the Dodd case Americans were being introduced to its replacement.

In addition, in earlier times staffers like those in Dodd's office would not have been so sanguine about the power of the press to legitimate them and their criticisms. By the mid-sixties, though, the media had become increasingly powerful in national politics. They were promoting more moralistic standards for judging political figures. Some journalists wrote and spoke of the Dodd case as a test of whether the Senate was a morally worthy institution, capable of holding itself to suitably high ethical standards. DODD INQUIRY PUTS PRESSURE ON SENATE, *The New York Times* headlined one story about the case. What the Senate was feeling, the *Times* said in the accompanying story, was the demand that it "examine its own conduct unflinchingly."[23] Dodd's outnumbered defender on the Senate floor, Russell Long, taunted his colleagues with their subservience to the press. Senators were going to vote against Dodd, Long said, because they were afraid that if they voted the wrong way, they would be subjected to "the same kind of calumny and smear" that Dodd had received.[24]

Finally, in prior times staffers like Dodd's would not have thought that they could ever bring Dodd down. By the time of the censure vote, though, Dodd's fellow senators felt pushed to act according to new standards and expectations. The Senate of the time did have its own unwritten ethical rules, and Dodd was not a shining example of compliance. Still, many in the Senate had done at least some of the things Dodd had. The senators did not censure him because his practices genuinely scandalized them. Instead, they did so because the political climate had changed and was pressing hard upon the Senate.

The senators may not have known at the time that they were staring into the newborn face of post-Kennedy American politics. They did see that the Senate was being held to higher standards than in the past and that the call to virtue had, for a change, some real political muscle behind it.

With these new sensitivities and political realities, many of them quite different from those accompanying the scandals of the preceding years, the country approached Watergate. That event would create a climate more severe and provoke reforms more thoroughgoing and comprehensive than even Mark Twain or Henry Adams could have hoped for.

CHAPTER 2

AN HONEST PRESIDENT

WHEN THE BREAK-IN at Democratic party headquarters was discovered in June 1972, the country had already been torn by political divisions more bitter than any since the Civil War. Watergate transformed this rancor into a near-universal feeling that official criminality was the largest problem facing the republic and into an equally massive consensus in favor of political reform. This post-Watergate spirit affected virtually every organization active in national politics and brought about many institutional changes designed to free political life from the surreptitious influence of clandestine cash and make it less susceptible to abuse of power. The same climate produced the 1976 election of President Jimmy Carter, who supported and continued the cleansing process. Yet Carter was eventually destroyed, in no small part, by the same new standards that elected him. By the time he was defeated for reelection in 1980, it was clear that our reformed political system posed great threats even to the most honest of presidents.

It is hard to add any fresh information to the millions of words that have already been written about Watergate. We need only recall here that from the time of Richard Nixon's election as president in 1968, many of his adversaries saw him as not merely an opponent but a fundamentally illegitimate force in American politics. This thorny mantle was his because of both the battle over the Vietnam war and Nixon's history as a bête noire of the left. Some of Nixon's men in the White House and the Justice Department thought of the antiwar activists with the same bitterness, treating them as criminals and threats to the basic structure of constitutional government. These officials indulged in futile mass indictments of the protesters. They tried to use the FBI and the CIA to go after antiwar groups. When the intelligence agencies balked, the Nixon aides suspected them of attempting a de facto coup against democratically elected authority. Out of such suspicions came the conviction in the White House that the president was justified in taking extraordinary steps to defend the country and his office.

These steps turned out, as we know from the Watergate story, to be extraordinary indeed. After an almost decade-long game of mutual goading between defenders and opponents of the war, it was the president's men who not only stepped over the line and did the indefensible but got caught sporting their disguises and spying on their enemies in the modern equivalent of the confessional, the office of Daniel Ellsberg's psychiatrist. As if these discoveries were not enough, in the middle of the uproar the vice president of the United States, Spiro T. Agnew, was forced to leave office for having taken bribes.

Watergate buffs still argue over whether the president might have saved himself, after the initial revelations, by launching a political offensive more sophisticated than the ill-fated coverup that occurred. They say he could have admitted error earlier, for instance, or fired more people or burned the tapes. But the anger and pent-up passions set loose by Watergate probably made it inevitable that Nixon would have to leave office, which he did in August 1974.

Today, those who are too young to have paid much attention to Watergate do not get as excited as their elders about it. Younger people do not shudder at the mere mention of terms like "ITT," "plumbers," or "CREEP." When former president Nixon appears before them in the press and on the best-seller lists these days, he is usually portrayed as a pleasantly graying guru of foreign policy and a figure of fascinating complexity. In the spring of 1991 there appeared a book, from a major publishing house, arguing that Nixon did not mastermind the Watergate coverup and that he was removed from office by a coup.[1]

If even the chief alleged criminal of Watergate has made this sort of comeback, we can be sure that we are, less than 20 years after the Watergate cataclysm, in the midst of revisionism.

As a result of this change, we now speak easily about the ideological and partisan roots of Watergate. We know that it was not simply a series of crimes but the product of a fierce struggle over national political power. At the time of the scandal, though, public discourse reflected a broad agreement that the event was to be seen as a legal and ethical crisis posing the gravest of threats to constitutional government and affecting all Americans equally. We get a sense of how pervasive this rhetoric was when we consider the phenomenon of Sam Ervin.

The Senate Select Committee on Presidential Campaign Activities, which held the nation spellbound in 1973 with its televised Watergate hearings, was chaired by folksy senator Samuel J. Ervin, Democrat of North Carolina. Ervin, a Harvard Law School graduate, carried a copy of the Constitution in his breast pocket and clearly thought he could interpret the document at least as well as any bunch of misguided liberal members of the federal judiciary. Moved in large part by this secular analogue of religious fundamentalism, Ervin voted against every major piece of civil rights legislation of the 1960s. This same fundamentalism was offended by the machinations of Nixon's White House. Ervin's ire drove him to take a dramatic role in the Watergate hearings, where his manifestly southern and conservative prominence helped persuade television viewers that the scandal was not just a bunch of phony left-wing charges against the president but a danger to liberals and conservatives alike.

The old civil rights battles forgotten, Ervin emerged as something of a liberal hero. His elevation was much like the widespread admiration that Watergate brought to federal judge John J. Sirica, who handled the cases of the original Watergate burglars. Before the break-in, Sirica had been regarded by liberals as a Republican party hack and a prosecutors' mouthpiece. But when Sirica pressed his Watergate defendants for more information about the caper by giving some of them draconian 40-year "provisional" sentences, only a few civil libertarians protested.[2] Here was another sign of how thoroughly the Watergate crisis had displaced more conventional political issues.

The federal ethics legislation that came into being during the Watergate years reflected the same view of where the nation's problems lay. Some of the reform measures passed by Congress after Nixon's resignation were directed at Congress itself. Even before Watergate, the legislators, responding to the prevailing climate of mistrust, had begun to tighten federal campaign finance legislation. In 1971, the first systematic revision of these laws in almost 50 years limited media spending in campaigns and expanded disclosure requirements. It also explicitly legitimated political action committees as means for collecting and distributing campaign contributions. The new law's proponents argued that these PACs, governed by strict rules, would become a wholesome substitute for rich individual campaign contributors exercising secret power over politicians. A mere three years later, in 1974, Congress substantially amended the law and set stringent limits on how much money an individual could contribute to a campaign for national office.

Both houses of Congress also passed new ethics codes for their members. The House and Senate expanded financial disclosure requirements, limited the gifts and outside income a member could accept, and forbade—11 years after the censure of Dodd—the commingling of a congressman's personal financial accounts with his political and public ones.

Yet most of the legislation spawned by Vietnam and Watergate was directed not to Congress but exclusively to the executive branch, as the legislators acted on their determination that the Imperial Presidency would not get the bit in its teeth again.

Some of this legislation aimed at making large, direct changes in the relative power of the president and Congress. An addition to a supplemental appropriations bill passed by Congress in 1973 forbade the government to participate in air warfare over Cambodia. In the same year Congress passed the War Powers Resolution, constitutionally controversial to this day, which forbade presidents to commit American troops anywhere abroad for more than 30 days without congressional approval. At the end of 1974 the legislators passed the Hughes-Ryan amendment, requiring presidents to notify several congressional committees of any American covert actions abroad. The Budget and Impoundment Act of 1974, intended to give the legislators more control over federal spending, greatly restricted the practice of impoundment that presidents had used to avoid spending money appropriated by Congress.

Other changes in law at this time tried to make government

more open to the public. In 1974 Congress, with bipartisan support, amended the Freedom of Information Act to require agencies to respond to citizen requests for information within 10 working days. If an agency resisted by claiming the documents were classified, federal judges were given the power to declassify them. Courts could also make the government pay attorneys' fees if it lost a case, and the judges could even turn recalcitrant bureaucrats over to the Civil Service Commission for punishment. Each agency had to send an annual report to Congress explaining every one of its decisions to withhold information from a citizen who had asked for it. The Government in the Sunshine Act, passed in 1976 after years of lobbying by reform organizations like Common Cause, directed some 50 federal agencies to start conducting all their deliberations in public.

In 1978, for the first time, Congress passed legislation to prevent government agencies from firing or demoting whistleblowers who had charged their superiors with waste or fraud. In that year the legislators also produced the Inspector General Act. The law created a dozen new inspectors general in six Cabinet departments and in specific government agencies from the Environmental Protection Agency to the National Aeronautics and Space Administration. The new IGs were to report not to the management officers in their agencies, as had been the case with IGs in the past, but directly to their department or agency heads. The new IGs were also to report independently to Congress every six months, and the heads of their agencies were forbidden by law to change anything in these reports. By the spring of 1991 the number of IGs established by law had increased five-fold.

The most famous post-Watergate statute, the Ethics in Government Act, was passed in 1978. In part, it tightened the executive branch's existing rules on conflicts of interest by devices such as further restrictions on the kind of lobbying that an ex-government official could do before his old agency. More significant were the procedural changes made by the new act. High-level officials would now be required to file detailed public statements of their financial affairs upon entering government and every year thereafter; until the Nixon administration, financial information of this sort had not even been systematically gathered, let alone released. The new statute also tightened the rules on when an appointee had to sell his financial holdings or place them in a blind trust in order to free himself from conflicts of interest.

In addition, the act established a new type of federal official, the special prosecutor. Before 1978, when high administration officials came under criminal suspicion they were investigated by the Justice Department. But after Watergate, the department was viewed as inherently suspect because it was headed by an attorney general who was the president's appointee and, in recent years, sometimes the president's friend or relative. Under the new act, when the attorney general got information from any source about possible lawbreaking by a senior official, he was to conduct a brief investigation. Then, unless the official was provably clean, the attorney general was required to ask a federal court to appoint a special prosecutor to continue the investigation. At this point, control of the case effectively passed out of the attorney general's hands. The special prosecutor could be removed from the investigation only for grossly improper behavior and only with the permission of the court.

The post-Watergate laws, like fossils, present a lasting record of the cast of the Watergate-era mind. Moreover, the laws provide important clues to understanding modern scandal politics, and the legislation played an important part in making political scandal into the industry it is today. The process of making the laws focused sharp public attention on the legal and ethical issues that Watergate brought to the fore, and this sustained scrutiny kept the subject of official turpitude bobbing high on the public agenda instead of sinking beneath the waves as it has done after other scandals. To the public, the continuing activity sent the message that the government's moral condition was abysmal. For insiders, the attention and energy absorbed by the lawmaking process ensured that the social concerns of the 1960s would not return to center stage. Along the way, some of the cultural tolerance of the sixties—toward sex, drugs, and a counterculture lifestyle—passed out of fashion.

The drama of the process helped make it self-reinforcing. As each once-impenetrable institution fell before the legislative onslaught, the light of the bonfire made other parts of the established system look more vulnerable to attack. Moreover, because some of the new legislation turned offensive behavior into crimes, the laws elevated sleazy politics into something more notorious, morally significant, and exciting. The politics of scandal became more interesting to the press and more glamorous to the government personnel enforcing the rules. For public officials who were potential targets, the new legislation, with its more exacting procedures and harsher penalties, steeply raised the costs of scandal and made American politics a considerably more dangerous occupation.

The Carter administration ("I'll never lie to you," candidate Jimmy Carter put it memorably in his 1976 campaign) came to office aggressively embracing the popular idea of ethical uplift and a highly moral government. "We *can* have an American government," he proclaimed, "that has turned away from scandal and corruption and official cynicism and is once again as decent and competent as our people."[3] For his top appointees, he devised the toughest conflict-of-interest guidelines ever seen in the federal government, and he sponsored legislation to apply the standards more broadly. His initiative played a large part in the passage of the 1978 Ethics in Government Act.

When the General Services Administration scandal broke in 1978 and revealed long-standing fraudulent practices among scores of employees and contractors, the Carterites were so eager to avoid charges of coverup that they allowed their crusading, media-savvy GSA chief to fire a deputy, not directly involved in the scandal, who was a close friend of Speaker of the House Thomas P. (Tip) O'Neill (D-Mass.). The incident helped cement O'Neill's enmity toward the administration and hurt its chances for success with Congress.

Despite all his attention to ethics, Carter did not manage to ride the reform wave successfully. Soon after taking office, his administration began to suffer from a string of scandals that ultimately crippled it. Though the new ethics system did not create the Carter administration's troubles, the post-Watergate climate turned familiar sorts of political controversy and antagonism into something much larger and more dangerous.

From the time they arrived in Washington, Carter and his aides aroused a good deal of antagonism not only from O'Neill but from others within their own party. This resentment stemmed partly from the administration's considerable talent for alienating those who should have been its allies. Yet Carter's situation also stemmed from the serious electoral trouble in which the Democrats increasingly found themselves over the course of the 1970s and from the fact that some Democrats rather gracelessly chose to point to Jimmy Carter as the source of their ills. Thus much of political Washington spoke of the president and his staff with contempt almost from the start. Here the capital had gone through the struggle of booting Richard Nixon from office only to see him replaced not by a group of cosmopolitan Democrats—Kennedys, perhaps—but by another dose of Sunbelt sleaze, this time of the smaller-scale Georgia variety. "White trash" is how a well-known journalist covering Washington in those years summed up the feeling of some of the permanent residents toward the newcomers. Early news stories about the administration complained of the clannishness of the "Georgia Mafia," disapproved of the blue jeans that some of the young Carter staffers wore in public, and reported that offices in the old Executive Office Building now looked like something out of *Animal House.*

The official involved in the administration's first big scandal—Carter's friend and director of the Office of Management and Budget, T. Bertram Lance—was not one of the young political junkies who had been targeted for the sharpest criticism by the Washington press. Lance was a prosperous 45-year-old banker, and observers of the administration had marked him as a force for stability and conservatism within it. Still, Lance had enough of the outsider in his and his wife's style to raise hackles. It soon became clear that he would be not only the president's budget officer but his most trusted economic adviser, overshadowing officials like the secretary of the treasury. Rumor soon had Lance a candidate for chairman of the Federal Reserve Board, which to some was a thoroughly alarming possibility.

In January 1977, during Lance's confirmation hearing, he promised the Senate Government Operations Committee that he would sell stock he owned in the National Bank of Georgia by the end of the year. This action was not required by law, but it was in keeping with the higher standard of ethics promised by the new administration. Six months later the value of the stock had dropped sharply, so Lance had to go back to the committee to ask for more time to sell his holdings and avoid a huge loss. He told the senators that he still owed a Chicago bank most of the whopping $3.4 million loan he had taken out in order to buy the stock. The committee seemed happy enough to give Lance more time. Indeed, several senators remarked that Washington's preoccupation with such matters was getting out of hand. The city, said Senator John Glenn (D-Ohio), was becoming "ethics-happy."[4]

But Lance's widely publicized trouble sent journalists digging around in banking institutions from Georgia to Illinois. They soon charged that Lance had gotten a sweetheart deal on his $3.4 million loan by having a bank he controlled in Calhoun, Georgia, deposit money—a "compensating balance"—with the lender in return. Other charges emerged. It was suggested that the Teamsters union had deposited money in Lance's Calhoun bank for political reasons. Lance went before the Senate committee again and, it was generally agreed, gave an impressive performance. The committee called off further investigations and President Carter happily expressed "absolute confidence" in his friend.[5]

But this resolution was only the end of Act One. (In modern political scandals, the show is not considered over until the accused is carried bleeding from the stage.) Another major player soon appeared: In July the Office of the Comptroller of the Currency, the Treasury Department agency that had investigated Lance before his appointment, got a new head comptroller. Distancing himself from the agency's previous probe of Lance, he ordered a new investigation, including an investigation of the old investigation, which news reports said had been closed out too quickly. In August the Comptroller's Office reported, saying it had found dubious practices but nothing criminal. "Bert, I'm proud of you,"[6] said Carter, in a line that would soon become a historic embarrassment.

That was Act Two of the Lance imbroglio, but still not the end. The scandal had reached critical mass and become capable of producing a continuous stream of fresh news with virtually no added external stimulus. The media began featuring stories about Lance's practice, already investigated by the Senate committee and the Comptroller's Office, of writing overdrafts on his account in his Calhoun bank. There were also new coverup questions in the press: Had a bank examiner been pressured to rescind disciplinary action against Lance just before the OMB appointment? Had the acting comptroller failed to tell Carter's transition team all he knew at the time of Lance's confirmation? Had Lance kept information from the senators?

Just as important as the aggressive press, government officials already involved in the Lance affair continued probing, and new official investigators joined them. The Comptroller's Office was soon said to be investigating Lance again, with help from the Internal Revenue Service. Republican senator Robert Dole of Kansas called on Democratic senator Abe Ribicoff of Connect-icut, chairman of the committee that had approved Lance's ap-pointment, to reopen hearings. Senator William Proxmire (D-Wisc.), chairman of the Senate banking committee, announced that he, too, was going to investigate. The Securities and Ex-change Commission said that it had begun looking at Lance's activities. House banking committee chairman Fernand St. Ger-main announced that he would hold hearings. The Federal Election Commission started investigating a prior race Lance had made for governor of Georgia. The avalanche was in rolling progress.

The Senate summoned Lance yet again, and once more he gave a good account of himself. By this time, though, the comp-troller had already sent one charge on to the Justice Department for further investigation. Common Cause had come out for Lance's resignation. So had Ribicoff and Republican committee member Charles Percy of Illinois. "I always could do my job at OMB," said Lance years later, looking back on his scandal time. "But sooner or later the cumulative weight becomes too much to handle. The pressure builds. People say, 'You're harming the president,' or, 'You're harming the party.' "

So Act Three of the scandal ended, at least as far as Wash-ington was concerned, with Lance's resignation on September 21, some 10 weeks after the major agitation had begun. But his ouster did not end the episode for Lance himself. Govern-ment agencies kept investigating and charging Lance with practices from unsafe loans to nondisclosure of required finan-cial information. Lance, by his actions and associations, kept providing grist for the government's mill. He was to spend the next decade in litigation with the government, including a criminal trial for bank fraud in which the jury acquitted Lance on nine counts of the government's indictment and deadlocked on three. The government, not surprisingly, decided not to go after Lance again.

But back in 1977 the Lance scandal did not sprout and flourish in the way it did because of the simple force of the charges against him. Who could remember, within two months after his leaving Washington, exactly what the bill of particulars against him was? Did we ever decide whether his bank overdrafts were a common practice, an embarrassment, or a significant sin? Did we ever learn which was greater, the pressure on government investigators to close the Lance case before Carter's inauguration or the pressure to look aggressive once the scandal broke? What did we think of the morality of compensating balances? Did we really know what compensating balances *were*?

Few of the untold numbers of lines spoken and written on the Lance scandal were devoted to examining the actions behind these charges. Instead, the accusations, coming one after another, served mainly as the pegs on which the scandal hung.

The press supplied these hooks with the facts it fed into the public arena each day, yet the journalists did not do the job alone: They got a lot of help from inside the government. They were aided by sources in the Comptroller's Office. They were given material by people like the ex-assistant U.S. attorney in Atlanta who, angry because a Lance-related case of his had been closed by his boss, decided to tell his story and fed the speculation that political pressure had been applied.

The many government people and organizations jostling each other in the Lance affair behaved aggressively in other ways, too. Each one of them did its job with assertive energy and mistrust. At the beginning of the scandal, the Senate Government Operations Committee behaved in the old-fashioned way: It raised its questions about Lance before confirmation and laid off afterward. But the Comptroller's Office followed no such rules. Neither did the SEC, the IRS, or the Federal Election Commission. Democratic committee chairmen—like Proxmire, St. Germain, and Robert Giaimo of the House Budget Committee—were sure that they, too, had something uniquely valuable to add to the store of knowledge about Lance. Republicans could not be expected to ignore this opportunity to embarrass the president; but with the cast of characters already so large, the opposition party was hardly necessary to the scandal's development.

Lance himself said of the scandal afterward:

> It's not the press that keeps something like this going. It's *government* that can't stop anything. When you institutionalize the process, you make sure this kind of

activity will be permanent. The competitive aspects cause it to be permanent. The people on the inside who are doing it aren't necessarily vindictive, but they reason that if they don't do it, somebody else will.

Yet the large scale and increased competition of present-day government do not fully explain the unstoppable forward momentum of the Lance scandal. The participants moving the ball were also hewing to changed operating rules and standards, of which two were of particular importance. The first new rule told all participants that when scandal strikes, it is far less dangerous to attack the alleged wrongdoer than to defend him or call for a suspension of judgment. The second new rule was the floating moral yardstick. Reporters and commentators often said during the Lance scandal that while he may not have done anything illegal, his behavior did not rise to the high moral level that Jimmy Carter had promised for his administration. Critics were justified, it followed, in treating Lance's deeds as seriously scandalous and in digging still further into his affairs in a hunt for yet more wrongdoing.

Most critics who used this argument could not really have believed that Carter's campaign language put forth reasonable operational standards of behavior for public officials. They must have known that Carter, like every president, would have to lie sometimes. They had to know from experience that no politician has totally clean linen. Yet they chose to judge Lance against Carter's unrealistic rhetoric. Some did so merely to prick the president's moral pretensions. Others did it opportunistically to make the Lance scandal look bigger. Still others talked and wrote this way because they were afraid that if they did not, they would not seem moral enough for the post-Watergate times. Their fear was a sign of the definite shift toward a type of modern Puritanism, a movement that had taken place in the political culture and its notions of morality.

This change in ideas became even clearer during another, later Carter administration scandal, a farcical replay of the Lance affair, which involved Jimmy Carter's brother Billy and became known as "Billygate." Carter's brother merited sympathy: He was an alcoholic and suffered from the problems of judgment that attend the disease. He also had the difficult job of trying to find a place for himself in the sophisticated world of the American presidency. On the other hand, the First Brother was also an entrepreneur not above capitalizing on his presidential relative in order to make a buck. Politics is full of operators with a jeweler's eye for human vulnerabilities like Billy Carter's, and by autumn of 1978 the president's brother was involved in business dealings with Libyan oil interests and with the Libyan government.

In view of the popularity of Libyan dictator Muammar al Qaddafi with the American people, Billy had made a breathtakingly poor choice of associates. Journalists like William Safire began, quite properly, to prod the administration to give a fuller explanation of Billy's ties to Libya. The Justice Department started investigating whether Billy had violated the Foreign Agents Registration Act by failing to declare his Libyan connections. In July 1980 the First Brother finally registered as a foreign agent, bringing himself into compliance with the law.

Yet finally complying with the law was not the end of Billy's scandal troubles. It was the beginning, for the public action made other journalists prick up their ears. Soon we began hearing more sinister things about Billy's Libyan connection: that the president's national security adviser had used Billy to communicate with the Libyans about the American hostages in Iran, that Billy had registered only after the attorney general had personally warned the president of trouble, that the attorney general was now covering up, and that the First Brother had used White House limousines on some of his forays to meet with his Libyan friends in Washington.

Media coverage of the affair exploded. News stories drew parallels to Watergate and spoke of the affair as a mortal political danger to the president. *Washington Post* reporter David Broder, writing later about Billygate, reported that on one especially heavy scandal day, Washington newspapers—Broder counted it up—did the following: reprinted a 1979 article on the psychology of Jimmy Carter's relationship with his brother, reported on the Senate majority leader's call to Carter to "lay out the facts" prior to the Democratic convention, printed press secretary Jody Powell's reply that the president would "do just that," told readers that Billy had "resurfaced" (meaning that the press had found him after having lost him) in Plains but was not talking, announced that a friend of Billy's had also registered as a Libyan agent, revealed that the Americans for Democratic Action had called for the attorney general's resignation, repeated the fact that Libya was trying to buy planes from the United States (though Billy seemed to have nothing to do with the project), highlighted the fact that Billy's foreign-agent registration papers did not say whether his Libyan connection had ended, reminded readers about the grim nature of the Libyan regime, printed a denial by the Justice Department's head of foreign agent registration that he had been pressured to bring a civil rather than a criminal case against Billy, asserted that Carter decision makers had made Billygate "their own national nightmare," and, finally, produced a long interview with Billy and his wife, Sybil.[7]

Yet at the beginning of August, after the president gave a press conference on the subject of his brother and performed reasonably well, the story began to sink like a tired balloon.

The offenses behind the Billy Carter scandal were not all trivial: We should know whether a First Brother is exerting influence on behalf of buddies like the Libyans. But the importance of the Billy problem was limited by the fact that Billy Carter did not have any appreciable influence on the conduct of American foreign policy. Furthermore, he was not going to acquire any such influence in the future, since his weaknesses were known to everyone in the White House, including his brother the president. These things were clear from the beginning of the scandal. Thus the scale of media attention to Billy Carter was slightly demented, as were some of the accounts of the danger his dealings posed to the republic.

After the Billy scandal was over, Broder found that no one in the press would claim responsibility for its vast size. Reporters said their editors had lashed them forward. Editors said their reporters had insisted on multiple stories. Journalists said they were merely responding to competitive pressure from their media rivals and vice versa. Billygate was driven by a pressure that in retrospect looks almost mechanical in its nature, so little is the deliberation that seems to have propelled it.

Yet this machinelike pressure grew out of human ideas and assumptions. In order to play the Billy story as a Watergate-like crisis in spite of the man's small political importance, press organizations had to put into play a kind of mistrust in the abstract, something apart from the actual facts of the case and separate from any real-world judgment about whether the theoretical dangers in Billy's case deserved significant worry. Some of the journalists working the story were doubtless genuine in their mistrust. For the rest, such suspicion was a convenient posture.

In addition to the scandal-breeding factors at work in the Lance affair and Billygate, something still more serious appeared after Watergate to increase the size and importance of high-level political scandals: Scandalous behavior could more and more easily become allegedly criminal behavior. In the Lance and Billy Carter affairs, the threat of criminal sanctions was always hovering at the edge of the uproar. In the case involving Carter White House aide Hamilton Jordan, the criminal law took center stage.

Jordan's difficulties with the Washington community started as soon as the new administration did. If Washington establishment types thought the presidential offices had become *Animal House,* Jordan was their Bluto. At the end of 1977, the White House aide's reputation for crassness of various sorts became indelibly public when *The Washington Post* told the infamous tale of Jordan and the pyramids.

The Washington Post's Style section has been entertaining its readers since 1969 with articles about the social mores of the nation's capital. The section is descended from the society pages that used to grace American newspapers, in about the same way Bette Midler is descended from an amoeba. Its features include profiles of the city's most powerful political figures. In these pieces, Style section writers are allowed to go beyond matters of verifiable fact and bring their personal sensibilities to bear, in order to guide the audience into the very heart of political life. While many readers enjoy the arch portraits that result, the reactions of interview subjects are sometimes homicidal.

In December 1977, the *Post*'s Style section ran a piece by staff writer Sally Quinn, reporting that the Carter administration's top officials were a living disaster when it came to social relations with the rest of political Washington. In fact, said the story, it was reliably reported that one evening at an elegant dinner party Jordan had looked down the front of the dress worn by the Egyptian ambassador's wife and ruminated, "I've always wanted to see the pyramids."[8]

Soon after the pyramids story came an even more colorful charge. In February 1978, writer Rudy Maxa reported in *The Washington Post Magazine* that Jordan, visiting a Washington bar named Sarsfield's, spat some of his drink—amaretto and cream, in distasteful particular—down the dress of a young woman who had spurned his attentions.[9] Press secretary Jody Powell, who thought he had underreacted to Quinn's earlier story, took no chances with this one. He actually tracked down a Sarsfield's bartender who had seen the exchange Maxa described. The bartender said the spitting never happened, and Powell issued a 33-page denial of the story. But the novella-length apologia itself became news, and the story lasted for weeks. All those defensive words of Powell's, ran the post-Watergate logic, meant there had to be a shameful secret underneath. How could any journalist afford to think otherwise? Who wanted to be taken in by another coverup?

Jordan was not the only administration member being accused of degeneracy. Press accounts at this time repeatedly referred to or hinted at recreational drug use by Carter staffers. In July 1978, Peter G. Bourne, a psychiatrist and Carter friend who served in the White House as special assistant to the president for health and who had publicly favored decriminalizing marijuana, was caught in a drug scandal. He had written a prescription for the sedative Quaalude, as Bourne later explained it, to be used by one of his assistants in order to help her sleep. At the time, Quaaludes were also popular on the illicit drug market. So, instead of putting his aide's real name on the prescription, Bourne said, he wrote it to a fictitious "Sarah Brown" in order to spare his staffer any bad publicity. But when a friend of the staffer's took the prescription to a pharmacy to have it filled, she got caught in the deception. Partly because of the rumors about drug use in the administration, the story got a good deal of attention. Bourne quickly resigned, and another stone was added to the pile of incidents casting suspicion on the Carterites.

Against this background of news and rumor a third, more serious story about Jordan appeared in August 1979. It concerned events that had occurred more than a year earlier, in April 1978, when Jordan and some friends of his had paid a visit to a trendy New York discotheque, Studio 54.

Actually, Studio 54 was more than trendy; it was, in its brief heyday in the late seventies, a reification of modern celebrity worship. Its owners filled it with the famous and the notorious, who swept into the discotheque every night trailing limos and glitter. Ordinary people strained against the ropes cordoning them off from the entrance, praying that something about them—exceptional beauty, perhaps, or mind-bendingly bizarre dress—would move one of Studio 54's quality control managers to pull them out of the crowd and allow them to cross the threshold.

In December 1978, federal agents raided Studio 54. They busted up the premises and carted away the establishment's financial records, along with garbage bags full of cash. Within hours of the raid, a crowd was once again dancing and engaging in its other customary pursuits at the disco. However, two of its owners, Steve Rubell and Ian Schrager, were indicted the following June on tax evasion charges. Their lawyers were soon plea bargaining with the U.S. attorney's office in Manhattan.

One of the defense attorneys, Mitchell Rogovin, informed the prosecutors that his client Rubell had seen Hamilton Jordan snort cocaine on the night of the White House aide's 1978 visit to Studio 54.[10] This sort of announcement is not unheard of in criminal cases. Defendants use various tactics, from offering to implicate bigger fish in crimes to threatening grave embarrassment for the government, in order to try to get themselves lenient treatment. By the time Rubell made his charges against Jordan, though, the 1978 Ethics in Government Act had gone into effect. Therefore the information about Jordan had to go to the Justice Department in Washington, and Justice had to decide whether to appoint a special prosecutor. Did the department have to go through this process even if the accusers were themselves criminal defendants trying to bargain their way out of trouble? Yes, even then.

The early phases of the investigation were supposed to be secret, but the story, predictably, leaked to the press. Once the charges became public, new charges, just as predictably, began emerging from the woodwork. A man named Barry Landau, identified variously as a public relations consultant and a Studio 54 groupie, was reported to have corroborated the Rubell story in an FBI interview. The defendants' attorneys were said to have gotten hold of a tape on which a drug dealer called "Johnny C" gave a detailed account of the alleged crime. This multiplication of charges, the interesting and the worthless alike, is routine in a high-profile criminal case. Yet the new charges, like the original investigation, were all seriously reported by the press. Johnny C himself appeared on the ABC news show *20/20* to tell his story in living color. Accusations then began emerging from the West Coast, where Jordan was said to have sniffed cocaine at a party in Beverly Hills and at a Los Angeles restaurant.

Meanwhile, back at the Justice Department, Attorney General Benjamin R. Civiletti said his preliminary investigation had turned up no corroborative evidence of the Studio 54 charge. Yet Civiletti could not absolutely rule out the possibility of a crime, and the new Ethics in Government Act said that under those circumstances the attorney general had to ask for a special prosecutor. Civiletti did so, and the court appointed attorney Arthur Christy to the job. That was how Christy, a former U.S. attorney who had made his reputation prosecuting mobsters Vito Genovese and Frank Costello, ended up pursuing a single alleged instance of cocaine use—a charge, all parties conceded, that would never have been pursued against an ordinary citizen.

Christy spent four months investigating both the initial allegations against Jordan and the charges that cropped up afterward. He and his staff of seven interviewed some 65 people and called 33 witnesses before a grand jury. He put Jordan's chief accusers through a lie detector test, which they failed. He took them down to the basement of Studio 54, where the alleged crime occurred, and tried to get them to reenact it. Christy took Jordan to the same basement—a "clandestine operation befitting a U.S. intelligence agency,"[11] the special prosecutor recalled later—and asked him about his actions on the fateful night. At the end of May 1980, he submitted a report that found, as was no big surprise, that the evidence against Jordan was not credible.

The investigation was costly in many ways. For one thing, Jordan's legal bills were said to be well over $100,000. Nowadays we are used to hearing about million-dollar tabs in cases like this one, but back in those innocent times $100,000 was still enough to shock. Jordan submitted a bill to the government for $67,000, but the government could not pay him because the special prosecutor legislation had no provision in it for the reimbursement of legal fees. Jordan was not an independently wealthy man or one who had used government service to enrich himself. The new law had forced him to mount an expensive legal defense that would not have been necessary had he been an ordinary citizen. Yet there was no way for him to gain redress for the financial damage.

After Jordan's time, the law was changed to allow reimbursement for officials investigated by the special prosecutor but not indicted. Yet even these new provisions did not cover all the legal expenses involved in a case like Jordan's. Any senior officials or political figures watching the struggle over lawyers' fees could see that they, too, might someday be eligible for bankruptcy because of the new system.

Another cost of the Jordan investigation was borne by Jimmy Carter. While Jordan was under investigation, the White House aide was handling, among other matters, talks with Panamanian leader Omar Torrijos about the Panama Canal, negotiations with the Iranians over the release of our hostages, and Jimmy Carter's reelection plans. Moreover, the cost to Carter did not end with the charges against Jordan himself. During the investigation of Jordan, Christy came upon charges of cocaine use by another longtime Carter aide, Tim Kraft. Christy duly passed these allegations on to the attorney general, who duly passed them on to the court, which in September 1980 duly appointed yet another special prosecutor. Kraft had to leave his job as national campaign manager of Carter's hard-pressed reelection effort, though the case was dropped after the election.

A final cost of the highly publicized investigation lay in the damage done to Jordan's reputation. On this count Jordan was lucky. His case was widely reported, but so was his exoneration. When the investigation was over, he was used as a leading example by people arguing that the special prosecutor law had to be changed to permit an attorney general to close a case early when the evidence warranted. The continuing debate over the special prosecutor law put Jordan repeatedly before the public as a wronged and innocent man.

Yet even under unusually favorable circumstances like these, a residue of doubt always remains. Not long ago an attorney familiar with the Jordan scandal agreed to spend a couple of hours talking about the case and its questions of evidence. He wanted to be anonymous, and that is important: The worst damage to reputations is done in places where speakers need not give their names. We went down the list of allegations against Jordan, and the lawyer explained how the supporting evidence for each one was, legally speaking, virtually worthless. Still, when the lawyer was asked the final question—"When you add it all up, which side do you come down on?"—the surprising answer was "guilty."

Why? "First," he said,

> I've been a criminal lawyer for 30 years; I have to trust my gut. Next, just from the circumstances. Some of the witnesses couldn't remember the event very well, and they would have been lousy on the [witness] stand. But [one of them] was very credible about other things that happened that night. . . . Plus, Jordan protested too loudly. . . .

"Besides," the attorney completed his list, snorting coke was "what Jordan was like." After all the special prosecutor's subpoenas and depositions, the old images, publicized still more by the investigation—the pyramids, the amaretto and cream, the presidential adviser in a decadent discotheque—still shaped the attorney's opinion of "what Jordan was like."

It was not the special prosecutor law that got Jordan into trouble in the first place. By the time Rubell made his accusations, Jordan's reputation had already been battered by the national press and the political establishment, and it was this tarnished image that made the charge of drug use plausible. But turning a problem like Jordan's into a criminal inquiry substantially inflates its importance, even if the probe is run by reasonable men and women working without a witch-hunt mentality. Taking a matter under criminal advisement, no matter how loudly everyone talks about the presumption of innocence, sends the message that something very wrong is going on.

Also, a news story about a criminal investigation includes the exciting possibility, even if remote, of someone's going to jail. If it is a powerful person who might be tossed into the slammer, as the appointment of a special prosecutor signifies, the news becomes irresistibly fascinating, and the story will get a great deal of attention. The more widely publicized the story is, the more the charges involved become fixed in people's minds; so even if the special prosecutor decides not to prosecute, his decision does not fully undo the harm. Television viewers and newspaper readers do not forget a piece of colorful scandal news just because someone later tells them it isn't so.

The Carter administration produced nothing like the huge number of political scandals that would later mark the Reagan years. Still, scandal was one of the forces that undermined Carter's presidency. His popularity and power depended crucially on his maintaining his status as a man who could and would give the country upright government. The scandals in his administration came often enough, and were played prominently enough, to call this status into serious question and thus undermine the moral foundation of Carter's presidency. In addition, two of the Carter aides hurt by scandal—Lance and Jordan— were perhaps his best and most experienced sources of political advice and judgment. Such things did not constitute the whole reason why Carter lost in 1980, but they were a significant part of it.

During the Reagan years, when scandals became more numerous, opponents of the administration claimed that the numbers were rising because of the Reaganites' low moral standards, while defenders of the administration often claimed that the scandals were merely a partisan tactic used by liberals against conservatives and by Democrats against Republicans. As we judge these claims, we should note that the modern scandal phenomenon began before Reagan came to office and that being a Democratic president did not provide Jimmy Carter with any solid protection against it. Ronald Reagan's election certainly contributed to our rash of modern scandals, but clearly the new system was not just a response to him and his political style. The system we see in operation today is surely partisan, but its partisanship is not that of Republicans versus Democrats.

By 1980 the Carterites' experience had already shown that the new laws, institutions, and attitudes put into place by Watergate would outlive the crisis that gave birth to them, persist in their effects, and present special hazards and dangers to anyone attempting to govern the nation. Ronald Reagan's administration fell, jumped, or was pushed into every one of the traps.

CHAPTER 3

THE RESPONSIBLE MEDIA

W HEN YOU ASK a public official what is responsible for today's surplus of scandal, the odds are that his first answer will be, "The press." And understandably so: Today's news media play an unprecedented role in our public life, and their power has shaped modern politics. "By the mid-eighties," writes Richard Clurman, press observer and former chief of correspondents for the Time-Life News Service, "the media had made themselves the cop on every beat. . . ."[1] Yet the press did not muscle its way to the top of the current political heap against the opposition of all other forces on the public scene. Nor did the media impose values on American public life that were foreign to the interests and attitudes of everyone else who plays an active role in the political process. Instead, the rise of the press as a power in politics was simply one result of the general distaste for conventional political institutions that has made its mark on almost every aspect of our public life over the past 25 years.

In the early 1960s, it is now widely recognized, American journalism was becoming increasingly visible, self-conscious, and eager for news that could be dramatically presented on TV. So it is no surprise that political protesters of the 1960s found the press such a useful vehicle for forcing themselves and their positions into the center of national political life. The confrontational politics of Vietnam and then Watergate, in turn, worked its own changes on the press, making journalists more mistrustful and adversarial.

Yet the bitterness of that era did not change attitudes in the press alone. The same political climate also reshaped other American political institutions, from government agencies to political parties, interest groups, and more. These institutions did not merely come under strong attack; they also lost self-confidence and began voluntarily to cede more authority and influence to the media. Journalists emerged from the process with more collective power than they had ever wielded before. As a result, their peculiarities of attitude and flaws of judgment, which would have been less consequential in a day when the press was not so powerful, have in recent years posed serious problems for American democratic politics.

Criticizing the American press has become, understandably, a popular indoor sport. Yet the common charges against the media—that they are too negative in their reporting, for instance, or are biased or have no respect for people's privacy—are extremely hard to judge in the abstract. We need concrete examples, and the first big scandal of the Reagan years was a classic case.

This scandal, involving Reagan national security adviser Richard V. Allen, was a quintessential example of what people are thinking about when they speak of the overweening national press. In November 1981, news stories charged that Allen had taken money from some Japanese journalists who had interviewed Nancy Reagan. The charge was officially investigated and Allen was cleared. But he lost his job anyway, partly because of the ineradicable suspicions created by the heated media coverage of his scandal.

Critics of Ronald Reagan who watched his administration take over the government in 1981 saw Richard Allen as an embodiment of what was wrong with morals, politics, and style in the new Washington of the 1980s. This distinctive climate had begun to settle over the city well before the 1980 election, but with Reagan's inauguration, his critics noticed—some of them seemingly for the first time—that the nation's capital was awash in money and in people who did not hesitate to spend it demonstratively. The city seemed to be in the grip of power brokers who, instead of doing their work in the tradition of secrecy, actually wanted and worked to get their names into the news-papers. If this press coverage suggested that they were influenc-ing government in some shady way, so much the better for business. The Reaganites, in their critics' view, were both the symbol and the cause of the new "if you've got it, flaunt it" spirit.

No one should have been unprepared for such criticism. The new president was unabashedly conservative, which in some circles was just another word for greedy. Moreover, Reagan's close friends were wealthy men—Justin Dart, Holmes Tuttle, and the like—who hailed from Southern California, a region even more culturally suspect than Jimmy Carter's Georgia.

The Reaganites and their wives swept into the capital during inauguration week in an unprecedented rush of furs and lim-ousines. Some of the California ladies, scorning Washington's traditionally understated style, appeared around town in hairdos so sculpted and lacquered that they looked like battle helmets. Jewelry collections seen in public places included large dia-monds and pearls the size of chocolate truffles. The First Lady herself showed a fondness for designer evening gowns decorated with beading that looked as if it had cost the entire gross na-tional product of Honduras. Henceforth, these clothes and jew-els announced, nobody in the capital would have to be ashamed of being rich.

Here was yet another, wealthier variant of the Sunbelt style. California had come to power at last, after more than a decade of strenuous efforts to prevent such a calamity. And the assault did not occur only at the top levels of politics and government. Washington, until then no culinary mecca, started sprouting fancy new restaurants to keep up with the growing demand. As public relations firms in the city increased their activities, jour-nalists began receiving expensively packaged press releases writ-ten with the depth of direct mail solicitations. Each missive was a graphic reminder of the newcomers' disagreeably slick style.

Yet the Reagans' world was not the only new Washington on the scene in 1981. The competing new style that had emerged from the political activism of the 1960s was also flowering in the city. This other style was not sumptuous but austere, and not only contemptuous of wealthy people but convinced of their im-morality and even criminality. Acolytes of this second faith looked at the federal government and saw crisis-level corruption, especially in the just-arrived Reaganites. The increasingly stern, ethics-oriented Washington set out to show the vulgar newcomers who was boss and hold the line against any influence that they would otherwise wield over government.

Richard Allen, ironically, was not really a creature of the mon-eyed culture that aroused such antagonism. He was a longtime conservative-movement activist, loyal over the years to ideas and colleagues on the right. He had served briefly in the Nixon White House and advised Reagan on foreign policy since 1977. Yet Reagan's critics saw Allen as a man perpetually on the make and therefore part of the distasteful new Washington. After his White House experience, Allen had gone into the consulting business and acquired a number of foreign clients. He soon attracted charges that he was using politics and public service as a way to line his pockets.

In 1976 a defense contractor accused Allen of having solicited a campaign contribution from him on behalf of Nixon's 1972 reelection effort and of having said that in return the adminis-tration would press Japan to buy the contractor's products. The charge was never substantiated. During the 1980 presidential campaign it was charged in *The Wall Street Journal* that Allen had passed inside government information to a Japanese busi-nessman in order to get consulting contracts.[2] Five days before the election, Allen had to leave the campaign while the story was investigated. He was cleared on the grounds that at the time of the incident he was no longer a government employee. The day after the election Reagan named Allen his national security ad-viser.

In July 1981 *The Boston Globe* charged that Allen had failed to disclose all his contacts with the government on behalf of the fugitive financier Robert Vesco.[3] The story died, but in Novem-ber 1981 came yet another mess, and by this time the idea that Allen had a penchant for shady financial dealings was well established in journalists' minds. "Richard Allen, President Reagan's national security adviser," sighed the lead of a UPI report on the latest accusation, "is no stranger to public contro-versy. . . ."[4]

The incident behind the UPI story took place on January 21, 1981, the day after the inauguration. On that day Allen received an envelope containing $1,000 from a Japanese reporter who had interviewed Mrs. Reagan. Not long afterward, Allen moved from his temporary office in the old Executive Office Building to permanent quarters in the White House basement. Some months later, military personnel on temporary duty at the White House took over Allen's old office and found the $1,000 in a filing cabinet fitted with a combination lock.

They reported their suspicious find to Edwin Meese III, a member of Reagan's troika of top aides and the one most friendly to Allen. But Meese was also the administration's law enforcement specialist; he promptly called the FBI and put the investigation into the bureau's hands. The FBI found that the Japanese journalists had handed the money to Allen so that he could give it to Mrs. Reagan as a gesture of thanks. Allen, in turn, had given the money to his secretary and asked her to store it until it could be handed over, like all such gifts, to the Treasury. Then everyone had apparently forgotten about the envelope. That, in the FBI's opinion, was that. Bureau director William Webster called Allen to tell him informally that the agents had found no dishonesty.

At the time, none of this was reported in the press. But news of the Allen probe was leaking out of Tokyo, where the conscientious investigators had done some of their checking. Acting White House press secretary Larry Speakes, in a standard preemptive move, gave the story to the media and explained that the incident was already over. When press reports of Speakes' briefing appeared, though, Webster's bosses at the Justice Department quickly announced that the department had in fact not declared the investigation closed. Journalists, noses atwitch, immediately noted that since Allen was a high government official covered by the then-still-new Ethics in Government Act, the Justice Department's continuing investigation could lead to the appointment of a special prosecutor. The story now vaulted into the major leagues.

Piece by piece, press reports added details that deepened the grounds for suspicion and fueled the scandal machine. On November 14, *The Washington Post* reported a claim from the Japanese press that the Japanese magazine interviewing Mrs. Reagan had anted up the $1,000 only after Allen had asked what kind of gift might be forthcoming. This news "indicates," the *Post* spelled out for its readers, "that . . . Allen played a key role in helping to arrange the meeting with Mrs. Reagan."[5] When the *Post* story appeared, Allen protested that he had merely passed on to others an interview request from a Japanese who happened to be a longtime friend of his. "Allen did concede for the first time that he had fielded the initial request for the interview," the next day's *Post* interpreted the new information.[6]

The White House response to such stories encouraged reporters to dig harder and give the incident full scandal treatment. At a presidential press conference, President Reagan, when asked about the Allen affair, spoke his formulaic line meticulously: "I cannot comment on [Allen's future in the administration] while it is under review."[7] Speakes told newsmen that Allen would keep his job—at least until the attorney general decided whether to ask for a special prosecutor. An administration source, of course anonymous, distanced the White House from Allen by leaking the news that it was a top White House aide who had started the probe in the first place.

In a sign that the scandal had escalated, news organizations began a stakeout of Allen's home (a "death watch," it is appropriately called) so they would not miss a single one of his comings or goings. Even when word leaked out that the Justice Department unit in charge of official corruption charges was not going to recommend a special prosecutor, the scandal did not abate. Michael K. Deaver and James A. Baker, the other two members of the Reagan troika, were said in press reports to be stepping up efforts to have Allen resign. White House communications director David Gergen, when asked about the national security aide's future, simply said, "Mr. Allen continues in his job."[8]

Any prospect that the scandal could be finally put to rest disappeared when subsidiary charges, the surefire mark of a sturdy scandal, began to emerge. From Tokyo came a report that a Japanese woman in the inauguration interview party had given Allen two watches as a present. Allen replied that the woman was an old friend of his family's and, in any event, that he had received the gift before he took office. Charge number two then popped up: It turned out that after the FBI's investigation of Allen, director William Webster had made not one but two phone calls to the White House aide, and press reports now suggested in vague and sinister terms that the FBI chief might have been delivering some illicit message. Then came charge number three: Press investigations revealed that on his financial disclosure form, Allen had listed 1978 instead of the correct 1981 as the year he sold his consulting company. Along with this seemingly portentous information came the news that the Justice Department had sent the FBI back to investigate Allen's activities further.

At the end of November, Senator Nancy Kassebaum (R-Kans.) joined Senate Democrats in calling for Allen's ouster. Allen took administrative leave from his job, telling reporters that he was departing so he could speak out more freely on the controversy. The ever-present anonymous source told *Newsweek* that Mrs. Reagan had joined the drive to oust Allen. "She'll get there," said the source, "even if [Allen supporter Ed Meese] has to go."[9] The endgame had begun.

On December 23, Attorney General William French Smith finally announced that he did not think a special prosecutor was warranted in Allen's case. Yet on New Year's Day, 1982, word leaked from the western White House that William P. Clark, a longtime Reagan friend then serving as deputy secretary of state, was likely to replace Allen as national security adviser. Allen's scandal aside, said an anonymous insider, Meese had made a study of Allen's staff on the National Security Council and found "confusion."[10]

Allen, now under attack on several fronts, asked for a face-to-face meeting with the president, which took place on January 4. Meese brought Allen into the Oval Office and, when Allen asked to speak to Reagan alone, excused himself. Allen asked for his old job back. "I can't do that," Reagan answered. By then, too many people for too many reasons wanted Allen out, and the president had indeed chosen Clark to fill the post. On the day Allen resigned, the White House counsel's office finished its own investigation of the affair and found Allen not guilty in his handling of the money from the Japanese journalists.

There is a postscript to this scandal. After Allen was back at his Washington consulting business, press reports continued to say—inaccurately—that he had been kicked out of office because he had improperly accepted $1,000 from the Japanese or because he had been found to have conflicts of interest in his dealings with Japanese businessmen. Allen decided to undertake the endless and expensive job of protesting every time he saw a news organization repeating these mistakes. He and his lawyer even developed a standard information kit to send to erring journalists. It contained the Justice Department report absolving Allen of the scandal's main charge. It also included examples of how other journalists and news organizations—including *The Wall Street Journal, The Washington Post,* and *ABC News*—had misrepresented Allen but corrected themselves or even apologized after receiving his complaints.

The package put journalists on notice: If they refused to rectify their mistakes even after such an explicit demonstration of their errors, they were opening themselves to that journalist's nightmare, the libel suit. Allen's combative technique has had a high rate of success.

The media's behavior in the Allen affair shows why the press is the institution that everybody loves to hate. The most visible aspect of press coverage in the Allen scandal was the overwhelming, sometimes physical, pressure that the media exerted on Allen and his family. "The press," in a big story like this one, does not mean a reporter or two or even ten calling for an interview but several dozen journalists who take sole possession of an official's life and telephone lines. "The press" is not a newsman with a microphone in his hand but a phalanx of equipment and people packed together and standing so close to the prey of the moment that he or she sometimes literally cannot move. The press can even be a troop of guerrilla fighters lying in ambush, tape recorders camouflaged, to catch their ill-starred prey.

At times during the Allen episode the stakeout of his home consisted of as many as 50 to 60 reporters and their crews, plus the television cameras, sound trucks, and all the cable that goes with them, camped out on the remains of his lawn and littering the premises with McDonald's Styrofoam. One group of reporters, Allen complained at the time, had even approached his six-year-old daughter, one of his seven children, and tried to interview her. These journalists, when they heard Allen's complaint, protested their innocence. They said they had merely approached the little girl and asked her nicely, "Is your daddy home?"[11] These reporters simply failed to comprehend the distastefulness of using the child's trusting nature as a means of entrapping her father. Such journalists probably also have a hard time understanding why juries in libel suits get such a kick out of awarding huge damages to individuals who have been harmed by press behavior, or why the public exhibited such thoroughgoing annoyance with the press and its values during Operation Desert Storm.

Every figure involved in a major political scandal during the past decade has gone through an en masse assault by the press, and every one of them remembers it graphically. One official new to such intense press coverage remembered in wonderment, "There were four to ten journalists in front of my house at all times—maybe more at the beginning." Some journalists, he continued, had even tried to search out his teenage child, then away at boarding school. Ed Meese recalled that when he came under criminal investigation in 1987, one of the joys of the experience was to have the family awakened every day at 5:30 A.M. by the bustling arrival of journalists for the day's stakeout. Some of them once stopped his wife as she was trying to drive away from home: It appeared that they thought she might have been smuggling the 200-pound Meese out of the house on the floor of the family car.

Another of the most visible press traits on display in the Allen affair is the reluctance of news organizations to correct errors. The mistakes that journalists made in writing about Allen's scandal were often very clear. Yet even in his relatively simple case, getting the press to apologize has been a major enterprise requiring resort to systematic legal warnings. There are good institutional reasons for media organizations not to roll over readily in the face of criticisms from the people they cover. But their reflexive defensiveness is yet another characteristic that infuriates the targets of attack. Allen is not the only one to have concluded in recent years that press dislike of certain people in politics is implacable and that when it comes to getting redress from the media, hardball is the only technique that makes an impression. So nowadays the Allen strategy—going aggressively after every press error—is increasingly used by public figures with the money, energy, and freedom to pursue it.

The Allen affair also displayed that mysterious phenomenon of momentum that so clearly governs press behavior during a scandal. Driven by a powerful, nearly primeval urge to keep the story going, the press corps on a scandal assignment surges forward to find new facts in the case, preferably facts that seem to provide evidence of the quarry's deeper and broader guilt. In the Allen scandal, news organizations certainly raced to find the stories within the story and dig up new accusations and accusers. The possibility that Allen was in any degree innocent was treated as remote.

News stories about the scandal were written in ways that dramatized the importance of whatever new information was available—or unavailable, if it came to that. "The Japanese press Friday," an enterprising American reporter wrote his lead out of Tokyo one day during the scandal, "took pains not to name names in the Richard Allen affair."[12] "There were lingering questions," another reporter reminded his readers during a lull in the proceedings. "To whom did Meese speak at the FBI? Did Meese initiate the calls? How many calls did Meese or any other administration official make to the FBI regarding the Allen episode? . . . Who initially reported the cash, and on what day in September?"[13] This sort of patter keeps a scandal alive and simmering until new hard information turns up to drive the affair still farther.

The process of keeping the old charges alive until new ones come along requires, of course, the habitual use of innuendo and suggestion to convey a sense of more importance in a story than the facts alone may warrant. This resort to unspoken accusation, which need not be substantiated, is among the press habits most hated by people who become objects of major media attention.

Scandal momentum is related to a more general press phenomenon whose growth worries observers today: sheer sensationalism, or the search for the most disgusting, sinful, or shocking possible facts about public life. This tendency has deep roots in the American journalism of the past two centuries, but only now are we starting to see what it looks like when expressed through the magnifying lens of television. The coverage of the Allen scandal clearly had its share of journalistic sensationalism. To see the practice in full flower, though, we must turn from the Allen story to one that unfolded not long after he left government: the page scandal that hit the House of Representatives in 1982.

Pages are teenagers chosen by their congressmen to spend up to a year in the nation's capital working as gofers for the legislators. In 1982 came shocking charges that pages were participating in organized homosexual activity and that a cocaine ring was operating on Capitol Hill.

On June 30, 1982, the *CBS Evening News* showed two young men sitting before the cameras with their faces obscured. Both of them, said CBS correspondent John Ferrugia, were former pages in the House. One of the ex-pages said he had been a target of homosexual advances and harassment while working on the Hill. The other claimed he had engaged in sex with three congressmen and procured male prostitutes for Hill staffers. Pages had to engage in homosexual activity, the second ex-page said, if they wanted to get ahead in the capital.

The CBS story had immediate impact. Other news organizations took up the tale, some saying that a dozen congressmen or more were involved in the scandal. Another scandal theme soon emerged: Rep. Robert K. Dornan (R-Calif.) told *The Wall Street Journal* that "at least six congressmen have been uncovered by investigators as 'user-consumers' of cocaine."[14] The House quickly ordered its ethics committee to investigate. The committee hired well-known attorney and former Cabinet official Joseph A. Califano to conduct the probe. The investigators, because they were armed with subpoenas, assembled a more detailed picture of a news story's development than most of us ever see. This behind-the-scenes tale was almost as startling as the charges themselves.

Califano's staff found contradictions in the stories of the young men who had made the charges about homosexual activity on the Hill. One of them had gotten into trouble while a page—for drug use, patronizing male prostitutes, and more. Indeed, when he finally left Washington, in a car not his own, his departure triggered an investigation by the Capitol Police. News of the investigation got around. CBS found the ex-page at home in Little Rock, Arkansas, and sought his story. But the young man admitted to congressional investigators that he had made up some parts of it and exaggerated others. He wanted to show people through his TV appearance, he said, that he was not the only page involved in the disturbing activities under investigation.

The second page in the CBS news segment said that CBS reporter Ferrugia had approached him, flattered him, and asked what the page knew about a ring of 25 to 50 homosexual congressmen (including a cocaine addict and a congressman who liked 8-year-old boys) and an employee in the House Doorkeeper's Office who procured pages for them. The page—"a 16-year-old kid satisfying his ego,"[15] he later described himself—started spinning his baroque and substantially false tale.

As for the alleged cocaine dealing, the investigators found that this accusation had come from a tipster named Larry, whose sister was keeping company with a former page. Larry suspected the ex-page—correctly, it turned out—of dealing cocaine. Larry also suspected a good deal more. He called the office of columnist Jack Anderson early in 1981 and accused one senator, two representatives, and several Hill staffers of drug involvement. An intern took the call and wrote a memo based on Larry's charges, calling him "my main source."[16] (Apart from the checking of names and titles, he was her *only* source.) The Anderson staff introduced Larry to an undercover police agent they knew named Michael Hubbard, and Anderson arranged for Hubbard to use Rep. Dornan's office as a cover while pursuing the drug investigation.

Hubbard helped arrest the drug dealer whom the tipster had fingered. But the police agent worried that higher-ups might not let him go further with his probe. So he did what comes naturally to the modern American mind: He blew the whistle, making a list of the congressmen he suspected of drug use and giving it to Rep. Dornan. Dornan began sharing these suspicions with the press. Jack Anderson publicized the story, naming eight congressmen as suspects and referring for his authority to what he called "an investigative document" that bore the same date as Hubbard's memo to Dornan.

The police investigator had gotten his basic information from Anderson's team. Then Anderson, returning the favor, had cited the investigator as his authority. The House probe later found that some drugs were indeed being sold on the Hill. But the story, feeding on itself in this way, had ballooned beyond the bounds of reality.

The Califano staff did discover two cases of improper behavior by congressmen toward pages, and as a result the House censured Rep. Gerry E. Studds (D-Mass.) and Rep. Daniel B. Crane (R-Ill.). The staff found that Studds had enjoyed a homosexual relationship with a page ten years before. As for Crane, the investigators found that he had had sexual relations with a 17-year-old female page three years before the scandal broke:

> At her deposition, the page testified under oath that . . . in the winter of 1980, she made a friendly wager for a six-pack of beer with Representative Crane on the outcome of a basketball game. . . . The page lost the wager. Sometime in the spring, she went to Representative Crane's office in the Cannon Building, around 8 P.M., carrying a six-pack of Heineken beer to pay off the wager.[17]

The predictable ensued.

In short, the real sins exposed by the page scandal were not much like what a TV viewer would have expected after hearing the original stories that the two pages told the nation.

The accusations made by and about the pages in 1982 would have caused a scandal in almost any era: The subject of sex and drugs among the powerful is about as close to a universal scandal theme as you can get. Nor is it new to see a journalist trying to squeeze news out of unsavory characters. Still, many observers agree that the competitive pressures on journalists covering national politics became worse after Watergate. One reason was the fact that the television networks were being pressed by more powerful competition, which started to grow when Ted Turner's new Cable News Network spearheaded the arrival of additional news alternatives for TV viewers. The race was on, as Martin Mayer has put it in his book *Making News*,[18] to gain and maintain popularity by featuring stories that appealed directly to people's emotions. TV newscasts need, as reporter Martin Schram has described it, "news that wiggles."[19]

The page scandal was an extreme example of what can result, but the problem is more pervasive. As Timothy Russert, Washington bureau chief of NBC News, put it recently:

> We've reached news saturation—maybe news overload. With satellites, everyone now has access to the

same pictures and sound bites, and news becomes old with amazing speed. Things have changed; networks are feeling the competition. We've become more aggressive. Sometimes this aggressiveness is viewed as arrogance and—even worse—uncivil behavior. That's a problem.

Also, 10 or 15 years ago, the networks acted as if there was a tacit agreement to be "highbrow" in their definition of news. Now we've got *Geraldo*, *Inside Edition*, *Current Affair*, and *Entertainment Tonight*. Will their presence drive us, consciously or unconsciously, to gravitate toward more sex and scandal coverage?

Probably so, though the popularity of CNN's round-the-clock news coverage of events from the Keating Five hearings to the Gulf war suggests that competition may prod the networks in healthier ways as well.

Still, despite the flaws of the press, the journalists—even with their tendencies to hound their targets, create scandal momentum, and sensationalize—are not the only players who have created our present scandal-filled climate. There are other major actors. For instance, growing numbers of private organizations are now in the business of gathering and disseminating information about politics and policy. Governments and corporations once had a hammerlock on the ability to provide the kind of information a political reporter needs in building a story, but they have lost their exclusivity. The newer organizations, including public interest advocacy groups, exist in no small part specifically to help and encourage journalists to expose malfeasance.

The most famous of these advocacy organizations belong to the Ralph Nader conglomerate. Press coverage was the source of Nader's power, and he established close relations with the press early in his career. Among other techniques, he provided reporters with negative information about his adversaries in government and business. This information, right or wrong, was defensible: A journalist could construct a story from it without fear of being embarrassed by patent inaccuracies. Just as important, reporters regarded Nader's information as untainted because it did not come from the powerful organizations and interest groups they so mistrusted. Nader shrewdly called himself a "noninstitutional source." He was, his biographer Charles McCarry notes, "virtually the first such source in history."[20]

Nader has by now become an institution himself. He has established, inspired, managed, or cooperated with many separate public policy organizations, from the Corporate Accountability Research Group and the Tax Reform Research Group to the Aviation Consumer Action Project, the Clean Water Action Project, the Center for Concerned Engineering, and the Freedom of Information Clearinghouse. Many of these groups have the ability to generate information—mostly unfriendly—about government and corporations in their policy areas. They, like Nader, are accorded the credibility given to noninstitutional sources. They make the climate in their respective fields distinctly user-friendly for reporters hunting scandalous material.

Similar help for journalists is provided by organizations like the well-known Common Cause. This group was founded in 1970 to oppose the Vietnam war but not long afterward turned its attention to classic good-government issues. During Watergate it sued the Committee to Re-Elect the President and forced the disclosure of large corporate contributions to Nixon's 1972 campaign. Common Cause championed the 1974 legislation that limited individual contributions to political campaigns, and in 1988 the group pushed for a congressional pay raise linked to a ban on outside honoraria for congressmen.

The organization's current clout comes partly from its grass-roots lobbying network and partly from its expertise. It keeps tabs on good-government proposals and on relevant legislation making its way through Congress: Common Cause knows its details, where it stands in the enactment process, and how to answer arguments made against it. The organization compiles campaign finance statistics to illustrate how much legislators owe to the moneyed people who help elect them. Journalists trust Common Cause's information as untainted, like Nader's. They know that if they use Common Cause information they are not likely to be accused of having been captured by some corrupt financial interest.

The Nader organizations and Common Cause are not exceptional. In 1990 the Washington-based Foundation for Public Affairs, after purging its files to eliminate marginal groups, still listed over 1,000 public interest advocacy organizations active in national politics, not counting narrower business and occupational groups. More than half of such public interest organizations were founded after 1960, and more than half not only do business in the capital but also have a permanent office there. Such figures give a sense of how much valuable nonofficial information today's journalist has at his or her disposal when setting out on a scandal hunt.

Increased aid from outside groups is not the only change that encourages scandal stories in the press. Journalists get some of their most important help from the government itself. To see how, let us return full circle to the Allen scandal. Even in this episode, where the press played such a large and visible role, journalists were no more important than a government reshaped by the changes in structure and climate that have taken place since Watergate.

As for climate, Ed Meese, the White House aide who received the original information about Allen and called in the FBI, said some years later that if he had gotten the same sort of report in pre-Watergate days, "I would have been able to call Allen directly and get the story more quickly. [The story of Allen's dishonesty] was implausible from the beginning. If he [had] intended to take the money for himself, he wouldn't have left it in the safe." But this was not the old days. "There was such concern that someone might think something was being done wrong," Meese continued, that taking the matter out of political hands was the only prudent thing to do. This decision guaranteed that even though dishonesty did not seem to be involved, the inquiry would go on.

Still, the episode might have ended when FBI agents found no evidence of impropriety and FBI director Webster phoned Allen to tell him so. But the Justice Department decided that the investigation was not closed. A major reason was the Ethics in Government Act, which made it almost impossible to end the probe at an early stage if there was any chance at all that wrongdoing might be involved. In any event, the law did not allow the FBI director to close the investigation; the attorney general himself had to examine the facts and authorize a stop to it. Also, by

1981 it was politically more dangerous for the Justice Department to close such an investigation quickly and informally than to continue it and thereby give itself some insurance against the dreaded charge of coverup.

The government's continuing the investigation gave journalists more time to dig at the story for fresh angles and increased the chance that damaging new information would turn up. Even more important, it was the official investigation that made Allen a possible target for a special prosecutor and thus gave the story greatly expanded news potential. The government's investigation also added the drama of a 90-day deadline, because under the new law the attorney general had only that long to decide whether or not to ask the court for a special prosecutor. In short, post-Watergate law and the functioning of a post-Watergate government gave the journalists their cues and openings.

The changed climate inside the government affected the news in yet another way: The journalists on the Allen story, for all their enthusiasm, actually got most of their information through leaks from inside the government. The scandal grew as big as it did not simply because of the media's determined nosiness but because players inside the government had decided to manipulate this trait.

Government insiders played an especially large role in the Allen affair because Allen was not a well-loved figure in the capital, before or after his rise to power. When Allen looked back on his scandal not long ago, he judged that a big part of his problem came from an ideological reaction by the liberal establishment against an intruding conservative. He also thought part of the antagonism came from the fact that he, unlike his predecessors in the national security adviser's job, had refused to serve as a major source for the press. According to Allen, soon after he arrived at his job the prominent columnist Joseph Kraft suggested:

> [M]aybe we should set up the same kind of relationship he'd had with previous national security advisers, where he'd meet with them on a scheduled basis. . . .
> I said that was nice for him, but I didn't understand what was in it for me. He said he'd be able to report on my views in a more informed way.

In other words, if I fed him he'd take care of me. I said no, I wasn't interested in the process. And he said that in that case, I wouldn't be interested in the results. . . . [N]ot long after that, the little jabs and barbs—"bad manager," "disorganized"—began to appear.

Kraft is no longer alive to give his version of the encounter. Still, the story clearly shows that Allen took the columnist's words not as an offer of cooperation but as a threat, and that the aide profoundly mistrusted established Washington figures and refused to work with them in the conventional way.

Allen had similar troubles with some of his colleagues inside the government. One middle-level foreign policy official said he had always felt insulted by the combination of "second-rate thinking" and "a certain arrogance" in Allen. When Allen first took over at the National Security Council, the official recalled, the staff told him that he should be doing certain types of national security studies. "Allen would say," the man remembered disapprovingly, "that they didn't need studies. They were just going to 'react prudently to events.' "

Some White House aides, Michael Deaver among them, were either personally hostile to Allen or sure that he was in over his head and bound for trouble. So when the $1,000 story hit the press, according to one witness, "They simply used the opportunity to get rid of him." Recognizing the investigation for the opportunity it was, shrewd White House operators saw to it that Allen received no public support. They got the president to stay neutral instead of expressing confidence in his aide. Just as important, the anonymous sources were set loose. They spoke to the press more frequently as the scandal wore on, assuring journalists that Allen was going to go.

If so much distaste was pouring forth from Allen's own colleagues, a journalist might be forgiven for assuming that the charges against him were somehow justified. In addition, these "inside" comments gave the press the plot line of the Allen saga. When journalists wrote their stories, they already had a pretty good idea of what the final chapter would say.

Leaks from the government to the press are as old as the two institutions themselves. In this country, news organizations have always served as bulletin boards for the national political community. Yet in recent years it sometimes seems that the press, by default, has become the only bulletin board in town. Certainly no bureaucracy in the federal government can conduct anything like private internal communications with its employees anymore. At the other end of Pennsylvania Avenue, congressmen increasingly talk to their staffs more than they talk to each other. The once-well-developed communications systems of the political parties have fallen victim to reform and are today a pale shadow of their old selves.

Such changes have made the press increasingly prominent tool of political warfare. In May 1991 *The Washington Post* began publishing excerpts from *The Commanders,* a book by its reporter Bob Woodward on the U.S. military structure.[21] The resulting gossip asked not whether high-level defense officials had talked to Woodward but only which ones had done so. The press was not the primary cause of these developments; it has simply and happily feasted on the disintegration.

Those who are skilled political operators—in the White House, on the Hill, within the bureaucracies, or in organizations outside government—see, of course, that the press has become more important in this way. They are therefore increasingly likely to step into the nearest phone booth and emerge as an anonymous source who knows how to keep journalists fed, watered, and thoroughly manipulated. Indeed, such a source is so often present at the scene of a scandal story that by now his appearance is itself a part of the tale, and one that the press feels almost obliged to report. Most journalists covering political scandals today are as dependent on these sources as old-style journalists were on *their* political sources. In the past, the typical sin of the source-dependent reporter was puffery. Today it is more likely to be character assassination.

So changes in our politics and in government itself, and not just the imperatives of today's news business, have helped create these scandal-filled years. There remains, however, what some consider the central issue: that of the political spirit in which modern journalists cover the news. Today's press is often said to have grown biased against conservatives, business, free markets, and traditional values. When we consider this accusation, we should remember that there is rarely anything new under the

American journalistic sun. In particular, press hostility to political and business authority is not a new development. Indeed, the phenomenon probably reached its height not among today's journalists but with the muckrakers of the late 19th and early 20th centuries.

The famed turn-of-the-century journalist Lincoln Steffens, for instance, when writing his autobiography, remembered that in the winter of 1905–1906, when the U.S. Senate was resisting Theodore Roosevelt's economic reforms, the muckrakers declared to one another that the Senate "was a chamber of traitors, and we used to talk about the treason of the Senate."[22]

David Graham Phillips, the novelist and muckraking reporter, took the title *The Treason of the Senate* for his famous 1906 series of exposés of the Congress. "Treason is a strong word," Phillips wrote,

> but not too strong, rather too weak, to characterize the situation in which the Senate is the eager, resourceful, indefatigable agent of interests as hostile to the American people as any invading army could be . . . interests whose growth and power can only mean the degradation of the people, of the educated into sycophants, of the masses toward serfdom.[23]

Elsewhere in the series, Phillips characterized Senator Chauncey Depew, one of his targets, as a man of "greasy conscience," "greasy tongue," and "greasy backbone."[24] They're not making reporters like that anymore.

Still, Phillips was a member of a very small elite. Today's animus is shared by a much larger corps of journalists, and observers are fairly clear that the general stance of the press is distinctly more antagonistic toward government and its officials than it was, say, 25 years ago. "When I was a young reporter," recalled *New York Times* writer Martin Tolchin, a 36-year veteran at the paper,

> we had assumptions about people in public life—that they had the interest of the public at heart, that they were honest and competent. It took a heck of a lot to overcome those assumptions. But today, some journal-

ists have no assumptions and others have the opposite of the old assumptions. The old way, if you covered a politician, you were a friend and part of an entourage. Today, politicians know that journalists are *not* their friends—that there's no such thing as off the record, background, or anything of the sort.

One sign of the changed spirit is the recent growth in the number of press people who think of themselves as investigative journalists. The term refers less to specific techniques or modes of research than it does to an attitude: the determination to fight the established powers for the information whose exposure will bring about some malefactor's downfall. In labeling themselves investigative reporters or saying they are devoted to investigative journalism, reporters and news organizations signify that they have adopted the adversarial stance those words convey. Investigative reporters have traditionally been pictured, for good reason, as tenacious, often lonely fighters against the established powers in behalf of political and social justice. Nowadays, though, they are no longer so alone.

In 1986 a survey aimed to find out from editors at the country's 500 biggest newspapers and top 200 TV stations whether they were doing more investigative reporting than they used to. The term was defined this way: "(1) it is a topic treated in an in-depth way, often using documents and records; (2) it reveals something significant that an agency or person wants to keep secret; (3) it largely is the result of a reporter's own work." Nearly 98 percent of the respondents said their organizations did at least some investigative reporting. Over half of them said they were doing more than they had done five years previously. More than 71 percent of the newspaper editors said the use of investigative reporting techniques had increased among beat reporters.[25] Recent budget cuts by some types of news organizations have cut into the numbers of investigative and other reporters. But the figures are still well above what they were when today's investigative wave started.

The modern investigative reporter can get organized professional aid in learning how to practice his craft. The biggest advisory outfit is Investigative Reporters and Editors, Inc., based at the University of Missouri, with a membership of around

3,000. The IRE holds frequent conferences devoted mainly to helping members develop reportorial tools and techniques. Most of the articles in its newsletter dispense practical advice, a journalistic version of Heloise's household hints, with stories such as "Bankruptcy Court Fertile Snooping Ground"[26] and "Investigating the Nuclear Power Plant."[27] Readers learn what information corporations are required to file with the federal government, when it is legally permissible to search other people's garbage, and how to use the Freedom of Information Act to maximum effect.

Advice of this sort probably does not make much difference at the biggest metropolitan newspapers, but it almost certainly improves the technique of reporters elsewhere in the country. In recent years, the Cleveland *Plain Dealer*, the *San José Mercury News*, and the *St. Paul Pioneer Press Dispatch* have broken scandals concerning national politicians. Some of the most significant reporting on the savings and loan scandal came from papers in Michigan and Ohio. Paula Parkinson was brought to us by the Wilmington *News-Journal* and Donna Rice by *The Miami Herald*.

One effect of this expansion is still more competition for the larger, more established news organizations. But there are other consequences as well, only partly accounted for by the simple pressures of competition. This country's great investigative journalists are a national treasure. Yet not long ago veteran investigative reporter Nick Kotz pointed to one of them when he commented on the recent changes in his field. "When I came to Washington in 1964, there was Jerry Landauer at the [*Wall Street*] *Journal*, Larry Stern and Morton Mintz at *The Washington Post*—damn few people doing the real, hard digging." Nowadays, Kotz continued, "There are so many *more* of them—or at least people who *call* themselves investigative reporters."

Kotz is not the only experienced journalist to have become uncomfortable about all the fresh troops "who *call* themselves investigative reporters." Another was star reporter Jerry Landauer, one of those mentioned by Kotz. Landauer worked at the *Journal* from 1963 until he died of a heart attack at the age of 49 in 1981.

If any reporter was ever "investigative," in the sense of being dedicated to uncovering malfeasance in American business and government, it was Landauer. In 1971 he broke the story of how the dairy industry had shoveled large amounts of cash into the Nixon reelection fund in return for a hike in dairy price supports. In 1973 he revealed the story of bribe taking by then–vice president Spiro Agnew. In 1975 he exposed payoffs by U.S. corporations to corrupt government officials abroad.

Landauer was as guileful as any other first-rank reporter when it came to getting information. After his death, his friend Kenneth Bacon, also with the *Journal,* told about a news story that the two of them had covered, involving a payoff of nearly $500,000 by the Del Monte corporation through a business consultant to officials of the Guatemalan government. The two reporters had the story from an anonymous tip but could not confirm it. So Landauer decided on a frontal assault and asked a Del Monte lawyer to meet the reporters for lunch at the Madison Hotel in Washington. Landauer's strategy, Bacon recalled, was very simple: "Since we knew almost nothing, we would pretend that we knew a lot and try to bluff the story out of him." At the Madison, said Bacon:

> I asked questions for hours and hours and the lawyer went through this very dull story. He finished with a great look of self-satisfaction and said, "You can see there's absolutely nothing here to write about."
>
> At which point Jerry went—slamming his hand on the table—"That's the most ridiculous thing I've ever heard! You mean you traveled 3,000 miles to tell us that? Look. Go back to San Francisco and talk to your clients who are paying you big money to come here and buy us lunch in the Madison Hotel and spend the whole day with us and tell them we need a few facts or we're just gonna have to say that your company paid $500,000 to a guy and you don't even know his name and you don't know what you got for it."
>
> So the lawyer went back to San Francisco and came to Washington a week later and delivered a pretty full account of what had happened. Afterward, I said to Jerry, "How did you know he was going to come back with the facts?" And he said, "The harder you kick 'em, the faster they come back."

This basic technique was not what you would call overly polite or truthful. It is, however, immediately recognizable to many politicians who have been caught in an investigative reporter's sights.

Yet when the Koreagate influence-buying scandal broke in 1977, Landauer was not on the investigative train, and in an article for the *Journal* he explained why. More than two years before the scandal hit the headlines, he explained, a South Korean defector publicly charged that South Korea was in effect buying the favor of U.S. congressmen with campaign contributions. "The media," noted Landauer in his piece, "ignored him."[28] But the Justice Department later began an investigation, *The Washington Post* reported on it in the fall of 1976, and the chase was on.

Press reports said that 22, then 90, then 115 congressmen were under investigation. The amount of money said to be involved mounted to $1 million a year. The scandal was said to be spreading—"scandals must always seem to be 'growing,' 'spreading,' or 'widening,' lest they appear stale,"[29] Landauer noted—to the Senate. Yet not a single senator was ever identified. When an indictment finally emerged, the case against sitting representatives involved less than $150,000 paid out over eight years, mostly in the form of legal contributions. Sources in the Justice Department and Leon Jaworski's congressional investigation staff said they were mystified as to where the hugely inflated numbers had come from.

Though some journalists did good reporting on the scandal, Landauer thought the way it grew demonstrated the dangers in the post-Watergate style of scandal journalism:

> [I]n the capital these days a scandal isn't a scandal until important segments of the media "discover" it. Once perceived, a scandalous situation is likely to dominate the news, for no newspaper editor or television executive wants to miss another Watergate. Then, as more newspeople pounce on the story, competitive pressures can overshadow fair play, resulting in overstated coverage that may not end until another "scandal" comes along to divert the media's attention.[30]

Shortly before he died, Landauer prepared a prospectus for a course on modern investigative reporting that he wanted to teach at Washington's left-leaning Institute for Policy Studies. The course would explore, he wrote,

> several major themes: Is the press too ardent in the pursuit of scandal? Is there a proper concern for fairness and accuracy? Has the emphasis on investigative reporting generated perceptions of wrongdoing where none exists? And does the press needlessly contribute to disillusionment with government and other institutions of society?[31]

That was the question Landauer left for his fellow reporters covering the Reagan administration, and it is the fundamental question that the disciples of investigative reporting must confront. For some time now, a debate has gone on about the ideological bias of the press. This bias clearly exists. But bias in the conventional liberal-versus-conservative sense may be less important in determining the scandal reporting we get today than the imperatives of the reporter's job as we have come to define it.

When Speaker of the House Jim Wright emerged in the spring of 1989 as designated scandal target of the season, the counsel to the House ethics committee started releasing damaging information about him and journalists started gobbling it up and spewing it out. Some liberal opinion makers in the press were clearly uncomfortable about the way they were cooperating in bringing about Wright's political demise, but the process did not stop. "All of us," said James T. Wooten of ABC News about himself and his colleagues in the press,

> are trying unsuccessfully to avoid the appearance of a feeding frenzy. You hear them say, "Here come the sharks," but what the hell are we supposed to do except find people to answer our questions?[32]

There is, indeed, often nothing else a reporter can do these days, for the aggressive, investigative, adversary style of journalism and the attitudes that go along with it have become the accepted measure of journalistic excellence. All good reporters, in this view, should mistrust official explanations, and reporters should occupy themselves by digging for things that established institutions do not want us to know. The central purpose of the journalistic craft, the argument continues, is to bring to citizens' attention the flaws in their institutions and leaders. If citizens learn more about nefarious political activities they will be better able to throw the bums out. Indeed, the basic reason for giving the press very broad protections and privileges in a democracy is that people need to know the bad news in order to perform their duties as citizens.

These principles can produce great acts of courage by individual journalists. The same principles can also provide a sure-fire recipe for increasing the amount of scandal put before the American citizenry. They do not necessarily constitute a bad way for the news media to function as a gadfly to government. But today's press is no gadfly; the nature of current politics has made the media more powerful than ever before in this century, and sometimes more powerful than any other single institution, in determining how our public life will be perceived and conducted.

Under these circumstances, when journalistic aloofness from political institutions edges toward nihilism, and reporters view every established leader or organization chiefly as a locus of possible crime, they can easily produce a steady scandal diet of the sort that will not do the job of encouraging citizens to be politically active and keep their public officials accountable. Instead, the constant scandal stories put forward by alienated news organizations can—and do—deter people from participating in politics at all. When this happens, the press stops helping people to be good citizens. And when it can no longer perform this function it loses the foundation of its own legitimacy.

Our modern journalism, teetering on this edge, is the lens through which we view and judge all the other actors in our scandal dramas.

CHAPTER 4

THE ETHICS APPARAT: INDEPENDENT COUNSELS

THE RICHARD ALLEN saga became a major news story in large part because of one question: Would Attorney General William French Smith be forced to ask for a special prosecutor in the case? The keen press interest in this issue reflected a political reality: If a special prosecutor were to enter the picture, the scandal would be invested with an air of momentous and sinister drama.

By the time of the Allen scandal, the office of special prosecutor had become a central symbol of post-Watergate politics. Following Watergate, Congress erected the institution as the grandest monument to its victory over Richard Nixon and the Imperial Presidency. The country urgently needed the new law, proponents claimed at the time of passage, because it was the only way to ensure that high officials were treated like ordinary citizens when it came to matters of criminal justice. This fair and equal treatment, in turn, was the only means through which we could rebuild public confidence in our political system.

Yet today, more than a decade after the act was passed, it is increasingly apparent that the advocates were wrong. If by "public confidence" they meant merely that the act would mute the short-run suspicions endemic among certain parts of the political elite, the legislation has succeeded. If we ask the more fundamental question of whether the criminal law system treats today's high executive branch officials more like ordinary citizens, the answer is clearly no. And if the issue is whether the law has inspired more trust in government in any long-term sense, there is not much sign of success. Indeed, the design of the act virtually ensures that there never will be.

The idea of a federal prosecutor wholly independent of the executive branch is a novelty in American politics. For more than 200 years, Congress and the president have been engaged in a sustained, constitutionally engineered low-intensity conflict over power, and the struggle periodically erupts into full-scale war. In the course of hostilities, Congress has used many sorts of sanctions against the presidency—budget cutting, investigations, and threats of impeachment, to name just a few. Yet until Watergate, the Congress, even in contentious times, never challenged the president's control over federal law enforcement, which both sides in these battles saw as the quintessential executive branch function.

From time to time presidents would appoint special prosecutors for important cases. Following this precedent, the Nixon administration's attorney general, Elliot Richardson, appointed Archibald Cox special prosecutor in 1973 to investigate the Watergate mess. In the fall of that year Cox insisted on his right to subpoena tapes of presidential conversations. As a result, Nixon fired him. The president, it is generally agreed, was within his legal rights to do so. But his own attorney general and deputy attorney general resigned rather than carry out the order, and the event generated a huge public outcry. Washington was swamped with 150,000 telegrams—the "heaviest concentrated volume on record," according to Western Union.[1] Almost all the messages protested the firing, and the uproar fatally crippled Nixon's presidency. The same public opinion forced the president to hire yet another special prosecutor and give him the broad powers necessary to continue the investigation. The new special prosecutor and the regular judicial system investigated more than 100 suspects and obtained several dozen convictions, on a budget of about $2 million a year.[2]

The lesson of the episode, you might think, was that our political structure could prevent a president from misusing his high-level law enforcement powers. Yet the post-Watergate Congress, in a sign of the times, found it an intolerable menace that the presidency had these powers at all.

Title VI of the 1978 Ethics in Government Act tried to remove this threat through a series of complex limits on the president and his appointees in cases involving charges of high-level executive branch wrongdoing.[3] The new law gave the attorney general, a presidential appointee, the sole authority to initiate the appointment of special prosecutors (renamed independent counsels in 1983). But the law also placed elaborate restrictions on this authority. The attorney general, whenever he received "specific information" that a federal crime had been committed by a senior executive branch official or officer of the president's campaign committee, was required to conduct a preliminary investigation lasting no more than 90 days. A court could give him a limited extension of time, but only if he showed good cause. During the 90 days, the attorney general was not allowed to issue subpoenas, convene a grand jury, or strike a plea bargain.

Unless this early investigation showed that the charge was "so unsubstantiated that no further investigation or prosecution [was] warranted," the attorney general was next required to ask a specially created division of the federal courts to appoint a special prosecutor. If the attorney general decided not to ask for such an appointment, he had to file an explanatory report with the court. If the original request for the investigation had come from Congress, the legislators, too, had to be provided with an explanation of just why the attorney general thought a special prosecutor unnecessary.

The court had full discretion in its choice of special prosecutors, and once appointed, such officials were almost entirely independent. A special prosecutor was to follow Justice Department policies, according to the new law, only "to the extent [he or she] deems appropriate." Unlike regular prosecutors, special prosecutors were quite free to make public statements during their investigations. When the special appointees were finished with their jobs, they were required to file a report with the court, which was expected to make it public. They had to ask the attorney general's consent only if they wanted to extend the scope of the investigation beyond what the court had already granted.

The attorney general could remove the special prosecutor only for what the law called "extraordinary impropriety," a phrase that was later changed to "good cause" in order to avoid clear constitutional problems. Even then, the AG had to file reports with both the court and Congress justifying the action. The fired special prosecutor could appeal in court to block his or her removal.

The act was notable for the independence it tried to guarantee for the special prosecutor. Just as important, the new law required the investigation of some accusations that a prosecutor operating under regular federal standards would reject as bases for criminal inquiry. Finally, the act provided for more publicity in the course of an investigation than a regular prosecutor, if he or she is an ethical one, usually generates.

The first aim of the legislation—to make the special prosecutor independent—has been achieved. Few people in and around national politics question the proposition that special prosecutors make their decisions free of executive branch coercion. It would be hard to find many opinion makers who believe that someone leaned on Arthur Christy to get him to decline prosecution of Hamilton Jordan. In the same way, a decade after the Jordan affair, critics found many faults with the Iran-contra investigation conducted by independent counsel Lawrence Walsh, but obsequiousness to executive branch authority was plainly not one of them.

This independence from the executive branch has lent special prosecutors and independent counsels great authority—so great that their verdicts sometimes have substantial political effects. In 1984, for instance, an independent counsel was named to investigate Edwin Meese III, one of President Reagan's top aides and his nominee for attorney general. The appointment caused bitter ideological controversy. Though politically shrewd, Meese—usually sporting an Adam Smith necktie and an unflappable smile—was viewed by his opponents as a kind of Southern California country bumpkin and conservative movement cheerleader. Worse, he had played a major role in designing the administration's civil rights policies, deemed by Senator Edward M. Kennedy a "disgrace."[4] Worst of all, there were whispers that Meese was being groomed for the Supreme Court, and civil rights groups were up in arms against the nomination.

This being the post-Watergate era, the dispute soon turned from ideological sparring to criminal investigation. A man named Roy C. Meyers, an aide to Senate Judiciary Committee member Howard M. Metzenbaum (D-Ohio), flew out to Meese's home territory of California to search for damaging information on the nominee.[5] At first he found none. But a former Senate investigator eventually steered Meyers toward records on Meese's sale of his San Diego home, which he had left upon moving to Washington at the start of the Reagan administration. When Meese appeared before the Senate Judiciary Committee for his confirmation hearings in March 1984, committee Democrats began asking Meese about charges that his financial dealings were unethical. Metzenbaum asserted that Meese, when selling the San Diego house, was given bank loans on specially favorable terms in return for getting federal jobs for two Californians connected with the bank.

There followed, in classic fashion, a procession of additional charges. The press revealed that Meese's wife had taken a $15,000 interest-free loan from a man who soon afterward became Meese's White House deputy. The loan had not been listed on Meese's financial disclosure form. Mrs. Meese had used the loan to buy stock for the Meese children in a company called Biotech, and documents showed that a Biotech subsidiary had been given a special exemption to make it eligible for a Small Business Administration loan. Rep. John Dingell (D-Mich.), chairman of the House Energy and Commerce Committee, called for a probe into the matter by the Securities and Exchange Commission.

Then the White House was forced to admit that Meese, after a trip to Korea, had kept a set of jade cuff links given to him by the South Korean government. The rules said a federal official could accept only gifts worth less than $140, but the cuff links were said to be worth $375. After that news, the army's inspector general charged that Meese had gotten an improper promotion in the army reserve. The mounting charges were pushing the nomination toward a quick doom. So Meese himself called for an independent counsel to clear his name and to break the scandal's momentum through a cease-fire.

Independent counsel Jacob A. Stein started work on the Meese case in April. For a while it looked as if Stein would be just one more juggler in a multiring circus, with Congress and journalists continuing to generate and expand on charges and suspicions. In early April, for instance, Metzenbaum produced a new public

accusation: Though financial disclosure rules required top officials to report all trips paid for by private groups, Meese had
taken 26 such trips over the preceding three years but reported
only 8. Meese's lawyers lodged a well-publicized protest with the
Judiciary Committee, claiming that the Metzenbaum charge was
an "inflammatory and political use of the media" that could be
"extremely prejudicial" to the important work of the independent counsel.[6] This argument that the independent counsel's
investigation was quasi-judicial in nature did not stop all extra-
curricular activity during the proceedings but had enough impact to limit it. The scandal's momentum was further slowed by
the fact that the independent counsel's office was relatively leak-
proof. The silence built a good deal of suspense about what the
final report would say.

In September the report at last emerged. It was said to have
gone through seven drafts to ensure that its language did not
give unwarranted aid to partisans on either side of the Meese
debate. "Nowhere in the statute or the order [appointing me] is
there a directive," Stein wrote, "to investigate and report on the
propriety or the ethics of the respondent's conduct."[7] So the
report simply marched through the charges one by one, saying
in each case that there was no evidence to warrant criminal
prosecution.

Stein produced no indictment and no verdict of innocence.
More politically significant, the report contained no language
that could readily be used against the nominee. Meese declared
himself exonerated. The opposition agreed that the fight was
over. "The questions examined and resolved by the special counsel," Senator Kennedy forthrightly ended the battle, "should no
longer be part of the confirmation process."[8] The nomination
was a cliff-hanger, but in February 1985, the Senate finally
voted to confirm Meese as attorney general.

Those people who opposed Meese's appointment had over-
shot the mark. Watergate had led to a perverse grade inflation
in charges of moral turpitude, so that Meese's critics felt they
had to accuse him of not merely incompetence or bad character but the actual commission of crimes. By doing so,
though, they placed the matter in the hands of an independent
counsel. At the time, the tactic looked as if it stood a good
chance of success. After all, the independent counsel was free

of control by the president and would surely respond vigorously to charges of executive branch criminality. But like most independent counsels to date, Stein chose to use a less metaphorical standard than that of Meese's accusers in deciding what was and was not criminal.

The final report thus disappointed the anti-Meese camp. But the opponents, most of whom had supported the establishment of the independent counsel's office as a guarantor of fairness, could hardly claim afterward that the verdict was illegitimate. Their attack on Meese damaged him badly for the long run, but their choice of the independent counsel's office as a weapon had bound them to acknowledge the counsel's authority and permitted Meese to survive the confirmation fight simply by not being demonstrably guilty.

The legitimacy of the independent counsels has been bolstered, it must be said, by an extralegal advantage: The first individuals appointed under the new statute had outstanding personal credentials. When people viewed the Hamilton Jordan case, for instance, they did not merely think that political figures had refrained from leaning on special prosecutor Arthur Christy. They also thought that Christy was not the kind of man who would have consented to be leaned on. As for Jacob Stein, Meese's independent counsel, he was past president of the District of Columbia Bar Association, a board member of *The American Scholar* magazine, and aggressively nonpartisan in his politics. It is not easy to make corruption charges stick against such individuals. Unimpeachable reputations have enabled independent counsels to stick within the narrow view of their job and resist pressures to make more comprehensive judgments. Insisting on the narrow view, in turn, may disappoint the political partisans in the audience but has helped counsels maintain a widespread acceptance of their decisions.

There is irony here. The aim of the special prosecutor legislation was to do away with secret decision making in the criminal investigation of high officials and replace it with openness and regularity. But the individuals who have filled the job have been chosen through a process marked by secrecy and favoritism. Independent counsels are picked by senior federal judges who need not account publicly for their decisions, and a certain amount of old-boy politics clearly influences the choices. These features of the process are anathema to the spirit that underlay the law's passage. Yet the same characteristics, by producing generally good personnel, have enabled the system to work.

The luck need not hold forever. Indeed, in recent years the independent counsels have begun to arouse more criticism. Whitney North Seymour, Jr., came under fire when he investigated Michael Deaver on charges of criminally violating federal lobbying laws but indicted the ex–White House aide only for perjury committed in the course of the investigation itself. Independent counsel James McKay received similar criticism for his broad comments following the report of his 1987 investigation of Meese on charges of financial impropriety and illegitimate exercise of influence. Alexia Morrison was widely criticized for the length of time—measured in years, not months—it took her to decide that Theodore B. Olson should not be indicted. Judge Walsh's office has been castigated for the length and expense of the Iran-contra probe.

If an independent counsel wants to behave improperly—if, for instance, he or she develops a liking for press coverage and limelight, or does not want to go back home to his workaday law practice in some faraway corner of the country—he has the power to wreak prolonged and frightening harm. His budget is unlimited. He focuses on one or a few individual targets instead of having to divide his time among many. He is almost impossible to remove from office. Choosing the right people for the job is especially important because there are fewer checks on an independent counsel than on almost any other government official wielding comparable power.

If the number of independent counsel investigations stays low, the court may well be able to keep filling the jobs with people whose personal stature buttresses the independent counsel's authority and who are unlikely to submit to temptation. If the number of these investigations grows, the independent counsels will almost necessarily become a more mixed bag. The reputation of the office may fall and we will probably see more abuse of its power.

While the office of the independent counsel has thus far done well in commanding acquiescence among the political elite, this quieting of the natives is not the same thing as making the system more just or increasing the citizenry's trust in government over the long run. By these standards the office has not done well at all. The failure in both areas has had two causes. First, independent counsels must often make public decisions about questions that are normally settled in private. Second, the office has never been fully able to escape the taint of its partisan origins.

We can illustrate the first problem, that of publicity, by looking at one of the most disturbing independent counsel investigations—an inquiry that was run, ironically, by one of the most respected independent counsels, Leon Silverman. Early in 1982, Silverman began investigating President Reagan's secretary of labor, Raymond J. Donovan. The process did not end until six years later. This marathon was not the fruit of some mad inquisitor holed up in his office tracking down one tenuous lead after another in an enraged refusal to admit defeat. In fact Donovan's special prosecutor twice finished the investigation only to be forced by events to take up the work again.

The reason for the investigation's length lies in the wealth of baroque detail that marked the Donovan case. Raymond Donovan, executive vice president of the Schiavone Construction Company in Secaucus, New Jersey, served as New Jersey state chairman of Reagan's 1980 presidential campaign. After the election Reagan prepared to nominate Donovan as secretary of labor. There were whispers that Donovan and his company were connected with organized crime, but the president believed in the principle of political loyalty and gave no credence to the rumors. Investigation by the FBI indicated that the stories were unfounded. Some of the people helping Reagan make these early personnel choices did not know enough about Washington to see how much trouble such a nomination would cause the new administration, whether or not the charges were true. So Donovan was named in December 1980.

By the time the Senate Committee on Labor and Human Resources opened confirmation hearings in January 1981, still more charges had emerged. The Schiavone firm was accused of keeping on its payroll a "ghost" employee who did no work for the company and was in reality a chauffeur for an official of the Teamsters union. The company was also accused of making payoffs to organized crime and corrupt politicians. At the confirmation hearings, though, an FBI official testified that its pursuit of these charges had turned up nothing to substantiate them. "If it were a criminal investigation," said the spokesman, "we would have ended it long ago."[9] On February 3 the Senate voted to confirm Donovan.

This was not the end of the story. In the Donovan case, *nothing* was ever the end of the story. A Donovan accuser named Ralph Picardo, who had been an FBI-protected witness at the murder trial of Teamsters official Anthony (Tony Pro) Provenzano, had appeared on NBC's *Today* show just before the vote and demanded a more extensive probe of the new secretary of labor. "Swans don't swim in the gutter," warned Picardo darkly.[10] Charges continued to circulate, and the Senate labor committee, prodded chiefly by Senator Edward M. Kennedy, reopened its investigation less than a week after Donovan was confirmed.

In June someone leaked the news that the FBI had not given the Senate committee all the Donovan-related material produced by the bureau's wiretaps. This problem, it later turned out, stemmed from the Senate's broadened access since Watergate to FBI nomination reports. By the time of Donovan's nomination, the FBI was in effect reporting simultaneously to the president and the Senate committee involved, and the two bodies were sometimes getting different versions of the same data. But in the confusion over who had what information, even Republicans on the committee, including chairman Orrin G. Hatch of Utah, felt betrayed.

Then a charge came to light from a man named Mario Montuoro, a former official of the New York Blasters, Drillers and Miners Union who claimed he had been fired from his job because of his efforts at union reform. Montuoro said that in 1977 Donovan had attended a lunch at which another Schiavone official had passed a $2,000 bribe to a union official. Montuoro described the lunch right down to the shrimp cocktail appetizer, and George Lardner, Jr., of *The Washington Post* wrote a sympathetic story about him.[11]

The FBI opened another investigation. With the appointment of a special prosecutor now inevitable, Donovan wrote to Attorney General William French Smith and requested such an appointment so that all the questions could be put to rest. Smith granted Donovan his wish. Donovan, treated with more solicitude by the White House than Richard Allen had been, stayed on as secretary of labor. The White House thought a Cabinet officer's departure in the face of mere allegations would set a bad precedent.

At the end of 1981 the court appointed a New York attorney of national standing, Leon Silverman, as special prosecutor in the Donovan case. In six months—not bad, as these efforts go— Silverman produced a report and wound down his investigation. In a press conference Silverman noted the "disturbing number" of allegations against Donovan. But some of the accusations were inconsistent with one another. Some were contradicted by credible witnesses. Some were controverted by records. After all the sifting, there remained "insufficient credible evidence"[12] —Silverman had coined this careful term—to warrant federal prosecution. The special prosecutor did not have much more to say to the press.

But just before the June 1982 press conference announcing the report, more charges had been lofted over the transom, involving bid rigging and an alleged payoff to the aforementioned Anthony Provenzano. Silverman started investigating once more.

The Donovan probe began to look like a cross between *Guys and Dolls* and *The Silence of the Lambs*. One informant, Nathan Masselli—son of reputed mobster Pelligrino William (Billy the Butcher) Masselli (who, contrary to what you might think, got his nickname because his trade was ordinary grocery-style butchering)—was shot dead sitting in his car. Press reports suggested, most probably in error, that the slaying was connected to the father's cooperation with the Donovan investigators. Some law enforcement officials started telling journalists that bungling in the special prosecutor's office had caused the hit and that Silverman did not know how to operate in the sensitive field of organized crime.

Two more reputed mobsters rumored to be connected with the investigation were found, seriatim, shot to death in *their* automobiles. On a more encouraging note, Donovan accuser Mario Montuoro won $2.5 million in the New York State lottery. He pledged to use part of the money to establish a fund for the aid of union dissidents.

In September 1982, Silverman submitted a second report dealing with nine new groups of allegations. Like the first report, the second one was filled with accusers retracting their statements and failing to take polygraph tests. Their accusations were sometimes denied by others. Sometimes there was simply no corroboration. Once again there would be no indictment, on grounds of insufficient credible evidence.[13]

Upon Donovan's second escape, the conservative Young Americans for Freedom threw him a 500-guest dinner, and President Reagan expressed public support of his labor secretary. Schiavone lawyers started trying to force retractions from press organizations that had printed accusations against the company, and perjury trials began. Schiavone was investigated by Congress for having hired an investigator to investigate those investigating the company. For a moment the episode seemed to be lurching toward a conclusion.

The moment was brief. The field of organized crime relates to ordinary law enforcement in the way a pot-au-feu relates to a cheese sandwich. Specialists in the area, including writers who become enamored of the subject, operate in a moving sea of leads, probabilities, lies, theories, and fantasies, interspersed with the occasional body in an automobile trunk. The area breeds elaborate and sinister conspiracy theories not likely to be dispelled by anything so straightforward as a special prosecutor's report. Moreover, the special prosecutor's investigations had made Donovan immensely newsworthy. So perhaps it should have been no surprise when in October 1984, shortly before the presidential election, the curtain rose again on the Donovan drama. Bronx district attorney Mario Merola, a Democrat with political ambitions, indicted Donovan and seven other people connected with Schiavone for larceny. At the time of the indictment, the press described Merola as "one of the best DAs in the state."[14] Some journalists began contrasting what they spoke of as Silverman's fruitless past investigations with the energetic, can-do prosecutorial spirit of Mario Merola. Donovan finally took a leave of absence from his government post in order to fight yet another battle.

Merola and Assistant District Attorney Stephen Bookin briefed reporters extensively on the case. The officials explained that Schiavone and Donovan had committed their crimes in cooperation with a dirt-hauling company called Jo-Pel from 1979 to 1984, when Schiavone was a contractor for the 63rd Street subway tunnel being built by the New York City Transit Authority. Because the project was federally subsidized, Schiavone had to meet federal affirmative action requirements by subcontracting part of its work to minority-owned businesses. So Schiavone gave Jo-Pel, half owned by a black New York State senator, a contract for a $12.4 million job. Then Schiavone received reimbursement from the Transit Authority.

The problem, said the prosecutors, was that Jo-Pel was not a genuine minority-owned business. It was only a shell of a company, without its own tools or capital. Therefore Jo-Pel had to lease its equipment from—you guessed it—Schiavone, for $7.4 million. This arrangement meant that Jo-Pel kept only some $5 million of the $12.4 million contract. Schiavone's $7.4 million "leasing fee," prosecutors claimed, was a theft from the citizenry and, in Merola's words, "a fraud upon the minorities of the people of New York."[15]

It took two years for the matter to come to trial, and on the way the prosecution's case started to collapse. The Transit Authority, from which Schiavone had allegedly stolen $7.4 million, stated that the company had actually compiled a good record in handling Transit Authority contracts over the preceding decade. The executive director of the National Association of Minority Contractors said that minority-owned firms often needed leasing arrangements like the one Schiavone gave Jo-Pel if they were to compete for big construction jobs. It was September 1986 before the trial finally started, and when the prosecution had finished presenting its case to the jury, the defense rested without calling any witnesses.

The jurors deliberated less than 10 hours before declaring Donovan not guilty. When the judge ended the official proceedings, Donovan turned to prosecutor Bookin and asked the now-famous question, "Which office do I go to to get my reputation back?"[16]

Yet the acquittal was—that's right—still not the last of the story. During the final week of the trial, the jurors had to be sequestered because a press report had appeared claiming that Silverman was investigating Donovan again. The report was true. Silverman had been called back into action in June 1985.

By this time amendments to the Ethics in Government Act had changed the title "special prosecutor" to "independent counsel," so Silverman became the only individual in history to have the honor of serving as both.

The new probe was started because in the middle of an FBI investigation unrelated to Donovan, two executives had told the bureau that the Schiavone firm and Donovan himself took kickbacks from suppliers. Donovan had denied such accusations during the first Silverman investigation, so the new one centered on charges of perjury. The independent counsel's report on this third investigation—finally, the last—appeared in October 1987. It did not say, as the other two had, that there was insufficient credible evidence for prosecution. This time the report used another carefully chosen phrase and found "some evidence to support an indictment," but not much chance of getting a conviction.[17]

There was only one direct witness against Donovan, the report noted. The man had already been used as a prosecution witness in another criminal trial and proved credible to a jury. On the other hand, he was old and sick with cancer. His story kept changing in significant details, and he got some concrete facts about the scene of the alleged crime completely wrong. He also happened to be awaiting sentencing for a felony, and this situation always gives a jury a somewhat jaundiced view of a witness's motives.

So Silverman's final report, like the previous two, failed to dispel the stubborn ambiguities of the case, and the Donovan affair ended not with answers but with questions.

The Donovan proceedings, totaling six years of inconclusive inquiries, were not only unfair but egregiously so. They were not unfair because Donovan was a minor official who happened to get caught in the law's net: On the contrary, he was just the kind of high-level political appointee for whom the law was designed. Neither were the investigations unfair because the charges against him were ridiculous: They were not. And the probes were not unfair because a publicity-hungry special prosecutor had sensationalized the case: Silverman had to do battle with journalists who resented his refusal to provide them with more headlines.

The problem lay deeper. Every day government prosecutors

have to decide whether individuals should be indicted. Sometimes the answer depends on the strength of the case itself. Sometimes it depends on the matter's importance to some general government policy. Sometimes it depends on a prosecutor's view of various technical factors: the credibility of witnesses, their probable appeal to a jury, the jury's general view of the offense being charged, or the overall likelihood of conviction.

From an ordinary person's point of view, some of these considerations are common sense, some are technical, some are cynical or shockingly Machiavellian, and many are extraneous to the issue of how bad the crime was or how good the defendant's underlying character is. Sometimes these questions cannot be answered with any certitude, and prosecutors have to make their decisions according to unspoken judgments, hunches, and predispositions. But because these prosecutorial decisions are largely made in private, they need not be openly explained or justified. This process has its serious drawbacks. It provides some protection, though, for individuals who are investigated but not indicted.

A public independent counsel investigation, by contrast, is a different sort of ordeal for the person being scrutinized. Donovan's case was complicated by the organized-crime charges involved, but the outlines of his problem were fairly typical. A high official is accused of wrongdoing. The charges are widely publicized by the press and, more often than not, some sort of congressional investigation. When the first wave of charges becomes public, the publicity inevitably stimulates still other charges. These additional charges, too, will be publicized.

When an independent counsel is chosen by the court, the appointment will itself bring more publicity to the accusations. Then, at the close of the investigation, an independent counsel must issue a report, which is almost always made public. The report requirement sets independent counsels far apart from regular prosecutors. First, the report system puts special pressure on an independent counsel to pay meticulous attention to each of the many charges that emerge during the investigation, even if they are implausible or not really worth an expenditure of prosecutorial time.

Second, when the report appears, it will lay out all these charges, from the serious to the remote, bizarre, or malicious.

Sometimes the evidence on an accusation will be complicated or confusing. Sometimes an investigation will turn up the fact that the official involved committed no crime but came close to the edge with behavior that was morally insensitive, in current parlance, or grossly flawed in judgment. Sometimes we will see in one of these reports that only some technical factor has kept the evidence from adding up to a prosecutable offense; the report will have given us enough commonsense evidence to say that the official did wrong. Sometimes the evidence leaves us without a definitive guide: It does not show a crime, but it does not exonerate, either. Finally, the sheer number of the charges enumerated in the report, whatever their disposition, will give us the suspicion that in among them somewhere is a real crime that simply did not get caught.

The traditional prosecutors' code dictates that they put up or shut up—in other words, that when considering a case they either indict or refrain from elaborating on why not. But by law, the independent counsel cannot shut up. Compared with a regular criminal investigation, the independent counsel process leaves fewer of the ambiguities of evidence and strategy on the legal system's cutting-room floor. If an independent counsel chooses not to prosecute, the investigation will still be especially likely to cause suspicion and cast lasting shadows over the official who has been the target. In this sense the new procedures are deeply unfair. Moreover, criminal investigations are hell for those under the microscope. A six-year purgatory like that given Donovan is extraordinary. That such a sentence should be handed out in a case that never came close to being prosecutable is simply unjust.

The publicity of the independent counsel process is also ill suited to promoting general confidence in the quality and character of federal officials. Political Washington may be mollified by it, but in the long run the effect is the opposite: Citizens learn from these investigations that they had more grounds than they ever imagined for mistrusting the morals and competence of their political leaders.

Trust is not something of which this age has an abundance. President Franklin D. Roosevelt's attorney general, Francis Biddle, when once asked about the possibility of removing himself from certain kinds of law enforcement decisions, is said to have replied that if he was not trusted to exercise such authority he would simply resign from office. This is a position barely intelligible to many people active in politics today, and in the independent counsel, such people have designed a system to cater specifically to modern mistrust. If the same system acts to perpetuate and broaden the mistrust on which it was built, that is not a danger the reformers take with any great seriousness.

The other major reason for the law's failures in the areas of fairness and public confidence is the incorrigibly partisan character of the legislation. The new law did not take political pressure out of the process of investigating high government officials but only gave the pressure a new configuration.

The legislation was, of course, partisan in its origins. And even after the 1978 Ethics in Government Act was passed, the president and Congress continued their tug-of-war over its provisions. Congress first amended the independent counsel legislation in 1983. Republicans controlled the Senate, and the political community had seen in the Jordan investigation what harm could occur when a prosecutor was required by the new law to pursue frivolous charges. So the 1983 amendments contained several important concessions to the presidency. For instance, the attorney general got more flexibility in deciding what to investigate: He could now reject a charge against a high official if it came from what he judged to be an inherently noncredible source. Also, the number of executive branch officials subject to the act was reduced, and an official investigated but not indicted would henceforth be reimbursed for attorneys' fees. Finally, the name of the office itself was changed to "independent counsel" in order to try to dissipate the cloud of presumptive guilt that the term *special prosecutor* carried with it.

In 1987, with the Democrats back in control of both houses of Congress, there were more amendments, but this time they all moved in the opposite direction from the earlier batch. Congress, looking back over the 10 years of the act's operation, concluded that the Justice Department had not asked for independent counsels often enough. So the 1987 amendments tried to squeeze the discretion out of the attorney general's role in the process, making it harder for him to turn off an investigation. The amendments limited the length of the initial "threshold inquiry" that Justice could conduct before formally launching the 90-day preliminary investigation. They set new standards of proof and evidence that made it harder for the attorney general to end an investigation without asking for an independent counsel. The amendments also instructed the judges who appointed independent counsels to grant them broad authority so counsels would not have to go back to the attorney general to ask for additional jurisdiction. Finally, Congress gave itself new powers to make the documents from these cases public.

The same political clashes that drove the amendment process have also driven individual cases. The leading example in this area is independent counsel Alexia Morrison's investigation of Theodore B. Olson, the assistant attorney general accused of lying to Congress during the 1982–83 Environmental Protection Agency scandal. On December 27, 1988, Morrison submitted a final report on her investigation of Olson's alleged crimes. In the report she announced that she would not seek prosecution of Olson for lying because what he had told Congress was not a lie. This news came five and a half years after Olson's alleged offense.

The Olson case began as a bitter ideological battle between the president and Congress over the future direction of the federal government's environmental policy. When the Reagan administration took office, one of its stated goals was to free this policy area from the heavy influence of activist environmental groups. To the Reaganites, the environmentalists were extremists who had nevertheless taken places at the very center of the establishment and built alliances both on the Hill and throughout EPA and the Interior Department. In order to break this hammerlock, the administration set about appointing senior environmental officials who could be trusted not to succumb to the environmentalist network's arguments, blandishments, and pressures.

The Reagan appointees could have succeeded only if they had acted shrewdly and made themselves immune from charges of corruption. They did neither, and their enemies had them for breakfast. President Reagan's first secretary of the interior, James G. Watt, came to Washington from a conservative public interest law firm and announced at the start of his tenure that he wanted the department to change its public lands policy so as to place less emphasis on preservation and more on development.

Soon the Sierra Club had collected more than a million signatures on a petition demanding that Watt be fired. Watt had a penchant for impolitic public statements, and his adversaries got their big break when he said about the composition of one of the Interior Department's advisory committees, "I have a black, I have a woman, two Jews, and a cripple."[18] He resigned shortly thereafter. He had given ammunition to those who wanted to delegitimate Reagan's environmental policies by portraying his appointees as not only wrongheaded but dumb, bigoted, and morally deficient.

Reagan's appointee as EPA administrator was ex-Colorado legislator Anne Gorsuch, who married while in office and became Anne Burford. Her political self-immolation was even more spectacular than Watt's. She aroused fierce antagonism among senior staff, especially after she agreed with administration plans to cut EPA's budget. Her critics soon charged that she and her fellow Reagan appointees in the agency were putting the health of the nation at risk by letting private and partisan interests rule the government's administration of the Superfund, a $1.6 billion pot of money that Congress had ordered EPA to collect from manufacturers and apply to cleaning up sites around the country where hazardous manufacturing wastes had been dumped and abandoned.

Scattered throughout EPA were people like Hugh Kaufman, a veteran at the agency and chief investigator of its hazardous wastes division when Superfund was born. In a later conversation Kaufman, still very much at EPA, explained that he thought of himself in broader terms. "I consider myself a policy entrepreneur," he put it. By the time the Reagan administration took office, said Kaufman, "I'd built my own network with the news media and on the Hill," and he worked it vigorously to fight the administration's policies. The process required much effort—for instance, in "continuously feeding the press pack with stories." Kaufman said the constant tending was necessary "in order to keep the heat on. You go to the files and feed them [a] case. You go to the files when you need something else. You need a backlog of cases to use for this purpose." While Kaufman stoked the press fires, he had to prod congressmen as well. As he explained, "You don't think they *cared* about environmental issues, do you?"

Care or not, by the fall of 1982, House panels chaired by Reps. Elliott H. Levitas (D-Ga.) and John Dingell (D-Mich.) were investigating the administration's handling of Superfund. Both chairmen, Levitas on September 13 and Dingell on September 17, formally demanded access to EPA's enforcement files. "I precipitated the fight over [these] documents," said Kaufman in his reminiscing. "I told the Dingell staff, 'Get all the consent agreements.' I knew the administration wouldn't release them."

Kaufman was just about right. The administration said it would supply most of the material but not "enforcement sensitive" documents, unless they showed evidence of wrongdoing. For two months administration lawyers negotiated with House staffers over the disputed documents, but negotiations finally broke down, with each side blaming the other's rigidity.

The president told EPA administrator Burford to withhold the papers on the constitutional grounds of executive privilege. She did so, and on December 16, 1982, the House declared her in contempt of Congress. The administration tried to block the action in federal court, but the judges would not rule on the issue without an actual case of contempt before them. The president and Congress would have to settle this one by themselves.

Once the court had spoken, the denouement of the crisis was swift. The administration gave the House access to the documents, and the House dropped its contempt citation. Burford herself had by then resigned, and the fight seemed over. But, instead, it was merely transmogrified into a criminal investigation.

During the documents fight, the individual most responsible for shaping the Justice Department's position on the controversy was Theodore Olson. EPA had traditionally been accommodating when congressmen asked for internal documents. But because the Superfund controversy was politically important, Justice got involved. As head of the department's Office of Legal Counsel, Olson was in charge of advising the executive branch on major legal issues that faced it, and he took the constitutional threat posed by the EPA case very seriously. It was Olson who wrote the memo to the president on which Reagan based his decision to assert executive privilege. Olson was never accused of having taken his stand in order to hide any actual wrongdoing from the eyes of Congress.

In March 1983, with the documents fight over, congressmen were still angry and suspicious at the way the Reaganites had behaved. On March 10, 1983, when Olson appeared before a House subcommittee chaired by Rep. Peter W. Rodino (D-N.J.) to testify on the Justice Department's annual budget authorization, subcommittee members used the hearing to probe for possible malfeasance behind the administration's decision to invoke executive privilege the preceding year.

Congressmen asked Olson whether the department had given the House all the documents relevant to the issue, including, said one congressman, "discussions reduced to writing on the various options." Olson answered, "Every draft, in a sense, presents options. . . . But I don't know of any option papers or anything of that nature." Another congressman asked whether EPA, as opposed to the Justice Department, had been willing to turn the documents over to Congress. "I don't recall having been told that by anyone associated with EPA," Olson replied. Asked whether anything was missing from the documents given to Congress, Olson answered, "I didn't include handwritten notes of my own," and "I'm not sure that we've included everything."[19]

The Rodino subcommittee could not get what it clearly wanted: either evidence of wrongdoing or the certainty that it had access to the executive branch's entire decision-making process during the documents fight, leaving no corners in which the private thoughts, schemes, conversations, and rude comments of Justice Department personnel could hide. Therefore the discontented subcommittee naturally launched a major investigation, undertaken, the subcommittee's general counsel later said piously, "in hope that a recurrence might be avoided."[20] What the investigation really did was to perpetuate the EPA scandal through an expanded search for malfeasance.

Two years later, in December 1985, the subcommittee staff produced a four-volume, 3,129-page report on the controversy. Chairman Rodino announced that he wanted an independent counsel to investigate the question of whether Olson, now out of government, had lied when testifying before the subcommittee. Rodino also demanded an investigation of two additional Justice Department officials involved in the executive privilege decision: Edward C. Schmults, deputy attorney general at the time of the crisis, and Carol E. Dinkins, assistant attorney general for lands and natural resources, who at the time handled EPA matters within the department. Meese, now attorney general, refused to ask for an independent counsel for the other two ex-officials, contending that the committee's evidence against them did not meet even the undemanding standards set forth in the independent counsel law. He went forward with Olson's case "only," he said later, "because the threshold [for requesting an independent counsel] is so low." Others, putting it less politely, saw Olson as a sacrificial lamb.

An independent counsel began work in April 1986. Within six months it appeared to counsel Alexia Morrison that "viewed in total isolation from the complex of surrounding events and based on evidence we had collected to that point, Mr. Olson's March 10 testimony probably did not constitute a prosecutable offense because it was literally true, even if potentially misleading in certain respects."[21]

The facts were this clear after six months, yet it took four difficult, costly years more to finish the job. During the investigation, after Morrison had declared Olson most probably not guilty, the statute of limitations on Olson's alleged offenses came near to running out. Morrison told Olson that if he did not waive his rights under the law she would indict him then and there. Such a tactic is not unknown among prosecutors, but in this case the pressures were special: In independent counsel cases the official under investigation cannot be reimbursed for legal fees if there is an indictment, even if he is acquitted afterward. So Olson's standing on principle would have cost him—as it turned out when the bills were finally added up—more than a million dollars. He waived his rights, and critics quite understandably started citing Morrison's move as an example of prosecutorial abuse.

The reasons for the delay in the Olson investigation were heavily political. For one thing, when Morrison began her inquiry she was treading ground already plowed by congressional investigators and doing so long after the event. By the time of her investigation, Morrison said later, a number of witnesses claimed—"with some credibility," she noted—an absence of recollection. In addition, because of the public record everyone involved knew what the allegations were and who had said what about them. Thus it was, she said, "harder to get straight stories out of witnesses, who worried about reconciling current testimony with their earlier version."

Morrison herself delayed the proceedings further when she decided that she wanted not merely to finish the Olson investigation but to expand it to cover an EPA official and the two Justice Department officials for whom Attorney General Meese had declined to request an independent counsel. Meese refused to broaden her jurisdiction to the two Justice officials, and the court upheld him. Shortly after the Olson case, the 1987 amendments to the independent counsel law considerably narrowed the attorney general's authority in this area. But in the meantime Morrison had lost, and the dispute had taken five months to resolve.

It is hard to imagine a regular prosecutor spending so much time on such an unpromising case as Olson's, but this was no regular prosecution. An independent counsel, as we have seen, has special incentives to follow every lead and exhaust every possibility. Such incentives are especially strong with a case like Olson's, in which Congress has a proprietary interest because of the huge amount of congressional time and effort already invested in the project. Thus, the way the Olson investigation persisted is no surprise. On the contrary, it would have been striking to see the independent counsel's office setting stricter limits to its own inquiry.

A final reason for delay in Morrison's investigation grew unmistakably out of partisan politics in the deepest sense: Opponents of the independent counsel law chose Olson's case as a vehicle for trying to have the legislation declared unconstitutional. With the 1978 independent counsel law, opponents argued, Congress had taken from the executive branch the constitutionally established executive function of law enforcement. Olson's case seemed like a good vehicle for the challenge. He was not accused of committing any crime for personal profit. Also, the length of his case showed how an independent counsel could use the office's vast discretionary power to visit harshly discriminatory law enforcement on individual government officials.

Olson's constitutional challenge to the independent counsel law was heard in April 1988 before a Supreme Court that included four Reagan-appointed justices who could have been expected to give the ex-official's argument a sympathetic hearing. But in June 1988 the court upheld the law by a vote of 7 to 1. Chief Justice William Rehnquist, in a scholarly opinion, denied that by passing the act, Congress had violated the basic constitutional doctrine of separation of powers.[22] The attorney general retained control, said Rehnquist, not only through his authority to remove an independent counsel for "good cause" but through his power to decide whether to ask for one in the first place.

The court's lone dissenter, Justice Antonin Scalia, wrote an opinion that bespoke not simply differences with the majority but amazement at its reasoning process. The attorney general's power to decide whether to ask for an independent counsel, wrote Scalia, was in reality an empty shell. "As a practical matter," Scalia said of the Olson case, "it would be surprising if the Attorney General had any choice"[23] in the matter. A House committee had asked for an independent counsel, sent the attorney general a monster report on the subject, and released the report to the public at the same time. Furthermore, the act ordered the attorney general to request an appointment except in the narrowest of circumstances. Refusing to do so would damage the president politically, and Congress had the power to retaliate if the administration did not act. "The context of this statute," went the opinion, "is acrid with the smell of threatened impeachment."[24]

As for an attorney general's power to remove an independent counsel for "good cause," said Scalia in a much-quoted analogy, "[t]his is somewhat like referring to shackles as an effective means of locomotion."[25]

In other words, Congress had taken the prosecutorial power not by legal means but through political ones. Under the new system, an administration could either keep helplessly investigating itself in one case after another or see itself portrayed as a bunch of crooks and obstructors of justice.

The majority opinion had clung to the undeniable fact of the attorney general's legal power to request or not request an independent counsel and had simply been silent on the political facts to which Scalia pointed. The omission was so conspicuous as to look clearly deliberate, as if the court, recognizing as clearly as Scalia did that the independent counsel issue was a struggle over political power, had chosen by ignoring these realities to excuse itself once again from the dangerous executive-legislative crossfire spawned by the EPA battle.

Six months after the verdict, Morrison finally wrapped up the Olson case. From beginning to end, the matter had been more a political dispute than a legal one, and in this Olson's example was no aberration. As we go down the list of public independent counsel investigations that have been launched since the law was passed, we see congressional thumbprints, for good or ill, on most of them. There would probably have been no independent counsel in the Donovan case had the Senate Judiciary Committee not reopened its confirmation hearings on him and provided a gathering place for the accumulating charges. The first independent counsel investigation of Meese was also triggered by a Senate confirmation hearing, where criminal charges against him were first floated. An independent counsel was appointed to investigate Samuel R. Pierce, Jr., ex-secretary of housing and urban development, after congressional hearings on HUD in 1989. The Iran-contra independent counsel investigation devoted itself largely to the issue of whether executive branch officials had behaved improperly toward the Congress.

In the case of Michael Deaver, Congress did more than force a subject to the attorney general's attention. In 1985 Deaver left his post as one of Ronald Reagan's top White House aides and set up a Washington lobbying firm. He had a quick, flamboyant success, which came to seem a prime symbol of the money culture that had invaded political Washington. Rep. John Dingell soon ordered Congress's General Accounting Office to report on whether Deaver was violating the conflict of interest rules set up by the 1978 Ethics in Government Act. Joining Dingell, five Democrats on the Senate Judiciary Committee asked Attorney General Meese for an independent counsel to investigate Deaver. An independent counsel was duly appointed, but Dingell kept right on with his own investigation. He demanded that Deaver appear and testify before Dingell's subcommittee, and Deaver complied. The subcommittee then sent the testimony over to the independent counsel's office, where it became a major basis of the perjury charges on which Deaver was finally indicted.

Congress's dominance in cases such as these leaves little doubt that Scalia did better than the Supreme Court majority when it came to describing how the independent counsel act really works. To judge by the record to date, when a congressman or committee decides to make a major effort to get an administration official into searing, consuming legal trouble, Congress will succeed. Because of this partisanship, as well as the problem of publicity, the independent counsel law has cost more in fairness to individuals and in the confidence of citizens in their government than it has gained us in stilled doubts in Washington about the system's integrity. And no senior government official can fail to have noticed the increased power—of a sometimes frightening sort—that Congress now wields through the independent counsel law. This awareness is perhaps the largest and most dangerous political fact created by the new statute, for such fear is a major means through which scandal politics and its demands come to pervade the operations of government.

CHAPTER 5

THE ETHICS APPARAT: A CAST OF THOUSANDS

THE OFFICE OF the independent counsel is a highly visible emblem of the nature of today's politics, but it is only that—an emblem. If this new institution had never been born, most of the cases it has handled would have been pursued anyway. For instance, the EPA scandal of 1982 showed an independent counsel vigorously pursuing Theodore Olson. But the only criminal conviction in the affair came about when regular Justice Department prosecutors brought perjury charges against Rita Lavelle, head of EPA's Superfund. This was no anomaly. Starting in the 1960s, the entire federal system for uncovering public corruption underwent fundamental change.

Today we have more federal laws against corruption than ever, including not only major pieces of legislation but scores of minor ones and thousands of internal rules promulgated by federal agencies. Congress has made more offenses criminal and increased criminal penalties for existing offenses. We also have, as we shall see, an unprecedented number of federal prosecutors, and many of them hold enlarged ideas about their role in preserving the integrity of our political system.

Agencies throughout the federal government are taking a larger role in rooting out their own corruption. They are making more use of criminal sanctions to press what used to be considered civil cases. We have a greatly expanded corps of federal investigators in the executive branch, many of them taking an increasingly broad view of their job; they now put considerable pressure on prosecutors to bring criminal cases.

Similar changes have occurred in state governments, creating competitive pressures for federal prosecutors. As the public grows to expect more criminal actions by the federal government, politics exerts its own pressure to prosecute more.

These organizational changes are based on changes in ideas. Throughout our legal system, individuals are being held personally culpable for more and more types of action by their firms, subordinates, and colleagues. More generally, government personnel in this area and the rules they enforce are parts of an increasingly self-conscious prosecutorial culture within the federal government. This culture is based on a mistrust of other public officials, and it insists on the enforcer's right to use not just ordinary means but less traditional ones, such as Congress and the media, in pursuing corruption cases. Those steeped in the culture argue that the reach of the criminal law should be ever expanding, in order to cover more and more official misbehavior. Finally, today's prosecutorial culture teaches that the best law enforcer is the one who pursues his quarry most implacably, no matter how heavy the political pressures in the case, how vexatious the conflicting arguments about where the public interest lies, or how strong the pull of compassion and sympathy.

This zeal is deemed appropriate not only in the pursuit of top-level government officials, for whom such hazards may be viewed as the price of power, but also in the cases of many more ordinary individuals as well. Sometimes all the vigor leads to serious abuse of official authority, as we shall see in the story of Ed Meese's friend E. Robert Wallach. Even when no such misuse of discretion is involved, this is no way to run a government, as both the case of space program chief James Beggs and the more general problem of defense procurement demonstrate.

One reason for the increased prosecutorial activity in political scandals over the past quarter century is that federal law enforcement organizations have grown more skilled at investigating public corruption. The leading case is that of the Federal Bureau of Investigation. Under the direction of the legendary J. Edgar Hoover, the bureau became famous for its clean-cut, shirt-and-tie agents and its pursuit of conventional criminals like bank robbers and interstate car thieves. By contrast, the politically astute Hoover was notably reluctant to put the bureau into the business of building criminal cases against public officials.

By the early 1970s the FBI had begun to change its character, and after Hoover's death in 1972 and the Watergate explosion the next year, the American political climate began to catch up with the organization even more rapidly. One quick way of gauging the change is to look at some enforcement figures on interstate car thefts, which once made up a large part of the bureau's caseload. In fiscal year 1963, over 26 percent of the inmates in the nation's federal prison system were there because they had been successfully investigated and prosecuted for motor vehicle theft. By 1980 that figure was 3 percent and by 1990 it was down below 1 percent. This decline was due to the fact that the FBI had begun devoting more of its time to investigations such as white-collar crime cases, which were often bigger and more complex. Along the way, aided by developing technology, the agency got progressively better at techniques such as undercover operations that were needed for the new tasks.[1]

The public received a dramatic demonstration of the change in the bureau in 1980, when the FBI undercover operation called Abscam exposed a particularly squalid sort of corruption in Congress. Abscam began when an informant working for the Justice Department's organized crime strike force claimed to his law enforcement contacts that he knew of corrupt federal officials. To expose them, FBI agents rented a comfortable house in northwest Washington, D.C., and posed as representatives of a wholly fictitious but compensatingly rich Middle Eastern businessman named Abdul. Amenable congressmen were brought to the house, where the agents told them that Abdul was willing to pay for some congressional favor, like passage of a private immigration bill on his behalf. "It sounded crazy," Thomas Puccio, then the Justice Department prosecutor in charge of the operation, later recalled the plan. "But," he smiled, "it was cheap."

Abscam nabbed seven congressmen. They or their agents were recorded on videotape agreeing to accept Abdul's money, and when the story broke, the country could watch fuzzy excerpts of the tape on the nightly news. "[A]ll the attention paid to Abscam *afterward . . . ,"* Puccio remembered the events that followed, "made it into a prototype." Undercover operations against suspect public officials, especially state and local politicians, became frequent. In early 1990 the FBI's methods got new attention when the mayor of the District of Columbia, Marion S. Barry, Jr., was arrested by federal agents for cocaine use in a sting operation run out of a downtown Washington hotel. Such operations are now well within the bureau's capability, and Barry's was only one spectacular example.

In June 1990, Barry was tried on multiple drug charges and convicted of a single misdemeanor charge of cocaine possession. By this time, there was a sense among many observers that the FBI sting operation against the mayor had turned into a type of entrapment. In this worrisome respect, too, Barry's case had a good deal of company. Entrapment, whether in its legal meaning or its more general sense, has become a familiar complaint against federal investigators and prosecutors by public officials in criminal trouble.

The FBI was by no means the only investigative agency expanding its activities at this time. One of the most concrete legacies of Watergate was to create more investigators throughout the executive branch of government and promote more aggressive behavior on the part of investigators already on the scene. The most visible examples of the trend are the new inspectors general, created by congressional statute, who are now at work in nearly 60 federal agencies and Cabinet departments.

The first inspector general was named in 1777 by the Continental Congress to look into cost and performance problems in the Continental Army. This move seems to have been part of an attempt to undermine the authority of the army's commander, George Washington. Since that ambiguous beginning, IGs appointed by agency heads have served in various parts of the government. After Watergate, though, and the GSA procurement scandal that followed on its heels, Congress began establishing IGs by law so that future agency heads would not be able to fire or muzzle them. Legislation passed in 1978 decreed that the new, statutory IGs would be accountable only to the heads of their agencies, instead of reporting as before to the agencies' regular management officials. Also, every six months the new IGs were required by law to bypass even their agency heads and send reports directly to Congress. Their superiors were forbidden to change or overrule anything in these documents. Charles L. Dempsey, who served as an IG both before and after the new law, said the change gave him vastly more clout in his department. "I had to educate the department about the new act," he remembered, pulling out a well-worn and underlined copy of the legislation itself, on which he had written the label BIBLE. "When people would tell me, 'You can't do that,' I'd say, 'Yes I can,' and show them exactly where it said so."

The IGs were made responsible for a wide range of inspections. Many of the new officials were career civil servants, and for some years after the 1978 act, the IGs had a low profile. But some of their offices have grown rapidly since their founding: Those at the Labor and Transportation departments, for instance, have nearly tripled in size.[2] In 1989 a large scandal broke involving the Department of Housing and Urban Development. The press was flooded with tales of theft in the field offices and influence peddling in Washington. The department's IG, it turned out, had been warning about some of these problems for months. The office of the inspector general suddenly hit the big time.

The IGs started getting more press attention, most of it announcing the results of new investigations and enforcement actions in areas such as generic drug fraud, supermarket cholesterol testing, private pension funds, or questionable expenditures at the National Science Foundation. The inspectors general also began fighting highly publicized turf wars. Some of the IGs began claiming the right to investigate not only inside their government agencies but in the broader outside territory that the agencies' other investigators had traditionally covered. A group of IGs launched a major drive to get permission for their investigators to carry guns just as regular criminal investigators did.

The coming of the IGs was only the beginning of the changes in the federal investigative force. Other investigative units, in places like the Postal Service, became more aggressive in taking their cases to the Justice Department and pushing for criminal charges. In news stories about federal criminal proceedings we began seeing new agency names, like that of the Naval Investigative Service, because people in such organizations were expanding their activities, taking more initiative, and learning how to use the press to push their projects.

During the 1970s the Justice Department itself was being organizationally changed by Congress and successive attorneys general with the aim of giving more attention to public corruption cases. In 1976 Congress established a specialized Public Integrity Section, with attorneys exclusively assigned to corruption work, in the Criminal Division of the Justice Department. The section gets its cases from its own investigations, from U.S. attorneys' offices, and from other government agencies whose watchdogs have discovered what they think may be crimes. Senior Justice Department officials can overrule the section's recommendation for an indictment, but as a matter of prudence they do so only in rare cases. Special care is taken to preserve the section's reputation for independence and ethics. Few of the unit's decisions, for instance, are made informally; such matters are written down. "In our section," one of its attorneys put it, "everything is a matter of record."

The Public Integrity Section has always been encouraged to use the criminal law creatively so as to bring new sorts of official misbehavior within legal reach. "It is the reality of the prosecutor/craftsman," one early head of the section remarked approvingly, "that is responsible for a number of relatively recent legal developments which can only be characterized as breakthroughs" in the public corruption area.[3] In 1977, the first full year of the section's operation, there were 507 indictments of public officials on federal, state, and local levels. In 1982 the figure was 729. The next year it jumped to 1,073 and has gone upward from there.[4]

The rising numbers and the "breakthroughs" referred to by the proud department official quoted above originated not only in Washington but in the offices of U.S. attorneys around the country. These officials, nearly a hundred of them, enjoy substantial freedom from Washington's control. In the past 25 years their staffs have grown rapidly. In 1963 there were 657 lawyers serving as assistant U.S. attorneys. By 1980 there were 1,695 of these prosecutors, and the number in 1990 was around 3,000. The number of criminal cases they handled, though, did not rise so fast. In 1963, U.S. attorneys' offices handled 33,235 cases, but by 1980 the number had declined to 29,120 before budget increases set the figure rising again. The prosecutors, like the FBI, were devoting less time to routine cases and giving more attention to complex cases that the attorneys themselves played a major role in developing.[5]

Among the complex cases getting more attention were those involving public corruption, and during the 1970s federal prosecutors moved to expand their jurisdiction over the area by using federal statutes in unprecedented ways. In 1970 the U.S. attorney's office in New Jersey used the Hobbs Act, a federal anti-extortion statute on the books since 1946, in a novel and ultimately successful prosecution of the Democratic administration of Mayor John V. Kenny in Jersey City, New Jersey. In 1973 a U.S. attorney's office in Illinois used an 1872 mail fraud statute to indict Judge Otto Kerner, Jr., for favoritism in the award of horse-racing dates during his term as governor of Illinois. The prosecutors admitted at the trial that Kerner had stolen no money from the state or its citizens. The prosecution made the novel argument that the governor had defrauded the citizens nevertheless by depriving them of his "loyal and faithful services" as their public servant.[6] Kerner was convicted.

In 1970 Congress, in part unwittingly, gave the prosecutors a great gift in their anticorruption campaign. At that time the lawmakers passed RICO, the Racketeering Influenced and Corrupt Organizations Act, a new law aimed at organized crime. The law's acronym was the name of the gangster played by Edward G. Robinson in the film classic *Little Caesar*.

Criminal organizations pose a special problem for law enforcement, because even if their individual members are convicted and imprisoned under ordinary laws, the enterprises can transfer the organization's assets to others and keep operating. RICO attacked this problem by saying that if a defendant had committed two related crimes within 10 years—from a list including offenses like murder and bribery—prosecutors could charge him with the further crime of being a racketeer. Under this charge, prosecutors could ask for a freeze on his assets before trial so that he could not transfer his money to safe places. They could introduce evidence into the trial that would not be permitted under ordinary law. Those convicted could be forced not just to pay fines but to give up all their ill-gotten assets. If third parties had already bought some of these assets, even in an honest deal, the purchasers might have to surrender the property to the government. Furthermore, private parties could sue under RICO and, if they won, collect three times the amount of the damage the racketeers had done them.

None of the individual pressures RICO can put on criminal defendants is unique, but the act is so broad that almost anything—from a corporation or government agency to an anti-abortion protest group—can be called a racketeering enterprise, and RICO's combination of crowbars gives a defendant power-ful reason to plead guilty and cooperate with prosecutors in implicating higher-ups. In white-collar crimes, including those of public corruption, everything may turn on the matter of the defendants' intentions and nothing can be definitively proved or disproved. Under these circumstances it is especially easy and tempting for a small RICO defendant to pay prosecutors for his safe conduct by offering to testify against a bigger fish.

Thus RICO gave immense power to prosecutors. The statute could be used well or abusively, depending on the attitudes of the prosecutors applying it, and these attitudes were undergoing marked change in some U.S. attorneys' offices beginning in the mid-1960s. The most visible example was the Southern District of New York, home to both Wall Street and the largest U.S. attorney's office in the country.

The young prosecutors in the Southern District had long had a reputation for being awesomely aggressive, and during the 1960s the office began to break new ground in the emerging field of white-collar crime. The Kennedy administration adopted a tough attitude toward big business, and in 1961, U.S. Attorney Robert Morgenthau brought this stance to the Southern District. Peter Fleming, an eminent New York defense lawyer who served under Morgenthau from 1961 through 1970, recently remem-bered:

> Morgenthau invented the idea of white-collar crime, and he was right to do so: There was a tremendous disproportion in the way these things were treated. He was creative. He'd give me a page he'd torn out of *The Wall Street Journal* and say, "Look at this."

"We understood," said another attorney who served in the office then, "that we were going to be the first to indict white-collar law firms, the first to get the Swiss banks."

The office started to seem more glamorous during the 1960s as the figure of the prosecutor, once seen as the embodiment of the social and economic establishment, became a symbol of the struggle against central parts of the same establishment. In the late 1960s some Supreme Court clerks finishing their terms began choosing the U.S. attorney's office rather than prestigious private law firms for their next jobs. Soon Watergate made the image of the creative, aggressive prosecutor more exciting still.

Yet today, a good number of Southern District alumni, not only defense attorneys but judges before whom the assistant U.S. attorneys appear, say that the ethics and quality of the office declined sharply in the 1980s. One judge said the biggest problem he had seen was that of competence: The office had grown so much and so fast that past high standards were impossible to maintain. He had also begun to see prosecutors with a troublesome attitude toward publicity in court. For instance, he said, it is natural for the press to object when a judge wants to conduct part of a proceeding in camera. But the prosecutors had started objecting right alongside the journalists.

This judge, like almost all critics of the present office, cited Rudolph W. Giuliani, who served as U.S. attorney in the Southern District from 1983 until 1989, as the man most responsible for turning the pursuit of white-collar crime and political corruption into a press-driven public spectacle. Other critics have accused Giuliani's prosecutors of being less than ethically scrupulous in putting pressure on criminal defendants to implicate others in their crimes. These are perennial defense complaints, but during the 1980s they came with unusually high volume and frequency. They even gave rise to the label "Rudyism," used by critics in summarizing the behavior of the U.S. attorney's office during those years.[7]

Most of the complainants say that the reason for the bad behavior was Giuliani's political ambition: In 1989 he resigned his office and ran unsuccessfully for mayor of New York City. But defenders of the Giuliani policies tend to reply like Bruce Baird, a recent head of the office's securities fraud unit, who has said, "I can be more sympathetic to someone who doesn't know any other world than the streets and committing crime than to someone who's gone to Groton, Yale, and Harvard Business School."[8]

Into the cross hairs of this increasingly powerful, decreasingly meticulous organization wandered the improbable figure of San Francisco personal-injury lawyer E. Robert Wallach, who went to Washington in 1981 with his old law school friend, Reagan adviser Edwin Meese III. Wallach, born in the Bronx and raised in California, was in no way a Washington type. Indeed, he was the sort of person that most of politically active Washington could not even look at without being overwhelmed by sinister vibrations.

They objected, for superficial starters, to his name. He did not write it in the conventional way but spelled it all in lower case letters, "e. robert (bob) wallach," like the title of a failed e. e. cummings poem. They also objected to his appearance. He was rail thin from following the diet of a longtime client, Dr. Nathan Pritikin, and his bushy eyebrows and the eyes under them stood out in relief. He sported what seemed to Washington a strange wardrobe, which looked as if it had come out of a cross between a Giorgio Armani menswear boutique and a Sausalito weaving and knitting workshop. Bobbing on a sea of dark suits, white shirts, and the ever-present Adam Smith neckties, these outfits of Wallach's made a statement, and they did not say "solid citizen."

Next came the mystery of just how Wallach was occupying himself in Washington. He had no clearly defined job. He seemed to spend a great deal of time entertaining, cultivating, and in turn being cultivated by people of widely varying type and character, including Washington lawyers as eminent as Robert Strauss, Max Kampelman, and Clark Clifford. In 1986 the Reagan administration named him to head the U.S. delegation to the United Nations Human Rights Commission in Geneva. By all accounts he did the job well, yet even when he was engaged in good works his name-dropping manner disquieted people.

More disturbing was the question of what Wallach was doing in the nearly constant company of his friend Meese, particularly since Wallach was a certified bleeding-heart liberal who had done a great deal of *pro bono* work back in San Francisco. Wallach looked out for Meese's health and tried to get the chef in the attorney general's private dining room to turn from the wickedness of Boston cream pies to the fresh-fruit-paved path of righteousness. Visitors to Meese's office would sometimes find Wallach simply sitting there. Wallach wrote Meese memo after memo on topics ranging from personal fitness to foreign policy. Since ideology was obviously not the basis of this friendship, Meese's colleagues and aides could not share or understand it. Wallach's attention to Meese's physical well-being only reminded suspicious observers of the hypnotic Rasputin.

Finally, Wallach had a habit of bringing together people who were totally inappropriate for each other's company. During the Iran-contra crisis of 1987 he held a dinner in a private room at Georgetown's Four Seasons Hotel for a small group that included both Meese and Washington real estate developer Jeffrey N. Cohen, a good friend of the city's much-investigated Mayor Marion Barry. Cohen suggested to the assembled group that the mayor's legal troubles were not much different from those of President Reagan: Both men were being attacked for what was really the behavior of unruly subordinates. The attorney general replied with his most affable smile that in the new federal prison then being planned for the District of Columbia, "There's going to be a special cell with Marion Barry's name on it."

Wallach actually thought that bringing different sorts of people and interests together in this way, outside Washington's normal categories and channels of communication, was one of the gifts he could give his country during Meese's tenure in the capital. Yet what he actually gave onlookers was a permanent case of anxiety. From early on, Wallach looked as if he was headed for trouble.

The trouble arrived approximately on schedule. In 1986 Giuliani's office in New York began investigating the Wedtech Corporation. The company had been founded in 1965 in the South Bronx to make high-tech, defense-related products using workers from an area of the city that many regarded as nothing but a wasteland. For some years the company was an exemplar to those who believed that public authorities could harness the private sector to change the lives of minority group members in the urban ghettos.

It turned out, unfortunately, that Wedtech's officers were equal-opportunity crooks who systematically bribed public officials in order to get government contracts and, in addition, stole the company blind. In January 1987 four Wedtech executives—indicted, appropriately, under RICO—pleaded guilty to various fraud charges and, with their sentencing in sight, began cooperating with federal prosecutors and naming names of others who they said were their partners in crime.

Two of the names were those of Democratic congressmen Mario Biaggi and Robert Garcia of New York. Both were prosecuted by the U.S. attorney's office and convicted of Wedtech-related offenses, though Garcia's conviction was later set aside by an appeals court: It turned out that the prosecutors had not been too careful about matching the crimes of which they accused the congressman with the evidence actually presented to the jury. Moving on to the executive branch of government, another name was that of Lyn Nofziger, political adviser and former assistant to President Reagan, who had done lobbying work for Wedtech. An independent counsel, James C. McKay, was appointed in February 1987 and prosecuted Nofziger for violations of the 1978 Ethics in Government Act. Nofziger was convicted in February 1988, but his conviction, too, was reversed. The problem this time was that Congress, in its zeal for reform, had not made the lobbying law intelligible, let alone clear enough to stand scrutiny as a criminal statute. The lawmakers soon cleaned up this detail in new legislation.

Meese, too, became a subject of McKay's investigation. When McKay released his Wedtech report on the attorney general in the summer of 1988, *The New York Times* announced, MEESE FOUND FREE OF SERIOUS BLAME IN MAJOR SCANDALS.[9] MCKAY REPORTS 4 "PROBABLE" MEESE OFFENSES,[10] said *The Washington Post* headline on the same day. Both were true. McKay had found no illegal behavior by Meese in the Wedtech affair. However, independent counsel investigations being what they are, McKay had also looked into many charges that had emerged during the investigation. For instance, Meese had made certain decisions affecting parts of the telephone industry while owning something over $10,000 worth of telephone stock, though "there is no evidence that he acted out of self-interest."[11] Meese had failed to disclose a $20,706 capital gain on his 1985 tax return, though this omission was a "one-time failure,"[12] not part of a deliberate pattern. In these instances, said McKay in the expansive manner encouraged by the independent counsel law, Meese had probably violated the law. But he should not be prosecuted, because a prosecutor would not go after an ordinary citizen in these circumstances.

The report damaged Meese, who resigned after it appeared. Yet the attorney general had once again slipped the legal noose prepared for him long ago by his enemies and left his opponents, as he often did, with a sense of grinding frustration. Bob Wallach, the attorney general's friend, was a good target for such unhappiness.

Wallach did not have the good luck to be pursued, like Nofziger, by a rather conventional independent counsel applying relatively conventional law. Instead Wallach was entrusted to the ordinary federal law enforcement system. When McKay found Wallach involved in the Wedtech affair, the independent counsel obligingly sent his case back to Giuliani's office, which was eager to have it. Thus Wallach was prosecuted by a team of Giuliani's assistants, who secured an indictment under RICO.

Wallach's involvement with Wedtech began in 1981, when the company was having trouble getting an army contract it wanted. Wedtech executives complained to a private investigator they knew that their competition must be paying bribes. (Since this was the way Wedtech officials did business, they would naturally have assumed that their competitors were doing the same.) The private eye—like Wallach, a Bronx-born San Francisco resident—knew the attorney general's friend and thought the Bronx-based Wedtech was the sort of project that would interest him. Wallach met with the Wedtech executives. In 1981 and 1982 he wrote a dozen memos to Meese, then still in the White House, describing Wedtech's problems and arguing that help to the South Bronx firm was a way for the administration to show a commitment to minority group progress.

This sort of lobbying, paid or unpaid, is quite legal, though, as it happened, Wallach got no payment at the time. Meese did help Wedtech: The company got its contract in August 1982. Wallach then stopped writing Wedtech memos to Meese. From this point forward, all parties agree, Wedtech did not use Wallach to lobby for it in Washington. The company had, we now know, several other means of access.

About a year after the award of the army contract, Wallach did start receiving payments from Wedtech. The fee agreement drawn up at the time said the money was for legal services dating back to October 1982—shortly after the date of the big contract award. Pursuant to this agreement, Wallach got one Wedtech check in 1983, for $125,000, and one check for $300,000 in 1984.[13]

The plea-bargaining and therefore cooperative Wedtech executives told the prosecutors pursuing Wallach that part of the money was really a late, secret payment of Wallach's lobbying fee. The gentlemen from Wedtech also said Wallach had told them at the time of the fee agreement that he was going into government in the future and that when he did (he never even came close), he would help Wedtech from the inside. The Wedtech executives told the prosecutors that the money they gave Wallach was, in part, payment in advance for these future services. The execs further said that in order to receive his money Wallach had, as they had agreed, submitted phony invoices for legal services connected with a capital acquisition.

According to the indictment, Wallach was a racketeer in RICO's sense of the word. Wedtech's payments to Wallach, the chain of reasoning began, were in reality fees for past lobbying and future services. The company could not legitimately capitalize these expenses. Therefore the full amount should have been deducted as an expense item from the year's income in order to figure out the firm's net earnings. But Wallach had knowingly and obligingly submitted false bills for legal services that could be capitalized. Therefore the full amount did not have to be deducted from the year's income. The net earnings figure was higher, giving an inflated impression of how well the company was doing. Wallach, in receiving his payment under false pretenses, was defrauding Wedtech.

Now let us step from fraud to racketeering. Wallach received his payment, it may be recalled, in the form of two checks. Each time, he took his check, written by Wedtech in New York, and deposited it in his bank account in his home state of California. Since the checks were fraudulently obtained—that is, stolen— each of these transfers was an instance of transporting stolen property across state lines. This offense is, as it happens, one of those on RICO's list of crimes that can add up to racketeering.

By depositing two checks Wallach had committed two related crimes on the RICO list within a decade. He could therefore be charged as a racketeer.

Because he was being charged as a racketeer, his assets could be frozen before his trial took place. At the trial itself, the prosecution could introduce evidence of other misdeeds, which would not be permitted in a regular case, in order to try to show that there was a racketeering-type pattern to Wallach's activities. If he were convicted, his sentence would be very long.

Despite its creativity, or because of it, the defense claimed that there were serious problems with the prosecution's theory. First came the inconvenient fact that beginning in the fall of 1982, the starting date on the fee agreement, Wallach did a great deal of genuine legal and counseling work—not lobbying—for Wedtech, and there were some 1,000 pages' worth of those voluminous memos of his to back up the claim. So why did the prosecutors say the money was actually for past lobbying and future services rather than genuine legal work? Because they chose to believe the plea-bargaining Wedtech officials instead of Wallach.

At the trial, the government said this choice was reasonable, explaining to the jury that Wallach's chief accuser, who was serving as a prosecution witness in a range of Wedtech cases, was a reliable witness even though a thief and con man. The man had to be truthful now: If he lied, his plea-bargaining arrangement with the government would be dissolved and he would be in great trouble when it came time for sentencing.

Another major problem with the prosecution theory was a type of paradox: How could you say Wallach had defrauded Wedtech when the company's officers set the terms of the agreement, knew what he was doing, and at the time of the agreement did not yet have any stockholders other than themselves?

There were other objections as well, and they worried observers with varying political views. Steven Brill, editor-in-chief of *The American Lawyer* and a shill for no one, least of all the Reagan administration, actually put Wallach's face on the cover of the magazine's June 1988 issue under the uncompromising title, THE LYNCHING OF BOB WALLACH.[14] One government lawyer, who had been at the Justice Department meeting that approved the Wallach indictment, told Brill:

We thought the case was weak. In another situation we might have urged them to wait and try harder or even to forget it. But you don't do that with Rudy Giuliani, especially in a case involving [the attorney general's] best friend when Rudy's gunning for the attorney general, or you'll read about it the next day in the papers.[15]

On the other hand, the Justice official added, "I have to tell you . . . that we didn't view it as any great injustice, since we all thought this guy Wallach was a sleaze from the way we'd read about and heard about how he'd traded on his friendship with Meese."[16] The costs of a bad reputation have escalated steeply in the post-Watergate years.

With RICO's complexities piled on top of the already convoluted theory of Wallach's fraud, the jury would almost surely not be deciding the case on the indictment's technical merits. By process of elimination, two other issues would be crucial. First, jurors would have to decide whether the genuine legal services Wallach performed for Wedtech were enough to justify the amount of money he got paid. Second, the jury would have to judge whether Wallach was the sort of fellow who would have gotten involved with Wedtech in order to reap illegal bonanzas or whether his motive was a more ordinary sort of pleasure at the chance to do well by doing good.

On the first question—whether Wallach's fees were reasonable—the defense could not score a win. It is almost impossible (probably for good reason) to persuade a normal citizen of the type likely to be on a jury that the huge fees charged by big-league lawyers are ever reasonable. So the remaining issue of character became a life-and-death one. When this is the case, particulars such as the qualities of the jurors, the judge, and the witnesses all count for a lot, and at the Wallach trial some of the particulars were riveting. The most dramatic moment of the trial, played prominently in the local press, came when Wallach's defense attorney tried to address the character issue by calling Avital Sharansky as a witness.

When Mrs. Sharansky was engaged in her eight-year campaign to free her husband, Natan, from a Soviet prison, Wallach, it transpired, had served as her chief American adviser. He spent hundreds of hours over several years, she said, helping her plan strategy, gain access to government officials, and deal with American organizations working for Sharansky's release.

When Sharansky was finally free, the couple settled in Israel with their relatives. At the time of Wallach's trial, in a circumstance of improbable drama, Mrs. Sharansky's mother was near death, drifting in and out of a coma. The young woman thought her debt to Wallach was overriding, though, so she arranged to fly to New York with her husband, testify, and fly back within 24 hours.

The Sharanskys arrived in New York at 5:00 A.M. and appeared in court that day. The defense had explained Mrs. Sharansky's predicament to the judge, Richard Owen, and tried to bring her to the stand. Chief prosecutor Baruch Weiss objected. A character witness could not testify as to just one good deed a defendant had performed, he said. Besides, he went on, Mrs. Sharansky's reputation was such that her appearance would be prejudicial to the government's case: The jurors would be influenced by her opinion.

Influencing the jurors' opinion is just what character testimony is supposed to do, and the issue was, by all accounts, the sort of question that trial judges deal with routinely on the spot. But in this case the judge, though he knew why Mrs. Sharansky could not stay in New York, said he would not rule on the matter immediately—not, in fact, until he had thought about it overnight. There would be no special arrangements made for Mrs. Sharansky, such as having the testimony videotaped for possible future use. The Sharanskys left the courthouse to go home, and the jury never learned they had been there. "I have seen only one trial in the Soviet Union—my own," Natan Sharansky said with a sardonic smile on the courthouse steps. "And now I have seen one in America."

Wallach was convicted of accepting payoffs: The jury believed that Wedtech officials had given him money for lobbying and for helping them once he entered government. The jurors acquitted Wallach, however, of conspiring with the Wedtech officials in either of these matters. The verdict bespoke some confusion, but the judge evinced none: He sentenced Wallach to six years in prison. Shortly afterward, the government conceded that the main prosecution witness against Wallach had perjured himself on the stand. In June 1991 the appeals court reversed the conviction on the ground that the government's chief witness had perjured himself and that "the prosecutors may have consciously avoided recognizing the obvious—that is, that [the witness] was not telling the truth."[17]

Meese's Washington scandals had turned into Wallach's criminal jeopardy in New York. Wallach ran afoul of the modern scandal production system, with all its self-feeding elements and their assumption that the job of restraint will be performed elsewhere. Traditionally, one source of such restraint has been the prosecutor's office, which decides what will and will not be treated as a crime. In this case, though, the decision was made by attorneys increasingly disinclined to exercise such restraint and armed with legislation making it unnecessary for them to do so. The result, at the end of the line, was an outcome palpably disproportionate to any facts that had been established.

The Wallach case is extreme, but it is of the sort that impresses itself on the minds of watching politicians and public officials. The lesson comes through clearly: Even deeds whose existence is uncertain, whose motivation is murky, and whose import is doubtful can have terrifying consequences. The line between self-promotion and criminality has grown uncertain, and political scandal has turned into a true blood sport.

The same spirit has infected many aspects of government and politics that are smaller in scale than the Meese-Wallach affair but more pervasive in their consequences. These effects have been quite visible, for instance, in the field of defense policy, and one of the many government investigative agencies affected by the aggressive post-Watergate climate was the Defense Contract Audit Agency. It was founded in the mid-1960s, and over the next 20 years the agency functioned as an auditing organization concerned with ensuring an orderly, responsible procurement process. Its auditors distinguished themselves from other, more ordinary government investigators, who often had no specialized training. James Brown, deputy head of DCAA in the early 1980s, spoke of the difference this way: "When you're dealing with white-collar crime, you need auditors who understand what the norms are in the field." Regular investigators often did not understand, because they had no core discipline. Therefore these investigators were, said Brown, forced to rely on the technique of looking at an isolated case and exploiting all its weaknesses. So the investigators tend to have no tolerance for less than perfection in an accounting system. Auditors know that there are ambiguities in the regulations and that each system embodies a lot of choices and exercises of discretion.

During the 1980s, as pressures grew to find and punish more fraud in the defense industry, the agency doubled in size within five years, to more than 7,000 people. This growth created its characteristic problem: The organization could not successfully assimilate so many new people at once. "There are a lot of untrained, inexperienced auditors now being released into the system," said Brown. During the same years, the agency had to cope with an even greater threat to its identity: pressure from Congress, which became vocally interested in just how many criminal cases DCAA was producing. "[T]he politicians," Brown remembered, such as Senators Charles E. Grassley (R-Iowa), William V. Roth (R-Del.), and Alfonse M. D'Amato (R-N.Y.), "kept looking at the auditors and asking how many referrals there'd been for criminal investigation." The auditors as a whole were not used to the new posture that Congress had thrust on them.

One of those referrals, born in the climate of the eighties, was the case of James M. Beggs, who in 1985 was head of the National Aeronautics and Space Administration. Beggs was a former executive vice president and director of the General Dynamics Corporation, one of the nation's largest defense contractors, and he had done a previous stint at NASA as head of the agency's advanced research and technology operation. Thus he had extensive personal contacts in NASA and Congress. Beggs was known as a hands-on, hard-driving manager. He had arrived as NASA chief in 1981, just after the flight of the first space shuttle, and steadily pushed the agency and the government as a whole toward the goal of an American space station.

On December 2, 1985, Beggs was indicted, along with three men who were still officials of General Dynamics, for having defrauded the U.S. government during the late 1970s and early 1980s. Federal prosecutors publicized the event by holding a press conference in Los Angeles, near the GD plant where the alleged crimes were committed. The story seemed especially big because the federal government was at the time pursuing wrong-doing by General Dynamics in a whole collection of other areas, ranging from insider trading to receiving kickbacks from sub-contractors. The action against Beggs fit very well into the larger theme of the company's misdeeds.

The story behind the indictment began in 1978, when GD and another company each got a $39 million contract from the army to develop a prototype for a new mobile, computerized antiair-craft system called the Division Air Defense, or DIVAD. The company that built the better prototype would get a much larger contract, as big as $5 billion, to produce the finished system's actual hardware.

The contract for building the DIVAD prototype, running to thousands of pages, was complicated even for the defense field. One basic type of government contract is a fixed-price contract: The government pays a flat fee to a contractor, who must in turn deliver the product even if producing it turns out to cost him more than the government paid him. Another general type of contract is a cost-reimbursement contract: The government pays the contractor back for the costs he actually incurred in making the product, plus some prearranged profit. But the DIVAD con-tract was an oxymoronic creature called a "firm fixed price [best efforts]" contract. The government would pay a flat fee for de-velopment of the prototype. The contractors promised to exert their "best efforts" to build it within the prescribed financial limit. The companies did not, however, agree to deliver the en-tire finished prototype for the amount of money the government had paid.

If at first glance the reader does not find these distinctions intelligible, he or she has the company of troops of experienced professionals who subsequently tried to understand the contract.

General Dynamics was not exactly unsupervised in its han-dling of government money during the DIVAD project. A team of auditors from DCAA had offices in the Pomona, California, plant where DIVAD was being built so that they could audit expenses continuously. The relationship between GD and the audit team was marked by mutual resentment, and GD people went to some lengths to ensure that the Pentagon auditors got no more information about the company's costs than was absolutely required by the rules. Company-government relations grew even worse when the DCAA team was changed as part of a regular rotation. The new auditors charged that GD owed the government money.

The DCAA auditors said that the DIVAD contract was a fixed-price agreement. In their view, GD was piling up serious cost overruns on the project. The company was fraudulently making the government pay these added expenses by wrongfully charging some of its DIVAD costs to other accounts it held with the government—like the pot of DOD money available to contractors for the sole purpose of preparing bids and proposals, or the government funds available only for research and development unrelated to a specific contract.

In olden days, this matter of who owed whom how much in which category would probably have been settled by negotiation. But the alert modern government investigators sitting in the Pomona plant noted that GD refused to give them some of the cost data from the project and pointed to this refusal as concealment, a sign of criminal fraud deserving criminal sanctions. The case went to the Justice Department's Defense Procurement Fraud Unit, founded in 1982 as a part of the Criminal Division in order to centralize defense-related prosecutions in Washington and bring more expertise to bear on these complex cases. Department lawyers, guided by the Pentagon auditors, decided to seek indictments.

General Dynamics lawyers protested that the DIVAD contract was not a fixed-price contract. The company was obligated to spend the government's money honestly to develop the prototype, but that was all. If GD spent its own money to finish the project, this money was not a cost overrun. The company did not have to give the government information about all the particulars and could legitimately charge the extra costs, if they qualified under the general rules, to other pots of available government money.

The prosecutors were not moved, and a year and a half of postindictment legal jockeying ensued. Evidence accumulated in favor of GD's interpretation. In mid-1986, in response to a Freedom of Information Act request by General Dynamics lawyers, the army unexpectedly produced 82 previously unseen boxes of documents on the contract negotiations, including more evidence supporting GD.

On June 19, 1987, the prosecutors asked the judge in the case to dismiss the charges. At a press conference three days later, Assistant Attorney General William F. Weld said to reporters, "The government is standing up and saying, 'We were wrong.' "[18] A year later the attorney general took the highly unusual step of writing an explicit apology to Beggs on behalf of the government. Near the end of 1989 the Justice Department actually had the records of the case "expunged"— administratively wiped out, so that Beggs, if asked in the future whether he had ever been indicted, could officially answer that he had not.[19]

The government has dropped prosecutions before without feeling compelled to make such elaborate amends. The legal error in this case, though, was very embarrassing. Also, the battle had generated a great deal of publicity, some of which had raised questions about Beggs' absence from NASA in late 1985 and early 1986 and what this circumstance had done to the U.S. space program.

When Beggs' indictment forced him to take leave from NASA, the Reagan administration was not sorry to see him go. From the time Beggs arrived at NASA he was at war with other parts of the administration over the future direction of the space program. His critics charged him with trying to make NASA's shuttle into the U.S. government's sole point of access to space. They wanted more scientific and military payloads in America's space future. The dispute was exceedingly bitter. "Of all the organizations I have dealt with . . . ," Reagan science adviser George C. Keyworth once said dramatically, "I have only seen one that lied. It was NASA."[20]

When Beggs' deputy at NASA retired in 1984, the White House tried to replace him with its own man, scientist and arms-control expert William R. Graham. Beggs managed to block the appointment for months, but the White House finally achieved victory in the fall of 1985. Then, eight working days after Graham officially arrived at NASA, Beggs was indicted. Though the administration had no wish to keep Beggs on the job at NASA after the indictment, Graham was very new. People in the White House were nervous enough about the possible consequences to NASA of replacing an experienced man with an inexperienced one, or at least about the bad appearances involved, so they allowed Beggs merely to take a leave of absence from the administrator's job and stay on at NASA to help with the transition. Graham became NASA's acting administrator.

When the switch from Beggs to Graham became public, one hawkish senior administration appointee phoned a friendly journalist and advised her not to thunder too loudly in print about the terrible loss of Beggs' expertise at NASA. Beggs was a bad character, explained the official, and Graham was a good man. Graham, for his part, later remembered that during this period he saw Beggs acting every day at NASA to "undermine my ability to keep the organization on an even keel." One day, Graham cited an example, he asked NASA's Beggs-appointed general manager to set up a meeting at which Graham and Beggs could discuss coproduction of shuttle propellants and electricity at the Kennedy launch center. Later that day Graham asked whether the meeting had been scheduled. The manager replied that he and Beggs had already held the meeting. Beggs and Graham barely spoke. The worst of all possible managerial outcomes had been achieved.

On a chilly January 28, 1986, the space shuttle *Challenger* was waiting to be launched from the Kennedy Space Center at Cape Canaveral, Florida. In a break with NASA practice, neither Graham nor his deputy was there, and the press would later remark pointedly on that fact. Instead, the acting administrator was in NASA's Washington headquarters, and an hour before the scheduled launch he left for an appointment on the Hill. Like Graham, Beggs was at headquarters that morning. So was Milton Silveira, NASA's chief engineer, who later recalled that he came into the office, looked at the monitor, and spoke to Beggs. "I told him," said Silveira, " 'We're going to get [criticism] from the press,' because we weren't going to fly." Both of them, Silveira said, were clear that there would be no launch that day.

Beggs later explained that he knew of no specific problems with the shuttle that morning, but he knew about the cold. "[I]t was in the twenties," Beggs recalled, "a rare occurrence. There are all kinds of apertures in the mechanism, and even a small piece of ice can clog a passage and the machine won't function. You don't know when. During the Apollo program, on one of the launches, we had a great deal of trouble with this."

Silveira remembered that on the morning of the *Challenger*

departure, as time wore on toward the launch, he told Beggs, "Those guys are still counting. I don't understand." Beggs responded, "Yes, maybe I ought to call Jesse [W. Moore, associate administrator for space flight, who was at Kennedy to make the final decision on whether to launch]." But the call seemed inappropriate to Beggs, and he never made it. "We probably couldn't have gotten through," Beggs mused later. "They shut off the phones an hour before launch. But we should have tried."

Challenger was launched and fell apart in midair; the shuttle program would never recover from the tragedy. The disaster, we learned from later investigations, had been caused by the failure of a shuttle component called an O-ring; the O-ring, in turn, had failed to perform properly because of the cold. Before the launch, NASA engineers had expressed doubts about the reliability of the O-ring but never managed to communicate the depth of those doubts in their conversations with higher NASA management. Now there was open speculation about whether the launch would have taken place had Beggs still been at NASA. His would have been another seasoned ear for the troubled engineers, and because of his Apollo experience he would have acted with an educated and acute fear of the cold.

A book on *Challenger* by journalist Joseph J. Trento told of Beggs' confidence on launch day that the shuttle would not go up.[21] So did a widely circulated article from the *Reader's Digest*.[22] *The Washington Post,* summarizing the Beggs case at the time his court records were expunged, said about the indictment, "As a result, Beggs took a leave from NASA that extended through the explosion of the shuttle *Challenger* in January 1986."[23] The suggestion was always that Beggs' indictment had contributed to the disaster. Some people at NASA became quite certain that the indictment was part of an administration plot against Beggs.

It is not possible, of course, to rewrite history in this way. Moreover, both the Beggs indictment and the *Challenger* tragedy had, like most events, more than one cause. As for the indictment, the consistent hostility of General Dynamics and its lawyers toward the government throughout the case contributed to the prosecutors' suspicions about the company. And as for *Challenger,* investigators of the tragedy have pointed out that during Beggs' tenure the organization was under strain, trying to meet the ambitious shuttle schedule he had set. Thus the agency ran an extra risk of accident no matter who was at the helm.

Yet there is a residue of responsibility that can not be explained away. At moments of stress in a fast-moving crisis, any organization depends vitally on its routines and established habits of communication. This is true even if—or especially if—those habits are flawed ones as a result of bad management in the past. Disrupting an agency like NASA at a time of climactic pressure is a serious act that must be presumed to have serious possible consequences.

Does this mean the head of an important agency should never be indicted for a crime? Of course not. But the case against Beggs was weak to begin with. Holding it off for a brief period would not have harmed it. In such circumstances there should be, somewhere in the decision-making system, someone with the authority and responsibility to say, if not Stop! then at least Wait! Or, at a minimum, Think!

But no one involved in the Beggs decision had these things in mind at all. The decision to bring the case was consensual, based on a broad agreement about the Justice Department's Defense Procurement Fraud Unit and what it was supposed to do. One lawyer who participated in the decision looked back recently on the government's embarrassment in the Beggs case and said with equanimity that defeats like that one were simply an inherent, unavoidable cost of the prosecutors' performing their job properly. "We've always thought of ourselves as being on the cutting edge," the attorney put it. "There is no one I know of who doesn't think that's where we should be." Being on the cutting edge means bringing not just the clear and airtight cases but the more novel and riskier ones as well. Taking such chances is the only way to broaden the law. Broadening the law is what cutting-edge prosecutors are in business for.

The prosecutors were not the only players with this view. In the Beggs case, Justice relied on Defense Department auditors who came to function as actual members of the prosecution team, and DCAA was looking over its shoulder at a Congress panting for criminal cases. No one was urging a modest view of what the scope and purpose of the criminal law should be in defense procurement. Anyone who spoke up on the issue was sure to be pushing the process in the other direction.

The unanimity was no accident. The Beggs case was part of a much broader attempt by the government to get tough with defense contractors as a way of cutting waste, fraud, and abuse in Pentagon procurement. This theme is a classic of American politics, and in recent years it has not only provided liberals with a chance to attack the military budget but also given conservatives an opportunity to fight big government and show that they are not creatures of a corrupt establishment. The defense fraud issue was introduced anew to the public agenda after Watergate, in Carter's presidential campaign of 1976, and began to produce concrete consequences during Reagan's first term.

In 1978 Congress passed the Contract Dispute Act, allowing the various armed services to suspend or debar contractors charged with contract abuse even before the charges were proved. In 1982, the year the defense fraud unit was set up in the Justice Department, a statutory inspector general started work at the Department of Defense. In 1985 Congress gave DCAA its own subpoena power for the first time, and an Office of Contracting Integrity was established in the general counsel's office of each military service to supervise the suspension and debarment of contractors charged with abuse.

Robert S. Bennett, a prominent Washington white-collar defense lawyer and the outside counsel appointed by the Senate ethics committee in 1989 to investigate U.S. senators involved in the savings and loan scandal, explained the difference such changes had made in the defense procurement field. After Watergate the Pentagon, through policy and organizational means, started using criminal actions to resolve disputes that had once been handled administratively. The department's various criminal investigative services, because of both their own changing attitudes and pressures from others, supported the change, and the result was more indictments.

Under the Pentagon's new, post-Watergate rules, if a contractor was indicted, rather than merely sued, it was relatively easy to suspend him from doing business with the Defense Department. And a contractor who was suspended was, in effect, left lying in the road hemorrhaging money until he could somehow clear up his troubles with the government. In other words, the new Pentagon system operated on the same principle as RICO: sentence before trial.

When a contractor is placed in a situation like this one, Bennett explained, "There is more incentive to plead guilty than to fight and win. You've got to think of your stockholders, and basically it's usually a better business decision. You must rise above principle."

As one procurement reform followed another, the figures on defense corruption got worse. In 1985 the Pentagon IG reported that almost half the nation's largest defense contractors were under criminal investigation.[24] In the last half of the 1980s the number of suspensions leaped upward. So did the number of guilty pleas by defense contractors in federal criminal cases. These numbers should not have shocked anyone. The rising number of defense firms under criminal investigation was no surprise in light of increasingly aggressive behavior by the Pentagon's investigative services. More contractors were suspended beginning in the mid-eighties in no small part because the Pentagon now had special new offices dedicated to suspending them. The rising number of guilty pleas appeared because the new system made it so much cheaper for a contractor to plead guilty than to proclaim innocence and fight the government.

Yet each new and larger statistic was simply proclaimed a sign of increasing misbehavior and the need to get tougher, and the early 1980s were marked by a number of big defense fraud prosecutions. Just before Beggs was charged in 1985, for instance, the government brought criminal charges against a General Telephone and Electronics subsidiary plus three individuals for dealing in classified Defense Department budget documents. The traffic in these documents was widespread, and the government wanted to crack down on it. Senator Charles E. Grassley of the Senate Judiciary Committee had publicly called for the prosecution and specifically told the Justice Department to go after not just the company but also the individuals involved.

The company promptly and intelligently pleaded guilty and settled with the government for $590,000. GTE then received a $4.3 billion contract from the army to build a radio telecommunications system.[25] The rest of the case, which involved the indicted individuals, proved almost as disappointing for the government as the Beggs disaster. It was hard for the prosecution to find a crime to charge the company with: There was no actual theft and no proof of bribery. So the government went out to the cutting edge once more and brought the case under the federal espionage laws.

The defendants, in order to show that no genuine national secrets were involved, subpoenaed some 80 government officials who had received copies of one of the documents and won the right to use classified information in making their argument. Two and a half years after the indictment, the government asked the judge to dismiss charges against two defendants (the third later pleaded guilty to one count of converting government property to his own use). "The Justice Department is not backing down," a spokesman said. "The case has been restructured."[26]

Senator Grassley charged that GTE was only the tip of a vast iceberg of defense scandal and that Justice Department officials had "turned their backs" on glaring evidence of crime.[27] He called Defense Department investigators to his hearings to testify to the fact. Meanwhile, some of the investigators looked elsewhere for prosecutorial muscle, and soon the Naval Investigative Service and the U.S. attorney in Alexandria, Virginia, near the Pentagon, were at work on an investigation they named Operation Ill Wind.

The probe began with a tip from an informant to the Naval Investigative Service about a defense consultant selling inside Pentagon information. This tip led to wiretapping that went on through most of 1987. In the spring of 1988 the government began a dramatic sweep of offices belonging to nearly 40 suspects and put the investigation in the headlines. The U.S. attorney, no fool, gave Senator Grassley a personal briefing.

Grassley announced that the new scandal "goes beyond our wildest imaginations"[28] and said that Justice could have broken the case years before if it had acted with sufficient vigor. Senator John W. Warner (R-Va.), ranking Republican on the Senate Armed Services Committee, described the Ill Wind allegations as "the most serious case in the history . . . of the Department of Defense."[29] Ill Wind was soon joined by yet another document investigation, from the same U.S. attorney's office, with the more pedestrian name of Operation Uncover.

In these cases, unlike the GTE fiasco, the prosecutors deliberately kept their charges to relatively simple ones. The new strategy met with courtroom success: As of the spring of 1991, the government had obtained pleas and convictions involving 41 individuals and 5 corporations. More than that, the government's decision in the early eighties to launch new criminal prosecutions in this area sent a clear signal to the defense industry. Indeed, before the GTE indictment in 1985 major firms had already seen what was coming and started changing their procedures to protect themselves. By the time of the Ill Wind cases, ironically, prosecutors were forced to work against statute of limitations deadlines because many of the offenses on which their cases rested were approaching five years old.

Yet as the culmination of a decade of concentration on the waste-fraud-and-abuse issue, the operations were a large disappointment, unsuited to their avowed end. Some of Ill Wind's charges exposed real bribery, reaching as high as a former assistant secretary of the navy. But fortunately, this type of corruption was not shown to be widespread. Most of the scandal involved a brisk trade in Pentagon budget documents among defense firms and the consultants that serviced them. The people dealing in these documents had, with few exceptions, the appropriate security clearances. And until the prosecutions of the 1980s, most forms of this information trading had not been considered criminal.

The practice was more a sign of systemic problems than of moral weaknesses. Defense companies wanted these budget documents so they could plan their future operations, make sure they had the capacity to do what the government wanted done, and lobby for those projects that would provide them with the most work. They hoped for an edge over the competition and a leg up in dealing with the government itself. At the time of Ill Wind, defense firms and consultants had been getting and circulating this information for a long time, and certainly by the 1970s at least part of the trading system was well in place. During the earlier years, said one defense executive who was there,

> It was accepted that if you were a contractor, you could find out certain things from the military about what they were planning. It helped the contractors make their plans and it helped the blue suits [Pentagon personnel] as well, because they could get the contractors to explore the bureaucrats' pet ideas and build up some force in their favor.

What happened to the system in the Reagan years is a matter of highly ideological dispute. Some say it has not changed much.

Others argue that it became sleazier during the eighties as military retirees set themselves up in business to make a living solely from their ability to get these papers from their Pentagon friends and contacts. Still others agree that the atmosphere grew grimier but lay the blame on the shrinking military budget and the consequently increased competition of the late 1970s. Some observers point to all the money sloshing around during the 1980s and all the discretion—with its opportunities for corruption—given to political appointees. Another group accuses the Reaganite appointees not of too much generosity but of the opposite flaw: introducing too much competition into the process and thus making contractors hungrier.

One change behind the apparent growth of the documents trade is less ambiguous: Since Watergate we have created many new rules and practices to control and fight corruption in the Defense Department. "There was a proliferation of rules," the same defense executive explained,

> and no one really understood them. I used to keep a copy of the procurement rules on my desk. Now I'd have to begin stacking them down on the floor to keep them even with the desktop.
>
> I don't think [the change took place] because the people involved are more evil . . . But the job is getting increasingly complex. We're being asked to do harder things.

This constant change and increasing complexity, added to the capricious character of the political process that produces the defense budget, means that the environment for defense contractors is unstable and has become more so. These firms, like all organizations, want information in order to reduce these uncertainties and make it possible to plan for the future. The official channels are so cumbersome that it is often very hard to get such information in a timely way through the regular system. Under these circumstances, middlemen will emerge to fill the gap and profit from it as inexorably as sidewalk vendors appeared on the streets of New York at the end of 1989 to peddle pieces of the Berlin Wall. Some kind of informal information network is the wholly predictable consequence of the combination of bureaucratization and marked instability in the defense field. The network can be genteel, but when circumstances change it can turn cutthroat, full of middlemen conning each other and everyone around them.

Perhaps the central question about the behavior revealed by most of these prosecutions is that of how it affects the system's ability to produce effective weapons and fulfill our defense needs successfully. Certainly our experience in Operation Desert Storm suggests that the military-industrial complex has not been gravely incapacitated by waste, fraud, and abuse. But such issues were ignored by Operation Uncover and Operation Ill Wind.

These two campaigns did not ask what impact the trade in documents had on the public interest as measured by money or job performance, or why people should not be given most of this budget information anyway in order to make the whole system of competition function more efficiently, or whether the roots of the problem lie in the politics of Capitol Hill. Yet these are the sorts of questions we should ask if we are really interested in mitigating the problem of all those clandestine procurement documents floating around the defense community. In fact, though the subject of improving Pentagon procurement is a daunting one, it is safe to say that in most cases the key to making the system work better is to get more information exchanged and give more discretion to the officials in charge, not less.

Procurement rules throughout the government are already becoming tighter and tighter. For example, when procurement officials evaluate a contractor's proposal as part of competitive bidding on a purchase, regulations make it almost impossible for them to take into account what they know about how well the contractor did on previous jobs for the government.[30] The prohibition follows a distinct logic. If we permit procurement officials to make subjective judgments like that one, the reasoning goes, they will be able to use their discretion to indulge in corrupt favoritism. Therefore we must remove this discretion.

The argument is coherent, but fighting corruption by forbidding government officials to make judgments has certain unfortunate side effects. If we do not let a procurement official use any judgment about the job performance of contractors, for instance, we have devised a surefire formula for inducing irresponsibility on their part. If the performance of a contractor in his present job cannot help or hurt him when he bids for the next contract, why should he worry about making his performance match his promises? In the same way, we can simply crack down on information flows between government and contractors and feel good about having done something for the cause of ethical government, but in doing things this way we leave ourselves with the flaws in the procurement process that gave rise to the information trading in the first place and can easily end by making the system work not better but worse.

Congress is in fact the chief author of the informal trade in Pentagon documents, because Congress has created the system that makes this process or something like it inevitable. Yet when congressmen hear of such practices, as they did when Ill Wind became public in 1988, they react with pious shock and proclaim a major moral disaster requiring a bigger crackdown, tougher penalties, and tighter rules.

Most enforcement efforts in the defense field today are admirably directed at ordinary, intelligible crimes, from financial fraud to test-result falsification. Yet alongside this necessary policing we have developed a new, quite different way of talking about crimes not only in the defense field but in others as well. We find an offense like document swaps or insider trading or aggravated sleaziness. Moved by the post-Watergate fervor among our legislators, investigators, enforcement officials, journalists, and good government groups, we decide to increase the penalties for the distasteful behavior or criminalize it or step up prosecution so that we can deter it more surely.

We act as if there were huge fishlike schools of offenses, those that are crimes and those that deserve to be, swimming out there in the turgid sea of business and politics. The better our enforcement of laws and regulations, the more of these fish we will catch. If some of the fish are slipping through the net, this does not mean they are undersized or misshapen and not worth catching. No, if we are not snaring these little fish we must simply shrink the size of the net's holes. Following this reasoning, we come to think of an expanding criminal law as a good criminal law and of progressively tightened rules as appropriate ones.

Yet scandal politics is a blunt instrument. When it is scandal politics of the criminal sort, it becomes blunter. Often offensive

behavior in government tells us less about the ethics of the perpetrators than about the system in which they operate. Where
this is true, a network of prohibitions and sanctions tight enough
to eliminate all undesirable behavior may also create a government incapable of accomplishing much that is worth doing, in
the defense field or any other. Thus apart from the problems of
justice that occur when our scandal politics becomes a matter of
criminal prosecutions, there are self-interested reasons why we
should not always be turning our policy, management, and political problems into law enforcement jobs. We do not govern
responsibly when we leave these matters to investigators, prosecutors, and the defense lawyers who face them from the other
side of the table.

CHAPTER 6

PROSECUTORS ON THE HILL

W HEN THE scandal broke in 1989 and exposed corruption in programs administered by the federal Department of Housing and Urban Development, congressmen expressed voluble shock. Yet HUD's inspector general, Paul Adams, had already warned Congress of such problems in his semiannual reports to the Hill and had not managed to capture the lawmakers' attention. Former inspector general Charles Dempsey recalled not long ago that he had seen the same congressional attitude at work during the Environmental Protection Agency scandal of 1982. When the big scandal broke, half a dozen congressional committees staked out pieces of territory and rushed into hearings. As the nature of the scandal became clear, Dempsey was sent to EPA to clean up the administrative mess and put tighter procedures in place. At the end of his nine-month effort he sent a report to Congress. "I never got a single phone call from that committee . . . ," he recalled. "The scandal was finished, you see. The headlines were over."

We send our congressmen to Washington in no small part to make nuisances of themselves by keeping an eye on the federal enforcement bureaucracy. Indeed, as the government's administrative apparatus grows, many people (including this one) feel they need their congressmen more. Yet too many congressional committees have become part of a scandal production system that makes a lot of noise, takes many hostages, does little discernible good, and sometimes makes government distinctly worse.

Historically, congressional committees have seldom paid sustained, serious attention to the operations of federal agencies and policy areas within their jurisdiction. The modern Congress carries on this venerable tradition. Indeed, congressional attention may have become even more erratic in recent years because the drive for media exposure has become stronger and the internal organization of Congress weaker. Congressional scholar Norman J. Ornstein, explaining the change, said recently that paying day-after-day attention to the normal operations of government has always been relatively dull stuff, attended to, as he put it, by "the congressional equivalent of high school nerds." Neither the media nor the voters ever cared much about it: "There was never credit outside the institution for doing it. There used to be some credit inside, but now there's not much of that, either."

During the 1970s, as Congress acquired a progressively larger sense of its proper role in the American political scheme of things, congressional staffs in the House nearly tripled in size, while Senate staffs doubled.[1] It has been noted by more than one observer that in this era of the budget deficit, the expanded staffs cannot fully occupy themselves with great, popular, and expensive legislative initiatives. In other words, large numbers of these new people are all dressed up with no place to go. There is little evidence that they have used their increased resources to become more sophisticated supervisors of government management. So what *have* they done? The answer seems to be that most congressional committees deliver the same kind of sporadic performance as before—but more of it.

Some committees now have the resources and the will to conduct what must be called a perpetual scandal hunt. They pursue their targets in a spirit of rivalry with the executive branch—a contest less muted than it was in earlier times by customs of civility or restraint from institutional leadership. Such committees show little interest in what is debatable, ambiguous, or tediously complicated in the problems they attack. Scandal is the only lens through which they view the objects of their attention.

As we shall see in the case of the Equal Employment Opportunity Commission, this combination of bitterness and myopia can throw a monkey wrench into the workings of government. Furthermore, as the case of Office of Management and Budget official Joseph Wright will illustrate, this cast of mind can punish individuals with disproportionate harshness. Finally, the case of Nobel laureate David Baltimore will show that this type of scandal politics can also wreak damage on society as a whole.

Most congressional scandal hunting does not occur during the big, famous scandals. Consider, for example, the huge but obscure fight that took place during the Reagan years between the Equal Employment Opportunity Commission and the congressional committees that supervise it. The commission was set up in Great Society days to help enforce the laws banning discrimination in employment, and it expanded during the 1970s to absorb the enforcement functions of several other federal agencies. The agency has suffered from endemic management problems during both Republican and Democratic administrations.

Clarence Thomas, who has since been named to succeed Thurgood Marshall on the United States Supreme Court, was appointed EEOC's new chairman by the Reagan administration in 1982. Thomas' views on civil rights enforcement, too liberal for some Reaganites, were too conservative for EEOC's congressional oversight committees and the civil rights organizations that worked closely with them. The committees and civil rights groups thought government should use "goals and timetables"—euphemisms for "quotas," in the view of their critics—to fashion remedies for discrimination. Thomas disagreed. Another ideological clash came on the issue of "statistical" civil rights cases against employers. Before Thomas' time, the agency had repeatedly gone to court with cases in which there was no direct evidence of discriminatory practices. Despite this absence, the government would argue, the number of minority group members in good jobs was too low to have happened merely by chance. Therefore discrimination must have taken place and should be remedied by the court. Thomas said these cases, sometimes covering an entire industry, were too big and too few to accomplish much, and he wanted to concentrate on cases with concrete evidence of discriminatory intent.

These disputes over racial policy soon turned into accusations of incompetence and wrongdoing at EEOC. In September 1985,

Rep. Augustus F. Hawkins (D-Calif.), chairman of the House Education and Labor Committee, asked Congress's Government Accounting Office to investigate EEOC performance in seven separate areas, with questions ranging from whether Thomas was faithfully following the enforcement guidelines established by his predecessor to whether the agency's career personnel were receiving arbitrary treatment. Rep. Hawkins also sent his own staffers to hunt for possible impropriety in EEOC field offices. They reported with alarm that the number of cases settled by the agency was declining; the commission's new management protested that the decline in settlements came not from shoddy performance but from a deliberate policy of holding out for better remedies.

The agency was also in charge of enforcing laws against age discrimination in employment. Here, too, Thomas raised hackles. The biggest controversy of his tenure involved a rule issued by the commission in 1987 saying that workers could, if they wished, take a lump-sum payment from their employers in return for retiring early from their jobs. Typically, in these retirement incentive plans, the payment would get smaller as the worker neared the age of 65: This reduction was meant as an inducement to workers to retire early rather than late. The practice sounds innocuous, but the American Association of Retired Persons objected, saying that because it treated workers of different ages differently, it constituted unacceptable age discrimination.

When the rule was passed, Thomas sent official notice of it to Senator John Melcher (D-Mont.), then chairman of the Senate Special Committee on Aging. Officials of AARP told the senator of their great unhappiness. Melcher sent Thomas a similarly unhappy letter announcing that there would soon be committee hearings on the whole issue.

This dispute turned into another wide-ranging search for agency impropriety. In late August 1987, Melcher's office sent a letter from the senator, "requesting that Committee staff be provided full access to any and all documents and records pertaining to age discrimination complaint/case management and resolution received and generated by the EEOC and its staff."[2] Thomas fought back against the huge, shapeless demand. He wrote to Melcher, asking the senator to make his requests specific and to send them through EEOC's established congressional liaison specialists.

Melcher escalated with a letter asking for 59 separate categories of information, covering six years and ranging over topics from case and backlog statistics to instances in which EEOC's general counsel had kept the staff from acting on specific cases. The great range and detail of these questions are noteworthy: Today's congressional committees, using their larger staffs and the increased accessibility of information about executive branch agencies, can make attacks more penetrating than ever before.

Melcher said he wanted the information within five days. By deadline time agency personnel had replied to 43 of the questions; the senator proceeded to give them 18 new ones. In October a committee investigator delivered many of the original questions directly to an employee down in the agency's Information Systems Services unit. Thomas wrote to Melcher in protest. Melcher replied with 43 more questions, similar to those on earlier lists.

Finally, in December, committee staffers and EEOC personnel met for the first time to try to agree on what the questions were, which ones had been answered, which had not been but could be, and which were impossible. Yet even this meeting did not bring a thaw in relations, for a new crisis intervened.

The committee, it turned out, was not beating up on an agency with an impeccable performance record. While the combatants were busy hissing at one another, Thomas was installing a new computer system at the agency. The innovation would eventually be a success, but the transition was very rocky. In the fall of 1987, internal EEOC audits gradually revealed that not all the important data on the agency's age-discrimination case backlogs were being entered into the new computer system. The agency started tabulating the unrecorded cases by hand. By December, Thomas had been told about the administrative horror story that was unfolding. Included in EEOC's backlog of unresolved cases were 900 age-discrimination cases for which the statute of limitations had expired. In other words, 900 people with age-discrimination complaints had lost their chance at a remedy under federal law partly through EEOC's failure of performance.

This being the age of full disclosure, or at least of the anti-coverup, Thomas quickly announced the bad news at a pre-

Christmas press conference. Later, when the Senate reconvened in January, he wrote to Melcher and officially informed him of the findings. Melcher replied with an angry letter accusing Thomas of having consciously withheld the information during the committee's fall investigations. In an answering letter, Thomas said, just as angrily, "I have not led you to 'falsely believe' anything, and I resent being called a liar."[3] He pointed out that Melcher's staff had never asked specific questions about the statute of limitations.

From here on relations deteriorated still further, if such was possible. At the end of February 1988, committee staffers served Thomas with a subpoena for information, this time to be drawn straight from EEOC field office files rather than the suspect Washington headquarters and to be supplied within two weeks. All five EEOC commissioners, Democrats and Republicans, jointly requested more time. Otherwise, they said, the agency might have to shut down all regular business in order to respond to the questions.

There was another year of this wrangling to go. By October 1988, according to figures prepared by the agency's career staff, EEOC personnel had spent 7,114 hours complying with committee demands and requests.[4] The feud ended only after Melcher was defeated for reelection to the Senate in November. Senator David H. Pryor (D-Ark.) succeeded him as committee chairman, and relations between the agency and the committee improved.

Well, not quite. There was still the case of Lynn Bruner to settle. In 1986 Bruner, an excellent investigator who had risen through the EEOC ranks, became director of the agency's St. Louis field office. Large backlog problems awaited her there. She asked for more staff, but there was a hiring freeze on; she got more funds when the freeze ended that December. The next year she received a bad performance rating from the Senior Executive Service's Performance Review Board, controlled by high-ranking civil servants. Ironically, in light of the controversy that would follow, the bad rating came about partly because of a dispute between Bruner and her supervisor over whether she was following agency policy and giving priority to age-discrimination cases nearing their statute-of-limitation deadlines.

When Thomas announced the agency's statute-of-limitations

foul-up in December 1987, local media started calling the directors of the field offices that had the most expired cases. Bruner, phoned by the *St. Louis Post-Dispatch*, said the problem was Washington's fault. "I pleaded with them,"[5] she said, but her superiors would not give her the resources to do a proper job.

Shortly after her words appeared in print, Melcher's staffers arranged for her to appear before the committee and help them document charges of wrongdoing by the agency's higher-ups. Bruner received her next performance rating in June 1988, just before she was to testify. Once again it was not good. One of her evaluators complained that Bruner had shown poor judgment after the Thomas press conference by talking to a journalist. She had given her bosses no warning that she was going to take a public shot at them, described her bad performance as a high-level policy dispute, and put chairman Thomas in a "negative light."[6]

Several months after her testimony, Bruner received a third bad rating. As personnel rules dictated, she was demoted, and she began an intragovernment appeal. As the current political system made likely, the Government Accountability Project, an organization devoted to protecting whistle-blowers, decided to represent her after congressional staffers referred her case to the group. And a congressman came forward to charge agency impropriety in her case. He was Rep. Tom Lantos (D-Calif.), chairman of the Employment and Housing Subcommittee of the House Government Operations Committee, which had been told about Bruner by the staff from the outgoing Melcher regime. Lantos said he wanted Bruner's demotion rescinded. Thomas and the senior EEOC career officials who had handled the Bruner case resisted the congressman's demand. Lantos made Thomas and these officials testify at a punitive hearing. The impasse was finally broken in the old-fashioned way, through politics. Senator Pryor simply told Thomas that he had better do what Rep. Lantos suggested if he wanted the new, "more cordial relationship" with Pryor's committee to stay cordial.[7] Thomas complied in June 1989.

A year after the dispute was over, Bruner, looking back on the scuffle, explained what was probably at the root of the expired-case problem. EEOC's age-discrimination cases, she said, had in previous years been handled at the Department of Labor, which treated most of them in an abbreviated way, well within the statute-of-limitations constraints. When the cases were moved over to EEOC for enforcement, the commission handled them in a more detailed manner—more like the way EEOC treated its race-discrimination cases, which had no statute of limitations. Over several years the two conflicting sets of procedures produced the backlog and expiration problems that emerged in 1987.

Yet there was little mention of such crucial but unglamorous matters in the battles between Congress and EEOC. The issue ". . . became a crisis," Bruner thought, "because the [Melcher] committee started investigating. It became a big political issue because age discrimination has gained such prominence."

In pursuit of the hot issue, Melcher's committee acted aggressively. When EEOC refused to provide access to all records, the committee replied with a list of questions so long it added up to the same thing as comprehensive access. Committee staffers repeatedly tried to bypass normal channels and create alternative sources among EEOC employees. The investigators acted as if they were dealing with an enemy, and a resistant and wily one at that.

Were they right? Partly so. To begin with, senior EEOC personnel were not exactly open and friendly with their committee keepers. When committee staffers tried to talk to agency people unofficially, senior managers would register a quick protest. When the committee asked for information that had already been supplied, the agency was prompt in pointing out the mistake.

More important, EEOC did not give the congressional investigators all the information they needed, but only the information they explicitly requested. It seems logical, for instance, that anyone interested in EEOC backlogs, as Melcher was, would want to have a wide range of information about statute-of-limitation problems. Yet if committee staffers did not ask the specific questions needed to extract the critical data, they were not going to get much help in rephrasing their requests. Finally, as the bad news about the expired cases unfolded at the agency, no one there chose to give his or her counterpart on the Hill an unofficial preview of the information crawling out from under the rock.

The committee response to each act of resistance was to devise even more draconian and ingenious ways to squeeze information out of the agency. This circle of mutual reinforcement calls to mind the ironic old saying, "This animal is wicked: When attacked, it defends itself." Anyone trying to supervise a government agency and keep it accountable must deal with the fact that few human organizations known to history have ever taken delight in disgorging information about their internal operations. Organizations resist with special force when the people doing the asking betray hostile intent. Those who ask questions or give orders in a threatening and legalistic way will get defensive and legalistic responses.

You will recall what kind of information the House Judiciary Committee got out of Theodore Olson when he testified at the end of the EPA scandal. Olson did not lie to the legislators, but he did not exactly pour his heart out. He did what any sane person would do in his circumstances: hunker down and talk with damage limitation in mind. Officials in this situation will not elaborate; they will use words as noncommittally as possible. As a result, the stories they tell will be incomplete, misleading, or unintelligible. Olson's testimony, a study in cautious brevity, was an example of how running a government through adversary proceedings can constrict the flow of information.

For some purposes, defensive answers are all a congressional investigator needs, and threats are the only way to get them. But congressional duties do not end when the lawmakers have asked their tough questions before the television cameras. The congressmen and their staffs, especially because of their increased resources, have some responsibility for the overall health of the government organizations in their care, and to fulfill this responsibility the inquisitorial style is not enough. Confrontation will not elicit much information about how an agency works from day to day, what factors actually influence the decisions of its personnel, or what problems are really on the minds of its managers.

At the time of the age-discrimination scandal, EEOC was clearly an organization with big problems, and there were interesting questions to ask about them. Bruner, in her recent remarks, addressed one of them: How—not who was to blame, but how—did the backlog develop? There are other such questions: What role, for instance, was really played by budgetary constraints? If there were differences in performance among the various district offices, why? To what extent was the agency's computer trouble only a temporary transition problem? A congressman or anyone else needs to know such things in order to help improve an agency like EEOC. A scandal hunt will miss much of this information. Indeed, when an agency has problems, inquisitors will often be the last to know. When they finally learn what has gone wrong, they will be embarrassed and angry about not having been told sooner. Their resentment will make them feel even more punitive toward the agency in their charge.

This destructive cycle also marked the particular treatment of Lynn Bruner. In her case, the committee approached an EEOC employee who had already run athwart her supervisors, and Congress publicized her critical opinions. Predictably, the publicity widened the gap of mistrust and increased the bitterness between her and her bosses. Congress then stepped in again, professing shock and trying to forbid the resulting unpleasantness. A Congress that uses whistle-blowers has more responsibility than this to gauge the effects such spectacles have on both the individuals and the agencies involved after the press coverage is over.

The same failure of responsibility that can jar federal agencies without improving them can also make congressional scandal hunts, as well as the hearings around which they often revolve, terribly unjust to individuals who get caught up in them.

Most congressmen, of course, do not grow fangs when they bang down the hearing gavel, and most committee witnesses are not only willing to testify but panting and eager to have their views influence the making of public policy. When a witness is treated harshly, there is sometimes more than enough reason. Still, a good many public officials and private citizens, and not just obvious miscreants, come away from their dealings with today's congressional committees complaining that they have been personally abused by a congressman or his staff. "Every one of us thinks we're Jimmy Stewart playing the role of the defense attorney," said Rep. Pete Stark (D-Calif.), acknowledging the widespread bad feeling. "The fact is that we're probably Darth Vader."[8]

The complaint about tyrannical, scandal-hunting, witness-abusing congressional committees is a grievance with a history. Such bodies are a perennial American phenomenon,[9] but during the Depression the Roosevelt administration and its allies on the Hill discovered the power of well-publicized congressional investigations to mobilize support for New Deal measures. The opinion grew more general that the investigating committees should have a great deal of power. It was this invigorated model of the congressional investigation that Rep. Martin Dies, Jr. (D-Tex.), imitated in 1938 when he took over the House Special Committee on Un-American Activities. Dies, in turn, provided a model for Senator Joseph R. McCarthy (R-Wisc.).

McCarthy was by no means the only politician after World War II who agitated the issue of Communists in American public life, but he became the symbol of the campaign. When he became chairman of the Senate Committee on Government Operations after the 1952 elections, McCarthy promptly awarded himself the additional job of chairman of the committee's Subcommittee on Investigations, a tactic he was not the last congressman to employ.

His hearings were archetypal exercises in scandal politics. They aimed specifically at exposing moral turpitude and criminality in his individual targets and were designed to highlight issues of personal guilt. McCarthy forced many witnesses to testify in open hearings so that if they had to incur suspicion by taking refuge in their Fifth Amendment rights, they would do so with maximum publicity. McCarthy's committee—and those fashioned after it—leaked closed-session testimony, refused to give witnesses and their lawyers access to relevant documents, and denied witnesses' attorneys the right to cross-examine accusers.

When the subject of political scandal was raised with liberals of the early 1960s, it called the McCarthy trauma to mind. McCarthy's sort of scandal politics left his opponents insisting that there must be definite limits on congressional and other government investigators when they took to examining individuals' lives and actions. McCarthy's adversaries did not merely share this conviction but defined themselves by it. Indeed, this general attitude was one reason why the political scandals of the early sixties were relatively contained affairs.

In the late 1960s, opinions shifted yet again. Liberals once more became partisans of Congress against a presidency they did not control and grew more approving of aggressive congressional investigations. The circle was complete. Today, because of the general climate and the demands of modern election campaigns, congressmen thirst with special intensity for media exposure, while competitive media scramble after scandal news. There is an acute temptation for lawmakers to provide such news by treating individuals indecently, in a punitive manner disproportionate to the sins involved.

This problem, like the problem of agency oversight, does not arise only in big, famous cases; it is an everyday dilemma. Typical of the more ordinary incidents was a year-long congressional attack in the mid-1980s on Joseph R. Wright, Jr., then deputy director of the Office of Management and Budget. A May 1985 story in *The Wall Street Journal*[10] set off Wright's troubles by accusing him of influence peddling.

Wright's father ran an Oklahoma company called the Anchor Gasoline Corporation, the target of a Department of Energy enforcement action for alleged overcharges under the Carter administration's labyrinthine, now-discredited oil price control program. The action had been pending since 1981 and sat for a long time on bureaucratic desks somewhere in one of the department's regional offices. At his father's behest, according to the *Journal* story, Wright phoned a DOE official in Washington in 1982. The department then moved the case from the regional office to Washington headquarters, where it sat for another two years. The department then issued an administrative complaint against Anchor.

By one of those strange Washington coincidences, just as the *Journal* story appeared, the ever-active House Energy and Commerce Committee's Subcommittee on Oversight and Investigations was starting to look into the matter, and the FBI had been called into the case. But the Senate Governmental Affairs Committee beat the House to the punch, summoning Wright within a week of the *Journal* article to testify about the fateful phone call.

At the Senate hearing, Wright told the committee a couple of things that the newspaper article had omitted. He had phoned the department, he said, to ask that the paralyzed bureaucracy move one way or the other, not to request leniency for his father.

Wright said he knew the call might be open to misinterpretation and did not want to give even the appearance of having asked for a favor. So he had gotten a staff aide to listen in on the phone conversation and confirm that no suspicious words, inflections, grunts, or pregnant pauses had passed Wright's lips. Senator Ted F. Stevens (R-Alaska), a committee member, deemed the call a lapse of judgment but said he would be "surprised . . . if Mr. Wright had done anything wrong."[11] Senator and then-presidential hopeful Al Gore (D-Tenn.) declared that the Anchor case had been, in the senator's word, "fixed."[12] The incident passed.

Six months later, though, Senator Thomas F. Eagleton (D-Mo.) demanded and got more committee hearings on the case. On the opening day of the new Senate drama, staffers stood at the door of the hearing room handing out press packets containing a chronology of events, an index of individuals connected to the case, a glossary of terms, and background information, both structural and financial, on the companies involved. The elaborateness of the package announced to journalists who received it that this must be one heck of a scandal.

Early in the hearing Senator Gore repeated his earlier line: "I think that Mr. Wright fixed this case."[13] Then came witnesses for the prosecution, lower-level Energy Department bureaucrats who said that the delays caused by department higher-ups in the matter were inexplicable. "Unless," said Senator Gore in case anyone was missing the point, "you wanted to fix the case."[14] According to the typical scenario, the next stage in this sort of hearing calls for the higher-ups themselves to testify so that everyone can watch their pitiful attempts to justify their actions. This time, though, committee staffers had stumbled and—in one of those moments of black comedy that help make politics worthwhile—produced a higher-up who was not your average sweaty-palmed witness but a pit bull of an adversary. Avrom Landesman was a Harvard Law School graduate who had been in the civil service for 23 years and was also, no less, an ordained rabbi. He was not going to be easy to topple from the moral high ground.

Landesman gave legal reasons for the decisions he had made in the Anchor case. "I don't think he's telling the truth,"[15] said Eagleton bluntly, beginning a sharp cross-examination. Landesman parried just as sharply. When Eagleton broke in on the testimony one time too many, the rabbi intoned understandingly, "I'm sure you're sorry for having interrupted me."[16] Finally, Eagleton snapped. "Oh, come now," he said to Landesman with angry sarcasm. "A *little* perjury is okay, but not *too* much."[17]

A congressman making even accusations as poisonous as this one is protected by the Constitution from the libel laws that govern ordinary citizens. Still, Eagleton had gone too far. Republican senators roused themselves to protest the accusation of criminality, and the hearing began to lose steam.

In January 1986 the Justice Department notified Wright's lawyer—there is, by now, always a lawyer—that it saw no evidence of criminal conduct. But this was not the end: The matter now had to go to the Office of Government Ethics, one of many such units created within the federal government after Watergate to force more attention to such problems. The ethics office concluded in March 1986 that Wright had, "albeit unknowingly," created the appearance of a conflict of interest.[18] Senator Carl Levin (D-Mich.) rushed to the barricades, demanding that OMB director James C. Miller III somehow punish Wright. In May 1986, *The Wall Street Journal* revealed to its readers that Miller had as yet taken no action.[19] Finally the director wrote a letter of "admonition" to Wright. The *Journal* gave prominent space to the event and to the opinion of a Levin staffer who found Miller's alleged leniency "troubling" and "planned to review the matter."[20]

This story was no tragedy. Wright's reputation was solid enough to withstand the onslaught. When Miller resigned as OMB director in the fall of 1986, Wright succeeded him. Yet something went seriously wrong with Congress's behavior in Wright's case. His was not an instance of an individual's actually committing a corrupt official act that serves his private interests while harming the public. We are not even talking here about the structural conflict of interest that occurs when an individual has official responsibility for public-policy decisions that affect his personal financial health.

We are talking instead about a more recent phenomenon, the "appearance of conflict,"[21] which underlies many of today's conflict-of-interest cases. When someone is accused of creating an appearance of conflict, he has not necessarily done any actual wrong by exercising official responsibility in an area or a way that affects his personal interests. Instead, the accuser charges that some third party, in viewing the situation, might well suspect the official of violating ethics rules. The accused, this charge continues, has created the appearance of an ethical violation, and creating the appearance of an ethical violation is an ethical violation in itself.

Public officials should indeed be wary of creating the appearance of conflicts of interest. For instance, in the Wright case it might well be argued that a deputy director of OMB is a generally powerful person, and federal officials who hear his voice at the other end of the telephone just might remember it vividly no matter how innocent the particular words he speaks. Therefore, high-ranking individuals should stay off that telephone altogether. This admonition, though, is a matter more of prudence than of basic tenets of ethics. Today's appearance-of-conflict standard, by contrast, speaks of prudential issues as if they were fundamental moral ones and leaves us with little ability to differentiate among varied offenses that range from lack of discretion to criminal behavior.

The new appearance-of-conflict standard is dangerous in another way as well, because the accuser's judgments play such a big role in creating the crime. To whom does there "appear" to be a conflict in these cases? Voters? Average citizens? Or is the relevant audience made up of political players like committee members, staffers, and journalists? If it is these last individuals who make up the audience, we have a special problem on our hands. Such individuals, after all, have personal incentives—from getting a good story to appearing on the nightly news—to claim moral shock early and often. In cases of this type, it is the scandal hunters who may have the most important conflict of interest.

The Wright phone call was a subject for some but not much moral excitation. Yet it prompted three separate sets of congressional hearings involving three different committees or subcommittees. The committees, in turn, set off an FBI investigation and consideration of criminal charges by the Justice Department, not to speak of the hundreds of hours spent by congressional staffers in becoming experts on the corporate structure of the Anchor Gasoline Corporation. During the probe, Senator Gore twice announced to the world that Wright was a major criminal and Senator Eagleton contributed a charge of perjury.

There was clearly more activity here than can be justified by the wrongdoing involved or explained by the pursuers' genuine moral outrage. In this respect, the Wright case was no oddity. Washington these days is flush with tales of congressional over-reaching, by staffers who routinely threaten a congressional sub-poena in the course of negotiations or look for excuses to deliver the subpoena in order to publicize an investigation and show the press that the other side in the negotiations is hiding something. Staffers who are asked to narrow their requests for documents sometimes say openly that they are calling for more information than necessary: They want their demand to be so broad that the target of the investigation cannot figure out what the committee is really after.

The complaints about testifying before some committees have become so widespread that in the mid-1980s the American Bar Association established a special Subcommittee on Congres-sional Investigations to address the problem. "[I]t is by no means unheard of," one of its cochairmen explained, "for Congress to call and interrogate witnesses, declare those witnesses to be guilty of crimes, and demand that they be prosecuted."[22] The ABA supplied a list of specifics: Some committees allow wit-nesses almost no help from their lawyers during hearings, or give witnesses no time to prepare testimony properly, or deny them access to their own documents or transcripts of testimony while using this unseen material to ambush them at public hear-ings.

In other words, some congressmen and staffers behave like prosecutors pursuing criminal defendants. Yet the legislature has more power than the prosecutors to threaten individual rights. Prosecuting attorneys, after all, must take account of the laws that limit their actions during criminal investigations, and their authority can be challenged in court. During con-gressional investigations, by contrast, there is rarely an outside judge to whom to appeal. The committees themselves are the judges and juries, and the members can ruin the reputations of witnesses without permitting them a right of reply. Congress is given this extraordinary latitude because its primary job is not to put individuals in jail but to consider broader policy questions. Yet some congressmen and their staffs use this uniquely wide discretion to go after individual targets, humiliate them, threaten their livelihoods, and put them in criminal jeopardy.

The ABA has proposed a set of model rules to prevent abuses in congressional hearings. Under the new rules, witnesses would (naturally) have a right to full representation by counsel, and witnesses declaring their intention to invoke the Fifth Amendment would not be forced into public testimony merely to dramatize that fact. Also, they would receive reasonable notice of hearings, get a chance to review relevant documents, be given copies of their previous testimony to the committee, and have an opportunity to rebut charges against them during the same session in which the charges were made.

A less polite response by targets of congressional investigations also started to appear during the 1980s. Stanley Brand, perhaps the best known of the Washington attorneys who now make a specialty of representing clients before bodies like congressional committees, was general counsel of the House of Representatives during the speakership of Rep. Thomas P. (Tip) O'Neill, Jr. (D-Mass.). Yet Brand cheerfully summed up his current approach by saying, "Congress has become like a grand jury. So my approach is very aggressive. I tell clients to say, Fuck you." The nation saw an only slightly more genteel version of this philosophy in the spring of 1987 when Lieutenant Colonel Oliver L. North, accompanied by counsel Brendan Sullivan, testified before the Iran-contra committees. Sullivan, frustrated by the limits the committees had placed on his participation, at one point raised his voice to declare, "I am not a potted plant!"[23] He thus gave voice to the anthem of what might be called the new Edward Bennett Williams school of congressional relations.

Sullivan had the protection of a charismatic client. Yet the lawyer also had leeway because key congressmen on the Iran-contra panel were worried about the bad reputation congressional investigating committees had started to acquire. During the HUD scandal of 1989, attorneys for congressional witnesses began to exploit that nervousness in a bigger way.

In the spring of 1989 President Bush's new HUD secretary, former Republican congressman Jack F. Kemp, heard from Inspector General Paul Adams the same warnings given to Congress about fraud in housing programs. Kemp promptly suspended one of the programs the IG had criticized. With Kemp's dramatic action, the HUD scandal hit the headlines, and department investigators began to expose additional abuses across the country.

Now Congress entered the picture, mainly in the form of the Subcommittee on Employment and Housing of the House Government Operations Committee, which hurried to hold hearings. The issues before the subcommittee—HUD's chronic vulnerability to fraud and past administrations' failure to deal with the problem adequately—were and are deadly serious. But the subcommittee did not want to waste all its valuable TV time talking about monitoring systems or hearing tales of small-time corruption in the boonies. It went for the big names. Congressmen expressed shock over news that private housing developers were hiring prominent Republicans as consultants in order to sidestep the complex HUD bureaucracy and get friendly hearings at the highest levels of the department for their grant and subsidy requests. The lawmakers summoned the consultants to testify and made a delicious catch in James Watt, the former secretary of the interior who had been a chief Reaganite scourge of big and wasteful government. Watt told how he and his partners had received $300,000 for one such intervention.[24]

Subcommittee members also wanted to hear, quite properly, from top HUD officials of the Reagan years who had been in charge when many of the abuses had taken place. Reagan's HUD secretary, Samuel R. Pierce, Jr., claimed that the influence peddling in and around the department had been directed by the woman who had served as his executive assistant from 1984 through early 1988, Deborah Gore Dean. So the subcommittee summoned Dean to testify. On the advice of her attorneys she refused to do so voluntarily, and the congressmen issued a subpoena. Dean's lawyers responded by opening negotiations with the staff for a deal in which she would testify in exchange for limited immunity from federal prosecution. The negotiations failed. The subcommittee, knowing Dean would take the Fifth and clearly not feeling bound by the ABA's model rules, set June 13 as the date for her public testimony.

On that day the hearing room had more lights in it than a

movie set, which in many ways it was. The dramatic press coverage conveyed the sense that Dean was running large risks and stigmatizing herself as a probable criminal if she chose not to testify. And when Dean refused to answer any substantive questions, congressmen used the highly visible occasion to express their indignation at her recalcitrance.

Yet the prospect of looking like a criminal had lost its terror, at least when compared with the possibility of actually being convicted as one. There would be no more Michael Deavers cooperating with congressional investigators in order to avoid looking shady.

Three other HUD officials also took the Fifth before the subcommittee, including, in his second appearance, the HUD secretary himself. When Pierce appeared before the subcommittee to invoke his Fifth Amendment rights, his attorneys added a new wrinkle to the proceedings: They took advantage of a little-used House rule that gave a subpoenaed witness the right to bar press cameras and recorders from the hearing room. This move made it a good deal harder for radio and TV journalists to gather the kind of dramatic scandal material they needed.

The congressmen were even angrier with Pierce than they had been with Dean. Newspaper editorials argued that the former HUD secretary was morally obliged to give an account of his stewardship of the department. Pierce's lawyers fought right back. In a piece on *The New York Times*'s op-ed page, they said Pierce would have been crazy to go before the subcommittee without procedural safeguards like those in a criminal investigation. They said that a subcommittee lawyer had denied Pierce a look at the documents he would be asked about during the hearings, maintaining that the proceedings were not a "1950s game show where contestants get the answers ahead of time." Pierce's attorneys portrayed him as a scapegoat—just like those created in the 1950s, they noted, by Senator Joseph McCarthy.[25]

Uncooperativeness from the main witnesses did not stop the subcommittee and its staff, of course. They saw to it that Pierce's case was referred to an independent counsel. They produced a new witness, a former Pierce aide serving time in federal prison for illegally accepting money while in office, who testified that Pierce had approved HUD grants for political and personal reasons. Congress referred this matter, too, to the independent counsel, and later broadened his investigation yet again. The two sets of investigators were at one point locked in combat over whether the committee was obliged to share information about its informants with the independent counsel.[26] The independent counsel threatened a subpoena, and the committee finally turned over the data. The broader policy issue of the underlying reasons why HUD programs were so open to hustlers and crooks moved to the periphery of the story. And once each former HUD official had acquired a criminal lawyer of his or her very own, it became a much more difficult task to extract a reasonably straight or complete picture of what had happened at the higher levels of the department.

Thus a lack of restraint in using official power against individual targets can be not only odious but self-defeating. Congressional witnesses who feel gravely threatened by such tactics will start refusing to go near a microphone without personal attorneys. These attorneys, in turn, will eventually learn how to be more aggressive and clever in fighting the congressional foe. It would be a sad and damaging thing to see congressional hearings strictly governed by regulations such as the ABA rules, which could turn investigations of controversial issues into full-dress adversary proceedings unable to do the job of providing the type of information Congress needs in order to govern intelligently. Yet even without ABA-style rules, lawyers for the unwilling witnesses summoned by Congress are increasingly turning investigations into battlegrounds, and it is hard to condemn these tactics. When threats of criminal penalties and public humiliation without a chance of redress permeate congressional hearing rooms like a bad smell, it is wholly foreseeable that those under attack, guilty and innocent alike, will defend themselves however they can.

This type of escalation can have worrisome consequences for the country as a whole—even, strange as it may seem, when congressional investigators are dead right in their choice of targets and when their opponents bear the heavier blame for the acrimony. Take, for instance, the five-year controversy involving biologist David Baltimore. In 1986, when the story began, the 49-year-old scientist had already won a Nobel Prize for his discovery of an enzyme that plays a key role in propagating certain cancer viruses and the AIDS virus. He was founder and head of the Whitehead Institute for Biomedical Research, affiliated with the Massachusetts Institute of Technology, whose research budget of $12 million included about $8 million in federal research funds.

More than most scientists, Baltimore knew how to handle himself in the world of politics and treated science as part of the country's political life. In 1976 he publicly criticized the award of a Nobel Prize in economics to Milton Friedman, on the grounds that Friedman had worked for the government of Chile.[27] On another occasion Baltimore suggested that representatives of labor, the poor, minorities, the law, and other such groups be allowed into the policymaking process to help form an agenda for a responsive science.[28]

In April 1986, the scientific journal *Cell* published a paper out of the Whitehead Institute on the ability of transplanted genes to affect an immune system's production of antibodies. The chief author was a postdoctoral student of Baltimore's. As head of the institute, Baltimore also had his name on the paper. Another collaborator, in a separate laboratory, was a Brazilian scientist of Japanese descent with the exotic name of Thereza Imanishi-Kari.

Tufts University was considering hiring Imanishi-Kari. A postdoctoral fellow named Margot O'Toole, employed in Imanishi-Kari's laboratory, approached the authorities at Tufts with the charge that there were serious errors in the *Cell* paper. O'Toole had copied 17 pages out of Imanishi-Kari's laboratory notebooks and said the data showed that part of the "successful" experiments published in the paper had in fact not worked at all.

A panel of Tufts scientists looked at the charges and decided the paper's problems were not serious enough to demand correction. The same thing happened when O'Toole took her complaint to authorities at MIT.

This was not the end of the story, because funding for Imanishi-Kari's part of the *Cell* paper had come from the federal government via the National Institutes of Health. Two scientists at NIH, Ned Feder and Walter Stewart, had begun devoting themselves to the mission of exposing scientific fraud. They learned of O'Toole's case and took it to the NIH misconduct office. Staffers at Rep. John Dingell's Oversight and Investigations Subcommittee of the House Energy and Commerce Committee heard about the fracas and got in touch with Feder and Stewart. The institute was persuaded to "lend" them to the investigation on a full-time basis; the practice is not uncommon, and the subcommittee picks up a number of off-budget staffers this way.

By this time NIH had appointed a panel to examine the whole affair. Dingell's staff put pressure on the agency to remove panel members who had professional connections with Baltimore, and NIH complied. But when the panel reported, the results were a disappointment to the *Cell* paper's critics. Though NIH forced the authors to write a correction of several points, the panel absolved them of "serious conceptual error."[29]

Yet the Dingell subcommittee had already launched another line of attack. Imanishi-Kari, under threat of subpoena, was made to hand over her laboratory notebooks to the subcommittee staff, which sent them to the Secret Service to be inspected for possible fraud. The subcommittee also commandeered documents and research notes from both the principals in the case and individuals on the periphery, like the researcher who had developed the mice used in the experiments. When Dingell staffers discovered that Baltimore's team had somehow heard in advance about part of the NIH panel's report, they asked for another official investigation, this time by an inspector general. Suspicions of coverup expanded to include at least nine scientists connected with the affair.

This campaign caused an uproar in the scientific community. Scientists saw Dingell threatening the community's authority to judge scientific work and were horrified at the subcommittee's techniques. In the midst of the controversy, a scientist and administrator at one major university said in conversation that after Baltimore had delivered a speech on the campus, someone from the Dingell staff had telephoned to say that the subcommittee wanted a tape of the talk. The administrator was scandalized at this type of official intrusion.

In May 1989, the subcommittee pressed forward with public hearings at which the alleged perpetrators were summoned to testify. These hearings did not go well for the subcommittee: The testimony of the Secret Service was equivocal, and much of the press coverage was favorable to Baltimore. But the staff kept working. A year later came yet another hearing, at which Secret

Service personnel had more to report. Under subcommittee supervision they had analyzed computer tapes that Imanishi-Kari had used to buttress her argument when it was questioned by her fellow scientists. The tapes, she claimed, were from experiments done in mid-March of 1985. But, said the Secret Service witnesses, from the identification numbers on the tapes and the color of the paper and ink it was clear that these tapes could not have been made until several months later. The chairman asked the Secret Service to share its information with the local U.S. attorney, who might be interested in criminal prosecution.

Even this blockbuster did little to faze partisans on the other side. They insisted that the difference in dates had little scientific significance: Whether the tapes were made in March or in September did not affect their validity. Besides, the data on those tapes were not even part of the *Cell* paper itself. But worse was to come, for yet another NIH investigation had been opened under subcommittee pressure. In the spring of 1991, a draft NIH report both reported that Imanishi-Kari appeared to have faked data appearing in the *Cell* paper itself and said that Baltimore was wrong to have defended her for so long. Baltimore asked that the paper be retracted and apologized to O'Toole. The recriminations began.

The Dingell subcommittee appears to have been correct not only in its view of Imanishi-Kari but in its more general concern with scientific error and fraud. In theory, the scientific community and the nature of the scientific discipline limit these pathologies. But accusations of dishonesty are normally heard and judged by scientists who, as in every other organization or discipline, belong to old-boy networks whose members do not like to trash one another's reputations. And as the scientific enterprise grows larger and more disparate, it becomes easier for error and fraud to slip in under the radar. Methods of scrutiny must adapt. Moreover, this country spends huge amounts of federal money to support scientific inquiry and relies on this research for the nation's well-being. Scientists are not very persuasive when they argue that politicians have no business in scientific affairs.

Yet there was another hand. Allegations of fraud in a field as notoriously "messy" as immunology are extremely hard to prove definitively: Even in Imanishi-Kari's case, it took elaborate Secret Service analysis to nail down the proof. Imanishi-Kari's colleagues made their inquiries by more ordinary means and did so in a spirit of collegial trust. Their resulting judgment was wrong and thus unjust to Margot O'Toole. Yet if the scientists who worked with Imanishi-Kari were slower to suspect her than the congressional sleuths were, this was not necessarily evidence of a conspiracy to conceal the truth.

The subcommittee met the scientists' resistance aggressively—through direct pressure on NIH to alter its investigative procedures, through recourse to the inspector general, and through the threat of congressional subpoenas. Staffers thought these were the only ways to deal with what they saw as such stubborn and corrupt individuals, but one unintended consequence of this strategy was to turn the substantive debate over the paper into a frontal, dramatic struggle over power. The dispute looked less like an argument over the merits of the paper than a tussle over who should be making such judgments. It was easy for scientists to see the episode as an attack on their legitimacy and respond, as many of them did, with fear and anger.

Congressional investigators, not surprisingly, saw this activity as yet another sign of the scientists' bad faith and another reason to act in a punitive manner.

The choice of aggressive tactics influenced the proceedings in another way as well: Because the investigation emphasized sanctions and personal culpability, the targeted scientists and institutions brought in lawyers. Thus the adversary nature of the process was guaranteed for all time, and every assertion came to be viewed primarily as a tactic. People in such a climate tend not to make thorough reexaminations of their views; Baltimore's apology to O'Toole came only after he had replaced his attorneys with a new team not previously involved in the dispute.

Personalities probably played less of a role than the newspaper reporting suggested, but they are never irrelevant. In Baltimore, the subcommittee found someone who rose vigorously to the bait: The same quality that had made Baltimore so certain of his moral superiority to Milton Friedman became the scientist's decisive weakness.

On the other side, from the subcommittee there emanated a deep animus against this country's scientific establishment. Just after the Secret Service presented its second round of evidence on Imanishi-Kari's notebooks, a committee source on the Baltimore investigation was asked whether this might be the time, now that the scientific community's consciousness had clearly been raised on the issue of fraud, for Dingell and Baltimore to make peace and voice their mutual dedication to good scientific research. "I don't think Dingell would sell out the staff that way," he said. "But why would it be a sellout?" the questioner asked:

> "Why can't everyone declare victory and go home?"
> "Because Baltimore and the rest covered this up."
> "You mean his humiliation is a necessary part of your enterprise?"
> "Yes."

It was necessary, the source explained, because science was so massively corrupt. "In science," he said during the discussion that followed,

> "you have to lie to survive."
> "You mean, for instance, that two-thirds of the scientists in this country have told some significant substantive lie in their careers?"
> "In their careers? I mean during the past *year*."

That is the language of resentment, not to say hatred. Its spirit was evident in the investigation and added to the sense of threat.

There is no doubt that a tough posture by official investigators generates action: Scientific institutions are now forming new boards and committees and writing new rules and procedures to deal with the fraud-and-error problem more formally. It is also quite true that the scientists with whom a congressman must deal may be arrogant. So if a congressional committee assumes a prosecutor's posture toward a group of scientists every so often, the adversary proceedings may be tolerable or healthy.

However, these techniques are not like the good china that gets used only on special occasions; such practices get to be a habit. For instance, even after NIH made its report in the spring of 1991 about Thereza Imanishi-Kari, the episode was not over: O'Toole refused to accept Baltimore's apology as adequate, and investigators were still pursuing a possible coverup, trying to discover exactly who knew about the fraud and when. The U.S. attorney in Maryland, where NIH is located, was said to have the matter under criminal investigation, and Imanishi-Kari began to give press interviews and describe her case as a "witch hunt." Feder and Stewart abandoned their scientific research in favor of fraud-hunting, and Stewart developed a new computer program that can run large-scale searches for scientific plagiarism.[30]

The Baltimore affair as a whole was competing for space in the newspapers with other stories, which had begun to appear with regularity, about science fraud allegations at various laboratories and universities. NIH itself was occupied with yet another massive scandal hunt—an unquestionably wasteful six-year inquiry, begun out of fear of congressional wrath, over whether NIH researcher Robert C. Gallo had or had not been the first to discover the AIDS virus. Meanwhile, NIH has been suffering an "extraordinary" exodus, according to *Science* magazine, of top researchers.[31] Apart from money, their major complaint is over what some call the "Dingellization" of their institution. "People are absolutely terrified of this Dingell business," said one researcher. "They're afraid to make a mistake."[32]

More ironically, in response to a suit by a scientist under investigation for misconduct, a federal court has struck down the procedures NIH uses in its inquiries.[33] The scientist deserved more due-process protection, said the judge, raising the possibility that these disputes will soon be as elaborate and protracted as full-dress criminal trials.

If a congressional investigator is persistent enough, he has the resources to force the scientists in his orbit to use much of their time creating records that will protect them when the next investigation comes. He can establish a powerful incentive for them not to stick their heads up and make themselves targets. He can make it much more attractive to them to take refuge in the judgment of committees. In short, he can help establish a climate that is anathema to high-quality scientific research, for such inquiry proceeds through hunches and uncertainties and flawed inspirations and personal injustices and judgments that could never be successfully defended in the bureaucratic courts.

To the extent that the scientific enterprise in this country is corrupt, Congress has a duty not to defer to scientists' opinions. Where test data are falsified or federal science grants are being used to pay impermissible overhead expenses at institutions that receive this largesse, we want the watchdogs to growl. Yet to view American science chiefly as a pool of corruption needing cleanup is about as responsible as viewing our defense industry chiefly through the lens of Operation Ill Wind. In general, science is not corrupt: If it were truly riddled with lies, it could not have produced the scientific progress we have enjoyed in recent years.

So, as congressional committees acquire the capacity to reach more frequently and more deeply into scientific research efforts, their members must take some responsibility for the well-being of the scientific enterprise as a whole and measure their investigations against that standard. If the job of overseeing science is not given to congressional people who respect it, flaws and all, Congress's power will do little more than help diminish the morale, attractiveness, and authority of one of the institutions on which we most depend. This, along with the fallibility of scientists, is a lesson of the Baltimore case.

In science and in other areas, we need Congress to root out wrongdoing. Yet if the watchdogs allow scandal politics to overwhelm the more mundane types of legislative kibitzing, carping, and consciousness raising, and if they do so long enough and intensively enough, they will corrode everything they touch. A congressional committee practices scandal politics when it treats administrative dilemmas as the acts of swindlers and prevaricators. It practices scandal politics when its first response to resistance from a bureaucracy is to start making punitive demands. It practices scandal politics when it treats individuals as presumptive liars.

Congressional investigators using such strategies may well win the particular fights they are waging, but they also become just another rung on a ladder of escalating hostility. Over time they may have to use bigger and bigger bludgeons to extract the information and behavior they want. Or they may exact compliance at a real cost to the ability of government and those who deal with it to get their primary jobs done.

CHAPTER 7

SEX

THE SCANDALS THAT rolled like a wave over our political shores after the mid-1970s were not propelled solely by greed and overweening ambition, real or alleged. There was also a fair amount of lust involved. Sex-related political scandals mesmerized us with their lurid dramas of passion and weakness, crime and punishment. Such scandals grew common because these years saw a great expansion in our views about how much politicians' personal character and conduct mattered to their public lives and how much the public had a right to know about their private behavior. The sex scandals became public extravaganzas because the media, to the delight of news consumers everywhere, did not stick to high-minded discussions of these issues but reported on them in exceptional, fact-filled, prurient depth.

These sex scandals, like our many financial scandals, have begun to pose real problems for our political life. They sometimes raise issues of fairness by applying a single standard of judgment to matters that are seen differently by people of different regions, social classes, and generations. Sometimes an individual is judged by two contradictory sets of standards at once. Some of the miscreants in these scandals escape lightly while others are unjustly destroyed. Worse, these sex scandals, sometimes justified on the grounds that we must know about our leaders' moral qualities, often do not really give us much insight into the character traits that affect a politician's behavior in office. We have come to know more personal details about our officials than we can successfully integrate into our political judgments. As a result, what we learn from sex scandals today is only a generalized distaste for politics and those who practice it.

The uneven and contradictory standards at work in our recent sex scandals were on display one night not long ago at the John Houseman Theater Studio in New York City. This small theater was established to present plays that are new, avant-garde, or produced by relative unknowns. It is in a basement down a narrow stairway, and its seats are chairs set on bleachers. Homemade baked goods are on sale in the lobby at intermission. On this particular night Rita Jenrette could be seen in performance at the theater, still struggling, almost a decade after she first gained notoriety, to be treated as something more than a joke.

Among the evening's plays was a high-toned drama featuring five characters on the deck of a cruise ship who wage a losing but highly articulate struggle to find meaning in their lives. One cast member was identified as Rita Jenrette. Was this the very same Rita Jenrette who as a sumptuous blond congressional wife had created a scandal by posing seminude for *Playboy*? It was. Could she act? Surprisingly well, considering her reputation as a woman with only one product to peddle.

After the performance Jenrette celebrated with friends. Their party, like her play, was a far cry from the glitzy galas of her celebrity days. The site of the postperformance festivities was a cheap and cheery neighborhood restaurant, and the crowd was made up of theater pals of Jenrette's and friends from the brokerage house where she worked during the day. She said there had also been a contingent from her church in the theater audience, and most of the roisterers at the party did not even drink beer. Later, in her small West Side apartment crowded with political photographs from earlier times, Jenrette sounded like the victim of a shipwreck. "I'm proud of having survived," she said, explaining how hard it had been for her to escape her past.

She was a graduate of the University of Texas, as she would repeatedly remind people in the years following her scandal, who, after a brief, failed marriage, went to Washington in 1975 at the age of 25 and took a job as a researcher for the Republican National Committee. Years later, author Rudy Maxa, chronicler and connoisseur of Washington scandals, remembered her arrival: "When Rita Jenrette came to town, I looked at her and knew immediately that she was trouble. . . . I cultivated her."

If the luscious Rita was trouble, then John Jenrette, the Democratic congressman from South Carolina whom she met and married in 1976, was a cataclysm. He had a long-standing reputation as a playboy, a hard drinker, and a man with large and frequent legal problems. Those problems grew worse in 1980, when Jenrette became one of the congressmen caught taking illegal money in the FBI's Abscam operation.

A big attraction at Jenrette's trial was his wife, Rita. One of the prosecutors in the case remembered:

> She'd come into a room and try to take over, then flounce out again. She wore a fur coat to the trial even though it wasn't cold. She'd come to court wearing a high-collared blouse, but at the same time she'd wear a skirt slit up to there. It was as if she couldn't help it.

Still, said the prosecutor, it would be a mistake to picture the Rita Jenrette of those days as an empty-headed party girl. "Rita was a highly intelligent woman," he explained, "who had the misfortune to look like a bimbo."

Rita may have made her loyal appearances in the courtroom, but the strain of Jenrette's trial and ultimate conviction sent their marriage down the drain. She turned for help to her friends Rudy Maxa and his then-wife Kathleen, also a journalist, and even moved in with them for a time. In December 1980, *The Washington Post Magazine* published an article by Rita Jenrette with Kathleen Maxa titled "Diary of a Mad Congresswife." It depicted a Capitol Hill seething with vice, from women to drugs and liquor. A memorable passage in the piece tells of Rita finding her husband, "drunk, undressed, and lying on the floor in the arms of a woman who I knew was old enough to be his mother."[1] When the article hit the streets, other congressional wives declared themselves outraged. Rita Jenrette stopped being a mere object of salacious attention and graduated to notoriety.

During that eventful fall of 1980, Jenrette also agreed to pose for the April 1981 issue of *Playboy* magazine. Kathleen Maxa conveyed the *Playboy* offer to Rita—"as a joke," Rudy Maxa later remembered. "It was no joke," as Rita recalled it. "I wish I had thought about it. I wish I had waited just one beat. . . ." By February the April issue of *Playboy* was on the stands, featuring luscious pictures of Rita and an article written by her with Kathleen Maxa. Here Rita divulged the immortal news that she and her husband had once made love, as she put it, on the steps of the U.S. Capitol. *Playboy*'s appearance created yet another sensation around Jenrette, and she embarked on a full-scale publicity tour to promote the magazine.

"She has been besieged by movie offers, TV movie roles, and media jobs," one journalist reported on Jenrette's subsequent progress. Sometimes Jenrette said she planned on becoming a media personality, "maybe a talk show hostess,"[2] and there was talk of ABC-TV's producing a movie version of her story.[3] Once she said she was going to be a country and western singer, while on another occasion she thought aloud about running for Congress from her home state of Texas.

Yet the dazzling future somehow never materialized. Jenrette moved to New York, then to California and back again, trying to build TV and movie credits. She appeared in a film called *The Last Picnic*, released under the somewhat different title *Zombie Island Massacre* (today a cult classic). In anticipation of the movie's release she posed again for *Playboy*. She became active in Norman Vincent Peale's Marble Collegiate Church and wrote a novel titled *Conglomerate*. Meanwhile, she was trying to pursue a real acting career and won some praise for her abilities. When she played in *The Philadelphia Story* in Los Angeles, a reviewer called her stage actions imaginative and said she had "a talent for comic situations."[4] In 1986 she made her off-Broadway debut in a play called *A Girl's Guide to Chaos*. Yet a 1987 *New York Times* "Where are they now?" roundup on women involved in political scandals summed up Jenrette's post-*Playboy* life by saying that she "is . . . said to be a still-aspiring actress."[5]

Eight years after her brief moment of fame, Jenrette was bitter. "I was used," she said of the journalists who had accompanied her down the path to *Playboy* and beyond. Rudy Maxa, responding to her charge, noted that if it had not been for all the publicity, "Rita Jenrette might never have gotten to act at all." Both are right.

Jenrette arrived in Washington with her flamboyant personality already formed, and she freely made the decision to embrace the world of *Playboy* photo spreads and scandalous exposés. Yet the opportunities and hazards suddenly laid before her in 1980 were the products of a certain moment in our political and cultural history, one preceded by a period of upheaval in the public discussion of sexual behavior. *Playboy*, which had grown steadily since its creation in 1953, was both a sign of this sexual revolution and its agent. The new movement brought us the message that sex was good and healthy and should be fun for men and women in much the same way. Many people, aided by the technological marvel of birth control pills, were happy to embrace the new sexual openness that the *Playboy* culture popularized.

By the early 1960s, people in national politics who considered themselves sophisticated and cosmopolitan lived by an upscale variant of the *Playboy* rules. Over the course of the 20th century, the American press had grown more reticent in its treatment of politicians' private lives. But journalists of the sixties, we learned afterward, knew more than ever about the private sexual practices of prominent political figures—and printed less. This press discretion bespoke the belief that sexual behavior was not a fundamental moral issue. Certain moments neatly encapsulated this attitude. In 1962, for instance, Marilyn Monroe appeared onstage in one of her famous poured-on evening dresses at a massive Madison Square Garden birthday party for President John F. Kennedy and sang him a breathy, seductive "Happy Birthday, Mr. President." That performance would not have taken place at any time before the early 1960s or, for that matter, afterward.

Over the years *Playboy* became quasi-respectable in many people's eyes. It was followed onto the scene by magazines like *Penthouse, Hustler,* and even more bizarre imitators that made the aging *Playboy* look wholesome in comparison. *Playboy* also legitimated itself by tactics such as running long, highbrow interviews with famous and well-established people. By the time of the 1976 presidential race, the magazine had climbed high enough to succeed in winning an interview with candidate Jimmy Carter—you could not get much more respectable. The 1981 issue of *Playboy* in which Jenrette appeared also featured an interview with Ed Asner, actor and politically serious man of the left.

By 1980, with the magazine at its peak circulation of around six million, it had become an institution, right up there in the barbecue–Little League–pillow fight mainstream of American culture. It shimmered on the horizon for any young woman who dreamed of rising in the world by capitalizing on her sexual allure. *Playboy* seemed like nothing to be embarrassed about. Jimmy Carter said so. Ed Asner said so.

Magazines like *Playboy,* by talking about sex more openly than ever before, both fed and stimulated the national appetite for news about sex. In the 1970s they were joined by publications like *People* magazine, which in the same manner fed a more general and also-increasing appetite for personal, private news about public personalities. With this combination, the sexual revolution, which had proclaimed that our private lives were nobody's business, became institutionalized in a way that made many private lives everybody's business, and in more explicit detail than ever before.

There was a growing market here, and new entrepreneurs naturally sprang up in the sex-and-gossip field to bridge the gaps between supply and demand. This emerging class of brokers and middlemen included journalists, literary agents, and personal managers. These people provided a sympathetic shoulder for a young woman to cry on if she had personal troubles, as she often did. They ran interference for her with the press and served as intermediaries in book, magazine, and TV deals. They provided coauthors to translate her experiences and inner thoughts into compelling prose.

What they almost never did was to tell her to call off the circus. Such friends were not likely to warn her that the publicity machine in which she had enmeshed herself was making a fool of her in front of millions of people, placing rather stringent limits on her future career options, and exposing her to contempt.

By Jenrette's time, the power of that contempt had been growing for some years. Hugh Hefner had barely installed the bunnies in his first Playboy Club in 1960 when social changes began that would wash him right up on the cultural beach. These changes, like so much else, were spurred by the moral intensity that marked the fight against the Vietnam war. For a time during the late 1960s this antiwar political fervor flourished in some of the very individuals who most enthusiastically embraced the idea of sexual liberation. But that moment of coexistence was brief, for the ideological passions of the era had stimulated the growth of a powerful women's movement, just as the great battles over slavery and Prohibition had spawned and shaped this country's earlier waves of women's activism.

The women's movement was internally varied, but in general it did not like the Hefnerite notion of sex as good, clean fun. Writers in the movement argued that sex was the arena not of women's freedom but of their slavery, in which dramas from rape and sexual harassment to oppression and spouse abuse were played out. Marilyn Monroe singing "Happy Birthday" was no longer funny. Whistles from construction workers were not funny. Moreover, sexual oppression was said to be inseparable from questions of the distribution of power in our society: "The personal is political," went the new motto. It followed that sex was not to be regarded as a sanctified area of privacy. Citizens had a right to know.

These attitudes were not new in American politics, but they were traditionally associated with the political right, which had often endorsed the proposition that public figures' personal morality could be the business of the whole community. The freedoms of the 1960s naturally produced an active opposition from such social conservatives, who increased their political activity in response. More surprising, the conservatives' opinions began to receive legitimation and strength from liberal sources.

On the one hand we were seeing new habits of explicitness and a growing market for news about sex and public personalities. On the other side we saw a growing hostility toward women who made a sexual display of themselves and an increasing disapproval of personal immorality in politicians. What the two trends had in common was the decreasing regard they fostered for the privacy of politicians' and officials' lives.

The two movements both clashed with and reinforced one another to make post-Watergate political sex scandals the blockbusters they have become. Journalists became the linchpin of the new order, steadily shrinking the area of public figures' privacy in order to produce more scandals and, just as steadily, growing more cynical about the result. It was no surprise that an ambitious young woman like Rita Jenrette could be propelled to instant recognition by the scandal machine and chewed to pieces by the same mechanism. Others besides Jenrette met the same fate.

Jenrette's sex scandal was atypical of these post-Watergate affairs in one respect: She did not bring down any national politician. John Jenrette obliterated himself quite effectively without his wife's assistance. By contrast, the more typical sex scandals produced by the scandal machine since Watergate have threatened the careers of prominent political figures. The latest example is that of Tai Collins, the beauty queen who accused Senator Chuck Robb (D-Va.) of having an affair with her. But the post-Watergate line of descent for these scandals begins back in 1974 with Anabella Battistella, better known by her stage name of Fanne Foxe. She had worked as a stripper at the Silver Slipper Club in Washington, where she was billed as "the Argentine firecracker." She was also the girlfriend of Rep. Wilbur Mills (D-Ark.), chairman of the House Ways and Means Committee. One night in October 1974, the U.S. Park Police stopped a car that was speeding past Washington's Tidal Basin with no headlights on. Mills and Foxe were inside. Foxe, in panic or attempted diversion, got out and jumped fully clothed into the shallow water.

It was just another fun-filled evening in the nation's capital. But an enterprising local TV station monitoring the police radio band rushed to the scene, and Fanne Foxe suddenly became a name familiar to all serious students of American politics. Mills was eventually forced out of office by the incident and subsequent revelations about his alcoholism.

Foxe did not, in the beginning, seek the publicity she got. Yet after the scandal broke she was showered with press coverage. Her example showed just what a girl could do with Washington's new combination of quivering sensitivity to moral issues and feverish media activity. Other women started acting more deliberately to get the same sort of attention.

In 1974, the very year of the Tidal Basin incident, *Washington Post* reporter Marion Clark met an attractive blonde named Elizabeth Ray on the Metroliner to Washington. In conversation, Clark said she worked at the *Post*, and Ray said she slept with congressmen. After the trip Clark and Rudy Maxa, her colleague at the *Post*, found that Ray worked for Rep. Wayne Hays

(D-Ohio), another powerful man in the House. The reporters tried in vain to arrange another meeting with the woman.

Two years later Ray called Clark from a phone booth. Hays, long separated from his wife, had finally gotten a divorce and married not Ray but some other woman. Worse, Ray was the only person on Hays' staff not invited to the wedding reception. When Ray had gone to Hays' office to complain, she told Clark, Hays had summoned the Capitol Police and actually had her thrown off the premises.

In another era Ray, angry at Hays' social snub and anxious about what he could do to her, might have sent an anonymous letter to his new wife, phoned some of his fellow politicians, or slashed her wrists and left a tragic, incriminating note. But Ray went directly to the press to take her revenge. A child of the *Playboy* culture, she did not in the least mind being revealed as Hays' mistress. Moreover, when she stepped into that phone booth she was confident that her story would be welcomed even by such a prestigious news organization as *The Washington Post:* After all, two *Post* reporters had avidly pursued her. Finally, our young woman had before her the shining example of Fanne Foxe. Ray could be confident that after her scandal broke, the media attention would be vast.

Ray's story of her trysts with Hays posed a problem from a traditional journalist's point of view: This sad relationship did not look like any of the public's business, since it had nothing to do with Hays' performance of his public duties. But the reporters luckily found that Hays had been paying Ray $14,000 a year for office work, and Ray claimed she had never performed any such labor. She was paid for being his mistress, she said: "I can't type. I can't file. I can't even answer the phone."[6] Here was fraud on the taxpayers of the United States.

After telling the *Post* reporters about her relationship with Hays, Ray let them listen at her apartment door when Hays visited her. She kept changing her mind about whether she wanted to cooperate, so the journalists had to work to keep the information flowing. Clark told Ray that when the Hays story ran in the *Post*, Ray and her dog could stay at Clark's home for security and comfort. Clark even took Ray to the *Post*'s press-room to see the young woman's story and picture being printed on the paper's front page.

When the story appeared, Ray indeed became very well

known. People's reactions, though, were not what she had expected: "She had wanted Hollywood, big bucks, the silver screen. Instead she had been dealt notoriety and sleazy tabloid reporters,"[7] who "asked all the wrong questions. How could she get off a one-liner when some nut from AP kept asking her if it was true she'd taken a typing course in high school? . . . They were treating her like . . . a criminal, not a star."[8] The two *Post* reporters tell us about these feelings of Ray's in an engrossing book they later published about this and other such scandals. They may have catered to Ray's pretensions while reporting the story, but with the tone of these passages they convey their unmistakable contempt. Five years after the scandal, Ray was living in New York City, still—as *The New York Times* said of Jenrette—"an aspiring actress."[9]

Liz Ray was part of a mid-seventies sex-scandal wave in Washington. In 1976, Rep. Joe D. Waggoner (D-La.) was apprehended soliciting sex from a police decoy in Washington, and Rep. Allan Howe (D-Utah) was caught in a similar act in Salt Lake City. Public authorities were becoming more reluctant to cover up incidents like these. A woman named Colleen Gardner accused Rep. John Young (D-Tex.) of having kept her on the public payroll, Wayne Hays–style, to have sex with him. Rep. Robert Leggett (D-Calif.) turned himself in to the authorities— that is, the *Post*—by approaching the paper to confess that he was supporting two families. He thought that if he were frank, the *Post* might not run the story, since it was irrelevant to public business. He guessed wrong: According to post-Watergate logic, Leggett's two families made him financially strained and thus an easy target for bribery. So the Leggett story ran in the paper.

Journalists carried this reasoning even further in the case of Rep. Don Riegle (D-Mich.), who in 1976 was running for the Senate. The *Detroit News* got hold of tape recordings of Riegle made seven years previously by a woman with whom he had had an affair. The tapes were ancient history and held no evidence of abuse of office or fraud on the citizenry. The *News*, pushing past the old boundaries between private and public, ran the story anyway.

The most famous example of this new spirit in action occurred in 1981 with the case of Paula Parkinson. In 1978 Parkinson, then 27, moved from Wichita, Kansas, to the nation's capital and became a lobbyist. She set about making friends among House Republicans, and one such friend was Rep. Thomas F. Railsback (R-Ill.). Railsback, in turn, introduced her to Rep. Thomas B. Evans, Jr. (R-Del.), who was becoming one of President Reagan's major spokesmen in the House. The Evans-Parkinson affair lasted several months.

"The advantage of being a pretty woman lobbyist," as Paula Parkinson later told the world in an interview, "is that you have a slightly better chance of getting into a congressman's office."[10] But Parkinson's looks were also her downfall, because she could not resist the siren song of *Playboy*. The magazine's November 1980 issue, billed as "The Women of the U.S. Government: Ten Pages of Unimpeachable Beauty,"[11] featured Parkinson wearing a scarf, stockings, and a garter belt. Once the magazine appeared, her chances of getting into a congressman's office quickly dropped to zero. Parkinson still thought she had a story to sell: She talked to *Playboy* about their doing a big photo spread on her, perhaps with an article for which she would collect material by secretly videotaping herself having sex with various politicians. *Playboy* did not bite. Neither did *Penthouse*. Traditionalists that they were, they could not see how Parkinson's escapades with politicians had a clear enough connection to the public's business.

But the zeitgeist was on the march. A reporter from the Wilmington *News-Journal,* Tom Evans' home-state newspaper, tracked down details of Evans' affair with Parkinson. It emerged that in January 1980, Parkinson had joined Evans on a golfing vacation in Florida, where they had stayed in a rented house with fellow guests including Railsback and then-Rep. Dan Quayle (R-Ind.). This, you might think, still did not justify a news story. But in a stroke of journalistic genius, the *News-Journal* reporter figured out that while Parkinson was cavorting with the guys in the Florida sun, she was also a registered lobbyist working against passage of a certain crop insurance bill. When the bill came to the floor, Evans had voted no.

In truth, House Republicans like Evans had voted overwhelmingly against the crop insurance bill. Evans would never have voted for it, with or without Parkinson. Yet the *News-Journal* ran the Evans-Parkinson story on March 6, 1981.

The story caused not only the ordinary sort of gossip on the

Hill but a distinct post-Watergate buzz. The article suggested that votes were being traded for sex. This was a crime, right? Indeed, rumor on the Hill had it that foreign governments might be using this same technique to influence legislation. Here was not only a crime but a threat to national security. So the system moved into overkill. Rep. Philip M. Crane (R-Ill.), seeking to "avoid a witch-hunt mentality"[12] toward the episode, formally asked Attorney General William French Smith to investigate. Smith put the FBI on the case. When the time came for the bureau to interview Parkinson, she and her attendant journalists made a publicity feast of the occasion.

Parkinson, like her predecessors, found it hard to translate her notoriety into any other distinction and eventually left Washington. However, the FBI investigation continued. After three months, Evans said some years later, he was told by sources in the FBI that because of his perceived closeness to President Reagan they had been asked by the Justice Department to keep digging. Finally, after six months of investigation, the Justice Department announced that no votes had been given to Parkinson in return for sex. The verdict was of little help to Evans: He lost a bitter campaign for reelection in November 1982, largely because of the Parkinson affair.

In the summer of 1988, the public was treated to a reprise of the Parkinson scandal. Senator Dan Quayle had been nominated by the Republican party as George Bush's running mate. From the bowels of NEXIS, the computerized information retrieval system used by many journalists, there emerged the 1981 story of Quayle's sharing a house with Parkinson on that famous Florida weekend. Parkinson, living in Texas, refused requests for interviews but suggested that she might sell her story. Two Parkinson attorneys soon appeared on the scene to provide particulars: According to their client, Dan Quayle had propositioned her on the single night they had shared the Florida vacation house. The lawyers bolstered their case by saying that Parkinson had told the FBI the same thing back in 1981 and that they had contemporaneous notes to prove it.[13]

In its 1988 election issue, *Playboy* ran its old seminude photo of Parkinson. "He wanted to," the magazine quoted the old-fashioned girl on the subject of Quayle, "but I was there as Tom Evans' date."[14] Keeping current with the times, Parkinson next showed up on *Geraldo,* one of the new TV talk shows that make the likes of *People* magazine seem vestiges of quaint gentility. Parkinson gave Rivera "chapter and verse," as he later put it, of her affairs with six Republican congressmen. But the show's co-owners canceled the episode because there was no corroboration. "How could we corroborate what happens in the bedroom?" the host protested. "Censorship stinks."[15] Freedom of the press finally won the day, for in a later appearance on Cable News Network's *Larry King Live,* Parkinson finally managed to let waiting America know the names of five of her six alleged congressional conquests.

No one seemed to care. Even Parkinson's old friend Rudy Maxa wrote about her 1988 reappearance with a tired air: "The scent of scandal again sent Washington players—the press, the politicians, and the blonde—to their appointed places on the stage."[16] In other words, Parkinson's charges were interesting this time around not for their shock value but for their elements of ritualistic theater.

Yet this increased cynicism and weariness had reached full flower even before Parkinson II, in the 1987 case of Gary Hart and Donna Rice. By then, the press had become more aggressive than ever in pawing through the private lives of politicians, and the growing cynicism of journalists toward these scandals was becoming ever clearer. In May of that year, the bumptious *Miami Herald,* acting on a tip, staked out a Washington town house belonging to Gary Hart, former senator from Colorado and front-runner for the Democratic presidential nomination. Reporters caught Hart escorting a woman inside and soon identified her as model, aspiring actress, pharmaceutical company sales representative, former beauty queen, and Phi Beta Kappa college graduate Donna Rice. At first Rice and the Hart staff denied everything. Then Rice confirmed that Hart had repeatedly phoned her from the campaign trail and that some months previously she had gone with Hart on a cruise to Bimini. They had stayed overnight, but only because of difficulties with the Bimini customs authorities, the Hart camp claimed. There had been no such difficulties, the Bimini customs authorities responded to eager queries.

Major scandal mania ensued. When Hart held a press conference to answer the charges, NBC even interrupted its normal afternoon soap opera and game show programming to cover it live. The scandal became a boon to stand-up comics across the land. David Letterman entertained his viewers one night with a list of 10 Gary Hart pickup lines, ranging from "Can a Kennedyesque guy buy you a drink?" to "Have you ever seen a front-runner naked?"[17] Finally, *The Washington Post* presented Hart advisers with evidence it had gathered of a liaison between the candidate and yet another woman. If Hart continued in the presidential race, his people were advised, the story would be made public. Hart withdrew.

Rice had a somewhat longer run. For a time after the scandal broke she was, in the parlance, "in seclusion." Journalists had to content themselves with running old publicity photos of her and researching her record. They found that her résumé listed a small role she had played in a wedding scene on CBS's *Dallas* but that CBS said there was no record of her appearance. The journalistic sleuths also discovered that Rice had attended a party on the yacht of then-multibillionaire Saudi businessman Adnan Khashoggi. Rice had her attorney report that she was angry at how the press was treating her.

As the scandal approached the two-week mark, there was a change: Rice was now reported to be telling her story to *Life* magazine and posing for accompanying photos. It was announced that in the *Life* article Rice would not talk explicitly about her relationship with Hart. "I feel like a hunted animal," she said in the article.[18] Next, *U.S. News & World Report* reported that Rice was looking for a literary agent to market a book she might write.[19] Rice had already acquired a Washington representative, who confirmed that Rice "realizes she needs to talk to America."[20] The young woman decided to do an interview with Barbara Walters on ABC-TV's *20/20*. "Donna Rice," went one advance report of her appearance, "who doesn't like the way the media has [sic] portrayed her, is turning to the media again."[21] Rice was prepared for the *20/20* encounter by a team including her lawyer, a personal "crisis manager," and journalist Rudy Maxa; Rice and Maxa were talking at the time about doing a book. "I feel," said Rice on the show, "like I've been exploited."[22] On grounds of "dignity," as she put it, she would not tell whether she had slept with Hart.[23]

At the peak of Rice's 15 minutes of fame, ABC Entertainment expressed interest in producing *The Donna Rice Story* to show, said a network spokesman, the lifestyle of the many young people who work hard but "like to go out and have a good time on weekends."[24] Soon afterward Rice signed a contract to do TV commercials for a brand of jeans named No Excuses. When the commercials aired on national television, one of them featured Rice announcing, "I make no excuses. I only wear them." In another she teased, "I've got a lot to say. But 15 seconds? Not enough time."[25]

This moment in the sun lasted only until December 1987, when the jeans company ended Rice's employment in order to replace her with a new No Excuses spokesperson, who turned out to be comedian Joan Rivers. Rivers said she had never met Rice, though "maybe I stepped over her at a party."[26] Rice, meanwhile, had begun looking for a new manager but "has complained," according to *People*, "that the people she's interested in aren't interested in her."[27] By May 1988, Rice was living in the Washington, D.C., area and working at various charitable and self-help projects. A corporation executive asked by a friend of hers to give her a job replied that he would rather not: "You can appreciate our position. Donna Rice is rather infamous."[28]

From the beginning of the Hart affair, the dance between Rice and the media was like an insect mating ritual in which one bug is sure to end with its head bitten off, and the decapitated member of the duo was not going to be the press. Even before anyone knew whether and how Rice would try to cash in on her fame, journalists were writing about her as a classic opportunist and a large joke. Near the beginning of the scandal, Stephanie Mansfield of *The Washington Post* imagined in print what the phone traffic must be like these days for Donna Rice's mythical agent Wifty LaSeur:

> "Wifty? It's Bob. . . . Bob Guccione. . . . We want Donna. . . . We want her to pose naked."
> "Would you take semi?"
> "Semi? That's Hefner's thing."
> "[C]an I put you on hold? Michael Korda's on the line."
> "Hello Wifty? Simon and Schuster's got a book deal here for your client. . . . *The Donna Rice Diet*. . . Blanched Hartichokes. Harts of palm. . . ."
> "Listen, Michael . . . Ted Koppel, Oprah Winfrey, Bar-

bara Walters, *People* magazine, *Entertainment Tonight*, and Geraldo Rivera are all on hold."

"What does Geraldo want? Is he doing an investigative report?"

"Sort of. He wants to open her overnight case on the air."[29]

The contempt was there, ready and waiting. Rice walked straight into it, trying to avoid the *Playboy* route but courting publicity enough to permit her media critics to call her a hustler. In between the promoters and the critics there was no room for a happy ending.

The moves in this sort of sex scandal are well choreographed by now, and each episode looks much like the one before. Journalists watching the woman involved assume that she knows just what she is doing: She does not just get publicity but makes publicity. To them she is, in historian Daniel J. Boorstin's term, a walking "pseudo-event."[30] Yet journalists' cynicism toward the woman in one of these scandals is matched by the contempt some of the more thoughtful of them have for their own role in the process, for they are no more innocent than she is. They know they are not simply doing the solemn job of revealing the character traits of national politicians but acting as integral cogs in the sensationalist scandal machine. They are part of a vast drama of manipulation, and in it they play the roles of both the manipulators and the manipulated.

Some are smart enough to feel demeaned by their participation. "You can't do a story like this without feeling grimy,"[31] a *Miami Herald* staffer put it. They try to separate themselves from the embarrassment by writing about these affairs with detached irony. This adaptation makes the coverage of such scandals even more cynical. In truth, cynicism in these matters is hard to avoid. A combination of prudery and prurience has produced a dazzling scandal display in recent years, but one that tells us less about the individuals involved than it does about our own shifting moral fashions. The process is indiscriminate, and at its end we are left not with increased insight into our leaders' character but with a weary disdain that colors the way we view all of them.

Not all post-Watergate sex scandals have been half-serious, half-comic reenactments of the Fanne Foxe story. Sometimes

See 311

the central issue is not funny at all, and the reporting is more serious. Such is the case when we deal with charges of sexual coercion or violence. Yet even here, where the moral questions seem least ambiguous, it can be difficult for an outsider to know what one of these scandals really shows.

Scandals of this sort were barely discussed 20 years ago, let alone dealt with seriously by public institutions. For a benchmark we can use the well-known Chappaquiddick scandal of July 1969, which began when Senator Edward M. Kennedy (D-Mass.) drove his 1967 Oldsmobile off a bridge on the island into Poucha Pond. The senator survived the plunge, but his passenger, 28-year-old Mary Jo Kopechne, died. Kennedy said he had made efforts to pull the girl out of the submerged vehicle, but when she was found dead the next morning, trapped inside the car, the senator had not yet notified the police. To this day the debate continues over whether the young woman might have lived if Kennedy had acted differently that night.

Yet Kennedy survived the accident physically and politically. Local officials cooperated with Kennedy lawyers and family friends to minimize the incident. When the senator pleaded guilty in Edgartown District Court to leaving the scene of an accident, the court gave him a two months' suspended sentence and lifted his driver's license for one year. The records of the inquest into the affair were ordered sealed until the indictment process was over, and there was no sustained outcry from the press. The controversy effectively removed Kennedy from contention for the 1972 Democratic presidential nomination, but in 1970 the people of Massachusetts enthusiastically reelected him to the Senate.

Less than 10 years before Chappaquiddick, the stories about the Kennedy brothers and their extramarital affairs had seemed glamorous. Now, in a major change, the rumors were about manslaughter. This was a big change. Yet from today's vantage point, the Chappaquiddick affair looks like an embodiment of the old order in national politics, with its relatively lenient standards for judging politicians' private sins.

Compare Chappaquiddick with an incident that took place in 1985 and involved charges of wife-battering. In February 1985, *The Wall Street Journal*, not exactly a steamy supermarket tabloid, published an article by investigative reporter Brooks Jackson about the personal problems of John Fedders, then the aggressive chief of enforcement at the Securities and Exchange Commission.[32] The *Journal* article revealed that some of Fedders' difficulties revolved around his recent separation from his wife of 18 years, Charlotte.

In 1984 Charlotte Fedders wrote to White House counsel Fred Fielding with her story of Fedders' violence, saying her husband had physically abused her and asking Fielding to do something about her domestic situation, which she said was inconsistent with President Reagan's promotion of family values. In the same year the *Journal* was told the story but did not print it. Fedders, when asked about the charge, denied it.

But during the couple's divorce proceedings the next year, Fedders admitted in open court that he had physically abused his wife on seven occasions. The *Journal* put the information in its article on Fedders, having concluded that it was a dirty job, but somebody was going to do it. The day after the story ran, Fedders resigned from his SEC post. In April 1986, his wife wrote an article for *Washingtonian* magazine telling of her ordeal. She later published a book on the same topic.[33] The book became the basis of a TV docudrama. What used to be called wife-beating, heretofore not considered fit material for the serious political press, had come out into the open in a big way.

Since the Fedders case, fully half the sex scandals connected with major national political figures have involved encounters marked by some kind of coercion or lack of full consent—sexual harassment, sexual assault, prostitution, or rape—rather than two or more consenting adults getting together for a good time. The charge of rape against a nephew of Senator Kennedy's is merely one of the more recent examples. Often the public learns more than anyone really needs to know about one of these incidents.

Rep. Donald E. (Buz) Lukens (R-Ohio), for instance, went to trial in 1989 on charges of exploiting an underage teen by having sex with her in his hometown of Columbus, Ohio, once in 1985, when she was 13, and again in 1988. Soon after the 1988 meeting, the girl's mother called Lukens and the two met at a fast-food restaurant to talk. Mama came with reinforcements: Doubting that the police would help her, she had approached a local TV station for aid, and they sent her into the meeting wearing a wire. They also videotaped the proceedings, which featured Lukens offering the mother a government job.

At his trial on charges of contributing to the delinquency of a minor, Lukens tried to have the girl's previous juvenile records admitted into evidence to show that she was already delinquent when he met her. But her record was ruled inadmissible, and on the stand she was a graphic witness. Lukens was convicted. House Republicans, wanting no association with him, took the lead in asking the House ethics committee to investigate. Lukens' constituents were palpably upset. "A lot of people feel all politicians have their hands out," said one citizen interviewed at a local mall, "and they take that for granted. [But] this was a moral offense, and there are quite a few religious people around here."[34] Lukens soon lost his congressional seat, and early in 1991 he served 9 days of a 30-day sentence.

Almost as raw was the case, in the same year, of Rep. Gus Savage (D-Ill.). In July 1989, *The Washington Post* said in a front-page story that Savage had sexually assaulted a female Peace Corps worker who had been assigned the job of briefing him on an official visit to Zaire the previous year. Afterwards, it was reported, the woman had to be sent home for special counseling designed to help victims of sexual assault.[35]

Savage made the proceedings memorable by telling a *Chicago Tribune* reporter who was trying to ask him about the charges that she should, as the Associated Press recorded it for history, "Get the fuck out of my face." The reporter persisted, so Savage said it again: "You heard what the fuck I said. Get the fuck out of my face."[36] In the following weeks Savage called the scandal a white racist attack on a black public official. His Chicago constituents, unlike Lukens', were not horrified at what he had done and, despite a rough primary, reelected him to Congress at the next opportunity. But three of Savage's fellow Democrats took the lead in asking the House ethics committee to investigate.

What the two foregoing incidents tell about the character of the perpetrators is fairly clear. The stories also show us how much our standards in these matters have changed. As recently as 25 years ago, the heavy odds are that neither incident would have become public, because the authorities were more protective of congressmen and because they did not consider such matters as morally serious as we do today. The House would not have mounted an official investigation into the wrongdoing involved. Today, by contrast, such matters are staples of House ethics committee activity.

Sometimes, though, these stories are a bit more complicated. In 1989 the House ethics committee "reproved" Rep. Jim Bates (D-Calif.) for sexual harassment of female staff members. The committee found that this harassment consisted of, among other things, demanding daily hugs, asking one staffer whether she would sleep with him if they were stranded on a desert island, and wrapping his legs around the leg of a female staffer, "in full view of other members of the staff."[37] A reproval is not the harshest of sanctions, and one of the complainants said she was outraged by the leniency.[38]

Bates publicly apologized for his lack of sensitivity, established a sexual harassment policy for his office, and went for counseling. When he spoke of the case some months later, he said of it, "I'd gotten carried away with myself." He added, "I'm not saying I'm totally innocent, or that there was no basis" for the proceedings. Yet he still betrayed some bewilderment at the way today's new standards of sexual behavior were being applied. Some of the words and gestures that became such points of contention in his case were, Bates explained, "just flirting around." Some were due to plain old grossness and indelicacy. None of it, he said, carried the threat implicit in what Bates called "real sexual harassment: Put out or get out."

The rules had indeed changed. Sexual harassment was once commonly thought of in just the way Bates defined it. Other sorts of sexual innuendo and aggression were thought to come under the heading of more general obnoxiousness. Bates' actions became a scandal not just because of his character but also because of our shifting notions of tolerable behavior.

Some sexual coercion scandals have an uncertain meaning because they involve public charges about private behavior that by their nature can never be proved or disproved. In September 1988, for instance, Senator Brock Adams (D-Wash.) called a press conference to try to defuse an accusation of this sort. The incident at issue took place in the spring of 1987, when Kari Tupper, a woman in her early twenties and the daughter of longtime friends of the senator's, made an appointment to meet Adams for dinner in a Georgetown restaurant on a night when his wife was out of town. According to her, she wanted to tell him to stop making passes at her.[39] According to him, she wanted to complain about her job on the Hill.[40] When Adams did not show up, she drove to his house. They had several drinks. According to her, she was then drugged by something Adams had put in her drink and woke up in his house the next morning to find him pawing her.[41] According to him, she was too drunk to go home, so he let her spend the night, alone, with no sex involved.[42]

Tupper filed a complaint against Adams. But the U.S. attorney's office declined to prosecute, because of significant evidentiary problems.[43] According to Adams, Tupper then demanded $400,000 in hush money.[44] She denied this.[45] By the following spring, *Washingtonian* had somehow been told Tupper's story. One of the magazine's writers asserted in conversation at the time that the story was believable. After all, he explained, Adams had a reputation as a skirt chaser. In the fall of 1988, having learned about the coming *Washingtonian* item on the incident, Adams began phoning Washington state political leaders to brace them for the coming storm. Seattle newspapers published the story, Adams called a news conference, and the scandal broke.

There was uproar in Adams' home state of Washington, of course, and the young woman's father mounted a campaign to defeat Adams when the senator came up for reelection in 1992. As for the rest of us citizens trying to judge the caliber of this man, what could we make of the incident? Next to nothing. Both Tupper and Adams were placed under permanent suspicion, she of being a spiteful hysteric and he of being an exploitative predator. All we could know for sure is that this was a far cry from the fun and bunnies that Hugh Hefner had promised us.

Despite such uncertainties, accusations of sexual coercion have emerged as a powerful tool of partisan politics. For instance, when the U.S. Senate in 1989 voted down the nomination of ex-senator John Tower to be secretary of defense, the rejection had several causes, but part of the fatal combination was the accusation that Tower was a womanizer. The meaning of the word as applied to the unmarried Tower was at first unclear, but it turned out that he was really being charged with sexual harassment and coercion. The stories circulated during the confirmation fight purported to show that Tower had forced his attentions on women who were not willing.

There were problems of evidence, as with the Adams case. The partisans debated whether Tower had, as charged, chased a secretary around a desk when he was a U.S. arms control negotiator in Geneva. This was impossible, Tower's supporters contended: The desk in question had been bolted to the wall. In a similarly enlightening dispute, a retired army sergeant phoned the FBI to charge that a drunken Tower had "fondled," as *The Washington Post* put it, a female flight crew member during a Tower tour of a U.S. military base.[46] Senators and journalists argued strenuously about the sergeant's emotional health and whether or not his spotty psychiatric record made him an unreliable witness.

The whiff of coercion shocked and offended the audience, enough so that Tower's opponents were able to benefit from the sex issue in the confirmation fight. At the end, though, there could not have been half a dozen people in the country capable of saying with any confidence whether these charges were true, much less what they showed about Tower's general character and temperament.

If it is sometimes hard to see and interpret the facts behind a scandal even when there is some sort of underlying moral consensus in the audience, as with sexual coercion, it is even harder when the moral ground is in the middle of an earthquake, as it is on the issue of homosexuality. A quarter century ago the subject of homosexual behavior by political figures was almost literally unmentionable. The silence was broken on an October day during the presidential campaign of 1964 when one of President Lyndon B. Johnson's closest aides, Walter Jenkins, was arrested for soliciting sex in the men's room of a Washington, D.C., YMCA. Jenkins agreed to resign quickly, and Johnson advisers Abe Fortas and Clark Clifford were dispatched to persuade local newspapers not to run the story. The two men might well have succeeded, but officials in the rival Republican campaign found out about the incident. The story leaked to UPI. The Republicans issued a statement charging that Johnson was covering up a matter of national security interest. The story became public and news of Jenkins' homosexuality reached the front page.

Yet in some respects the Jenkins case was dealt with according to older, quieter standards than ours. Dean Burch, Republican national chairman in 1964, recently recalled, "LBJ handled it very well. He didn't disown Jenkins, he said he was sorry about the human frailty, then he got him out [of town] quietly. It certainly wasn't a scandal by today's standards."

Only 15 years later, the taboo against the public discussion of homosexuality was breaking down. One consequence was that things became more dangerous for homosexuals in national politics: The media could now publicize homosexual activity, but such revelations still meant political death. For instance, in October 1980, during his campaign for reelection, Rep. Robert E. Bauman (R-Md.) went before a judge to answer a misdemeanor charge of sexual solicitation. At that time local law enforcement officials were cracking down on such offenses because they were worried about organized prostitution rings and an influx of young male prostitutes to the Washington area, and Bauman was a beneficiary of their energetic police work.

Before the scandal Bauman, a prominent conservative in the House, had seemed a sure bet for reelection. Now, however, his opponent in the 1980 congressional race, Democrat Roy P. Dyson, did not even have to make an explicit issue of homosexuality. Bauman lost his seat.

By 1982 the climate had changed again. In the 1982 congressional page scandal, the House censured Rep. Gerry Studds (D-Mass.) for his involvement in sexual relations with a male page. But Studds—unlike Dan Crane (R-Ill.), censured at the same time for having sexual relations with a female page—did not apologize. While his fellow congressmen were voting his censure he stood in the well of the House, as required by the rules, but he turned his back on his colleagues and their vote. When he was reelected in 1984, he returned not only to the House but to the good graces of many of his fellow congressmen.

This same change was demonstrated more dramatically in May 1987, when 47-year-old Rep. Barney Frank (D-Mass.) announced in an interview with *The Boston Globe* that he was homosexual.[47] The expected reaction of shock and disapproval did not take place. Several days later Frank said the general reaction among his colleagues had been "enormously supportive."[48] Those who were less than supportive kept relatively quiet. Homosexuality, it seemed, was being domesticated in national politics.

Part of the nonreaction to Frank's news was idiosyncratic, for Frank, in the House since 1981, was a favorite there. He still talked like a street kid from his hometown of Bayonne, New Jersey. He had gone to Harvard and moved into Massachusetts politics carrying a reputation for outspokenness and an awesomely detailed fund of knowledge about the nuts and bolts of American political life. He was solidly on the ideological left, but his wit and grasp of practical politics gave him a wider circle of friendly colleagues and made him popular with the press.

If the private behavior of politicians can reveal character flaws that will mar their public performance, this was the wrong case to choose as a demonstration. Before Frank's announcement, his colleagues already knew all they needed to know about his public performance. There was no evidence that he had been hampered as a lawmaker by any personal characteristic, whether it was homosexuality or bad teeth.

The other reason why the machine did not begin grinding its gears upon Frank's revelation lay in changing general attitudes toward homosexuality, even outside Frank's tolerant state of Massachusetts. By the time of his *Globe* interview, opinion among people who considered themselves enlightened had moved from thinking homosexuality a moral vice to viewing it as a psychological disorder to seeing it as a trait that might well be genetic in origin—that is, not a vice or a problem but a fact. The American Psychiatric Association had already voted to remove homosexuality from the list of disorders in its *Diagnostic and Statistical Manual of Psychiatric Disorders.*[49] Frank's case seemed like yet another milestone on the inevitable road to the acceptance of gays in national politics.

Yet the coverage of homosexuality in public life, like the coverage of heterosexual extramarital affairs, was affected by today's public focus on the seamy and coercive side of sexual behavior. Soon after Frank's announcement in May 1988, *The Washington Post* ran a front-page story detailing the strange habits of a man named Tom Pappas, the chief aide to Maryland Democratic congressman Roy P. Dyson, who had taken Robert Bauman's seat in 1980. An ex-staffer charged in the *Post* that Pappas had told him not to date for a year. Pappas, said the *Post*, told a male employee at an office retreat to do a striptease, though the staffer refused. "These aides," the story summarized, "were among those in a long line of young men, often seeking their first job on Capitol Hill, who were recruited in sometimes unorthodox ways to work for Dyson. . . ."[50]

All this was on the front page. On an inside page, those who read further found that Pappas' demands for staff socializing did not, by all accounts, extend beyond the various dinners and events he organized. Yet as columnist Georgie Anne Geyer noted several days later, "There was one overwhelming and unmistakable purport to the story. . . . Mr. Pappas was a homosexual and was using his congressional position in effect to lure pretty and innocent young boys from the hinterlands into his lair."[51]

There was some evidence in the *Post* coverage that the campaign against Pappas was partly an act of revenge by a fired employee. There were also charges of financial irregularities—charges that turned out to be at least in part well founded. These issues were never examined closely, though, because the day after the first *Post* story there came another front-page article about Pappas, this one headlined, DYSON AIDE DIES IN LEAP AT N.Y. HOTEL.[52] Pappas, in New York for the weekend, had read the previous day's *Post* story about himself and jumped from his 24th-floor window onto an adjacent 8th-floor roof. His successor in Dyson's office, Katie Tucker, said Pappas had received an anonymous letter almost two months previously, threatening, "The fun and games you are having in your boss's office will catch up with you soon."[53] A friend said Pappas had viewed the *Post* story as the work of people who were out to get him and "weren't going to stop at anything to achieve that goal."[54] News stories do not cause suicides single-handedly, but in this case the connection was uncomfortably close.

The story about Pappas was interesting not only for its effect but also for its politics. The account can easily be seen as a fairly straightforward exercise in gay-bashing. It used slender evidence to conjure up the classic homophobic nightmare of lascivious men preying on innocent young boys. Yet it is clear that this problem did not exercise much influence over the decisions of the story's reporter and editors. Instead, the journalists looked at the facts and saw in them the theme of sexual coercion, which had become so prominent in Washington's collective imagination.

Even the Barney Frank case, that emblem of growing tolerance, came back to public attention recast as a tale of prostitution and abuse of trust. On August 25, 1989, readers of *The Washington Times* picked up their newspapers and saw this banner headline: SEX SOLD FROM CONGRESSMAN'S APARTMENT. FRANK'S LOVER WAS "CALL BOY."

The Washington Times was founded in 1982 as competition for *The Washington Post,* which had been without a rival in the city since the demise of the *Washington Star* in mid-1981. The backer of the new newspaper was the staunchly conservative Unification Church, headed by the Korean religious Reverend Sun Myung Moon. At that time Moon's young disciples—Moonies, they were called—were highly visible in big cities, standing on busy street corners soliciting money from strangers. People had heard stories about nice children from good homes who had been brainwashed by the group into disowning their parents. Though the paper's editors said Moon's views would not affect their operations, critics contended that Moon stood for a regimentation that was anathema to the free, inquiring spirit of American journalism. They did not treat the *Times* as legitimate competition.

Yet the paper survived. It developed sources, especially in conservative circles, who gave its reporters news that readers sometimes could not get elsewhere. The *Times'* strong local reporting gained it support in Washington's black community, some of whose leaders considered coverage of their affairs by the *Post* condescending. The *Times,* finally, had no qualms about reaching deep into politicians' private lives, including those of favored liberals like Barney Frank.

Here is the account of Frank's doings that emerged from nearly a week of *Times* stories written mainly by reporter Paul Rodriguez: In the spring of 1985, before Frank had publicly announced his homosexuality, he answered a classified ad placed by a call boy in *The Washington Blade,* a gay newspaper (the *Times* thoughtfully reproduced the ad for its readers[55]). A man named Stephen L. Gobie appeared at Frank's door, and the two had sex at a cost to Frank of $80. Over the course of several such meetings, the two became friends, and Frank hired Gobie to do various housekeeping and chauffeuring chores. Gobie took the opportunity to begin running his own escort service out of Frank's apartment, and he claimed that Frank knew about the sideline. Frank said he did not know and that when he found out about it in 1987, he kicked Gobie out and broke off relations with him. The House ethics committee later said it had found no evidence to support Gobie's charge.

The facts about Gobie and Frank presented the *Times* with the old Elizabeth Ray problem: Frank had paid Gobie with personal funds, and what the congressman had done did not seem to be any of the public's business. Yet there was, as usual, a way out of this journalistic dilemma. Hiring a prostitute, first of all, was a crime. Moreover, Gobie had a past. He had been convicted in 1982 for oral sodomy, production of obscene materials involving a 15-year-old juvenile, and possession of cocaine. In 1985 Gobie was convicted in Virginia for cocaine distribution, and as a condition of his probation he was ordered not to live outside the state. Frank wrote letters to Gobie's probation officer—on congressional stationery—explaining that Gobie was working for him and should therefore be allowed to live in Washington. Here was an abuse of Frank's congressional office. The *Times* ran copies of the letters as evidence.[56]

In later stories the newspaper shored up its theme of malfeasance. One article accused Frank of violating the tax laws by not reporting to the IRS the money he said he had paid Gobie in wages over the months of their friendship.[57] In another story the paper charged that Frank had used his congressional prerogative to cancel Gobie's parking tickets.[58]

The House showed no great eagerness to haul Frank before the bar of justice. A number of congressmen, when asked for their opinions of the scandal, were heard to mouth some version of the statesmanlike formula, "Let his constituents decide." Rep. Matthew McHugh (D-N.Y.), who had once joined Frank in asking the House ethics committee to investigate Gus Savage, remarked that bringing discredit on the House—an offense under House rules, and the offense that Frank had doubtless committed—would have to be better defined in the future. "That's a very broad standard," said McHugh. "I think that's the standard that's ill defined in everyone's mind."[59]

The ethics committee put off investigating Frank until the following session of Congress, and it was almost a year after the scandal broke when the committee finally recommended that the House reprimand him. On the House floor, Frank's critics pushed for a stronger sanction, such as censure. Frank himself, indulging in a piece of postliberal ugliness, threatened to reveal the names of conservative homosexuals in the House if his enemies kept agitating the issue. Yet in the end, the vote to accept the committee's recommendation was a lopsided 408 to 18. For all the rawness of the facts in the case, few congressmen were ready to let it determine their general opinion of Frank.

This tale was a quintessential example of the sort of information about a public figure that you wish you could simply stuff back into its box. Trafficking in prostitution is not merely a private vice but a publicly corrosive one. But to destroy, under these circumstances, a congressman who is a clear asset to the House would be a sign that our concern with politicians' personal morals was becoming suicidal. The House did about as well as it could in an area that has become almost impossible to treat constructively.

So even when we manage to get some sense of what really happened in these sex scandals, we face the more basic challenge of deciding what relationship a politician's sin has to his public capacities and his character as a whole. Will the politician cheating on his wife cheat on us as well? Does it make a difference whether the wife is a saint or a monster? Whether the other woman is a bimbo or a classy professional? Is the congressman's suggestive remark to his female staffer a sign of his general insensitivity to women's issues or of the persistence of old habits? Do politicians who hide their homosexuality act out of a broader deceitfulness that the public has a right to know about? Or is such deception simply the necessary price they pay for surviving in public life?

The increasingly aggressive reporting on politicians' private lives has raised increasing numbers of these questions and given us no help in answering them or in connecting the answers to our more general opinions of political figures. That is why modern sex scandals have not done much more for our public life than increase general disillusionment with it. We need more of a sense of discrimination in talking about these scandals, and here are some rules of thumb that may help: (1) In politicians, major private sins do matter. These people are not technicians, after all, but elected leaders. Their lives have symbolic meaning for their communities. To require them to conform to prevailing mores is not too high a price to exact in return for the power of public office. (2) The preceding rule is not immutable. It has exceptions. It does not absolve politicians or journalists of the need to exercise moral judgment in deciding whether to expose private wrongdoing. (3) Exposing sin among politicians is not a goal that ought to absorb major press resources or be used to justify significant invasions of privacy. We are, after all, not merely a democracy but a liberal democracy, dedicated to the notion that the public does not have a limitless right to restrict or inspect an individual personality. We must show our disapproval when we learn of private misdeeds by public officialdom, but we should not spend much time hunting for them.

CHAPTER 8

THE SCANDAL OLYMPICS:
IRAN-CONTRA

THE IRAN-CONTRA CRISIS was in one sense a rarity among American political scandals. While most of our scandals have involved common and largely domesticated sins such as cupidity and lust, Iran-contra was different. Like Watergate, it stemmed from charges that the president and his men were usurping political power and subverting the Constitution. This was grave business, and Iran-contra revealed flaws in the workings and leadership of our government as deep as those illuminated by Watergate.

The Iran-contra scandal also gave us a look at the various parts of the post-Watergate scandal system operating in high gear. The president hurriedly separated himself from the mess. The administration quickly asked for an independent counsel, lest anyone suspect that the White House was in any way controlling the investigation of the affair.

This withdrawal by the president left the field wide open to other players. Congress, in an almost automatic response, set up Watergate-style investigating committees to deal with the scandal's revelations. These committees, in an equally automatic move, arranged dramatic hearings heavy with big-name witnesses and cross-examination. Journalists behaved very much as we would expect, giving Iran-contra massive coverage and focusing overwhelmingly on questions of criminal or quasi-criminal guilt and innocence. The independent counsel began a series of criminal investigations that at this writing had already lasted four and a half years. Here, in short, was a scandal that had it all.

The result of this activity, though, was a succession of contradictions, collisions, and confusions. The congressional committee members most supportive of the president and his policies were often those who roasted his subordinates most aggressively, while those pursuing the president most doggedly were willing to let the underlings claim that they were only following orders. The committees helped build the excitement surrounding the scandal but came in for harsh criticism when they failed to deliver on their unspoken promises. Congress and the office of the independent counsel, each with an immense view of its mandate and importance, fell into a public dispute over who had first dibs on the juiciest witnesses. The independent counsel was spoken of as the official best able to ensure that the Iran-contra tale would be told and that sufficient punishment would be meted out to the offenders, but his office proved no better than Congress at getting complete stories from scandal figures, and the chief punishment meted out to them so far has been the investigation itself.

Finally, the elusive Ronald Reagan was a deeply unsatisfying villain, and his subordinates had not acted for personal gain; in this sense, the scandal was hollow at its core. By its end, Iran-contra had proved a disappointment to scandal-hunters. The behavior of some of the institutions involved in exposing it diminished their stature. The long, costly, endlessly publicized process ensured that not much attention would be paid to the most important and fundamental dangers that Iran-contra put on display.

Like Watergate, Iran-contra grew out a deep ideological fault line in American politics: the Vietnam-spawned struggle between ideologies, generations, classes, and institutions over the general direction and control of U.S. foreign policy. One theater in this war was the domestic controversy over U.S. policy toward the Sandinistas who governed Nicaragua and toward the contras who were in rebellion against them. Our domestic war, like so many of the foreign conflicts it affected, was an endless guerrilla conflict. Both sides operated on many fronts, avoided direct engagement, refused to accept defeats, dug in for the long haul, and made generous use of secrecy.

In 1979 the Sandinistas overthrew the Somoza dictatorship that had ruled Nicaragua since the 1930s. During the new regime's first months in power, its repressive and bellicose character became increasingly clear, and debate began over the proper U.S. response. More hawkish types said the Sandinistas were Communists of a classic stripe who would turn Nicaragua into a staging ground for further Soviet incursions into Central America. The conciliation camp countered that we should avoid the risks of interfering in an area peripheral to our interests and that we owed the Sandinistas a fair chance, without our obstruction, to create better conditions in their small country.

The Carter administration, during its last months, grew more antagonistic toward the Sandinistas. Then the election of 1980 produced a new president who had already announced an explicit policy of active support for the counterrevolutionary forces. The political figures who opposed Reagan's position organized for protracted warfare. These adversaries turned out to have great staying power, because they enjoyed strong institutional bases of support. Some of the mainline U.S. churches, for instance, were active in their aid to the Nicaraguan government and passionate in their criticism of official American policy. The doves were also solidly entrenched in the Congress, especially among the Democratic majority in the House.

Every facet of the civil war in Nicaragua—how well the contras were doing militarily, for instance, or which side was running up more human rights abuses—became a battleground on which the two camps in our own internal war could continue their struggle.

The post-Watergate Congress would not cede the primary control of this issue to the president. Instead, it tried to direct policy by aggressively using its power of the purse. Thus Congress passed a series of measures putting limits on both the amount of money to be given to the contras and the purposes for which the funds could be used. But ideological divisions, along with the increasingly fragmented power within the Congress, meant that our lawmakers spoke with a cacophony of voices on the subject of Nicaragua. True, almost no one on the Hill had a good word to say about the Sandinistas, at least in public. Yet in funding the contras, Congress was—to put it delicately—erratic.

In 1981 the United States gave covert support to the contra guerrilla fighters. But in 1982, Congress passed the Boland amendment, named after Rep. Edward P. Boland (D-Mass.), chairman of the House Permanent Select Committee on Intelligence, stating that the U.S. government could not give the contras any aid for the "purpose of overthrowing the government of Nicaragua."[1] Since the administration could hand the contras all sorts of military aid while claiming that the purpose was only to force the Sandinistas to negotiate, this restriction restricted very little. In 1983 Congress removed this limitation, yet at the same time the legislators cut the amount of aid.

In October 1984, with a presidential election approaching and Congress stalemated over the aid issue, the lawmakers in the House and Senate passed the second Boland amendment. It said that the CIA, the Defense Department, and "any other agency or entity of the United States involved in intelligence activities" were forbidden to spend money to support, "directly or indirectly, military or paramilitary operations in Nicaragua...."[2] The measure would apply until Congress took yet another vote on contra aid, which could occur as early as February 1985.

The Boland amendment, meant to mute the Nicaragua debate until after the 1984 elections, was designed to gain the consent of congressmen with a wide range of views on the basic issue of contra aid. It is no surprise that different congressmen had varying notions of what they had meant in passing the measure. In June 1985, their confusion became academic, because at that time Congress took its next vote on helping the contras. This time it decided to allow them "humanitarian aid."[3] A few months after this decision, Congress declared that the U.S. government could also give the contras communications aid. In the fall of 1986 Congress resumed full funding of the contras at a level of $100 million.

In sum, congressional policy toward the contras bounced from one position to another in a sustained bout of inconsistency and mixed signals. We hear much debate nowadays about what Congress can and cannot constitutionally do to rein in the president's foreign policy actions, and there can be no doubt that the legislators have the constitutional power to place the president in a very small box. Yet when they exercise this power with as little discipline and clarity as they did on the contra issue, they erode their moral and practical claims to it, no matter how broad their legal rights may be.

One effect of congressional indecision about the contras had particular importance for the Iran-contra scandal to come. Beginning in the spring of 1980, congressional decisions led to the deployment of military and civilian American personnel in support of the contras. This contingent of Americans developed the attachment to the contras, and the consequent sense of obligation toward them, that is the natural result of this type of activity and without which the job cannot be done effectively. When policymakers bob and weave the way the congresspersons did on Nicaragua, they can be sure that the people on the ground carrying out the orders will resist the constant changes and that the people implementing policy will develop a certain amount of contempt for the authors of the confusion. Growing angry when things work this way is about as morally impressive as railing at the law of gravity. Congress's negligence bore no small responsibility for the behavior, on the part of American personnel, that the legislators found so offensive when it was exposed at the end of 1986.

In fighting the war over the contras, the executive branch, for its part, chose as weapons its claims of inherent foreign policy powers, its ability to influence public opinion, and its trained suppleness in evading congressional interference. The president and his high-level advisers showed almost as little inclination as Congress to marshal their resources behind a settled policy.

The congressional action that posed the greatest threat to the administration's contra efforts was the version of the Boland amendment that passed in the fall of 1984, with its broad directive that intelligence agencies not spend money to support military activities in Nicaragua. From the beginning, those involved in implementing the amendment thought it ambiguous in meaning and authority. For instance, even under the new amendment, some sorts of communication with the contras would still be constitutionally permissible, but no one knew how much. In addition, the amendment applied to intelligence agencies and "entities," but it was not clear whether the law applied to the National Security Council, which had traditionally been considered part of the presidency itself rather than some separate "entity" or agency. In other words, the breadth of the amendment's restrictions on the president's ability to carry out the country's foreign policy looked as if it might be unconstitutional.

Yet the administration was in no shape to exploit these uncertainties. Reagan had just been reelected president by a wide margin, but in his campaign he had declined to risk his personal popularity by asking the voters to reaffirm particular Reagan policies such as contra aid. Thus he came to the contra issue in his second term without a renewed mandate.

Meanwhile, the upper levels of the administration's foreign policy apparatus were in embarrassing disarray. There were personality clashes, like the feud between Secretary of State George Shultz and Secretary of Defense Caspar Weinberger and the bad feeling between Chief of Staff Donald Regan and National Security Adviser Robert McFarlane. High officials refused to act in a disciplined fashion. Open meetings were rancorous. Not surprisingly, officials found it easier to do their work through informal, private channels—if not exactly behind their enemies' backs, then at least in a way that avoided open confrontation.

On the contra issue, there were more specific differences among the foreign policy advisers. Some wanted to face down the Congress over the Boland amendment while others counseled staying out of sight and waiting for the climate to change. Some members of the team talked brave talk to the outside world about the need for a strong contra posture but declined to advocate bold action when it came time to make policy in the National Security Council.

So the president did not veto the Boland amendment, oppose it in court, or otherwise publicly challenge Congress's right to dominate policymaking toward Nicaragua. The administration decided to live with the legislation and work around it. At one and the same time the administration accepted the legitimacy of Congress's role and tried to undermine Congress's verdicts. By trying to make policy through evasive action against the Hill, Reagan's aides made themselves into yet another guerrilla force. It is no wonder that their underlings at the National Security Council adopted a guerrilla's attitude when dealing with Congress and its demands.

In a nice encapsulation of post-Watergate politics, Congress would not give the president foreign-policy power and could not itself exercise such power decisively, while the president found it too politically dangerous to make a frontal attempt to get the power back. Thus, in this type of irresponsibility characteristic of modern American politics, no one governed.

When the second Boland amendment was passed in the fall of 1984, President Reagan told his national security aides to keep the contras and their organization alive until the next vote on funding came up a few months down the road. The president, as we later learned from Iran-contra documents, later reiterated this wish forcefully. Since the center ring of the administration's foreign policy efforts during those years was filled by issues such as arms control negotiations with the Soviets, the job of keeping direct watch over the contras was handed off to marine Lieutenant Colonel Oliver L. North, an NSC staffer then working in the area of Central American affairs. In his new job, North made presentations and sometimes gave White House briefings to private citizens who were contributing money to the contras. He asked Richard Secord, a retired air force major general, to help the contras procure arms with private money, and North gave counsel to this procurement operation.

North also advised the contras more generally. He pressed them to broaden their political base and make themselves more attractive to American policymakers by strengthening their commitment to democracy, and he shared intelligence information with them.

Meanwhile, as we know, North also worked on the administration-approved shipments of arms to Iran that began in 1985. News of the calamitous Iran initiative was one of the triggers for the huge scandal that followed, but the mistakes behind the Iran attempt were, though large, more ordinary than those reflected in the contra operation. On the one hand, when deliberations on Iran took place, the poor communications among high administration officials meant that several experienced voices were absent from the table. Certainly the initiative was never controlled closely enough, and the Reagan aides involved were almost laughably manipulated by men better versed in Mideast politics. On the other, the project was not some piece of dangerous free-lancing by National Security Council operatives: The negotiations were launched because Ronald Reagan wanted the American hostages held in Lebanon to be returned home and said so repeatedly. The ensuing debacle stemmed mainly from the Americans' complicated and grandiose notion that with U.S. arms shipments we could make an opening to Iran, do something for the hostages, and strengthen the internal opponents of the Khomeini government, all at the same time.

The idea that the so-called Iranian moderates were powerful enough to carry out a deal was at the least premature. The assumption that we could accomplish so much at once, without waiting for events to unfold and present their concrete opportunities, was much too ambitious. The refusal to consider what would happen if the story leaked was grossly imprudent. Yet today, as we see Iran starting to emerge from the Khomeini rubble and as we consider the area's alternative powers, such as Iraq, the 1985 Iran initiative does not look so bizarre. The mistakes in its planning were huge but garden-variety sins compared with the pathologies of our contra policy.

The link between the Iran initiative and the contra issue was, simply, Oliver North. After the Iran-contra scandal broke, there was much discussion of the overzealous, manipulative, and secretive personal qualities that North had displayed in his work. But zeal, cleverness, and a penchant for secrecy were the requirements of the contra liaison job as defined by the president, and it is no accident that such jobs find themselves filled by people like North. When government policies are implemented in a furtive manner, they tend to get carried out by the kinds of people who are comfortable doing things furtively.

North made his distinctive contribution to our nation's history with a piece of his cleverness: his seizing upon the "neat idea" that some of the money hauled in by the Iranian arms sales should be used to help the contras.[4] North's ingenious plan to tie his different activities together made it likely that if the Iran initiative were revealed, the contra operation would soon be exposed as well, and soon after the spectacular story of the Iranian arms negotiations became public in the fall of 1986, it was.

With the combined Iran-contra discovery, the system moved into its by-now-established scandal response mode. National Security Adviser John Poindexter resigned. North was fired from his job. The president established a fact-finding commission headed by ex-senator John Tower. Journalists started digging for lies and conspiracy, and an independent counsel was appointed. He was Lawrence E. Walsh, a former New York federal judge who had retired to Oklahoma City but would now be back at the center of the action in Washington. A number of congressional committees began investigating all at once, but Congress pulled itself together long enough to set up a joint investigating committee in order to expose what the overwhelmed White House chief of staff, Donald Regan, called "horror, horror, sheer horror."[5]

Watergate was on everyone's mind. Even before the scandal broke, fear of impeachment had hovered in the background as the administration shaped its policy toward the contras. After Iran-contra became public, Watergate analogies moved to the forefront. Certainly, those who dug for the facts of the Iran-contra story had Watergate very much in mind. Journalists, of course, behaved as Watergate had taught them to, dogging the investigators for evidence of high presidential crimes and misdemeanors and judging the newsworthiness of items by how close they placed Ronald Reagan to the scene of the malfeasance. As for Congress, it had before it the model of the Senate Watergate committee, chaired by Sam Ervin, which had mesmerized the nation with its televised hearings and made its members famous.

When the Ervin committee was formed in 1973 to investigate the Nixon administration's misdeeds, senators did not exactly climb through windows to be on it. Most senators viewed the job of investigating a president as risky and unpalatable. So the committee could be kept small: It had only seven members. Ervin not only chaired the proceedings but could generally count on the complaisance of the three other Democratic committeemen. Thus he was in a position to give his majority counsel near-plenary authority. The committee's size allowed each member a good deal of television exposure, and the central direction added to the drama of the hearings. So did the fact that the committee started its public proceedings by questioning relatively minor figures and gradually worked its way up.[6]

In addition, the Watergate committee appeared statesmanlike because it generally kept partisan issues well below the surface. The opponents of Richard Nixon were to a great extent allowed to couch their case in terms of highly consensual values such as respect for truth and law.

By 1986, when Iran-contra exploded, Watergate had already shown politicians what great benefits they could glean from serving on an investigating committee in a blockbuster scandal. The press attention would be massive. A congressman would have the chance to appear before his constituents—indeed, the nation—early and often, and display, by turns, indignation and sagacity. So the Iran-contra committee ended up with 26 members, who naturally had a harder time than their predecessors in attracting substantial media attention.

Size was not the worst burden the committee had to bear. In addition, the Iran-contra congressional investigation lacked the central direction of Ervin's effort. The new committee was actually two committees, one from the House and one from the Senate: Though the two houses had displayed enough statesmanship to join their Iran-contra hearings together, the House could not manage to leap over the next huge crevasse and agree to merge the House and Senate staffs and operations. So the investigation proceeded with two majority staffs, one in the House and one in the Senate, and two corresponding minority staffs.

These divisions guaranteed additional disorder and conflict, not to mention cost. On the Senate side of the Iran-contra committee, relations between the majority and minority staffs were civil and sometimes cooperative. On the House side the majority Democratic staff tried to operate, one participant noted, as a "one-party state," freezing the Republicans out of as much of the action as possible. Minority staffers in the House found it easier to get documents and information from the Senate's Democrats than from the House majority staff. When a witness was going to be deposed, the House Republican staffers would sometimes know about it only because of word from the Senate. Meanwhile, Republican committee members were themselves divided between those who wanted to go easy on the witnesses and those interested in assigning them as much blame as possible, so as to exonerate President Reagan.

This fragmentation hurt committee effectiveness, of course. Moreover, the notably partisan spirit of the House Democrats, marked by a willingness to roll right over the minority, would play a role in later scandals: It was precisely this quality that would make House Republicans so determined, two years later, to kick Rep. Jim Wright (D-Tex.) out of his post as Speaker of the House. In the Iran-contra scandal the House Democrats' efforts at domination did not even succeed in producing a show of unanimity. Power over the investigation was simply too fragmented for that, and the House Republican staff was able to wage its own form of guerrilla warfare.

In yet a third difference from the Ervin effort, political battles were more overt on the Iran-contra committee than with its Watergate predecessor. When Ronald Reagan's opponents spoke of the scandal as a battle between the rule of law and an overweening executive, their lofty characterization of their own motives did not go unchallenged. One reason lay in national politics, where an increasingly articulate conservatism had emerged since Watergate. Another reason lay in experience: Conservative and Republican politicians had seen during Watergate how the rhetoric of respect for the law could be used as a cover for less lofty partisan motives. They would not be surprised or unprepared a second time.

Indeed, people on all sides in national politics had taken lessons from Watergate. Congressmen, for instance, had grown accustomed to using television and TV journalists as aids in conducting an investigation. But as Oliver North soon demonstrated, two can play the TV game. Before North's appearance at public hearings, he and committee staffers skirmished over the usual staff questioning of witnesses that goes on prior to public hearings. North's attorney argued that the questioning should be strictly limited: After all, under committee rules anything North said in such a meeting was open to possible perjury charges. Staff attorneys agreed. Thus at the subsequent public hearings, questioners had a relatively meager script to work with in trying to shape and control the drama.

As North emerged into the public spotlight on the hearings' opening day, it quickly became clear that the cameras and microphones were going to be kinder to him than to most of the congressmen and staff attorneys interrogating him. Part of his advantage was a visual one, of course: What seemed like every communications outlet in the country got a picture of him—strong-jawed, clear-eyed, and clothed in battle ribbons that spoke of patriotic blood and sacrifice—taking his testimonial oath. The image was a hard one to beat. The committee counsel

who asked many of the questions in the hearings looked nowhere as noble as the lieutenant colonel did in his uniform.
Indeed, the two main staff questioners, attorneys Arthur L.
Liman and John W. Nields, Jr., both came under public criticism for insufficiently photogenic or symbolically inappropriate
hairstyles. As for the congressmen peering down at North from
the heights of their seats in the Senate caucus room, they were
the picture of a crowd in the Colosseum casting its callous eye
on the noble gladiator in the arena below.

Not all of North's strength came from the TV images, for
viewers clearly liked what they heard as well as what they saw.
North's verbal description of himself as a pawn in a struggle
among higher-ups certainly corresponded with most people's
notion of how the world works. Congressmen on the Iran-contra
committee noted the public reaction to North's testimony. When
they did, the investigation's political utility to them declined
rapidly, and the hearings' dramatic tension ebbed. The post-
Watergate operating rules had boomeranged on the legislators,
who discovered that he who lives by the tube can die by the tube.

Yet one Watergate-induced factor keeping the committee in
check was not a matter of political forces or calculations. Back in
the days of the Watergate hearings, the people who wanted to
impeach the president had no sense that the deed could really be
done and had never seen the consequences of such an act. By the
time of Iran-contra, we all knew that it was quite possible for
such an investigation to destroy a president. This knowledge
gave some of Ronald Reagan's congressional critics pause as
they considered whether or not to go for the administration's
jugular. Few of the congressmen wanted to put the country
through another Watergate, and this sense of responsibility
made them weaker combatants than they might otherwise have
been, less willing to press every point or drown out opposing
voices.

Though they revved up the engine of the scandal machine,
they could not satisfy the expectations created by all the noise.
The committee, therefore, took criticism for what some called
insufficient zeal. At the end of the investigation some House
majority staffers wrote additional, highly partisan material for
the final report and presented the names of a sizable number of
new people that they said the investigation must depose before

shutting down. Their material was rejected, the investigation was not extended, and coverup charges began in the press. Some journalists belabored the committee for not going further in the search for the real secrets, which would be so shocking that they would surely lead to an impeachment. Yet the committee did, in general, find out what had happened in the Iran-contra scandal. There were subsequent revelations: Perhaps most important, the trials left the impression that President Reagan was somewhat more personally involved in Iran-contra policymaking than we had known.[7] But overall, the later news did not substantially change the story or its import for public policy.

The coverup charges were directed at a congressional committee whose image had already been weakened by its fight with another child of Congress, the office of the independent counsel. During Watergate the relationship between Congress and law enforcement authorities had been relatively pedestrian: Congress held its public hearings and the Department of Justice—including the special prosecutor, who was a part of the department—proceeded to try the Watergate defendants. This happened in the old days, before we had all become so sophisticated and cynical about political scandal: Officials of that time did not automatically ask for immunity when their local congressional investigator rang the doorbell.

After Watergate, though, we had a new system built around the independent counsel. This independent counsel had become the dramatic center of journalists' interest in political scandals, and the independent counsel's office was seen as the locus of civic virtue in scandal investigations. In this view, we could gauge the commitment to truth telling and respect for law on the part of the president and Congress by looking at how freely the independent counsel was permitted to function. In other words, criminal investigation was treated as the best and most important way to deal with crises like Iran-contra. Other activities—hearings focused on discovering the systemic causes of the disaster, for instance—were seen as distinctly less significant and less morally or dramatically compelling.

The fight between the independent counsel and Congress took place over the issue of immunity. When the Iran-contra committee was formed in January 1987, its members, even apart from the desires some of them harbored for maximum-impact publicity, wanted to get the hearings over before the 1988 presidential election season got into full swing. The committee needed the testimony of the main Iran-contra players, but these people were under investigation by the independent counsel and thus in criminal jeopardy. Prosecutions had not even started and would surely not end for months or years. Therefore Congress gave some of these witnesses, chiefly North and Poindexter, a limited immunity from future prosecution. If the independent counsel indicted them, he would not be able to use their congressional testimony to build a criminal case against them.

Washington's discussion of the immunity issue respected only criminal investigation and its imperatives. Anything that hampered the independent counsel was viewed as tantamount to obstruction of justice. Walsh protested Congress's grants of immunity, warning that future criminal prosecutions might be hopelessly compromised, but continued his investigation. Not surprisingly, the independent counsel emerged from the press coverage of the fight seeming much more high-minded than Congress did.

Today, with more of the story known, it is fairly clear that the congressmen made the right choice. Iran-contra revealed political dangers facing the country that were more urgent than the need to make criminals out of individual wrongdoers, and it was more important for the public to hear their testimony promptly than to wait three years and more for the criminal verdicts. The independent counsel did not acknowledge this possibility and proceeded full speed ahead with his criminal investigations. As a result, he produced seriously flawed prosecutions: We now look back on Walsh's investigations with the knowledge that after the North trial, an appeals panel reversed one of North's convictions and vacated the others on the grounds that the trial court had not inquired closely enough into the problem of whether immunized testimony had somehow seeped into the proceedings.

Even before this reversal, though, the Walsh team's efforts showed that there are serious problems with our recent habit of using criminal investigations by the independent counsel as the means of putting out political scandal conflagrations.

The independent counsel's office disposed of ex-national security adviser Robert McFarlane first, in part because his involvement in the contra episode was more limited and manageable than that of North or of McFarlane's successor, John M. Poindexter: McFarlane was out of office by the time North's efforts culminated in the contra supply drops that stood at the Iran-contra scandal's center. Yet even McFarlane's relatively small case showed the limitations of criminal inquiry in attacking political and policy problems.

McFarlane, a career marine officer, had a personal and government background whose symbolism was quite perfect for an official dealing with America's contra involvement. He was the son of a congressman. In 1965 he led the first American combat unit ashore in Vietnam. During the Nixon administration he went to the White House to work for National Security Adviser Henry Kissinger, and in 1975, still in the White House, McFarlane had the job of deciding when to cut off the airlift evacuating South Vietnamese from the roof of the American Embassy as Saigon fell. McFarlane—not surprisingly but ironically, in light of his later fate—was known in the Reagan White House as a dove on the subject of contra aid and defiance of Congress.

McFarlane became national security adviser in the fall of 1983 and left in December 1985. He was in office when Congress imposed its strictest Boland amendment requirements on the administration and when the first arms transfers were made to Iran. Just before he left office, he recommended that these transfers be stopped (though they were not). Yet in the spring of 1986, as a private citizen, McFarlane flew to Tehran for the U.S. government to try to gain the release of American hostages.

In December 1986, soon after the Iran-contra scandal broke, McFarlane began to testify to congressional committees about his knowledge of the affair. Because other Iran-contra figures were claiming their Fifth Amendment rights and refusing to testify without grants of immunity, McFarlane, who did not take the Fifth, was one of the few major witnesses available. So much of the early publicity about the Iran-contra scandal centered around McFarlane's statements. On the night of February 8, 1987, McFarlane tried to commit suicide. Before he did, he wrote notes to the chairmen of the House and Senate intelligence committees apologizing for having withheld from them, in his testimony the previous December, information about a Saudi contribution to the contras.

Ten days after the suicide attempt, in the Bethesda Naval Hospital, McFarlane testified to the Tower commission. Two months later, informed that he was not a target of the independent counsel's investigation, he testified to a grand jury three times. Several days after his last session he testified to the Iran-contra committee, which had by then begun hearings. Two months after that, in July, he was back before the committee, which had asked him to reappear and refute testimony by Oliver North. In October 1987 Walsh's office informed McFarlane that its intentions toward him had changed and that the independent counsel was now thinking seriously about bringing criminal charges against him.

McFarlane's biggest problems with the independent counsel's office, it transpired, stemmed from events in the summer of 1985. (Pop quiz: Which version of the Boland amendment was in force at this moment?) Stories appeared in the press saying that the National Security Council was giving substantial support to the contra effort. The NSC had clearly not been very successful in keeping a low profile.

Rep. Michael D. Barnes (D-Md.), chairman of the Subcommittee on Western Hemisphere Affairs of the House Foreign Affairs Committee and a strong opponent of U.S. aid to the contras, wrote a letter to McFarlane, then national security adviser, asking whether he was complying with "the letter and the spirit" of the Boland amendment.[8] The Barnes letter also posed a list of more specific questions. Rep. Lee H. Hamilton (D-Ind.) and Senator David F. Durenberger (R-Minn.), chairmen of the House and Senate intelligence committees, sent similar letters.

McFarlane had White House lawyers go through office files identifying the documents that they thought might point to Boland compliance problems. He looked at each of them and had North draft answers to the specific questions. McFarlane then wrote replies saying that the National Security Council had complied with the letter and spirit of the Boland amendment.

Now, in 1987, the prosecutors in the independent counsel's office wanted to indict McFarlane for conspiring with North to violate this same Boland amendment through the answers they gave to Congress. The core of the prosecution's case was a group of six memos from North to McFarlane that McFarlane had examined before writing his answers to the congressmen. The prosecutors said the memos showed that illegal activity was going on and that both North and McFarlane knew about it.

In one of the memos, North said he had met with a Chinese official in order to solve a problem for the contras.[9] China had agreed to sell arms to the contras, but the end-user certificate prepared for the shipment said the arms were destined for Guatemala. North assured the troubled official that the end-user certificate was only a cover, and the arms were shipped.

In another memo, North wanted to stop the ship *Monimbo*, preparing to deliver a suspected supply of arms to the Sandinistas from North Korea.[10] Still another memo was a package of two separate documents, one on top of the other.[11] The first, submitted for McFarlane's signature, was a proposal to McFarlane's fellow members of the NSC that the United States increase its aid to the government of Guatemala on the grounds that the country was facing increased danger from guerrilla activity. In the explanatory paper underneath the letter, North said the aid should really be increased in return for the Guatemalan government's help to the contras.

A fourth memo from North asked McFarlane to talk with other U.S. officials about the idea of raising humanitarian aid money for the contras through a private tax-exempt foundation, with the president kicking off the fund drive.[12] Another memo reported that the contra force "has responded well to guidance on how to build a staff" and asked McFarlane to try to get more money for the contras from the foreign governments that were already aiding them.[13]

The last of the six memos, written at the end of May 1985, when Congress was expected to vote soon to let the CIA resume aiding the contras, said the NSC's activities in this area were being transferred to the CIA, except for "the delivery of lethal supplies," which would be "sustained as it has since last June."[14] The prosecutors took this to mean that the NSC might actually have been running the contra arms-supply operation, in gargantuan violation of the Boland amendment. McFarlane had seen these memos, said the prosecutors, so he could not possibly plead ignorance of North's illegal activities.

McFarlane and his lawyers were of course ready to dispute almost every guilty interpretation. For one thing, whether North's ideas were illegal depended very much on one's particular interpretation of the much-disputed Boland amendment. In addition, in the whole pile of documents there was only one instance in which an arguably illegal act—North's helping the contras pry their arms shipment free—was actually carried out. The documents, moreover, never showed McFarlane approving any of the proposals that North floated. The evidence all ran in the other direction: Except for clearly innocuous suggestions, McFarlane's notations on the memos all disapproved or asked for assurances that the contemplated acts were legal. Such evidence did not add up to lying, said the defense lawyers, let alone conspiracy.

The other disputes between the prosecution and the defense followed the same pattern, and the struggle went on for eight months after McFarlane's grand jury testimony. "We have to charge him with *something*," an exasperated Judge Walsh said at one point during the negotiations. The prosecutors did, just as Judge Walsh said, need to have McFarlane declared guilty of something. The main activity occupying the independent counsel's office at the time of the McFarlane negotiations was not the former national security adviser but the coming trial of chief target Oliver North. The prosecution needed McFarlane to testify that North was doing something more than just following his superiors' orders and to say, more specifically, that North had not violated the law on instructions from President Reagan.

If the prosecutors broke off negotiations with McFarlane and simply indicted him, the Fifth Amendment's protection against self-incrimination would take over, and McFarlane could not be made to testify at North's trial. On the other hand, if McFarlane came to the stand unindicted or with immunity from prosecution, a jury would surely wonder why the higher official had gotten off scot-free while the working stiff was taking the rap.

Finally a deal was struck. On the one hand, the prosecution would get its guilty plea from McFarlane. On the other, he would not be charged with perjury or any other felony. Thus, in 1988, McFarlane pleaded guilty to four misdemeanor counts of withholding information from Congress. He was sentenced to two years of probation, a fine of $20,000, and 200 hours of community service.

To achieve this Solomonic result, the prosecution and the defense had spent months parsing texts and arguing over the meaning of particular details. Yet there is no great profit in trying to decide which side had the better argument, for the whole debate was simply impossible to resolve. Those precious documents fought over by the two sides were not composed in moments of deliberation or prepared as legal depositions. Neither did anyone read the documents in moments of great deliberation or meticulous attention. The documents were essentially political in their purpose, and the words were chosen to serve the aim not simply of dispassionate accuracy but of persuasion, protection, and politics in the executive branch and its environs.

The same can be said about the great majority of written communications used in making government decisions. Pieced together with other information, they can tell us a good deal about how the government works, but many of them are hopelessly ill suited to the job of providing evidence in a criminal case. They rarely constitute either a smoking gun or clear exoneration. Indeed, when a government document does provide clear evidence of an official's innocence in an imbroglio like this one, it is a good bet that the piece of paper in question was created not just for working use but for the files and eyes of future investigators.

A further complication for the document sleuths lies in the fact that the letters from and to the committee chairmen were not the sum total of the communication on the subject of Boland. Indeed, on sensitive matters the normal practice of the executive branch in the foreign-policy area until recently has been to deal with Congress through a combination of written contacts and more informal oral ones. The practice was meant to bring some secrecy, deniability, and civility into the making of foreign policy. Thus McFarlane, after he wrote his letters, met with intelligence committee members and gave a fuller account of North's activities, arguing that they did not rise to the level of Boland violations. Material from North's diaries, which became public in the spring of 1990, included notes of a similar briefing given to a group of congressmen in the spring of 1985.[15] Such communications make documents like the six memos even less definitive as a record of what really happened.

The documents certainly raised many questions. How many congressmen, for instance, were seriously concerned about what North was doing? What happened to the North ideas that were vetoed by his superiors? Did President Reagan ever hear about any of them? The list can be readily extended. Such queries soon lead us, though, away from criminal matters to political ones. For the prosecutors, these questions had to take second place to the need to construct a winnable criminal case.

In order to build such a case, the prosecutors let McFarlane off with misdemeanors. For the same reason, they narrowed their concerns a great deal as the time of the Oliver North trial approached. The prosecutors had at one point planned to present their case on the basis of complex theories of criminality that defined secrecy in foreign policy decision-making as a species of fraud. They had intended to go after violations of the Boland amendment. But the administration had strongly resisted these ideas, partly by refusing to release some of the classified documents needed to support such a broad case. More important, interpreting the Boland amendment proved to be something like tying up Jell-O; some of the prosecutors realized that the task was too complicated for the courtroom.[16] Thus, when North finally went to trial, it was not on great charges of fraud and conspiracy. The central issue of North's diversion of Iran arms sale funds to the contra effort was nowhere to be seen.

The indictment accused North of making false statements to Congress, lying to Attorney General Edwin Meese when the scandal first erupted in late 1986, and doctoring and destroying documents in the days when the scandal was becoming public. Two of the accusations were more personal: North was charged with using traveler's checks from the contras for personal expenses and with not only accepting a home security system as a gift but also backdating letters to make it look as if he had offered to pay for it. Finally, one count accused North of committing tax fraud in raising money for the contras.

The prosecutors had a big job ahead of them. They would have to use McFarlane's testimony to help persuade a jury to convict North of felonies for acts similar to those for which McFarlane—his boss—had been charged only with misdemeanors. In this uphill struggle Walsh's people failed. They had extensively prepared McFarlane, but once on the witness stand he did not deliver powerful testimony against North. Instead, McFarlane gave answers that seemed deliberately obscure and complicated—so much so, in fact, that at one point the trial judge,

Gerhard A. Gesell, admonished him for his convolutions.[17] The prosecution's decision to settle with McFarlane and use him against North had been a bad bet.

To ensure impartiality, the North jury was chosen from among men and women who had seen and heard virtually nothing of the Iran-contra uproar that had filled the nation's newspapers and television screens in the preceding months. At the end of the trial the jurors acquitted North on nine counts and convicted him on three. Two of the convictions involved physically doctoring and destroying documents, while one was for taking the security fence.

The prosecutor in the case, John Keker, promptly proclaimed that the verdict had vindicated "the principle that no man is above the law."[18] Prosecutors say this a lot, especially when they lose. The application of the principle to a case like North's is not clear. If it means that a uniform standard of law should apply to all citizens, then it does not fit North's case very well, since he got the kind of single-minded investigation that no ordinary citizen has to put up with and was indicted for offenses that were as political as they were criminal in nature. In a sense, though, the "single standard" principle was indeed upheld. The real message that the North verdict sent was something like: You cannot steal money for yourself. You cannot tamper physically with government documents. That is, you are not above the reach of ordinary law. But we are not going to make a felon of you because of a fight that Michael Barnes was having with Robert McFarlane.

This is not a bad outcome for a half-political, half-criminal trial. Perhaps jurors uninformed about high politics are at an advantage in such a proceeding, for they are better at separating out those things that are crimes in the commonsense meaning of the word from the charges that are largely surrogates for partisan or ideological grievances. Such juries and verdicts are exactly the opposite of what we need, of course, if we are to learn anything fuller or more complex about the political forces that brought Iran-contra into being. Such contradictions are common when we try to fashion policy through the courts.

The trial of former national security adviser John M. Poindexter was even less illuminating than North's in this regard. This time the prosecution's charges were even more simplified than in North's case, in hopes of better results and, at last, a clear win. Thus the counts of the Poindexter indictment charged concrete, relatively simple acts of lying and obstruction. Two of the charges stemmed from the way Poindexter had answered questions put to him by Congress, when he was national security adviser, about the perilous Boland amendment. Three others stemmed from the aftermath of the Iran arms sales, when the deals were first exposed and Poindexter had to give Congress testimony and documents about them. Even where the charges were similar to those in North's case, Poindexter was more vulnerable because he was one of those high officials who had presumably given the orders to underlings like North. So Poindexter, unlike North, had no boss except the president to point a finger at.

Admiral Poindexter's lawyers did try to draw Ronald Reagan into the chain of command and succeeded in forcing him to testify. The former president, his memory seemingly riddled with large holes, came nowhere near saying anything specific enough to help his ex-national security adviser, and none of the examining attorneys went very far in the unenviable task of trying to press the former president for fuller information. Poindexter was convicted of the charges against him.

Back when Iran-contra first broke, Poindexter had told congressional investigators that the buck was going to stop with him, and that is where it did alight in the end.

When Iran-contra first became public, many congressmen were most angered by what they said was the Reagan administration's lawbreaking as it evaded Congress's will in the form of the Boland amendment. Yet as the criminal system proceeded against its main targets—McFarlane, North, Poindexter—the substantive crime of violating the Boland amendment receded farther and farther into the background. The amendment was so complicated in its history and subject to varying interpretations—so political, that is, in origins and meaning—that criminal violation would have been difficult to establish. So the criminal cases came to focus on crimes like perjury and obstruction. While these are very serious offenses, they consist not of doing something that is itself substantively criminal but of lying to people about it. By the time of the Poindexter case, the prosecution had figured out how to win an unambiguous Iran-contra conviction: by removing from consideration the substantive acts that had ignited the Iran-contra scandal in the first place. The independent counsel's office expressed great pride that in the Poindexter trial it had finally scored a clear victory and a six-month jail sentence.

Relying on criminal proceedings to deal with a political scandal has its dangers. Just as he who lives by the tube may well die by the tube, he who lives by criminal proceedings can occasionally get a stiff uppercut from one of them. Criminal proceedings are tempting to scandal hunters because they carry the worst threats of punishment. To bring criminal charges, though, is to submit to the rules of the courtroom. These rules, luckily for us all, can be quite unexpected in their effects.

For instance, the independent counsel's office took elaborate steps to ensure that no one could accuse the prosecutions of being tainted by contact with immunized testimony from the Poindexter and North congressional appearances. Nevertheless, when North and Poindexter appealed after sentencing, each argued, among other things, that the trial evidence had indeed been contaminated by immunized testimony and that the trial judge had not investigated the possibility thoroughly enough. A circuit court panel ruled in North's case that the defendant was right: The trial had failed to meet the strict standards that the Supreme Court had established in the early 1970s, over the objections of conservative law-and-order advocates, for the protection of criminal defendants. The Supreme Court would not take Walsh's appeal from this verdict. The independent counsel's lawyers now faced the prospect of a court hearing in which they would have to demonstrate, line by line, that they had not used tainted evidence. Whatever the final result of the legal battles, the appeals court's judgment showed that the years of work in the independent counsel's office could easily be wiped out by the technical workings of the adversarial legal system.

Dealing with a serious political scandal like Iran-contra through criminal indictments has other costs. Perhaps the most fascinating question of the Iran-contra story, for instance, is the one about the various routes by which Ronald Reagan's aggressive pro-contra positions and exhortations were turned into concrete action by his aides. But because the question was asked as part of a set of criminal prosecutions, those who knew the answer were not likely to offer it.

When perjury charges are in the air, participants in a scandal and witnesses to the deeds under investigation tend to minimize their involvement in the accounts they give the authorities. They also know that if they change their original stories they are open to criminal prosecution. Often these early stories, because of self-interest or simply bad memory, are not correct. Yet throughout the proceedings that follow, the participants remain wedded to their initial versions of events and keep busily arranging and rearranging facts, whether consciously or unconsciously, to fit in with their previous statements. The result is reams of testimony that can enormously distort rather than enrich the historical record. No documents can make up the loss.

Making criminal proceedings the center of attention in Iran-contra had a still higher price, for it threatened to distort our fundamental understanding of the scandal. The Iran-contra revelations showed us a Congress that had produced five different contra funding policies in four years yet insisted on the right to an equal role in the operational direction of our foreign policy. The debacle also put on display Cabinet-level officials who paralyzed administration decision-making with their personal quarrels and bemoaned the erosion of presidential power in foreign affairs while doing nothing useful to stop it. This combination of pathologies turned policymaking on the issue of Central America into a long-running, reckless game of chicken.

The absence of a real locus of power and the consequent escalation of the traditional quarrel between the executive and legislative branches in foreign affairs—common symptoms in post-Watergate Washington—are what led to Iran-contra. Focusing on particularized crimes will not help us deal with the problem. Indeed, criminalizing more and more tactics in executive-legislative disputes will almost certainly make the emergence of foreign policy leadership less likely and ensure that our problem grows worse.

The Iran-contra scandal—fortunately—made all sides so sated with the subject of executive-legislative relations in foreign policy that they seem to have lost the stomach to keep agitating the issue as bitterly and tenaciously as they used to. Congress's last-minute decision to support President Bush in waging war on Iraq was in part a sign of this weariness: Iran-contra may have served a policy purpose simply by being such an unattractive spectacle that no one on any side wanted to repeat it. Meanwhile, the office of the independent counsel investigating the affair, by the time it had been in existence for four years, had spent more than $28 million,[19] a figure that omits many associated expenses not included in the official accounting. Financially speaking, *this* was where all the bucks stopped.

With all the millions spent, the independent counsel had extracted five guilty pleas out of Iran-contra defendants, including one that led to a jail sentence on a tax evasion charge. There were two convictions—including one six-month jail sentence—that proved highly vulnerable to legal challenge. It is fair, finally, to start asking why we allowed our Watergate-bred fears and angers to take the control of our politics away from us, as the scandal hunt surely did in the Iran-contra affair.

CHAPTER 9

CONGRESS IN THE DOCK

THE WISE POLITICIAN in a democracy always remembers the boomerang rule: The ingenious new weapon you hurl at your political enemy will soon return to hit you in the face. Congress did not heed this warning in the years after Watergate. The lure of scandal politics proved irresistible, especially to congressional Democrats who found it a politically cost-effective strategy against the Republican executive branch. But it was not long before Congress's scandal hunt turned around and headed straight back to the Hill, where it fastened greedily on congressional targets. By the late 1980s, both houses were immersed in the quicksands of self-investigation.

While the boomerang was turning toward home, one of the biggest policy disasters in our history, the savings and loan crisis, was growing in the cellar like the small monster in a horror film who eventually gets big enough to devour Tokyo. We did not pay much attention. No one was getting visibly hurt, and we had important things to do: tightening our conflict-of-interest and revolving-door rules, crusading against government secrecy, pursuing our cops-and-robbers scandals, lamenting Reaganite tackiness, and buzzing about politicians' sex lives. Even now, when the S&L scandal is inescapable, the legacy of 15 years of scandal politics is making it harder to find the way out of the morass.

During the 1970s, Congress did not wholly exempt itself from the spate of new ethics rules it devised. The 1971 and 1974 federal campaign finance law reforms applied to Congress as well as the presidency. In 1977 each house of Congress adopted an internal ethics code limiting congressmen's outside income and requiring them, for the first time, to disclose all their income—including honoraria—and its sources. In this same period, the ethics committees of both houses grew more active in investigating ethics charges against congressmen.

Washington attorney Stan Brand recently recalled that in the 1970s, when he was general counsel to the House of Representatives, he had warned congressmen that if they went too far in their push toward tougher standards everywhere, they would simply give federal prosecutors new tools against elected officials. "[E]thics is good," he remembered having said at the time, "but you're setting yourselves up with all the new rules. . . ." He explained, "I always saw the executive branch trying to encroach on the legislature through prosecutions." Brand was prescient. Over the course of the 1980s the new post-Watergate rules, meant to improve congressmen's behavior, produced an increased number of congressional scandals involving sexual and financial sins. These scandals were often overblown, yet the sheer number of them created the picture of a Congress awash in crime and corruption.

The sound of Richard Nixon's footsteps had barely faded from the White House halls when Congress was hit with a series of financial scandals. The first was the Great Hunting Lodge Caper, a grandson-of-Watergate drama. Because of a stockholder suit over illegal contributions to Nixon's 1972 campaign by the Northrop Corporation, a large defense contractor, the public learned that in the early 1970s the company had rented a goose-hunting lodge and used it to entertain not only Defense Department officials but congressmen and congressional staffers. Other defense contractors, it turned out, had done the same.

Before the scandal was done, 17 congressmen admitted having visited one lodge or another. The chairmen of both the House and the Senate ethics committees were on the guest lists. Congress investigated and criticized the Defense Department's internal probe of the matter but did not touch the legislators involved.

Another spin-off of Watergate and of the detailed attention paid to the 1972 Nixon campaign was the Gulf Oil scandal. A post-Watergate corporate investigative committee formed by Gulf reported to the Securities and Exchange Commission in December 1975 that its illegal 1972 contribution to Nixon was not an aberration due to exceptionally brutal arm-twisting by the president's fund-raisers. Over the previous 10 years the company had forked over some 5 million illegal dollars in contributions to candidates for federal office. Dozens of congressmen were implicated. In the end, one representative pleaded guilty to a misdemeanor charge stemming from a failure to report a Gulf contribution. Senate Minority Leader Hugh Scott (R-Pa.) admitted that he had received a hefty $45,000 from Gulf. According to some reports the true total went as high as $100,000. Yet the Senate ethics committee voted not to investigate the senator, who retired in 1976.

The third and final major congressional scandal of the mid-1970s was Koreagate. Though the publicity attending the scandal was overwrought, the headlines—about influence peddling by agents of a foreign government—were enough to alarm any news reader. Yet only one congressman, Rep. Richard T. Hanna (D-Calif.), was declared guilty of a crime. He pleaded guilty to conspiracy to defraud the government and served a year in prison. The House ethics committee recommended reprimands for two California Democrats and the harsher sanction of censure for another Democrat from California, Rep. Edward R. Roybal, who had taken $1,000 in cash from the South Koreans and failed to report it. But the full House reduced Roybal's punishment so that he, too, got only a reprimand.

Then came the 1980 Abscam revelations, fulfilling Brand's prophecy of increasingly aggressive federal law enforcement against legislators and opening a new era in congressional scandals. At the start of the 20th century, federal investigation of fraud in the transfer of federal lands led to the indictment of four congressmen. But two were acquitted, one had his conviction overturned, and the last had his conviction on appeal when he died.[1] Abscam was different. In addition to Rita Jenrette's husband, Rep. John Jenrette, six legislators—Senator Harrison A. Williams, Jr. (D-N.J.), and five congressmen—were caught in the net. Rep. Raymond Lederer (D-Pa.) was shown by the video camera taking $50,000 in a paper bag. The no-nonsense Rep. Michael (Ozzie) Myers (D-Pa.) got his cash in an envelope. Rep. Richard Kelly (R-Fla.) was recorded asking whether his share of the money made bulges in his suit. Prosecutions and convictions inexorably followed. Here was a scandal to confirm the darkest suspicions of the populist mind.

Abscam did not reveal the way most of the Congress worked or even how most congressional corruption worked, for the FBI agents had offered the congressmen who came to Abdul's rented house an opportunity much more attractive than anything the lawmakers were likely to come across in normal life. The money was exceptionally good, especially for passing a one-shot immigration bill that involved no continuing entanglements. The assignment to be carried out would not hurt anyone, or so a congressman could easily tell himself. Thus the job was easy on the conscience. Real life rarely presents a politician with a deal so perfect.

Abscam was also more dangerous than most real-life deals. As one of the federal attorneys involved in the Abscam prosecutions put it:

> This setup, with explicit deals and strange people in strange places, was very unusual. In the real world, most [official] corruption takes place among friends, neighbors, relatives, longtime associates. Most corruption doesn't even require words. It's done with just a wink and a nod.

So Abscam told us less about patterns of real-life legislative behavior than it did about the increasing scrutiny that this behavior would henceforth receive. You might think that Abscam would have given Congress all the warning necessary to see that the post-Watergate spirit could pose as big a threat to the Hill as to the presidency. Yet it is a hard thing for a political party to surrender a marvelous weapon such as the ethics issues had become, and even harder for a politician to give up his or her identification with the forces of law and order. Not many paid attention to the message that the early scandals sent.

Congressional scandals continued to proliferate throughout

the 1980s. More important, over the course of the 1980s such scandals came to be seen as parts of a pattern. A systematic critique of congressional ethics fed by reformers, journalists, the executive branch, and congressmen themselves took shape. It came in different versions, but often it centered on the behavior of political action committees.

These PACs were, ironically, the legacy of the preceding wave of 1970s campaign finance reform, in which Congress gave political action committees the legislative seal of approval and triggered a dramatic increase in PAC activity. It must be remembered that PACs were meant to be instruments of morality in politics: They were going to replace dirty corporate and individual political contributions with election funds from organizations that were aboveboard and accountable. It must also be recalled that PACs have been a success at fulfilling these goals. These organizations operate in the open, making their political contributions publicly and giving the federal government elaborate reports on their activities. The reports have provided the press with much new information about the financial connections of national politicians. It is worth noting that none of our recent scandals has centered on illegal activity by PACs.

Of course openness and regularity were not really the only aims that the campaign reformers of the 1970s had in mind. The tight disclosure rules imposed on PACs were also meant to cut down the influence of the interests that PACs represented. A congressman taking PAC money, went the logic, would have to report the contribution publicly. The risks of such publicity would create a new political counterweight to PAC power.

This theory of campaign finance reform promised that we could destroy the beast of special-interest influence by exposing it to the sunlight of publicity. Imagine the shock when we hauled the creature up out of its dank hole into the legislatively decreed daylight and the monster simply refused to melt as contemplated. There we were, doomed to stare into its ugly face forever.

The increase in PAC activity, along with the increase in political campaign costs that has accompanied it, is a consequence of electoral reforms in a more indirect way as well. These reforms, over the past quarter century, have weakened the role not only of individual contributors but also of political parties in congressional election campaigns. In a recent conversation Rep. Barney Frank, a liberal who is as conversant as anyone in Congress not simply with political scandal but with the entire machinery of American politics, summed up the story of rising campaign costs and the increasing congressional dependence on PACs:

> It has a lot to do with the decrease of [political] party voting. Twenty-five years ago, a large percentage of the electorate voted for one party or another. Now more votes are up for grabs: You know, "Vote for the man and not the party," the good-government formula. Now the market is larger.

The decline of party brought other changes in its train: the disappearance of the old unspoken agreements on campaign spending limits, the new reliance on sophisticated technologies to reach large numbers of voters, and the usefulness of PACs as money-raising devices. The very people whose prior reform efforts did so much to cause these changes now recoil from the consequences. "People are always asking me," said Frank, "about PACs, and not about other contributions. . . . Why is it somehow bad to take money from a bank PAC but not to take the same amount of money from five bankers?"

Not everyone is so coolheaded. Many critics are appalled by the openness with which the PACs operate, and it is certainly true that the PACs, in filling the financial vacuum created by the 1974 limits on individual contributions, have made the fund-raising process much more elaborate and public. The Democratic House and Senate Council, for instance, publishes a convenient directory of fund-raising events sponsored for various Democratic congressmen and the amount of money required of each contributor who wants to go to one of these parties. A typical segment of the May-September 1989 list included these entries:

> May 1: Congressman Charlie Rose, North Carolina 7 [7th Congressional District]. North Carolina "Pig Pickin' " reception, Alexandria, Va., Committee for Congressman Charlie Rose. $500.

May 2: Congresswoman Beverly Byron, Maryland 6. Reception, National Democratic Club, Byron for Congress. $500.

May 2: Senator Max Baucus, Montana. Reception, home of Mrs. Pamela Harriman, Friends of Max Baucus. $1,000.

May 2: Congresswoman Jolene Unsoeld, Washington 3. Reception, the Lewis house, 456 N St., S.W., Jolene Unsoeld Congressional Campaign Committee. $300.

May 3: Congressman Tim Valentine, North Carolina 2. Reception, National Democratic Club, Valentine for Congress. $350.[2]

Such examples of matchmaking can be multiplied manifold. Not long ago Rep. James Scheuer (D-N.Y.) commented that when he set out to raise money for his 1988 campaign, after several years in which he had not been forced to do a great deal of fund-raising, he found that the process had changed. There are fewer campaign volunteers now, he noted. More of the fundraising is done by outside specialists. "They ask you for a list of your friends," the congressman said:

They want to write letters to your friends. They *call* your friends. They use aggressive pitches, which you are seemingly powerless to control. Your friends assume all of this emanates directly from you. They have a right to feel offended and put upon.

This newly open, increasingly organized congressional fundraising system sprang from the same causes that brought about the louder, brasher corps of professional lobbyists and consultants increasingly in evidence on the Washington scene during the 1970s. In both cases, the logic was the same: When political community declines, and quiet, private communications can no longer get the work of politics done, everybody has to start advertising. In the 1980s, PAC critics began to deride this adaptation as another greedy and brazen symbol of the Reagan era.

Some of the critics also blamed PACs for the rising cost of political campaigns. Part of the reason for this increased recent cost, it is generally agreed, lies in the expensive modern technology—mainly television and computerized direct mail—on which campaigns increasingly depend. But according to the anti-PAC critique that began to gather steam, the rising campaign costs were also part of a circular process: The PACs themselves drive costs upward by pouring rivers of money into political campaigns and forcing cost increases through competitive pressures. The rising costs then force politicians into still greater reliance on PAC money. The only way to break the cycle, in this view, is through more reform legislation to limit campaign spending or even, were it possible, through public financing for all federal campaigns.[3]

In something of a contradiction, the same PACs that were accused of keeping congressmen scrambling desperately for campaign money were also accused of helping to insulate congressmen from electoral competition and keep incumbents in office more safely than ever before. In making this second argument the reformers found themselves joined by Republicans who were discontented with their party's seemingly perpetual minority status in the House of Representatives. Republican spokesmen were happy to inveigh against the corrupt PAC system that, they thought, made the Democrats a permanent House majority.

The critics noted, quite correctly, that the PACs tended to behave like the textbook model of a rational political actor, giving their money to whoever could help them most. That meant they gave by far the biggest part of their funds to congressional incumbents and to the Democrats who made up the House majority. After all, the Democrats were the ones with leadership and power. Since incumbents were overwhelmingly likely to be reelected, PACs contributed to them simply to be on the side of the winners. In a corrupt, self-feeding political circle, PACs gave to incumbents; the fat PAC contributions made the incumbents even more likely to remain incumbents, chiefly by scaring serious potential challengers out of running; and, after reelection, the PACs gave to these incumbents again.

The statistics were clear. By 1990 the average Democrat running for reelection to the House was getting $239,434 from PACs. His Republican challenger got $11,769. Republican incumbents did well, though not as well as their Democratic counterparts: These Republicans got an average of $183,236 apiece. On the other hand, Democratic challengers did much better than Republican challengers: The Democrats got an average of $34,965 each in PAC money. Indeed, PACs thoughtfully gave money to some incumbents who did not even have challengers in their campaigns for reelection.[4]

Yet the PACs, said critics of congressional ethics, were not the only reason why almost all the congressmen running for reelection were victorious in 1988. The other major cause was said to be the assiduous way in which congressmen used the power of their incumbency. In 1989 the average representative had a staff budget of about $400,000, which paid for an average of 17 staffers.[5] Some of these employees kept busy trying to get their bosses' names in the press by means such as running investigations of executive branch malfeasance and waste. Other staffers were caseworkers. Their growing numbers enabled them to do more of Congress's traditional job of servicing constituents back in the congressmen's home districts by handling complaints about everything from taxes to Social Security payments to annoying regulations placed by the federal government on local savings and loan associations. Political commentator Alan Ehrenhalt had described this state of affairs as a type of hyper-responsiveness on the Hill.[6]

Legislators also enjoyed free mailings, and in fiscal year 1988, House members sent out 548 million pieces of literature devoted in no small part to telling the citizenry what a terrific job they were doing.[7] In addition, a congressman could have subsidized radio and TV messages made for home-state stations in Congress's own broadcast facilities.

This picture, though overdrawn, contained a lot of truth. In 1990 our congressmen's reelection rate was approaching 99 percent and the Soviet Union was in the midst of its tortuous passage through the wrenching, mesmerizing process of *glasnost*. Soviet citizens were allowed their first free elections since the Bolshevik revolution. On their ballots, Russian voters could cross out names they did not like. If no candidates were approved, there would be another election. In March of that year, the cartoonist Toles drew a memorable political cartoon that first appeared in *The Buffalo News* and featured a Soviet election official explaining the new system to a lumpish, fur-hatted average Soviet citizen. The new voter, taking hold of his now-meaningful ballot, looks over his shoulder at us and smiles slyly,

"Eat your hearts out, Americanskis." America's general opinion of Congress has never been high, but this joke surely represented some kind of new, bitter low.

Congress was a better scandal target than ever. American politicians being as inventive as they are, the Republicans found a way to exploit this state of affairs, largely through the efforts of Rep. Newt Gingrich (R-Ga.). Gingrich brought scandal politics unmistakably home to the Congress and the Democrats by working from inside the House itself.

Gingrich was—and is—a political entrepreneur who helped found a group of House Republicans called the Conservative Opportunity Society. This organization aimed to do the considerable job of turning the Republican party into the recognized party of ethical government and economic progress for members of minority groups. The COS argued that the Democratic-controlled House of Representatives now constituted the most entrenched branch of the federal government, constantly manipulating the system to make it harder for challengers to oust incumbents from office.

Gingrich, with his first-class strategic mind, saw that among the most valuable tools he had to work with in trying to put the Democrats on the moral defensive were those developed during the preceding 25-year period of enthusiastic scandal making on the part of the political left. Gingrich explained not long ago that with the rise of the new left in the mid-1960s, the cosmopolitan, sophisticated liberals of the past were replaced by a generation on the left that thought of politics as a secular religion complete with minimum tolerance, maximum hypocrisy, demons, and absolution of sins for those who hewed to the proper political faith. "All we did," said Gingrich of himself and his allies,

> was to universalize their selective standards . . . to say, "If they're going to apply to Republicans, they'll have to apply to Democrats. If they apply to the executive branch they apply to the legislature. If you want to write new rules, fine. But you can't have it both ways."

One of Gingrich's working assumptions was that the individuals who led the Democrats in the House, especially House Speaker Jim Wright (D-Tex.), were great practitioners of selective morality who did not really believe the rules applied to them. Gingrich's other major assumption was that in the bureaucratic political system established to run the welfare state—replete with grants, subsidies, and tax breaks—corruption was endemic. On these bases he began attacking the Democratic party and Speaker Wright.

The state of the television art gave Gingrich a special advantage in his campaign. The same improving technology that had created so much new competition for journalists in the capital during the 1980s had also produced more extensively televised coverage of House proceedings than ever before. In the evenings, Gingrich would take the floor of the House to discuss issues such as the behavior of Speaker Wright and the scandal of congressional incumbency. Sometimes Gingrich spoke after the House had adjourned for the day, when there were no congressmen on the floor to hear him. Through the miracle of cable television he delivered his message to the nation nonetheless.

Gingrich was shrewd in choosing Wright as his number-one target. Just as the coming of Watergate owed a good deal to the personal idiosyncrasies of Richard Nixon, the Wright affair owed much to the speaker's style. For starters, Wright looked the perfect picture of the crooked politician. His pointed, bushy eyebrows were a match for those of E. Robert Wallach. The speaker's voice was high and somewhat oleaginous, his phrases pious and orotund. He could not talk of public virtue, no matter how sincerely, without reminding many of his listeners of Elmer Gantry.

Though Wright had the manner of an old-style southern politician, he did not have much old-style charm or collegiality. Indeed, he was capable of acting like a hard-edged ideologue. Instead of trying to work compromises in the Nicaragua dispute that divided the House, he increased the bitterness of the dispute by initiating his own personal foreign-policy dialogue with Sandinista president Daniel Ortega, independently of what had once been thought of as the U.S. government. The speaker also acquired a reputation for using his office in a fiercely partisan way. He repeatedly employed his mastery of House procedures to render its minority Republicans without a voice, and they grew resentful of him as they had not with his immediate predecessor, Tip O'Neill. In May 1988 the entire House Republican leadership, in a highly unusual move, took the floor of the House to give speeches one after another about the tyrannical way in which the Democratic majority, led by Wright, was exercising its power.

In May 1988, Gingrich, escalating his campaign against the speaker, filed charges against him with the House ethics committee. At that time Gingrich had a reputation among his fellow Republicans for being something of a bomb thrower. Still, when he sent his complaint to the ethics committee he was able to persuade 71 of his fellow Republicans to sign the document along with him. Wright's personality and the partisan animus he aroused play a large part in explaining why.

Personal idiosyncrasies were not the sole explanation for Wright's downfall any more than they were with Richard Nixon. By the time Gingrich filed his complaint, rising criticism of Wright had led the reform organization Common Cause, not known for any personal antagonism toward the speaker, to send its own letter to the ethics committee asking for an investigation of Wright's possible violations of House ethics rules. In post-Watergate style, Common Cause also asked that the committee hire counsel from outside the House to direct the investigation and lend it credibility. The ethics committee responded by launching an investigation of Wright in June 1988. To serve as counsel they chose trial lawyer Richard J. Phelan of Chicago, a Democratic party activist. Some people muttered when Phelan was appointed that the investigation would be a put-up job: A Democrat like Phelan would never act with the vigor necessary to run the speaker to ground, and the committee's choice was just another sign of the self-perpetuating lock that the Democrats had on the House. These early doubters did not understand the moving forces of modern American politics.

Eight months after Phelan began, he produced, as outside counsels tend to do, a wide-ranging report. In it he recommended that the ethics committee charge Wright with various violations of House rules. Wright's main problems, it turned out, were in three areas. First, he was accused of having been overzealous in defending savings and loan operators from his home state of Texas against punitive actions by federal regulators. In one instance he was reported to have let regulators know that the size of their future appropriations depended on whether they dropped their lawsuits against a Wright constituent who ran a savings and loan institution. In another incident, after the Federal Home Loan Bank Board had removed a Wright ally from his post as head of a Texas S&L, the speaker was said to have put heavy pressure on the chief of the bank board to force a reversal of the action. Still other stories had Wright asking regulators to put off closing a crumbling Texas S&L, whose owner, Don Ray Dixon, had—among other favors—lent his yacht to Democratic party bigwigs.

Another set of accusations against Wright stemmed from a book written under Wright's name titled *Reflections of a Public Man.*[8] A friend of Wright's had published the book, and the arrangement gave the speaker unusually high royalties: a whopping 55 percent of the book's sales. Sometimes when Wright made a speech to an organization he would sell the group his book, in bulk, instead of collecting an honorarium. In this way, said Phelan's report, Wright got around the limits set by House rules on the amount of money members could earn in outside speaking fees.

A third set of problems for Wright stemmed from his friendship with a Fort Worth, Texas, businessman named George Mallick. Mallick had done Wright favors such as hiring the Speaker's wife and allowing him use of a car and apartment. The report said Wright had failed to report some of these gifts properly. Moreover, House rules forbade members to take gifts from people who had some personal interest in federal legislation. It was charged that Mallick had just such an interest in federal programs to aid economic development in the Fort Worth area, an issue on which Wright was understandably active in the Congress.

The committee, following Phelan's recommendations, voted to charge Wright with violations involving his book and his friendship with Mallick; a number of Democrats defected from party ranks to vote against their speaker. But the committee decided not to bring charges against Wright on the most serious matters of all, those involving the speaker's intervention with savings and loan regulators on behalf of shaky thrift institutions. Wright's actions in these cases, said his fellow lawmakers circumspectly, lay within the bounds of what a congressman customarily did to promote the interests of his constituents.

Now that the Wright scandal was fully out in the open, it began, in the usual way, to sprout branches. Indeed, with the Wright scandal the House and the Congress as a whole embarked on a veritable scandal orgy. There were new charges regarding Wright himself: For instance, *The Wall Street Journal* said Wright had inserted into the *Congressional Record* a pitch for a home video program made by a company that had employed his wife.[9]

The Wright scandal also developed subplots. For example, House Democrats launched a counterattack by asking the ethics committee to investigate Newt Gingrich, who—like Wright— had published a book with the aid of outside backers, including prominent conservatives. Common Cause wrote another grave letter to the House ethics committee, this one saying that Gingrich, too, should have an outside counsel to investigate him.

The Gingrich scandal grew. The *Atlanta Business Chronicle*, in Gingrich's home state, reported that some Gingrich staffers who had taken unpaid leaves from their government jobs to work on his previous congressional reelection campaigns had been given temporary raises when they got back to their congressional posts, in violation of House rules.[10] The wily Gingrich made a counter-counterattack, claiming that more than half his fellow House members did the same thing and supplying the press with the names of 14 House Democrats who, said Gingrich, had serious ethics problems.

Gingrich was never charged by the House ethics committee. Over in the Senate, though, the ethics committee had begun investigating yet another book deal that looked as if it were designed to evade the rules on outside income. This time the target was Senator Dave Durenberger (R-Minn.), and the investigation of this and other charges would finally result in the senator's being denounced by his colleagues in the summer of 1990.

The Wright scandal also spawned a subscandal of a darker type. On May 4, 1989, *The Washington Post* Style section ran the story of a woman named Pamela Small, 36 years old. One evening in 1973, the article said, Small went shopping for window blinds in a northern Virginia home furnishings store. She accompanied the night manager, a young man, into the back storeroom to look for the item she needed. There the man suddenly turned on her in a vicious physical assault. He pounded her head with a hammer, opening her scalp down to the bone. Then he carried her out to her car, dumped her inside, and left her to die. Miraculously, Small came to and drove herself to a service station to get help, and she survived the attack.

The manager, 19 years old, was apprehended, convicted, and jailed. Yet he served only a little over two years in a Virginia jail before he was released on a work program. He was eligible for the program because he had been promised a job as a file clerk by Rep. Jim Wright, whose daughter was married to the criminal's brother. By 1989 the man who had bludgeoned Small, John P. Mack, was the executive director of the House Democratic Steering and Policy Committee, a top aide to Wright, and a power in the House of Representatives. The *Post* story was not the first report of the Mack affair, but it was the first with Small's name and picture included. The story quoted Mack as saying he would always feel sorry for what he had done to Small. The same story had Small answering that Mack had never made any attempt to apologize to her.[11]

"I was flabbergasted," Mack later said of the *Post*'s phone call and story. He said he was not surprised by the newspaper's attack on him, but he was bitter: "I wasn't accused of anything except rising too high. They never talked about the years I spent as a $9,000-a-year filing clerk, working my way up." Washington politicians and press did not fall all over themselves trying to develop and expand the story. House Majority Whip Tony Coelho (D-Calif.) defended Mack by saying that a criminal's debt was to society, not to an individual victim, and that Mack had paid the whole penalty society had demanded of him.

Coelho's statement described rather accurately the rehabilitative ethic to which our criminal justice system has been dedicated for many years. Yet by the time Small told her story to the *Post,* this view of punishment had lost some of its appeal, and public attitudes toward crimes like Mack's had changed and hardened. Across the country, in newspapers and on the critical radio talk shows, there was a strong response to the Mack story, and the anger flowed back to Washington. The grapevine started spreading the word that this was the fatal blow to Wright's defense efforts.

Wright clearly did not think so. He beefed up his team of

lawyers, and they started a counteroffensive by approaching the House ethics committee to accuse Phelan of having misused his privileged position as committee counsel by acting like a prosecutor in a criminal case. The committee, said the defense, should start acting like a judge in the same criminal case and have only formal contacts with him.

Hell hath no fury like a congressman accused of being led around by the nose. Committee chairman Julian C. Dixon (D-Calif.) not only denied the defense motion but also added that it was "an exercise in bad judgment."[12] Perhaps Speaker Wright was learning what congressional witnesses mean when they complain about being subjected to criminal-type proceedings without criminal-court protections.

The difference between a courtroom and the modern-day Congress was demonstrated again on May 23, when Wright's attorney Stephen D. Susman, a well-known Texas litigator, finally had the chance to meet Phelan in public argument before the committee. Susman, lawyer-like, addressed the charges against Wright in an orderly manner. First there was the question of whether Wright had violated the rules by selling his book to organizations he addressed as a way of evading limits on speaking fees.

House rules, said Susman, clearly did not count book royalties as regulated outside earned income. This was true whether the royalties were taken in lieu of speaking fees or to buy poor children Christmas presents or anything else. In making this claim, Susman had support from, among others, Rep. David Obey (D-Wisc.), chairman of the commission that drew up the House ethics code in the first place.[13]

Susman attacked the Mallick question in the same way. According to the rules, Wright's attorney said, a congressman could accept certain gifts from a genuine friend, which Mallick was. The rules did forbid taking such gifts from individuals with an interest in federal legislation. But Mallick's general interest in the economic development of his hometown, Fort Worth, was not direct and specific enough to fall within the meaning of the rules. On this point, too, Obey supported Susman's interpretation.

If the House wanted to change the rules, Susman argued, well and good. But the committee could not properly judge Wright guilty of violating rules that did not exist. "The very meaning of a [dividing] line in the law," Susman quoted legal giant Oliver Wendell Holmes, "is that you intentionally may go as close to it as you can if you do not pass it."[14]

Phelan's talk to the committee, in a nice contrast to Susman's, used the more expansive language of the newer politics. On the matter of George Mallick's relationship with Wright, for instance, Phelan made the ringing declaration, "To suggest that every member of the House has a friend like George Mallick is to demean this institution."[15] In point of fact, Phelan was speaking to an audience of congressmen, many of whom did have a friend like George Mallick. Such relationships between congressmen and well-heeled friends are common and run the gamut from corrupt to harmless. Yet Phelan's rhetoric allowed for no such differentiation. Committee members, this kind of talk threatened, could not feel safe taking refuge in Susman's careful reasoning about the distinctions dwelling in various provisions of the House ethics rules. The lawmakers had to aim not just to keep on the lawful side of the line but to be so far away from it that no journalist could place them and the line together in a single photograph.

Looking back on the crisis, Susman later recalled that within a week or so after he had joined the case, he realized "that I wasn't going to be able to pull the rabbit out of the hat." The case had been going on too long, Susman said, and when people spend a year in investigation they look foolish if they come up with nothing. Moreover, Phelan had produced hundreds of accusations, and people were paying attention to things like the John Mack story. The committee simply wasn't focusing on the specific charges against Wright.

But Wright's reluctant judges on the committee did not have to decide between Susman's and Phelan's ethical styles. The congressmen were let off the hook without having to decide whether to press forward to more formal charges against him, for Wright announced after the arguments that he would resign the speakership and his congressional seat at the end of June. In his farewell speech to his House colleagues he asked them to stop the "mindless cannibalism" that he saw in the attack on him. He talked of the "feeding frenzy" that characterized the behavior of the press.[16] He sounded very like one of Ronald Reagan's more embittered executive branch appointees.

On the way to resignation, Wright briefly paused to consider whether after leaving his congressional seat he should turn around and run for it again. He quickly discarded this idea: It would have been suicidal to return to continuing investigation and uproar. Nevertheless it is no wonder that the notion occurred to him. Even at the height of the scandal, a poll of his constituents showed that 65 percent of them stood ready to re-elect him.[17] Part of this approval reflected a personal popularity built over the years. Still, it was also striking that the intense press coverage of the scandal and the showy, quasi-judicial proceedings in Washington had somehow not managed to persuade the voters that Wright's actions were egregious.

The Wright scandal was not the end of the congressional travails. Even before it was over, another one arose that was almost as big. By the time Wright finally left the House, his second-in-command, House whip Tony Coelho, had already resigned his seat. In a sense Coelho's leaving was more important than Wright's, for Coelho had become the symbol of the congressional campaign politics that the critics called in-eradicably corrupt.

In 1981, when Coelho was angling for the post of whip, he became head of the Democratic Congressional Campaign Committee, where he proved himself an effective, enthusiastic, and unabashed fund-raiser. Coelho was the party official who, perhaps more than any other, saw to it that the PACs understood just how beneficial it would be for them to fork over substantial amounts of money to the House Democrats. He was the party's chief practitioner of the new political hardball. In 1988, *Wall Street Journal* reporter Brooks Jackson, who had spent a great deal of time covering Coelho, published a book, mainly about the congressman, called—no shilly-shallying here—*Honest Graft.*[18] It explained in some detail how Coelho made the new money-raising apparatus work. It did not say Coelho was personally venal. It did say, more dangerously, that he was a human metaphor for the disturbing ethical problems that beset the whole modern fund-raising process. The book was widely quoted, and the House whip started walking around with a bad case of political vulnerability.

In April 1989, with the Wright scandal already in flower, *The Washington Post* reported that Coelho had bought, then sold for a nice profit, $100,000 worth of high-yield junk bonds underwritten by the securities firm of Drexel Burnham Lambert.[19] Drexel's name had a sinister aura, since it was the ex-firm of Michael Milken, who had been marked by federal law enforcement authorities as the embodiment of Wall Street greed and was under indictment on myriad complex criminal charges. The junk bonds Coelho had bought were of a type not usually available to small investors, and to buy them he had gotten a loan from a savings and loan executive whose institution was a major Drexel customer. This man was also a major contributor to Coelho's Democratic Congressional Campaign Committee.

These facts did not really add up to much on the wrongdoing scale. But the searchlight was now on Coelho, and soon the public began to see other small creatures scurrying around in it. In mid-May, just before the Wright hearing, Coelho's attorney admitted in response to press queries that his client had underpaid his taxes on the profits from the sale of the bonds by $2,000. The error was said to be a mistake by Coelho's tax preparers.[20] Then word came from Milken's home territory of Los Angeles that the Justice Department had begun looking at the Coelho connection.[21] The congressman was also accused of conflict of interest for owning an interest in a dairy management firm while pushing a dairy subsidy bill.[22]

Coelho acted quickly. On May 26, five days before Wright's resignation announcement, the House whip said he was leaving. Coelho not only escaped prolonged bloodletting but left Congress to a round of highly public parties and fond farewells. To all appearances, no shame or guilt attached to the departure. Instead, other Hill denizens expressed admiration and even gratitude for Coelho's wisdom in getting out fast and avoiding more harm to himself and his party. The ex-congressman soon became managing director of the investment firm Wertheim Schroeder—thus giving the lie to the old nostrum that haste makes waste—and remained an honored member of the political community. In fact, since his departure from the House he has been spoken of as the man of the future in national Democratic politics and a potential chief of staff in a Democratic White House.[23]

The uproar of sex and money scandals on the Hill and the unseating of not one but two House Democratic leaders brought a moment of sobriety to some of the journalists who had covered these imbroglios. After 15 years of scandal reporting they now rather suddenly started to worry about, as *The New York Times* put it, about "the degree to which they feel manipulated by politicians on the attack" and the possibility that "pressure resulting from competition among news organizations can lead to a lowering of standards of inquiry."[24] The press soon steadied itself, however, and went on to more of the same.

Almost as soon as Wright had left, the fickle finger of accusation swiveled and pointed straight at Rep. Julian Dixon, House ethics committee chairman and investigator of Jim Wright. On June 12, Dixon reported that in the preceding year his wife had earned more than $100,000 from an investment in a company that had a lucrative concession to operate gift shops at Los Angeles International Airport.[25]

Mrs. Dixon was a bona fide businesswoman, and the ethics committee's ranking Republican declared that there was no evidence of dishonesty. But the bipartisan seal of approval could no longer still doubts when a scandal was straining to be born. Press sleuths looked further and found that some of the investors in Mrs. Dixon's company were friends of Los Angeles mayor Tom Bradley, who had awarded the airport concession to the company. It next emerged that the company's minority-group participants had been recruited by an Atlanta firm that ran a sort of rent-a-minority operation, connecting such investors with companies that needed them in order to meet government affirmative-action regulations. Then came news that two months before the gift shop franchise was to be awarded, Rep. Dixon had given the lawyer who headed the airport commission a job with the House ethics committee.

So what? So nothing, apparently. That spring's reporting about Dixon led nowhere. All it did was encourage anyone who followed the story to believe that somewhere in the middle of this thick smoke sat the head of the House ethics committee, assiduously lining his wife's pockets and his own.

The same thing happened shortly afterward to Rep. William H. Gray III (D-Pa.), who had entered the race to succeed Tony Coelho as House whip. At the end of May 1989, in the middle of Gray's campaign, *CBS News* told the nation that the congressman's office was being investigated by the FBI. Gray called a news conference to say that FBI agents had indeed visited him but that the visit had concerned one of his employees. Gray was as upset as an indicted Reagan administration official about the leak from the prosecutors. He thought it was outrageous. "You may find it amazing," said Gray. "It is. You may find it unbelievable that it could happen in America."[26]

Gray was elected House whip despite the bad publicity, but the episode was not over. Rumors about his financial affairs kept circulating around Washington. At the end of June, *The Washington Post* produced a front-page story on Gray's finances. The article explained that Gray was not only a congressman but also pastor of Philadelphia's Bright Hope Baptist Church, as were his father and grandfather before him. When Gray was elected to Congress in 1978, his church—"represented by two of Gray's close political allies,"[27] the story thought it pertinent to point out—bought Gray's house to use as a permanent parsonage. Gray's mother, as widow of the former pastor, could live there at no cost. Gray, too, lived at the house when he went back to Philadelphia some three weekends a month to preach, gratis, at the church. He also gave the church the part of his honoraria, received from his other speaking engagements, that was above the amount House rules allowed him to keep.

If this account has not made you suspicious, you are still not in the right frame of mind to understand today's politics. Here is the theory that the *Post* was investigating: By letting Gray live in the house at no cost on weekends, the church was giving him outside income that Gray did not have to report. Then Gray paid the church back, you see, by giving it his extra honoraria—the speaking fees that the rules said he could not keep for himself anyway.

There were, however, problems with this theory, and the *Post* conscientiously reported most of them. For one thing, free housing might not count as outside income under House rules. And the housing might not even be a gift from the church: One trustee said the right to occupy the house had been granted to Gray's mother, not to Gray, and that when Gray stayed there he was accepting hospitality from his mother, not the church.

To generate this information on Rep. Gray, the diligent reporters on the story had interviewed church folk and Gray's lawyers, consulted the Philadelphia tax rolls and commissioned a computerized search of real estate prices, looked at FEC records, and gotten hold of Gray's mother's voter registration data to check on when she had actually moved into the house. All this effort produced over 50 column-inches of material that left readers saying to one another, "I don't get it. Where was the scandal?"

Yet sometimes the consequences of investigative activity of this sort come in the long run. Rep. Gray's scandal-immune system had been seriously breached, and within a year his office was said to be under investigation again. The rumors persisted, without much hard evidence to support them, up until the time when Gray announced his resignation from Confress in the spring of 1991.[28] And the idea of the corrupt congressman-preacher had clearly taken hold: In the summer of 1990, another such lawmaker-cum-minister, Rep. Floyd H. Flake (D-N.Y.), was indicted for enriching himself through his church. The case went so badly for the prosecution that the government dropped it in the middle of the trial. Two of the jurors showed up at Rep. Flake's Queens church the next Sunday to hear his sermon.[29] Once again the arcane subject of church finances had proved impenetrable to the scandalmongers.

While Congress was virtually swimming in these tawdry and inconclusive scandals, one of the great embarrassments of its history was unfolding. This was of course the savings and loan scandal, which has presented taxpayers with a mind-boggling bill variously estimated at anywhere from $130 billion to $500 billion, the amount it will take to make good on the federal insurance covering thrift institutions that failed during the 1980s. Despite the wishes of political entrepreneurs in both parties, the S&L scandal cannot be traced to a single villain or ideology. Instead, the history of the crisis is a cameo of some of our pronounced and characteristic policy failings of the past quarter century—a story, as Judge Stanley Sporkin put it in a ruling in a savings and loan case, "that demonstrates the excesses of a misconceived and misapplied regulatory program along with a group of individuals who were bent on exploiting these excesses."[30]

It will be a long time before we get a definitive account of how the crisis came to be, but some of the policy-relevant parts of the story have become clear. The social spending of the 1960s and then the American involvement in Vietnam brought pronounced inflation. This inflation, and in the 1970s the instability surrounding the collapse of the old Bretton Woods system of exchange rate regulation, wreaked havoc with institutions whose success depended on a more stable economic environment.

For instance, our public policies had long encouraged the existence of a group of savings institutions separate from commercial banks and dedicated to providing mortgage money for American homes. These thrift institutions, as they were called, lent money in the form of home mortgages at fixed rates of interest. The thrifts got their profits from the difference between these mortgage rates and the historically lower interest rates that they paid their depositors. But sustained inflation—and in the early 1980s, ironically, the government's efforts to curb inflation—sent general interest rates rising steeply. The earnings from the S&Ls' low-interest home mortgage loans were not enough to allow the thrifts to compete for depositors by offering the prevailing high interest rates.

Federal policymakers responded by capping the rates that thrifts and commercial banks could pay depositors. The ceiling for thrifts was just above what commercial banks were allowed to pay for the same types of accounts. The thrifts were thus given a fixed advantage. But the ultimate result of the controls was a huge outflow of money from the S&Ls to still other institutions, like money-market funds. These upheavals would ultimately have their effects on commercial banking as well as the thrift industry, but at first the S&Ls suffered alone. Congress showed no inclination either to increase regulation of money-market funds or to let the thrifts meet the challenge by making adjustable-rate mortgages, whose interest rates could rise and fall competitively.

By the end of the 1970s, the thrift industry was clearly obsolescent. One early-1980s estimate predicted that if then-current trends persisted, the last S&Ls would fail and close their doors by 1986. The federal savings and loan insurance fund was even then greatly inadequate to the task of reimbursing depositors if the thrifts simply shut down.[31]

In the early 1980s the government began trying to make its way across this economic minefield that it had assiduously laid for itself. First, Congress lifted the thrifts' interest-rate ceilings. Since this change increased what the thrifts would have to pay for deposits, large thrift institutions extracted a quid pro quo in the legislation: Federal deposit insurance was raised from $40,000 to $100,000 per account. Federal regulators instituted adjustable-rate mortgages and broadened the S&Ls' investment powers. The thrifts' capital requirements were eased considerably, in part through explicit new standards and in part through more permissive accounting rules.

Some proponents of these changes seem to have thought that expanded opportunities would make the thrifts profitable and stable on a long-term basis. Others hoped only that they could close down the worst-off S&Ls while making the healthier institutions valuable enough so that they would be bought by other financial institutions.

At first the policies seemed to work: Deposits and capital started to flow into the thrifts. Federal regulators began to close down and sell troubled institutions. Soon, however, two of the policymaker's nightmares made their inexorable appearance. First, the law of unanticipated consequences took effect with a vengeance. Also, the disparate interests and ideologies behind the movement for thrift deregulation started pulling the project in contradictory directions.

As for unanticipated consequences, the effect of the $100,000 deposit guarantee, which made no distinctions between blue-chip institutions and breathtakingly risky operations, was disastrous. The policy violated the first principle of proper deregulation by making it impossible for the market to balance yield with risk. The combination of uncapped interest rates being offered by the S&Ls with the government's guarantee of absolute safety brought deposits flowing indiscriminately into conservative and high-risk thrifts alike, and favored those institutions that offered the highest yields. The hefty interest that the thrifts were obliged to pay on such deposits created great pressure to invest in risky high-yield enterprises.

Congress's generosity in bestowing its $100,000 deposit guarantee was not unusual. On the contrary: For the past 50 years we have increasingly used federal loans, loan guarantees, and insurance schemes in areas from housing to economic development and agriculture as a way of giving out benefits we assumed we would never really have to pay for. We have repeatedly tried to get a political something for a budgetary nothing. The results can be huge taxpayer liabilities and radically skewed incentives.[32] Under these circumstances, good policymaking is very difficult and even ordinary sorts of policy failure can have extraordinary consequences.

The atmosphere that began to pervade the thrift industry, smelling of big risks and big returns, began to attract high rollers and crooks. More important, even basically honest S&L managers, who greatly outnumbered the criminals, were often not well equipped to manage their institutions' money in the more complex and dangerous world that government policy changes had created. Losses in the industry mounted.

Unanticipated consequences made their appearance in other places as well. For instance, some thrifts were chartered not by the federal government but by individual states, though the federal treasury still insured the deposits. When Congress and federal regulators began liberalizing the rules for federal S&Ls, state institutions started switching to federal charters. In part to lure back the thrifts and recapture the money they had once paid to state governments, some states began liberalizing their investment rules well beyond what federal legislation had done. The opportunities to lose money broadened and multiplied.

Even with the continuing losses, the drop in interest rates in the mid-1980s gave the thrifts as a whole a nominal profit. It may be, as some of the earlier thrift regulators claim, that this was the time to move quickly to reorganize the industry, but no such thing happened. When the real estate market began to falter after the tax changes of 1986, whatever window of opportunity there might have been was closed, and the situation grew irrevocably worse.

Real estate collapse or no, the idea that thrift regulators would be able to fine-tune their policy to meet changing circumstances was unlikely from the beginning. The varied and conflicting interests of the players in the thrift arena ensured that this would be so. For instance, the original thrift deregulation strategy would surely have had a better chance if the federal regulators had operated with an enforcement staff well able to root out crooked practices and shady accounting. Yet for the administration's Office of Management and Budget, deregulation meant reducing the budgets of federal regulatory agencies. The budget office strongly resisted increases in the size or salaries of the enforcement staff, though by the mid-1980s the number and quality of supervisory personnel did start to rise.

More important, some deficit-conscious, constituent-sensitive top administration officials were happy to remove constraints on the S&Ls but unwilling to close down institutions that had failed. The policies of the early eighties had advocated selective forbearance for potentially healthy thrifts, but selective forbearance soon turned into a generally blind eye.

Richard T. Pratt, chairman of the Federal Home Loan Bank Board from 1981 to 1983, has said that in one shareholder lawsuit against the board for closing an insolvent thrift, a high Treasury Department official actually testified for the plaintiffs.[33] When Pratt's successor, Edwin Gray, began asking for more enforcement staff and making new rules to restrict the activities of the worst thrifts, presidential chief of staff Donald Regan let Gray know that he wanted the chairman to resign before the end of his term. In late 1986 the White House helped feed a scandal in which Gray was shown to have accepted favors, primarily meals and hotel rooms, from the thrift industry he was regulating.

An OMB official who consistently fought Gray's budget requests later recalled, "We knew him as a public relations guy out of California. We thought there was no problem with the board and that he had started creating these troubles." The official paused, then asked musingly, "Or did Regan create this impression? I heard lots of bad-mouthing of Gray, and it certainly made me less receptive to what he had to say."

These conflicts reduced any chance of intelligent action. Still, the Reagan administration cannot carry off the honors in the question of who was most enthusiastic about giving the S&Ls new freedom and least willing to permit the failure of thrifts that had misused that freedom. Well after the White House had started trying to deal with the worsening S&L crisis by means such as shoring up the deposit insurance fund so that failing thrifts could be closed and their depositors paid off, Congress blocked legislative action, in order to keep thrift institutions from being shut down and to give them a chance to make the final, desperate investments that might produce mountains of life-saving profits. Congressmen also used their power of the purse to try to get the regulators to go easy on individual S&Ls belonging to constituents and campaign contributors.

It may be remembered that in 1986, Rep. Jim Wright, then House majority leader, caused a major delay in the recapitalization bill for the insurance fund by putting a "hold" on it and used the threat of congressional inaction to try to get better bank board treatment of Texas S&L owners who were constituents and contributors. But Wright had a lot of company in his attitudes. To take one example, another congressman who delayed the insurance fund's recapitalization bill in 1986 was Senator David Pryor (D-Ark.), who held up the legislation more briefly while writing to Gray to complain about the board's "deliberate harassment" of Arkansas thrift institutions. "Before the Bank Board receives any recapitalization authority from the Congress," said Pryor in his letter,

> you need to assure us that your supervisory resources are being used effectively and fairly. . . . I have put a "hold" on the Senate recapitalization bill and am anxious to receive assurances from you that you will correct the abuses which have been taking place in Arkansas and other states.[34]

Pryor was a member of the Senate ethics committee, which would soon be considering the cases of five other senators, some of whom had done not-dissimilar things on behalf of the S&L industry.

Indeed, perhaps Wright was lucky to get out of Washington when he did, for week by week the climate was turning harsher on the subject of Congress and the S&Ls. The Lincoln Savings and Loan Association of Irvine, California, became the symbol of this change of mind. Lincoln was purchased in 1984 by Charles H. Keating, Jr., who from the beginning of his tenure was at odds with federal regulators over how broad Lincoln's investment authority should be. In the spring of 1986 the conflict escalated as federal investigators began a detailed examination of Lincoln's affairs. A year later they were still investigating.

To plead his case and try to get the regulators off his back, Keating was able to mobilize, in various degrees, five senators (aka the Keating Five) to whom he had made a total of some $1.3 million in political contributions: Alan Cranston (D-Calif.), Dennis DeConcini (D-Ariz.), John Glenn (D-Ohio), John S. McCain III (R-Ariz.), and Donald W. Riegle, Jr. (D-Mich.).

Keating had put his money into these senators' campaigns and favorite causes.

Though their case has been contentious, the outline of its facts is fairly clear. In April 1987, with legislation pending to recapitalize the insurance fund, bank board chairman Gray was summoned to a meeting with four of the five lawmakers (there was later testimony that Riegle had arranged the meeting, but he did not attend) and told to bring no staff along. According to Gray's later accounts, the four senators wanted Gray and the bank board to withdraw a new regulation, being challenged in court by Keating, whose application limited Lincoln's ability to invest in undeveloped land. The senators also wanted to know why the regulators' examination of Lincoln was taking so long.

After this meeting, the San Francisco–based bank board staffers actually performing the examination of Lincoln were called to Washington to provide more specific information in a meeting with all five senators. The lawmakers again asked about delays in the investigation. They accompanied their speeches with some version of this disclaimer by Riegle: "If there are fundamental problems at Lincoln, okay"[35]—that is, go ahead and take action against it. Otherwise, the unspoken part of the message continued, get the investigation over with. After some discussion, one of the San Francisco examiners said, according to notes taken by a regulator there, "We're sending a criminal referral [of the Lincoln matter] to the Department of Justice." The notes show that the senators quickly subsided,[36] though after the meeting, two of them—Cranston and DeConcini—kept trying to help Keating despite the regulators' mention of a possible criminal case against him.

As matters turned out, the senators probably did not have much effect on the timing of the bank board's actions against Lincoln. But the case suffered great delays: It was another two years before Lincoln was finally taken over in the spring of 1989 amid charges that Keating had run reckless risks with the institution and milked it for himself and his family. When Lincoln was taken over by federal authorities, the bill to the taxpayer was estimated at $2.5 billion—about twice the cost, said regulators, of closing the institution when they had first advocated it two years previously.

When news of the senators' meetings with bank board personnel emerged in May 1989, the S&L scandal shot into orbit.

The Justice Department pledged a massive special effort to hunt down the crooks who had looted S&Ls. Congressmen rushed to ask department officials in stern tones why the enforcers were not hiring still more attorneys for the job. Campaign finance reform proposals got a push forward in the Congress. The Senate ethics committee started investigating the five senators involved in the Keating affair to determine which Senate rules they had violated.

Conventional scandal politics, in other words, became the first lens through which we viewed the crisis. As the S&L scandal burgeoned, press comment and official action focused heavily on the criminality of individual S&L operators and the evils of our campaign finance system, which was said to force congressmen into corrupt dealings with the unsavory likes of Charles Keating.

As for criminal S&L owners, they were surely and prominently in evidence. Some were massively crooked and colorful, and they made terrific copy. Their conspicuous presence in the S&L scandal established without doubt that the tradition of Billy Sol Estes is alive and well in entrepreneurial America. Still, the most plausible estimate of how much of the S&L bill stemmed from out-and-out individual larceny ranges from 5 to 10 percent:[37] The overwhelming majority of the losses stemmed from mere garden-variety cupidity or basic lack of shrewdness and brains.

More important, we have harbored crooks in the American marketplace since its beginnings, but never before have they been permitted to present the citizenry with a $130 billion to $500 billion bill. The size of the S&L scandal was monstrous not because there were thieves in the industry but because public policy had permitted the stakes to become so high. The strategy for saving the thrifts was a complicated one that needed constant adjustment and proceeded not so much by deregulating an industry as by putting existing institutions into what was in many respects a new business. The regulators lacked control of some of the forces most important in determining their success or failure, from the $100,000 deposit guarantee to the actions of state legislatures. Finally, backers of thrift deregulation had a collection of inconsistent aims that guaranteed policy incoherence.

The S&L crisis revealed, in short, serious and characteristic tendencies toward irresponsibility in our politics and government. Yet at the moment of maximum publicity, public discussion gravitated automatically toward issues such as the question of who gets how many years in the nearest minimum security facility. And it will be hard to dispose of the S&L mess itself, or the bank crisis that has followed it, as long as we refuse to address the nonpersonal structural factors, such as the distorted deposit insurance system, that underlay the crisis in the first place.

Press coverage of the S&L issue certainly contributed to the skewed public attention. As the scandal finally broke open in 1989, the emerging evidence of the size of the crisis stimulated journalism reviews and press seminars to ask why American journalists had missed the importance of the S&L problem so completely. As it happened, local newspapers had done some substantial reporting on the S&Ls in their circulation areas. But for the national press, it was a good question.

One reason for the failure, surely, is that the S&L story was abstract, at a time when the media were becoming ever more interested in news they could personalize. Another reason seems to have been that for a long time few of the players in the S&L field happened to have a personal or political interest in predigesting the negative version of the story and presenting it to investigative journalists.

In 1989 a newspaper in Dayton, Ohio, where Keating had ties, finally asked ex-chairman Gray about the story of the five senators and ran it on a slow news day.[38] The Associated Press picked it up. Around the same time, congressional hearings featured testimony from elderly Californians who had lost money in the collapse of Lincoln.[39] Journalists now saw that here—in Charles Keating, the senators, and the old folks—were the personalities and the personal scandal necessary to make the S&Ls a big story.

After a quarter century of journalists' declaring that they were no longer in anyone's pocket, the press proved to have been as dependent as ever on its sources and those sources' interpretations and interests. And years of scandal politics had made journalists increasingly uninterested in policy stories unless they could find some personal malfeasance in them. It is no wonder that news consumers of the 1980s had no inkling of the gathering storm or who or what was to blame: They could not be expected to tell the players without a program, and the press was providing none.

In November, safely after the 1990 elections, the Senate ethics committee began hearings on the senators associated with Charles Keating. Just as the case of Raymond Donovan drew a high-quality independent counsel who had to cope with an impossible subject matter, the Keating Five hearings were supervised by an extremely skilled special counsel, Robert S. Bennett, who was forced to deal with an issue that seemed to drive the committee, witnesses, and onlookers into an ambivalence as thorough as in the case of Tom Dodd a quarter century before.

On the one hand, Keating had given the five senators enough money so that they would have looked suspicious sending him a birthday card, let alone ganging up on a regulator and barring witnesses from the confrontation. The public climate demanded that the committee take some punitive action, and this demand was not simply the cry of a mob thirsting for blood. The awful consequences of congressional behavior in the Keating case and those like it showed that something improper and out of the ordinary had surely taken place.

On the other hand, the committee clearly had problems, feigned and real, in deciding just what their colleagues had done wrong. When special counsel Bennett made his early investigative report to the committee, he recommended cutting loose senators Glenn and McCain, the two men least involved in the affair, and going on to a more formal probe of the other three. The committee refused to make any such distinctions. Committee members both declined to set Glenn and McCain free and refused to open more formal proceedings on the others. Instead, the committee set up "fact-finding" hearings in which McCain and Glenn would be put through the same public wringer as the Keating episode's three ringleaders.

Democratic senators like committee chairman Howell T. Heflin (D-Ala.) spoke of the hearings as an exercise that could actually improve the image of the Senate by showing the public that senators had in fact not caused the savings and loan crisis, and he tangled with Bennett when the counsel resisted this educative—or public relations—approach to the proceedings.

Once the televised hearings opened, both press attention and the live coverage of the sessions by the Cable News Network produced a storm of public indignation. Yet some of the senators in the dock argued strenuously to the committee that their ethics were in fine shape. Their connections with Keating were legitimate constituent relationships, they said. Prestigious accountants had vouched for Keating's case against the bank board. As senators, they were not only allowed but obliged to speak up for Keating. Indeed, forbidding congressmen from intervening with regulators under these circumstances amounted to sanctioning a bureaucratic tyranny over the American people.

Furthermore, as Senator Cranston and Senator DeConcini insisted in their opening statements, in helping Keating they were merely doing what all other senators did. Finally, there was no rule forbidding such practices. If Congress wanted to write such a rule, senators made the familar plea, well and good, but it simply was not fair to find individuals guilty of violating a rule that did not exist.[40]

The questioning of the witnesses by ethics committee members poked at this defense but raised no concerted challenge to it, and in its final actions, the committee bought the bulk of the defendants' arguments. Only Cranston, the committee ruled, would be placed before the full Senate for discipline; to the other four, the committee merely sent admonitory letters whose varying degrees of severity were distinguishable only to very careful readers.

It is easy enough to see why the committee was dubious about some of the arguments offered by political moralists in the Keating affair. For instance, the lesson of the Keating Five, we frequently hear, is that we can no longer tolerate old-style congressional representation of constituents and donors, because the high costs of today's election campaigns have turned congressmen into such thorough lackeys of the PACs and other money raisers. Yet the Keating affair was in reality not testimony to the evil effect of PACs in today's politics. The money Keating gave to the five lawmakers included no PAC contributions. Instead, Keating used other channels, from individual campaign contributions to support for voter registration efforts. If Keating's activities taught a lesson in this area, it was that abolishing PACs would be no more a guarantee of cleaner politics than was the creation of PACs that took place in the 1970s wave of reform.

Perhaps more interesting, the behavior on display in the Keating scandal was not really the product of today's high-cost political campaigns. We need look back only as far as the Gulf Oil scandal to be reminded that people with economic interests had figured out how to seek political advantage through large-scale political contributions even before the advent of PACs and 1980s-level campaign costs. And in past eras, contributors almost surely got far better results through one senator than Charles Keating did with five.

Instead, what the Keating Five scandal best illuminated was the gamut of destructive possibilities inherent in our modern political reforming impulse. Out of distaste with the grubby realities of democratic politics, recent reformers managed to weaken those centers of power, like political parties, where much of the fund-raising and favor-giving in politics once took place. Today, such activities must be more closely attended to by individual officeholders themselves. While this change was taking place, the same antipolitical distaste brought about new rules making all the wheeling and dealing much more visible than ever before. We are now given a more detailed view of our officials doing decreasingly exalted things. The distaste thus increases, as does the pressure for more reform.

Indeed, the problem of Congress's solicitude toward S&L owners was not even merely a problem of money in politics: The thrift institutions had their political clout not just because of their cash but because they were located in every congressional district in America. For decades the well-being of S&Ls had been closely tied to the general fortunes of the communities they served, and people had come to think of the two as nearly identical. Without these associations, the thrifts could have given just as much money to politicians with nowhere near so much effect.

Does this mean that the senators in the dock were right when they argued that they were scapegoats, on trial for actions that were ordinary, prevalent, and permissible under the rules? No. Cranston and DeConcini, the senators who had pushed most persistently for Keating, had not simply worked in the classic, unexceptionable way to get a hearing for a private interest. At a time when the dire state of the thrift industry was already widely known, they chose to give credence only to those experts who supported their constituent and contributor. They refused to doubt Keating even after the government had surely given them enough grounds for suspicion.

They presented their views to the regulators in a way that suggested organized coercion rather than the more normal inquiries, persuasive devices, and veiled threats of everyday politics. "If I'm sitting on a park bench," Bennett explained the difference,

> and an 800-pound gorilla comes along and says, "Excuse me, I'm just making a status inquiry if there are any seats available," you say, "You're damn right, there's a seat available."[41]

Some of the senators in the Keating case were clearly making gorilla noises. And when Senator DeConcini chose to defend himself by making a massive public attack on the character of his Arizona colleague, Senator McCain, he reminded us that some forms of political incivility can be more dangerous to democratic politics than the simple trading of favors for money. Such activities crossed, in other words, the line—fuzzy but existent—that a democratic representative must always tread.

Yet this type of transgression cannot easily be described as a violation of some definite rule. In fact, the focus on specific prohibitory rules may make us less rather than more able to control the offending behavior.

Some 25 years before the ethics committee's Keating hearings, Senator Thomas Dodd had been charged with a series of unsavory practices ranging from double billing to influence peddling. Senator Russell Long defended Dodd by saying that the accused senator had violated no clear Senate rule. Long was right. The standards Dodd had violated were not chiefly written rules but some of the unwritten standards of senatorial behavior. Yet Dodd was not censured for having crossed the invisible line. Instead, the force behind his censure came from those who did not think the unwritten rules were powerful enough to limit official discretion and provide justification for punishing miscreants severely. These critics wanted the standards to be stricter, more explicit, and more binding. From the desire for more open, distinct standards came the many new government ethics rules and investigative procedures of the 1970s and 1980s.

Yet in 1991, as in 1966, the senators guilty of misbehavior did not sin because they had violated some written rule. Instead, the sinning senators transgressed the unspoken standards and sense of proportion on which political decency and responsibility depend.

In other words, all our ethics reform and rule writing over the past quarter century have not been able to create more moral politicians or make us any less dependent on the unwritten understandings of politics. Yet the Senate ethics committee, in the absence of a specific rule to which to cling, proved unable to come to any coherent ethical judgment.

Afterward it was said by critics that the Senate, which had been happy enough to embrace the idea of government ethics with enthusiastic sanctimony when it came to the executive branch, discovered prudence when the same political spirit came knocking at the congressional door. If this had been all that happened during the Keating Five case, it would have been no very bad thing. But the committee did not simply display prudence. Something worse had been revealed: Years of punitive legalism had left the ethics committee incapable of making the sorts of ethical judgments on which a political system truly depends.

Worse still, the enormous S&L scandal, more costly than all the rest of our 200 years of scandals added together, was an indictment of practices and habits deeply embedded in our national politics. It took shape while the media were tracking down Gus Savage and Buz Lukens, while prosecutors were moving heaven and earth to give Bob Wallach six years in prison for the way he had submitted his bills to Wedtech, while an independent counsel was spending years trying to parse one morning's worth of testimony by Ted Olson, and while a congressional committee was commandeering the resources of the Secret Service to bolster the view that the scientific community is corrupt.

During these years, scandal politics made its way from the Hill to the White House and back again, but that was not the most important occurrence of the years between Watergate and the S&L scandal. More serious was that our frantic appetite to take hold of every scandal of intention harbored in the depths of national politics left us no time or energy to occupy ourselves with scandals, like that of the S & Ls and the recent BCCI crisis, involving more dangerous problems of competence and of political will. The same view of political life drives us repeatedly toward solutions that assuage the thirst for political cleanliness without taking much care for political performance.

CHAPTER 10

PERSONAL EFFECTS

THE SCANDALS OF recent years have been dramatic productions mounted on the world's most visible stage. They have more spear-carriers in their casts than a Wagnerian opera, and they play to an audience of millions each day and evening. No wonder they succeed in turning every political transgression into a mini-Watergate and elbow aside more serious issues and more deeply scandalous public problems. Yet nowadays, because we are increasingly adept at rooting out offenses by public officials, most people assigned to starring roles in these scandals are not gross offenders. More and more we have to deal with the small-time, garden-variety influence peddler or the agency head who schedules work-related trips on the weekends when his son is playing football nearby or the official who calls a colleague in another agency and asks him to speed up a decision, one way or the other, in some regulatory matter.

Therefore we must worry more about the personal costs exacted by modern scandal politics, out of range of the lights and cameras. Political scandals take a huge personal toll on the mounting number of individuals under attack and on their families. Despite all of today's personality journalism, the press does not pay much attention to such travail. Perhaps one reason for the scant coverage is that many of those who hunt and publicize political scandal do not want us to look too closely at this type of personal injury. Indeed, they try to avert their own eyes from it as well.

We should not exaggerate in describing these personal costs, so let us start with a modest example. Theodore Olson was investigated by Congress and an independent counsel for more than five years before he was exonerated in 1989 of a charge of lying to Congress. Despite the long inquest, it is hard to view Olson as an object of pity, for he was exceptionally well equipped with the resources necessary to withstand the ordeal. Before joining the Justice Department, Olson had been a partner in a large Los Angeles–based law firm, and he returned to the firm when he left the department in 1984. "I was lucky. The firm has given me a lot of support," he reflected later. Olson did a prodigious amount of legal work for the firm during the years when the investigation was dragging on. "He's got more ability to compartmentalize things," his wife explained afterward, "than anyone I know."

Still, Olson later remembered the investigation as a nightmare. It ate up time, of course. Olson had to deal with its demands almost every day. Not infrequently, he recalled, "I'd spend the entire day on the phone with my lawyers."[1] The process also did real damage to his legal career. "I had one case," Olson gave an example,

> that a client said he'd have me argue all the way to the Supreme Court—except that it wouldn't be a good idea, what with my own case before the court. I had another client take my name off a Supreme Court brief. And then there's the stuff you don't know about, the people who never call you in the first place.

Even worse, the investigation put Olson's life in a state of radical and sustained uncertainty. For over five years he had to face the threat of indictment, conviction, jail, and professional obliteration. Worst of all, the investigation's far horizon retreated each time Olson thought he was about to reach it. "When the independent counsel investigation started [in 1986]," he recalled,

> I figured it was going to last a month. The longest investigation up to then had been six months. And in

my case, the crime I was supposed to have committed was committed in public, with 250 witnesses and a court reporter taking down my every word. People had already investigated the issue, so the independent counsel had the documents. I couldn't imagine it being long.

Then McKay [James C. McKay, the first independent counsel assigned to the case] quit, because of conflicts that he never quite specified, and Alexia Morrison [McKay's assistant] took over. But . . . I figured she already knew things, and it wouldn't take too much extra time. She herself had represented someone before one of the independent counsels. So I got my mind ready for six months.

As the time got nearer and nearer to six months, and I saw that it wasn't happening, I got more and more upset. . . . After six months Alexia Morrison said that to date she had found no prosecutable offenses by me. I thought that meant it would be over soon.

But it was not. There were still more than three years of misery left to go. "The worst part," Olson summed up, "is not knowing when it will end. The big trick is to keep busy and to learn how to live with this thing hanging over you."

Scandal was very hard to take even for Olson, who had a secure livelihood and a particularly stable personality. When the same thing happens to someone whose professional life and temperament are more volatile, a scandal becomes a seemingly endless emotional roller coaster. Here are the words of another Reagan appointee describing the personal effects of his scandal:

There were sleepless nights, of course. I was into the bottle at night so I could get to sleep. I would wake up in the middle of the night in panic sweats, and I'd have to control the urge to call my lawyer at 3 A.M. I gained weight and developed high blood pressure. I bitterly resented my children when I heard them laughing about anything. There were fights at home about whether I should resign and go home. I had to be told over and over again that in Washington, if you survive, no matter how, you win. If you leave, you lose.

Whenever I wasn't invited to a meeting, I was half sure it was due to the cloud of scandal around me. Because of the nasty leaks from [my] agency, I stopped talking and traveling even when I shouldn't have. I felt constantly embarrassed. When I was in an elevator and other people were silent, I was sure they were thinking about the scandal publicity. If I saw two or three people talking together I was sure it was about me. I became so paranoid that I went home to [my home city] and cleaned out all my business files from before I was in government, even though they were innocent.

I kept having fantasies about [a certain journalist covering the story]. In some of them I would kiss his feet and ask him to let up for the sake of my children. Sometimes I would think about how to put out a contract on him. I visited a psychiatrist for help.

Clearly this man is not Olson's type. The two stories, though, display elements that appear over and over in the tales told by those who have lived through political scandal. Such individuals find their scandals overwhelming their lives at work and at home because of the time the scandals take up, because the highly public nature of these troubles makes the people experiencing them feel especially isolated, and because the long-running uncertainty of these affairs threatens them with a loss of control over their lives. The result is often a state of nearly constant fear.

The most concrete, immediate threat faced by many of these individuals and their families concerns money. An official involved in a scandal will probably lose his job. Worse, he may find his prospects for getting another one severely reduced. Even if he was only tangentially involved in the scandal, he will carry with him some of its sinister scent. If the official stays employed, he will face severe financial problems anyway, for his legal bills can be staggering. Near the high end, Michael Deaver's legal fees hovered around $2 million. Olson's legal bills amounted to over $1 million, just as he had feared, during his independent counsel investigation. Lyn Nofziger's bills came to nearly $1 million. The court denied him reimbursement even though his conviction was reversed, on the grounds that the legal system had treated him just like any other citizen, and he had borne no special costs meriting compensation.

These cases involved independent counsels and a great deal of publicity. Yet the not-so-famous also get hit hard. After federal appellate judge Douglas Ginsburg was nominated for the Supreme Court in 1987, he was accused of having smoked marijuana some years previously. He withdrew his name. In the course of the scandal explosion, though, Ginsburg was also charged with serious conflicts of interest dating from the time when he headed the Justice Department's antitrust division. Justice Department attorneys began investigating, to see whether an independent counsel should be appointed. They decided that the charges did not meet even the law's accommodating standards and that the case should not go forward. The preliminary investigation alone, though, gave Ginsburg legal bills estimated to be in the six figures.

Even tangential involvement in a scandal can be expensive. In any sizable scandal with criminal possibilities, lower-ranking participants are commonly called before the grand jury along with the major players. In today's climate, this means personal danger, and the subordinates need lawyers. The government often refuses to pay the bills, so more or less ordinary people end up saddled with tens of thousands of dollars in debt.

During Iran-contra, Howard R. Teicher, head of politico-military affairs at the NSC, was one of those who came under scrutiny. He proved to have played very little part in the affair and was never under serious criminal investigation. Still, he recalled several years afterwards, he and his lawyers were called upon to talk to two committees each of the Senate and House, the Tower Commission, the FBI, the independent counsel's office, and the grand jury, not counting the inevitable dealings with the media.

Teicher's legal bills came to some $50,000. He applied to the government for reimbursement under an executive order allowing such payments to officials who are criminally investigated but not charged. The government refused to pay. "They said," Teicher recounted, "that I didn't *need* a lawyer." He finally received partial reimbursement only after four years of battling for it and only under a carved-out exception that allowed him repayment for the legal work done in connection with his congressional testimony.

The penalty for loitering in the neighborhood of a scandal can be even higher. For instance, in one offshoot of the Iran-contra affair, Richard R. Miller, whose media consulting firm had done work for the State Department's efforts in the contras' behalf, came under investigation and in 1987 pleaded guilty to a one-count felony charge of conspiring to defraud the government by abusing the status of a tax-exempt organization. At his sentencing the judge, having considering the gravity of the offense, put Miller on probation for two years and ordered him to do 120 hours of the now-popular community service.

Miller's operations were a natural and proper field of inquiry for government investigators, but the probes got out of hand. "At one time," Miller later explained his decision to plead guilty to the tax charge, "they had seven investigations of me going." One was mounted by the Justice Department. One was from the House and one from the Senate. The IRS was conducting an elaborate audit called an income probe. The Federal Election Commission was investigating Miller to see whether he had ties to any illegal political contributions. The Defense Department was auditing his consulting firm's contracts, and the State Department was investigating grants the firm had received from the U.S. Information Agency.

The legal and accounting bills from these processes, Miller said, ultimately came to more than $500,000. During the investigations, when he was deciding whether to fight the government's indictment of him, "My lawyers told me that if I decided to go to trial, the defense would cost [another] $500,000, unless we piggybacked on Ollie North's defense." Yet becoming a target alongside North was a perilous enterprise. So Miller pleaded guilty.

Financial costs are only one part of the legal problems frequently faced by these people. The possibility of being branded a criminal or even going to jail looms even larger. "At first," said the spouse of one scandal-mired official describing the process of engulfment, "it's hard to understand that you're in trouble. [My husband] read the early newspaper reports of the scandal and still didn't see how it could involve him." Next comes the realization that the marked man or woman needs a lawyer. "What happens then," the spouse went on, "is that they tell you that you can't talk at all to the other people involved [in the scandal]. That sometimes includes people who are your friends or the ones you would want to turn to in a situation like this. It's very isolating and very frightening."

Each time the scandal spawns a new legal crisis—before a deposition, or a hearing, or the filing of court papers, or a trial— the lawyers and their demands come to dominate the official's life not only at work but also at home. "When my husband testified [to Congress]," a wife recalled, "it stopped everything for weeks. The files and the papers came pouring into the house, and they were a surprisingly big physical intrusion. They wouldn't let you forget that event hanging over your head."

These crises weigh even more heavily on those going through them because, as Theodore Olson pointed out, a target often has no sense of when the suspense will end. This long purgatory is not just a natural part of a scandal, like the thunder that follows lightning; it also results from the fact that a lot of people have an interest in not seeing these scandals finished. There are journalists who want to keep pushing a story because they hope to find more damning evidence and because the process of pushing can itself produce a lot of news. There are investigators and prosecutors who try to keep their searches open-ended in order to preserve their freedom of action, put pressure on the people they are after, or avoid admitting defeat.

This sort of indefinite sentence can be visited on even the most politically advantaged figures. In July 1984, for example, columnist Jack Anderson wrote a story suggesting that Senator Mark Hatfield (R-Ore.) had exercised improper influence on behalf of a Greek businessman named Basil Tsakos by writing letters in support of Tsakos' idea for an oil pipeline across Africa. Tsakos had paid Hatfield's wife, a prominent real estate broker in Washington, $55,000 for professional services, and some ex-employees of Tsakos said the payment was really meant to buy influence with her husband.

The Senate ethics committee investigated and found no corruption on the senator's part. But the Justice Department had begun its own criminal investigation and would not close it out. The legal pressure continued until 1987, when the senator wrote a letter to the department demanding to know one way or the other what it was going to do about his case. Only then did

Justice say that it had found no grounds for prosecution. Hatfield's was a highly privileged position: Most people undergoing criminal investigations are not in a position to force the authorities to announce their intentions in this way.

And even in Hatfield's case, the Tsakos affair proved to be the opening wedge for investigations that would put the senator in much deeper trouble in 1991, when he was shown to have accepted undisclosed gifts.

James Towey, one of Hatfield's aides during the Tsakos scandal, afterward described the unremitting pressure generated by the long siege of uncertainty:

> We were on the networks every night and on the front page of *The Washington Post* every day. The reporters were definitely influenced by the post-Watergate mentality. . . . [T]hey would come to you with accusations made by their sources, which were no good in the first place. . . . [I]n this way they would force a press conference. . . .
>
> The emotional toll . . . is nearly unbearable. You're beaten down and physically tired. You can't eat or sleep well. . . . [B]ut you can't show they're getting to you, because the more you say on this score, the more they'll write about your instability.

The press, as Towey's remarks show, is the agent that brings many of the feelings of shame and powerlessness. Sometimes this harm comes from particular press techniques, which are not always as visible as a stakeout on the front lawn or a microphone thrust into the face of one of the family's children. The invasion's landing craft is often the ordinary telephone. Journalists are very good at ferreting out even the most closely held home telephone numbers. They call at all hours. Some of them do not give their names, thinking that by not identifying themselves they have a better chance of drawing a beleaguered official to his telephone doom. Soon, each ring of the phone comes to remind those inside the home fortress how very vulnerable they are to the hostility of the world outside.

These manipulative techniques would not be so galling, though, were it not for the corrosive character of the news stories they produce. From the point of view of our politics as a whole, the way the press behaves in a major political scandal is often worrisome; but to the people written about, it is searing. "It's the labels," a spouse began explaining the personal effects of the experience. "They'll never mention his name now without the label 'former Iran-contra figure.' "

In addition, scandal press coverage exposes not just the event itself but the personal life of the official involved. Some journalists in these circumstances think it permissible to report on anything from the official's alcoholism to the most delicious facts about his sexual habits or video-renting practices. "I was astonished," said one scandal figure who had been burned, "at how much private information others can learn about you from public places like police stations and telephone companies, and I was even more astonished at how many people are willing to report it."

These details give outsiders a great deal of knowledge about the private life of the official and his or her family. One woman, during a time when her husband's name was too often in the press, visited a possible elementary school for their child in the coming term. When she announced her errand, the school's admissions officer looked at her skeptically and said, "Do you think you're really going to be here next year?" This sort of publicity creates great anxiety in individuals at having to face the world without ever being sure of what strangers have read or heard about their weaknesses or personal lives. Lyn Nofziger, after the end of his Wedtech-related scandal, described the feeling: "You walk down the street wondering what people know."

The publicity brings not just embarrassment but further social isolation. From the point of view of those involved, the path of a scandal is usually marked by personal betrayals. First on the list of those who act badly come most of the journalists whom an official may have considered friends back in pre-scandal days. "We only lost one friend," said a spouse in recalling her family's scandal experience, and she named a prominent columnist. When the troubles came, she said, and her husband needed support from the press, this writer who had seemed so close somehow could manage to write only a single grudging and backhanded defense of his buddy. "It was more general than that, though," said the wife, her hurt still apparent. "He just did not look at the things that were happening to us from a friend's point of view."

Another wife described the same kind of long-lasting pain. One seemingly friendly journalist, she remembered,

> said he was going to write a piece supporting us. Then he didn't. Later he apologized to my husband for not writing it. [My husband] was pleased with that. I had a different view. Why should this guy get credit for an apology? How does this make up for the harm he caused us by not writing when he said he would and when we needed him?

Even with journalists who are not special friends, the objects of news coverage are often startled by what they see as personal treachery. Officials and their families are furious long after the fact over what journalists think they can do to another human being's life without being held morally accountable. "This was an aspect of Washington," said a spouse, "that I've gotten to feel more bitter about. They say, 'We can beat you up one day and have a drink with you and slap you on the back the next, and that makes everything all right.' Well, it doesn't to me."

One normally tranquil wife of a scandal-plagued official said that even years after the event her feelings—"pure venom," she called them—had barely cooled. "For a long time afterward," she said, "I wanted to meet [the reporter who covered the scandal]. At first I wanted to hit him. Then I decided," she went on sweetly, "that I'd just like to go up to him and tell him he's going to burn in hell." The behavior of journalists like this one, she said, was "pure immorality." They insisted that they were only doing their job, "but . . . they're ruining families' lives. Why don't they ever put themselves in their victims' place? Who gave them the right not to?"

The government tends to behave toward a scandal-plagued official in approximately the same way journalists do. If an official involved in scandal was a member of the executive branch, he or she often lists the president and his top aides as a big source of personal nonsupport. "The White House," said one woman sarcastically about the president's staff during a scandal in which she was involved, "was, shall we say, not communicating. In fact they cut and ran."

The response by the political bosses is not always so cynical. If a president has a personal tie to an official in trouble, the disengagement will be longer in coming. In general, though, presidential staffers have increasingly been taught that their job is to keep the president as far as possible from the scene of a political scandal. Today the risk of supporting an official in scandal trouble is greater than ever, since such aid may well be portrayed as a high-level, Watergate-style coverup.

As for congressmen investigating a scandal, the family of an official involved will often see them in a public hearing that is being televised. Because these congressmen want to appear before the cameras looking prepared, coherent, and full of a satisfactory amount of indignation toward the miscreants sitting before them, the lawmakers are especially and visibly dependent on their staff aides. Family members sitting at one of these hearings see a questioning process that is full of artful planning and devoid of genuine, spontaneous anger.

"There was this aide there, Peter Galbraith [on the staff of the Senate Foreign Relations Committee, chaired by Senator Claiborne Pell (D-R.I.)]," said one relative in remembered shock. "He would keep handing the senator material and whispering in his ear. And the senator would do nothing but read the stuff, sometimes even stopping at the wrong places in the text." Under these circumstances it is no wonder that the congressmen's moral outrage seems merely manufactured for public consumption. The targets and their families do not accept this fact of life easily.

The smell of hypocrisy is even stronger when such officials and their families see congressmen talking very differently in private from the way they do in public. One spouse remembered bitterly, "After all the public cruelty, [one of the senators] had the nerve to say after the hearing, in private, that he was sorry it had all happened and that the next time [my husband] came before him, he would treat him well." Gaps between public and private behavior that are tolerable in everyday politics are enraging to individuals being destroyed by congressmen's public professions of indignation.

As for the friends of an official in trouble, many commit their small acts of betrayal one by one. A few remain loyal. "The people who were supportive," remembered one spouse, "were the *old* friends we had here." Even longtime friends sometimes sidle toward the door. One spouse of a Reagan administration official who lived through a minor scandal remembered that during the family's troubles, "There was an old friend of [my husband's] who moved here to Washington. It wasn't until eight months after the scandal was over that he told us he was here." The spouse had an even worse example to report: "A friend from college actually wrote a nasty letter telling [my husband] that he had betrayed all the principles of decency."

Those Washington colleagues who are not good friends disappear even faster. In the spring of 1991 Teicher recalled that when he had tried to get a job after being forced out of the White House during Iran-contra, a number of his fellow policy analysts in think tanks around Washington "wouldn't return my phone calls." An executive of one such institute, Teicher remembered, "said I couldn't go to their study groups because I might embarrass them."

Unlike most others in his situation, Teicher survived to see the wheel of fortune come around again. In the White House he had been a hard-liner against U.S. overtures to Iraq, and during the Persian Gulf crisis his expertise was rediscovered. "I got inundated," he smiled ironically. "First by the PBS's of the world, then even by the U.S. networks, and finally in the current issue of *Time*."

One longtime Washingtonian, wife of a man hit by scandal, was both philosophical and cynical about the process:

> Scandal behavior is just an extreme version of the way Washington behaves anyway—that is, according to whether you're in or out of power. In Washington you have a lot of acquaintances that you may see a lot of, at the dinners and parties you're invited to. You may like them, and you pretend you're real friends. But when you leave a high government post, especially under the circumstances [my husband] did, the invitations start to dry up.

She paused, and her detachment left her: "[Y]ou're especially grateful when someone prominent and powerful makes a point of inviting you to something and not leaving you out of things."

This is not to say that a public figure struck by scandal is always ostracized in the obvious sense. At social gatherings, people do not actually turn their backs on the besmirched individual. We long ago lost the sense of public propriety needed to do such things, and scandal has become so prevalent in national politics today that it has been robbed of some of its status as a badge of shame.

Still, many of the Washington acquaintances who are civil or even seemingly understanding toward a scandal-ridden official stop well short of being willing to defend him publicly or run any risks on his behalf. One prominent indictee was told that when his legal troubles became public, the talk about him at Washington parties was sympathetic. "A lot of people were nice in private," he replied bitterly. "But I did not get one word of public support from any of them."

If an official has children, the weight of a scandal is much harder to bear. Sometimes it is pure pain to hear how children are affected by one of these crises. "One evening I was sitting in front of the TV with my son, who was 12," Deaver remembered,

> and the news about my case came on. I asked him if he minded that I was being called an alcoholic, and he said no. Then I asked him if he minded my being called a liar, and the tears spilled out. Children think the most important thing in the world is to tell the truth.

Sometimes in these circumstances parents start seeing obvious behavior problems in their children. At other times the changes are more subtle, especially if the children are young. "The other kids would say," said one mother recounting her child's experience at school, " 'I saw your daddy on TV,' or 'My mom and dad watched TV and saw your daddy.' " None of these kids seemed to comprehend that this meant trouble.

"But it was different with his teacher," the mother went on:

> She tried to be nice to him and to talk about it and be sympathetic. This didn't help. In fact it made things worse. I could see my child starting to act upset at home. When I finally figured it out, I had to go to school and tell her it would be better if she didn't try to talk about it.

Another mother said her children had escaped trouble at school because they and their friends were too young to know what was going on. "But were they affected?" she repeated the question with a laugh. "How could they not be, with me lying on the couch with hot packs on my back and cold packs on my head?

"The more serious problem," she went on, "comes as the children get older and we have to discuss the issue with them. Now [my husband] explains to them that he used to work for the president, and the president doesn't need him anymore."

Individuals who have lived through these scandals can sometimes look back on them with some detachment. When first hit by a scandal, though, almost no one reacts calmly. Even Nofziger, an individual of some equanimity, said of his experience, "For the first month or two, I was panicked." For those who are not so experienced, the initial panic can have disastrous consequences.

When Superfund head Rita Lavelle became embroiled in the EPA scandal of 1982–83, some of her fellow EPA employees accused her of having taken part in a Superfund decision involving her former employer, a company named Aerojet. The agency's attorneys made Lavelle affirm in a sworn statement that she had recused herself from the case one day after learning of Aerojet's possible involvement, but others insisted that she had waited for three weeks before doing so. The Justice Department had her indicted for perjury. She told the jury that when she first heard the news about Aerojet she did not believe it, and that she got real confirmation only three weeks later. She also said, somewhat inconsistently, that she had signed her sworn statement under pressure from EPA's lawyers. The jury was not impressed, Lavelle was convicted, and in 1985 she served four and a half months in a federal prison.

The original conflict-of-interest charge against Lavelle was minor league. She had made no actual decisions affecting her old company and had picked up no information likely to help it significantly. Yet as the criminal walls closed in on her, Lavelle panicked and threw herself into what the jury found to be a coverup much more serious than her original sin.

Lavelle's type of panic appears with increasing frequency in Washington figures hit by scandal. People accused of having done something wrong will always try, consciously or unconsciously, to reconstruct the event in question so as to put the best face on their actions. At a certain level of deliberateness, the process becomes coverup. Today's improved means of detection—more records, more agency openness, more invest-igators—make it more likely than before that the dissemblers will get caught. Further, in today's fearful climate, these indi-viduals will not find many people willing to protect them. And when a public figure in this situation becomes panicky, he or she is almost guaranteed to make a misstep and get blown up half-way through the minefield.

The coverup then becomes a scandal bigger than what the original malfeasance could ever have produced. There are even some prosecutors and investigators who deliberately manipulate this panic syndrome in order to get their quarry into additional trouble.

Telling individuals that they are about to become scandal tar-gets is a reliable way to make some of them behave scandal-ously. The more fearsome the threatened penalties, the higher the proportion of officials who will succumb. Thus do modern scandals beget still other scandals among those who are weak in character or short of luck.

After the initial shock, some officials and their families start to cope with their situation through aggressive openness. They em-brace their scandal as the dominant fact of their lives. For one group of the scandal ridden, the result of this embrace is obses-sion. Because they are forced to spend most of their time and energy defending themselves for months or years, the search for vindication becomes their career. It is sometimes the only one open to them.

They meticulously collect documents related to their case. They search out every lead that might give them information about bad motives or misconduct in those who pursued them. They come to have no subject of extended conversation except their scandal experience. They write articles that are not printed and letters that go unanswered. They collar friends, acquain-tances, government officials, and journalists, trying to get out-siders to listen to the details of the scandal and to understand how much injustice was done. As time goes on, fewer and fewer people are interested even in listening to them. Their isolation is compounded instead of alleviated.

Even when there is no obsession, a bout of scandal often

leaves an official or politician and his family anxious about themselves and bitter about Washington, politics, and public service. "Time doesn't really heal these things," said a spouse who had lived through a scandal. "Very gradually, it quiets down. But even now, every time we meet someone new, my husband feels he has to talk about it, to explain it and make sure the person doesn't just keep walking around with that label 'scandal' in his head."

She continued, "At one time, I wanted to leave Washington entirely. [My husband] thought we had to stay—that if we left, we'd leave government to those jerks. But I'm not impressed by Washington anymore. I'm a girl from a small town, and these are very important people, but I'm just not impressed anymore."

So scandal uproots lives and wreaks traumatic psychological damage in a wide variety of ways. But so what if the people involved in these scandals suffer? Why should we, as citizens or human beings, care about their allegedly tragic stories? In the opinion of a good number of the investigators, prosecutors, journalists, public interest groups, and assorted partisans of good government who conduct our modern scandal hunts, we should not care much at all.

Does the alleged perpetrator in one of these scandals find his ulcer acting up? Does his wife cry every day? Has his little boy recently set fire to the family dog? These details are interesting, of course. The lost job, the broken marriage, and the turn to alcohol are good entertainments and vivid examples of how the mighty can plummet. Yet, in the view of the scandal hunters, these personal problems should not be allowed to move us when we discuss ethics in government or decide how to treat a public figure involved in scandal. And such distress is certainly not the fault of all the sleuths, publicizers, and others on the case. They are only doing their job and fulfilling their obligations.

This attitude among the scandal hunters is exactly as it should be when they are dealing with the Al Capones of modern politics. Such malefactors certainly exist: Even now they are concocting large and larcenous schemes to defraud the government or taking bribes or falsifying records in ways that directly endanger the health, safety, and pocketbooks of their fellow citizens. But there are also the scandal targets who are moved simply by a more ordinary desire to cut a corner or who are in trouble mainly because of panic or gross imprudence. Each of these officials may well deserve some kind of sanction, but by no reasonable standard do such lapses merit application of the Capone rules. In these less heinous cases, the scandal hunters are not justified in wrapping themselves in the crime fighter's mantle and refusing to look at the faces of the individuals they pursue in search-and-destroy missions.

Most of today's invocations of the superprosecutor's code, it is safe to say, are not based on genuine necessity. Instead, most such citations of the Capone rules are based on the fear that more complicated good-faith moral reasoning would lead to more leniency. These rules are very convenient for people who move forward in their careers or fulfill their own political or psychic needs by always pushing for the highest possible kill rate. This reality is one of the dirty secrets behind much of the high-minded talk about the need to be stringent in enforcing ethics in government.

When scandal entrepreneurs operate in this way, the result is a moral disproportion between crime and punishment, and the imbalance is sometimes huge. A classic case is that of Rep. Geraldine Ferraro, a congresswoman from Queens since 1979 who ran for vice president on the Democratic ticket with Walter Mondale in 1984.

When Ferraro was nominated, she looked like a politically shrewd choice: She would add excitement to Mondale's underdog campaign, and her style and politics did not automatically raise the hackles of cultural conservatives in the way that those of some other well-known political women did. As soon as she was nominated, the press began subjecting her to massive attention. "I was an unknown," she explained several years later, "and the first woman in this position." *The Philadelphia Inquirer,* she said, had sent "at least a dozen" investigative reporters out on her story, thus judging her the equivalent of a large natural disaster. Besides the twelve from *The Inquirer, The Wall Street Journal* contributed six reporters, *The Washington Post* five and *The New York Times* five.[2]

In New York City all the seats in the usually quiet Hall of Records were jammed after the nomination with reporters searching for housing code violations in buildings owned or managed by Ferraro's husband, real estate developer John A. Zaccaro. Journalists combed the rolls of Zaccaro's tenants and the lists of Ferraro's past campaign contributors for Italian-sounding names that might belong to underworld characters. The sheer size of this press coverage fed the notion that there must be a big story in there somewhere. That conviction, in turn, made each suspicious tidbit look significant and worth printing.

The investigating journalists first discovered from public records that at the very beginning of her career in Congress Ferraro had run into trouble with the federal campaign finance laws. In her 1978 campaign she had taken a $130,000 loan from her husband and children. The Federal Elections Commission subsequently declared the loan illegal, and Ferraro repaid it. Another, more serious, financial problem quickly emerged. Ferraro had declared on one of her financial disclosure forms, those gifts to American journalism, that she would not report assets belonging to her husband because they were separate from hers. But she had also listed herself as an officer and stockholder of her husband's real estate firm.

"It was not clear," *The New York Times* put it delicately, "how Ferraro could be an officer and stockholder of her husband's company without deriving or expecting to derive any economic benefit from his assets."[3] House Republicans and conservative organizations asked the Justice Department and the House ethics committee to investigate. It was hard to remember that only 20 years previously, President Lyndon Johnson had insisted that the Texas broadcasting station KTBC, owned by his wife, posed no conflict-of-interest problems for him, and most journalists and politicians had taken him at his word.

Soon after the uproar over her husband's assets, controversy broke Ferraro's stride again. The candidate said she would release her tax returns. Her husband would release a statement about his tax returns, she added, but not the returns themselves. Ferraro joked about her husband's sensitivity on this point, saying, "You people married to Italian men, you know what it's like."[4] The joke was clearly benign in motive, but old-style ethnic humor, once a staple of American political conversation, had no place in the new era of heightened sensitivities. Ferraro got a cascade of huffy criticism for ethnic stereotyping. "For the Democrats," liberal columnist Mary McGrory wrote, "the euphoria is gone. The honeymoon is over."[5]

Ferraro regained momentum after the tax return controversy and kept it, to all appearances, for the rest of the presidential campaign. FERRARO'S CROWD APPEAL SEEMS TO SURVIVE STORM,[6] one typical headline put it. But the probing into her finances had begun to spread like a metastasizing cancer, and new charges against her and her husband kept appearing. The most sinister was the suggestion that the two of them were connected to organized crime. *New York* magazine reported that a corporation controlled by Zaccaro had once owned a building listed as the address of a Gambino crime syndicate underboss.[7] *The Washington Post* weighed in later with the news that a Zaccaro-owned building in Little Italy housed Star Distribution, a pornography dealer "with alleged links to the Gambino organized crime family."[8]

One reporter, Jonathan Kwitny of *The Wall Street Journal*, had questions about whether Zaccaro's father, dead 13 years, had been connected with the mob. Kwitny could not get answers from the Mondale-Ferraro campaign, so he printed his queries in the form of an article in the newspaper. He wanted explanations for suspicious circumstances such as the fact that Ferraro's father-in-law had had his gun license confiscated in 1957 because of connections to "a notorious crime leader, Joseph Profaci."[9] Such facts "could have innocent explanations," Kwitny commented in a later story. "But if they were innocent, why couldn't we be provided the answers?"[10]

The reason the campaign had stopped responding to such questions was, Ferraro later said, that "we had learned that for each of those questions we answered, we created another 20." The Kwitny piece upset her more than any of the previous accusations. "I'm hurt for my mother and my mother-in-law," she said. "These are two elderly women. What in God's name did they ever do to anyone to deserve this type of thing? . . . I'll make it up to them. I'll spend the next 50 years making it up to my husband and his mother and my mother."[11]

By the last part of the campaign, all this scandal reporting on Ferraro had begun to produce concrete troubles for her family. In August a New York court held a hearing on Zaccaro's behavior as the court-appointed conservator of an elderly woman's estate. The previous year Zaccaro had borrowed funds from the estate at commercial interest rates. Six months later Zaccaro was told that the loan was improper and paid the money back. Because Zaccaro had been advised—wrongly and, it was later discovered, by a disbarred lawyer—that the loan was proper, the hearing judge absolved the candidate's spouse of any dishonesty. But Zaccaro was removed from the conservator's job anyway. Scores of journalists were in the courtroom to witness the decision.

Soon afterward, in September 1984, the House ethics committee opened its formal investigation into Ferraro's treatment of her husband's income on her financial disclosure forms. In yet another arena, word leaked out that the Manhattan district attorney's office was investigating one of Zaccaro's real estate deals.

Mondale lost the election in November. By then, though, the trouble train was traveling on its own steam. Before it was through it made a lot of stops. In January 1985, Zaccaro pleaded guilty to a misdemeanor fraud charge for inflating a statement of his financial worth in getting financing for one of his real estate clients. The project had been handled by the same attorney who provided the advice about the conservatorship loan, and Ferraro later recalled that Zaccaro had pleaded guilty because, as their attorney had pointed out to them, the case would have cost $500,000 to fight in court. She regretted the plea: It made the family seem like an easy target for the other prosecutors and enforcers who followed.

In the first effect of the plea, the real estate licensing board decided to hold a public hearing in April 1985 on whether to take away Zaccaro's license. Zaccaro told the board about the disbarred lawyer and said that because of the upheavals caused by the 1984 presidential campaign, "I have to start my business all over again. I think I've suffered enough. I want to go back to work."[12] But in June 1985, his license was suspended for 90 days.

The Justice Department was conducting its own criminal investigation of Ferraro's campaign finances, and by December 1985, the probe was 16 months old and still not finished. Ferraro was forced to announce that she would not run in the 1986 New York senatorial race against Senator Alfonse D'Amato. The next month, Justice Department sources let it be known that the department had no plans to prosecute her.

Much worse was to come. Less than a month after the Justice Department declared the criminal investigation of Ferraro moribund, local police in Middlebury, Vermont, arrested her son, John A. Zaccaro, Jr., who was then attending Middlebury College, for selling a quarter gram of cocaine to a female undercover police officer who had gone to his apartment to make the buy. Local police publicized the arrest and told the journalists who quickly converged on Middlebury that the younger Zaccaro was a major dealer, although this accusation was never substantiated. When Ferraro and her husband arrived in Middlebury for a pretrial hearing, they found a large group of reporters and photographers waiting for them outside the courthouse. "You people haven't changed," she said. "You guys are all vultures,"[13] he added.

John Jr.'s lawyer asked for dismissal of the charges, arguing that his client was being prosecuted selectively because his mother was so well known. The state's attorney countered—successfully—that prosecuting well-known people in order to attract publicity was not unconstitutional. The young man was convicted and served three months under house arrest.

By the time of the cocaine trial, the family was in even more serious trouble. In October 1986, the Queens district attorney indicted John Zaccaro, Sr., on charges of attempting to solicit a bribe in 1981 from a cable TV company trying to get a city cable franchise. When the case finally came to trial a year later, the man the prosecutors claimed had been threatened by Zaccaro said that Zaccaro had not made a threat or demanded a bribe but only warned him about "a process that was corrupt."[14]

After Zaccaro was acquitted, the prosecutor, Paul W. Pickelle, commented on the outcome of the case by reciting the creed of the modern prosecuting attorney: "We have no apologies for bringing this case. We'd much rather be explaining why we brought it and lost than why we never brought it at all."[15] It was as if prosecution were transcendently valuable, like honor or love itself.

The sheer prominence of the Zaccaro clan evoked a special type of behavior from every public institution the family dealt with in Washington, in the national press, in the Vermont criminal justice system, and back home in New York. After Zaccaro's first legal case, for instance, the real estate licensing board could have simply fined him as it often did in such cases. It did not have to hold a public hearing. Yet anything less than an open hearing and a suspension ran the post-Watergate danger of being called a mere slap on the wrist. As for the cocaine conviction of Ferraro's son, half the first offenders convicted of this charge in Vermont served no time and got off with a suspended sentence. State criminal justice officials said afterward that the young man's sentence was unusually stiff.[16] But any leniency would have aroused complaint. Indeed, even his serving his time under Vermont's house arrest program provoked protest: It was said that he was being allowed to cool his heels in too nice an apartment.

Finally, when it came to the elder Zaccaro's indictment bribery, one attorney familiar with the way the charges arose observed that they were definitely related to the family's being so well known. "There's [press] coverage," said the lawyer, "and then the rumor mill gets going, and then there are always those trying to ingratiate themselves with law enforcement officials. . . . So the system tends to focus on high-visibility cases."

Were Ferraro and her family without sin? By no means. Did her experience blight her life forever? No: By 1991 she was publicly contemplating a run against New York Republican senator Alfonse M. D'Amato, himself under investigation by the Senate ethics committee, which recommended no action against him. Should we let concern for widows and orphans stop us from trying to catch crooks? Of course not. Yet nowadays our whole scandal-production system is beautifully engineered to allow its personnel to avoid considering these human factors at all. The reporter is only going where the facts lead him and doing what his editor tells him to do. The editor is only putting his trust in his reporters and acting aggressively enough to meet the competition. The investigator is only bringing information to the attention of the proper authorities and fighting off encroachment on his territory by other investigative agencies and committees. The prosecutors are only putting the facts before the judge.

Probably few of the people who pursued Ferraro actually set out to condemn the family to the vast purgatory of real and threatened sanctions in which they were trapped for almost five years. Still, none of these pursuers felt obligated to think about whether the punishments they sought were becoming disproportionate to whatever misdeeds the family had committed. In other words, none of the hunters would admit to any ordinary ethical obligations.

If the number of our modern political scandals and the punishments meted out in them are disproportionate to what is deserved, we clearly have something to worry about. But how many of these excesses really exist? Isn't the plea for understanding actually an apologia for the Republican executive branch appointees who quite properly fell into scandal trouble during the Reagan years? Isn't the call for moderation merely a screen for the defense of well-off white-collar criminals already treated too lightly when compared with poorer, less powerful people who become enmeshed in the criminal justice system?

The charge of pro-Republican or pro-executive bias in a book like this one might have seemed cutting five years ago. By now, though, the growing numbers of Democrats and legislators involved in these imbroglios have clearly shown that modern political scandal is not a party phenomenon. The other issue—that of whether it is seemly to criticize harshness toward high-level offenders when common criminals are treated worse—is more substantial. The problem has too many parts for this book to encompass. They include the question of deterrence, for instance, and the extent to which people can justifiably be singled out for harsh treatment, especially in the criminal justice system, as an example to others. The questions also include the debate over whether or not crimes of physical violence pose a special danger to society and demand surer, more severe punishment than peaceable frauds do. And those who deal with the issue must face the question of whether it is an "illusion," as Murray Kempton recently put it, "that injustice to the poor can be remedied by even severer injustice to the rich."[17]

Yet we can address one part of the question by first agreeing, as we probably do, that punishments ought to vary with the gravity of the offense. We should also be able to agree that the more severe the sanction involved, the stronger an official's claim that he or she should receive no worse than equal treatment with others who are accused of similar misdeeds. And when we deal with today's scandals, it is not impossible to say something about just how bad these misdeeds are. As one approximation, I divided the 80-odd scandal-plagued individuals in this book into a half-dozen categories.

First came scandals involving serious misconduct that would also have seemed quite serious, say, 50 years ago. This category encompassed the Abscam defendants like Rep. Michael (Ozzie) Myers, people convicted of perjury such as Rita Lavelle and Michael Deaver, and those guilty of crimes of violence, like John Mack. I counted 30 of these. It is highly unlikely, we must remember, that the public would ever have learned about most of these sins in previous eras, either because we did not then have investigative resources like an FBI committed to exposing public corruption or because people did not discuss the private behavior of politicians and officials in today's detail. This fact does not detract from the seriousness of the offenses, but it must be part of any judgment we make about the moral caliber of our own day compared with that of times past.

In a second category I put scandals involving similarly genuine but distinctly less serious sins. These included Peter Bourne's writing a prescription on behalf of a nonexistent patient, Douglas Ginsburg's past use of marijuana, and Gary Hart's dalliance with Donna Rice. By my lights, 12 of the scandals fell into this category.

In the third and fourth categories were scandals based on actions that were treated as misconduct primarily because recently changed rules and standards declared them to be so. These changes sometimes involved what is now thought of as serious behavior, as with Robert McFarlane's misleading Congress in the Iran-contra affair or Jim Wright's leaning extremely hard on federal regulators in the savings and loan area. There were eight of these. Sometimes changing the rules of conduct made scandal fodder of more minor matters, like Joseph Wright's phone call to the Department of Energy or Mark Hatfield's letter for Basil Tsakos. There were, by my count, seven of these.

There were some scandals in which the officials involved were by and large not guilty of the charges against them but must be considered at significant fault for the notably flawed judgment they displayed. These would include Anne Burford in the EPA scandal and Edwin Meese in some of his financial dealings. I counted six of these.

Last came the scandals that involved, in the end, no persuasive evidence of significant misconduct. To my mind, this category would include cases like those of James Beggs and Theodore Olson. I found eight of these.

The above numbers have no real precision, for any reader of this book would argue with at least some of the judgments I made about what scandals belonged in which categories. A few of the individuals involved here were admirable. Of others it might be said that they and their scandals deserved each other. Some apparently got their entire political education on another planet. Still, sorting the scandals in this way makes two things fairly clear. First, when people judge our era a scandalous one, they do so largely on the basis of scandals that would not have come to being in any time but our own. Some of the change has come about because of rising ethical standards among the public. Much more has stemmed from the operations of our new, improved scandal machine and its cogs. Second, a significant part of our current scandals—almost half, I would say—involves offenses that in the larger scheme of things simply do not pose any great danger to the republic.

The narrow vision necessary for pursuing the big crimes can be immoral when applied to cases of wrongdoing that occurred long ago or were minor or stemmed from some combination of cross-pressures such as panic, avoidance of responsibility, and self-delusion.

After an observer watches the scandal hunters behave repeatedly with a characteristic moral blindness and realizes that their narrow perspective serves their private interests very well, the punishments meted out in many scandals come to seem arbitrary. Those who play the hounds do not look at all ethically superior to those who end up as hares. The very idea of ethics in government, as enforced today, comes to seem worthy of profound cynicism.

To say that the pursuit of politicians and their wrongdoing is a morally complex enterprise is only to begin the debates that are possible on these issues. We can disagree about which offenses by political figures merit the most severe type of treatment. We can argue over the extent to which individuals accept tougher rules of punishment when they choose to have public careers. These questions are wholly legitimate ones. But before we can discuss them we must ask a prior question: How much moral responsibility do the scandal hunters bear toward their human targets? And the answer cannot always be "none."

CHAPTER 11

A CULTURE OF MISTRUST

I**F THE CONCERN** with how scandal targets get treated is not a frivolous one, neither is worrying about the substantial costs that these scandals have imposed on our politics and government.

Nowadays we often hear the argument that even if the federal government as a whole is honest, the performance of government has fallen in quality because there has been a decline in the intellectual and ethical quality of high-level political appointees. Those who take this position often argue that Ronald Reagan is at fault, because he denigrated the importance of government and thus made it a place attractive only to the ambitious and morally deficient. Critics cite episodes like the HUD scandal as a sign of how far we have fallen. They long for the days of great public servants like President Franklin D. Roosevelt's brain trusters or the post–World War II foreign-policy establishment.

Albert Hunt, Washington bureau chief of *The Wall Street Journal* and a close observer of the capital for more than 20 years, recently said of this unease, "The Reagan appointees weren't sleazier. But they had more ethical insensitivity and not as much reverence for government." As Hunt suggests, the changed ethos that upsets today's critics is not simply a sign of personal corruption. There is indeed a problem of quality in government today, but it has more numerous and complicated roots. And the solutions put forward by ethics-minded reformers will make the situation worse.

The number of political appointees in the federal government has grown in the past quarter century, in absolute terms and when compared with the government as a whole: This was a period in which civilian employment in the federal government was relatively stable but the number of presidential appointees subject to Senate confirmation more than tripled.[1] Turnover in such positions has also grown. As a result, people in these jobs are now a less elite group than they used to be and, just as important, a younger and less seasoned one. In addition, the Reagan election of 1980 brought an especially large turnover at the political level and an influx of new, untutored appointees to Washington. When such revolutions take place, the old guard can be counted on to complain that the new people have no class, morals, or taste in neckties. In the case of the Reagan turnover, this clash was made more acute and visible by the active hostility of important bureaucrats to the Reaganite policies that came with the new appointees.

In addition, we saw more of the weaknesses of the appointees of the 1980s because of the reforms of the 1970s. The decline of political parties, fat cats, and back rooms made it necessary for influence wielders to advertise the connections more widely. Post-Watergate disclosure rules and practices gave us more information about these people's personal and financial affairs.

Moreover, when we found these officials wanting, it was by holding them up to considerably higher standards than had ever been used before. In the post–World War II years, no one asked whether Dean Acheson had properly recused himself from State Department decisions directly affecting the huge oil, munitions, and communications companies he had represented while in private law practice. If we had been able to apply modern standards to Roosevelt brain trust member Thomas G. (Tommy the Cork) Corcoran, later a Washington lobbyist, he would probably have been under continuous indictment for offenses such as attempted bribery and conspiracy to make illegal campaign contributions.[2]

By contrast, in the spring of 1991, President Bush's chief of staff, John Sununu, became involved in a considerable scandal over whether he had misused his White House airplane and chauffeur for several trips that were personal or political rather than official in nature. Such behavior would simply not have been controversial in the pre-Watergate era. Even Clark Clifford, whose political perspicacity and survival skills were admired in Washington for some 40 years, has had the end of his career marred by a post-Watergate scandal involving questions about whether he lied to federal regulators about foreign ownership and control of a bank of which he was chairman.

So it is highly unlikely that the personnel problem of the 1980s has its roots in a fundamental moral decline among the political class and public officials. Our current personnel situation is a consequence of our general political condition and partly a sign of our moral progress. When critics of today's government ignore these factors and talk as if our politics were in a state of degeneracy, needing yet more correction, it is hard to escape the thought that their dissatisfaction with our public life and their distaste for the political component of it are probably perpetual.

Even a relatively clean sort of politics is, after all, modern democratic politics. It requires the building of coalitions, and what builds coalitions is doing favors. Therefore politics and government must sometimes treat people unequally and judge them by something other than a purist's notions of merit. Democratic politics also requires some degree of secrecy and duplicity, for no politician has ever succeeded in working a compromise without saying different things to people on different sides of a dispute. Finally, modern government requires a certain degree of competence and must recruit skilled individuals even if this means—as it often does—associating with the organizations that produce such personnel.

In the way we talk about our public life, as in our modern theories of political morality, we have become increasingly intolerant of these necessities and of the conventional politics of which they are a part. Back in 1962, when President John F. Kennedy was defending his secretary of agriculture, Orville Freeman, Kennedy expressed this general view of corruption in the American government: "We have over two million employees, you've got a good many people that take advantage or attempt to influence them to seek private gain—a good many of the decisions that these men make involve large sums of money, contracts, and all the rest—pressures are put upon them. Some succumb. Most do not." Such acceptance of some corruption as the price of democratic politics is foreign to the spirit of today's ethics campaign.[3] We demand a politics of virtue and good motives. We are no longer satisfied with a public official's producing good results while not giving away the treasury. We also want to know that he has no ties to objectionable interest groups: He should not lunch with them too often or entertain thoughts of working for them after he leaves government. We no longer think it the right of these interest groups to help shape the public policies that affect them; we now speak of such influence as tantamount to corruption. We no longer accept the idea that a politician must be allowed to do some favors for his contributors so that we can maintain an electoral system not owned by the government; instead, we now hear the strong call for public financing of campaigns precisely so that the need for these favors can be obliterated.

It is no wonder that our scandals have come to resemble little more than primitive cleansing rituals through which we declare our intention to expel the impurity of politics from political life. Naturally, the banished politics, primordial ooze that it is, will reemerge somewhere, and the cycle of dissatisfaction will go on without end. It is just as unsurprising that our current scandals have done little to improve the performance of our government and have in some ways made it worse. If there is demoralization at the higher levels of politics and government today, it owes less to Ronald Reagan's ideology than to the more concrete workings of our new scandal system.

The great American scandal machine that we have built for ourselves is up and running with ferocious momentum. It is no longer merely a tool of partisan politics. Tightened rules and beefed-up corps of investigators guarantee that we will hear a steady stream of ethics charges. Congressmen and their staffs, dependent on the media, vie to turn these accusations into public drama. News organizations, increasingly competitive, stand ready to spread the word.

Though Republicans and Democrats have bloodied each other so badly with scandal politics that most of them would doubtless subside gladly into the peace of mutual assured destruction, too many people now have stakes in the scandal machine to let it run down. And as the routines of scandal making persist, they become more powerful, for increasing numbers of aspiring scandal hunters learn that they will never get ahead by displaying any hesitation in chasing after their quarry. They forget the very words with which to argue for leniency or a weighing of conflicting public goods or anything else that might stop the process.

The consequences are not trivial. Today's steep rise in public alienation is fed by incessant scandal, and our mistrust has created political habits and institutions whose workings are almost sure to produce more scandal and more mistrust. In addition, these scandals have made it harder for government to do a good job.

We have built ourselves a system that knows how to create a public outcry over even the appearance of an appearance of a conflict of interest but could not get itself interested in the policy sins that underlay our savings and loan crisis until Charles Keating had personalized it for us. We have invented a machine that will spend tens of millions of dollars to try to put Oliver North in jail while it strenuously ignores the systemic sores that caused the worst of the Iran-contra scandal and that continue to fester.

In each of these cases the great wrongs were those of politics and policy and should have produced a huge scandal by virtue of the incompetence involved. Instead, we seemed—and still seem—able to focus only on scandals of intention, moral failing, and criminal liability. In this sense, scandal hunting since Watergate has almost certainly made our government worse instead of better; in our pursuit of more virtuous politics and government we have fallen into a deep trap.

The new conditions have made things considerably worse by making it harder to recruit senior officials to the federal government. A vivid example of one reason for the difficulty is the case of John C. Shepherd. On April 5, 1988, Attorney General Edwin Meese offered the post of deputy attorney general to Shepherd, an eminently respectable St. Louis attorney and a past president of the American Bar Association. The day after the selection was announced, Shepherd's hometown newspaper, the *St. Louis Post-Dispatch*, ran a story on the nomination, including charges that had recently been made against the attorney by a 29-year-old ex-bookkeeper with his law firm who was improbably named Denise Sinner.[4] The firm had accused Sinner of embezzling

$147,000 from its coffers. Sinner protested that Shepherd had let her take the money because the two were having a love affair. A jury, not impressed by her story, had already found her guilty. Shepherd had told Meese of the incident.

"A former bookkeeper convicted of embezzlement," that day's UPI story began, ". . . reiterated her charges. . . ." Sinner "was found guilty last month . . . but is appealing the conviction."[5] In this version of the story, the verdict sounded like an open question. The *Post-Dispatch* next reported in a front-page story that Sinner would be willing to testify at Shepherd's confirmation hearing.[6] The day after that, *The New York Daily News* made Sinner's charges into a banner headline.[7] Two days later, the *Post-Dispatch* reported on the *Daily News* coverage.[8]

The *Post-Dispatch* quoted a Senate Judiciary Committee staffer saying the controversy could be serious for Shepherd, because it "has to do with credibility."[9] Then another news account reported ominously that Shepherd had been selected "without the customary White House clearance and FBI background checks."[10] Reports of Shepherd's imminent withdrawal began to circulate, and on April 20, he finally withdrew his name, citing intolerable pressures on himself and his family. The same day, the *Post-Dispatch* reported that it had investigated Sinner's account of her background and found nearly every one of her assertions about it to be false. Sinner's judge, when sentencing her 10 days later, called her a "pathological liar."[11]

Sinner's unsupported charges had bounced around from one news outlet to another, picking up altitude and velocity each time. Senate Judiciary Committee staffers and their White House counterparts had given Shepherd no support and even fueled the fire. This story of nonsupport for the nominee became big news in the general and legal press, and individuals interested in government service who read the tale were almost certain to ask themselves whether going to Washington might not be slightly less attractive than serving a tour of duty on a police bomb squad.

In conversation not long ago, Charles G. Untermeyer, then President George Bush's director of personnel, explained that it is getting hard to fill high-level government posts partly because the scandal machine puts such obstacles in the way of people who want to serve. The near certainty of hostile questioning in the Senate means that the FBI must check each nominee's background with special care. The special care takes extra time, and the extra time allows opponents to do a better job of mobilizing against a nominee. If new allegations against a nominee emerge at any point during the confirmation process, the administration must investigate each one thoroughly or open itself to the charge of coverup. These new constraints have generated new abuses. For instance, Untermeyer said, "It is now known that if you want to stop a nomination, you can do so by sending anonymous letters." He noted that such accusations have already held up several high-level appointments.

Untermeyer also gave a compendium of reasons why potential appointees these days, including some of the most talented, reject the idea of government service even before any nomination:

> It's the totality of all the disincentives that keeps people out of government. . . . [Low] pay is part of it—though I've never thought of that as number one, since everyone takes that for granted. . . . There's the financial disclosure requirement and the divestiture requirement. Then there are the postgovernment employment restrictions, which mean that some people can't return to the field from which they were recruited. With the post of under secretary of defense for acquisitions, there are legends about the number of people they had to talk to in order to fill the job. This was a classic example of the postemployment problem: The person who holds this job deals with *everything* in the way of acquisitions. It would be hard to find a postgovernment employer he *hadn't* dealt with.

The current atmosphere not only keeps some people from going into government but helps push government employees out the door. In 1989, when the most recent legislative attempt was made to tighten the revolving-door rules, agencies reported a spate of high-level retirements. People said they wanted to leave before the new code went into effect because the new rules were so confusing that you could never tell when you might be in criminal jeopardy. The outcry was so loud that the administration, in a highly unusual move, got Congress to back off the project temporarily as part of a budget compromise. Rep. John Conyers, Jr. (D-Mich.), chairman of the House committee that had produced the new rules, said, "We have given the procurement process back to the companies that have brought us Operation Ill Wind and similar scandals."[12]

The fear among civil servants over how ethics rules will be interpreted is not paranoia. Consider the recent case of a doctor and researcher who worked for the National Institutes of Health. He was a gifted specialist who had always kept a small private practice, to which his colleagues often sent difficult cases. When he was appointed to an administrative post, he voluntarily began to close down his private practice, except for those patients whom he thought he could not transfer to other physicians in good medical conscience.

Executive-branch rules then changed and forbade administrators like this doctor to have any outside income. The government's now-substantial ethics bureaucracy interpreted this to mean that while the doctor could treat his remaining patients, he could not take any money from them. The doctor offered to stop charging these patients for anything but the cost of the malpractice insurance he had to carry in order to maintain a private practice. The ethics officials said this would not do: There was no provision in the rules for taking expenses into account in this way. The issue ricocheted inconclusively among agency, department, and White House ethics officials for five years, during which our researcher, still in government, routinely received job offers to run major medical schools at twice or three times his existing salary.

As of this writing the great and grave issue is still unresolved. It is hard to know how to characterize all this application of bureaucratic energy except as organized lunacy. More recently, a glitch in the process produced new ethics regulations that forbade federal employees in general to earn any outside income at all for speaking or writing, even if it was on a subject totally unrelated to their government jobs. An amendment was promised to correct the mistake. Given the spirit of the times, it is not hard to see how the oversight occurred.[13]

Even experienced Washington hands can be forced out by the

scandal machine. In the spring of 1989 Richard Armitage, assistant secretary of defense for national security affairs and the Bush administration's choice to become secretary of the army, resigned his job and withdrew his name from consideration for the army post. Defense Secretary Richard Cheney accepted the resignation "with profound regret," Washingtonese for "I'm not just saying I'm sorry. I really *am* sorry." It is no wonder: Armitage was a widely respected figure, an Annapolis graduate who had served in Vietnam, been in public service for many years, and won the Defense Department's highest civilian award four times.

Yet over a long career in government any official piles up some troublesome pieces of history, and Armitage was no exception. For instance, there was the great stationery scandal of 1984. In that year Washington-area police arrested a Vietnamese restaurant owner for operating an illegal football pool. Armitage knew the woman from the days when she had run a restaurant in Saigon, and her lawyer asked him to write the judge a letter—a proper thing to do—identifying himself, explaining that gambling is socially acceptable among the Vietnamese, and asking that the woman's offense be viewed accordingly. Armitage wrote the letter, not only identifying himself but also doing so on his Department of Defense stationery. During 1986 and 1987 columnist Jack Anderson wrote no fewer than four pieces castigating Armitage for the incident.

Armitage also had a more serious entanglement. He was one of the senior government officials trying to get the Vietnamese government to account for all American soldiers who might be prisoners of war or were still missing in action in Vietnam. The atmosphere around the issue was filled with rumors, bitterness, and charges that the U.S. government was not doing enough. One of the less reputable critics accused Armitage of being involved in the drug trade in Southeast Asia from the mid- to late seventies. The charge was bizarre: During most of the years when Armitage was said to have been in Bangkok running a drug ring, he was actually sitting in an office on Capitol Hill working for Senator Robert Dole (R-Kans.). But the charge had been made before—by an organization called the Christic Institute as part of a massive conspiracy suit, later thrown out of court, against officials connected with American policy in Central America. And in early 1987, around the time of the great stationery scandal, Texas entrepreneur H. Ross Perot, who was doing free-lance work on the POW/MIA issue, repeated some of the charges to then-vice president George Bush in an attempt to force Armitage out of office.

Meanwhile, as Armitage prepared to go to the Senate for confirmation in his new job, he and the Bush administration were involved in a policy quarrel with Senator Jesse Helms (R-N.C.) over whether Japan should be allowed to codevelop this country's FSX fighter aircraft. Helms wanted to use the confirmation process to push the administration toward a more protectionist position. Armitage soon heard from friends on the Hill that certain staffers were out to get him; one Helms aide had already asked the Defense Intelligence Agency for information on Armitage and the POW/MIA issue, saying he wanted the material for the confirmation proceedings. Cheney heard that some were going to try to make the nomination "another Tower."

Armitage, educated by experience, foresaw what would happen: In a confirmation hearing, unfriendly senators would start by asking hostile policy questions. Then some senator would raise Jack Anderson's charges and question Armitage's personal morality. By the time the hearings got around to the drug-running story, even this accusation might look plausible. The Christic Institute zealots who had originally made it would try to use the hearing as a way to get maximum media exposure for themselves and their ideas.

Knowing these things, Armitage opted out. He did not mean to stay away from government forever; indeed, in 1990, President Bush would make him representative to the negotiations on U.S. bases in the Philippines. But in 1989, Armitage recognized that conditions were life threatening. It had become easy to make a highly visible scandal out of even the most grotesque charges born on the shadiest fringes of our politics. As a result, government service had become a much more dangerous place. "Combat is a little easier," Armitage compared Washington with his war experience. "The fight is a little fairer."

You cannot get an exact count of people who leave government or stay out of it in the first place for reasons like these. Champions of our new system of ethics and exposure claim that the horror stories point to a problem that does not really exist: If

certain sensitive souls think they are too good to subject themselves to the requirements for holding high federal office today,
plenty of other people out there will be happy to take those
federal jobs.

Of course there will always be applicants for high-level federal
positions, at both civil service and political levels. But are the
willing candidates good enough? By the time we know the answer, it may be somewhat late to make corrections.

The current atmosphere causes worries not just for those coming and going but for those at work inside government agencies.
One of the biggest problems has to do with paper. People inside
government are afraid to make an honest written record of their
actions for fear that some enemy will get hold of it and use it to
damage them. "The clearest effect [of the current atmosphere],"
one political appointee in the State Department put it, "is that
things that used to get written down do not get written down."
Another government manager said:

> We joke all the time about not taking notes. In fact a
> [House committee] staffer interrogated us not long ago
> on *why* we had no notes. When we do take notes, we
> dispose of them right away. If you want a written anal-
> ysis of a problem, you can't get one. I never even write
> in the margins of papers I'm reading without knowing
> that someone else may read the notes.

The official continued in a more serious vein: "It's very dis-
abling to decision-making. We have to make phone calls instead, and hold meetings. We're in meetings all the time."

Former solicitor general Charles Fried, who has himself never
been in the neighborhood of a government scandal, remarked
on the same widespread fear of making a paper record and told
how he saw it affecting officials' day-to-day operations. "Sometimes," he said, "when A writes a memo to B about something,
B doesn't write A a memo back."

"Why?" asked the author cooperatively.

"If B wrote A a memo back," Fried patiently explained,

> then a copy of A's memo would be in B's files, along
> with B's answer. And A would have to put a copy of his
> original memo in his files, along with B's answer.

Instead of all this, B will put his comment on the bottom of A's memo and send it back to him. If there's nothing more to be done, A is likely to wad the thing up and toss it in the wastebasket. It's a very convenient way to avoid making a record.

"But," Fried sighed, "the distortion of history involved in all this—now *that's* a scandal."

Charles Horner, who served as a Reagan appointee in the State Department and the U.S. Information Agency, remembered the time when in the course of his work he came upon a set of reports written by government science advisers during the Eisenhower administration. He marveled at how clear and frank they were. "I was astonished," he said:

> You never get something of this quality coming out of the federal government today. Then I realized why: In Eisenhower's time, when these people wrote, they were confident that what they said would stay secret. No more. Everyone writes everything thinking about how bad it could be made to look on the front page of *The New York Times* or *The Washington Post.* So we just don't get writing at this level of sophistication.

"And you can't substitute telephone calls," he added. "With some of these considerations, if they don't get written down they'll never be brought to bear on the process."

Getting good decisions out of government is hard under any circumstances. It is nearly impossible when officials speak to one another in a public language too mealymouthed to be of any use in making sensible choices. In a system that requires an approved, sanitized language even for internal written communications, officials who actually want to get their jobs done will be mightily tempted to do their most sensitive and important work through informal contacts or without written records.

The new system also brings other sorts of demoralization in its train. For one thing, officials simply spend a great deal of time and attention these days dealing with scandal or trying to prevent it. Dwight Ink, one of the country's leading experts in public administration, has served several tours of duty in the federal government. During the chaos of Watergate he was deputy administrator and then acting administrator of the General Services Administration. He had to deal with explosive subjects such as access to Nixon's Oval Office tapes, the improvements made by the government to Nixon's home in San Clemente, and the former president's gift of his papers to the federal archives in return for a controversial tax deduction.

Ink's most recent government assignment, ended in the fall of 1988, was as assistant administrator of the Agency for International Development. There are no systematic statistics, Ink said afterward, on how much time government executives spend dealing with the new ethics rules and conditions. But, he added, he has sometimes kept his own informal records of the way he spends his time on the job. During Watergate, he found that he was spending something over 30 percent of his time on issues involving the rules and procedures designed to prevent and deal with corruption and scandal. In his more recent job the figure ranged somewhere between 30 and 40 percent—and this was in a time of normal operations, with nothing like the crisis of Watergate on the agenda.

These numbers will come as no surprise to anyone who has served in government recently. And when a government executive is personally involved in a scandal, the proportion of time spent on it shoots skyward. As one Washington spouse remembered her husband's scandal:

> You may not want to spend all your time on it. You may want to get on with doing other things. But when you try to do those other things you find that you can't do them. You can't do anything unless you survive, and you can't survive unless you deal with the scandal.

Apart from the expenditure of time, officials who are constantly aware of the possibility of scandal—forming a "culture of mistrust," as one high-level civil servant described current conditions—may hesitate before pursuing policies that might stir up debate. Even if such a controversy starts out as an argument over policy or methods or ideology, an official can bet that these days the dispute will turn into charges of corruption or abuse. Some government managers not only hesitate to enter areas of potential danger but try not even to get close to them, so that the forbidden territory gradually grows in its extent.

This expansion, said the civil servant, might be called the "halo effect": Federal managers who want to avoid trouble retreat ever farther from policy areas, positions, or personal connections that are or might be on the "disapproved" list. Scandals in any governmental system, at any time, bring Byzantine and poisonous politics with them; when the number of scandals reaches a critical mass, these qualities pervade government as a whole.

The new system also brings the sort of demoralization that attends hypocrisy. For instance, new government ethics rules make it harder for managers to have contacts with the people they regulate. Naturally, the regulatees do not like these limits. More important, even noncorrupt federal managers often think the new prohibitions are bad. "Usually," one of them put it, "this sort of [now-forbidden] communication is constructive." Therefore the new prohibitions do not carry much moral authority. They are seen as obstacles to be gotten over, around, and under.

Some clever souls, ingenious Americans at work, will always figure out how to evade the rules. For instance, corporations often buy tables at the many Washington dinners given by think tanks, charities, and other worthy organizations. The corporations used to invite government officials as their guests. Now, under the new, cleaner regime, the officials cannot accept these invitations unless they reimburse their corporate hosts, and the cost is prohibitive. So in some places a new system is evolving. The corporations still buy their tables. The think tanks and charities themselves invite the government officials whom the corporations want at the dinner. These government officials somehow find themselves sitting next to the same corporate vice presidents for public relations who used to hand out the dinner invitations directly. Some ethics officer somewhere in government must think this situation morally preferable to what went on in the bad old days.

Then there is the boat trick. One Washington lobbyist holds dinners on his company yacht from May through October. The lobbyist invites an official to dinner and asks who else the official would like to have along for the ride. The official naturally names a group of charming and politically useful individuals. On the boat, everyone has a lovely time networking. Afterward the official reimburses the lobbyist for dinner, just as the rules demand. The amount of $15 was the tab for one such recent meal, a price far below what all the wonderful contacts were worth. The official does not forget the lobbyist's favor. The critics who deplored John Sununu's use of military planes were soon shocked to learn that, to escape further criticism, he had turned to the more problematic use of corporate planes. With ethics rules as with other such systems, there is no free lunch.

Another kind of demoralization comes about because the new system gives us so many scandals that scandal loses its power to stigmatize. Former president Richard Nixon, the very emblem of the scandal-destroyed politician, is now enjoying yet another political reincarnation, managing to draw a crowd of 50,000 supporters to the 1990 opening of his presidential library in Yorba Linda, California.[14] His return is a huge thumb in the eye of Watergate's moral certainties. Ex-speaker of the House Jim Wright went back to Fort Worth, Texas, to find a huge, festive welcome home party waiting for him. Reagan White House aide Michael Deaver, less than two years after the harrowing experiences of his trial and conviction, reopened his consulting shop, and his wife, Carolyn Deaver, has served as assistant chief of protocol in the State Department. Former Reagan aide Lyn Nofziger, when he was under indictment, actually had to turn away people who wanted to contribute money to his defense. The late senator John Tower, after the scandal that denied him the post of secretary of defense, was appointed head of the President's Foreign Intelligence Advisory Board, before his death in 1991. The board is one of the most prestigious such presidential bodies.

A good number of these rehabilitations are helped along by our current tendency to treat habits like excessive drinking as diseases, amenable to medical treatments and casting no aspersions on the sufferer's character or morals. Not all the people involved in scandals rebuild their public careers, but the number of well-known recoveries is increasing. This is no surprise: Today's many scandals engulf not only officials whose acts are unambiguously bad but those whose offenses not many people can understand or remember. Such officials can plausibly portray themselves as victims of political assassination. Sheer numbers are giving scandal something of a good name.

Not good enough, though: The final demoralizing effect of the numerous scandals on our politics is to make us feel perpetually dirty. This is not a feeling that bedevils the entire citizenry. In their capacity as consumers, most people seem to have a boundless appetite for scandal news. In their capacity as citizens, they seem to be able to maintain the view that politics has crooks in it—always did, always will—without concluding that the republic is going to hell in a handbasket. Those who help set the public agenda show less equanimity: They have placed corruption at the very center of their political concerns and thus permitted scandals to dominate political discourse.

There is no other developed country whose political life displays anything like this tendency of ours. Here is just one example of how big the differences are, even when we are compared with the foreign political culture closest to our own: In 1988, after a series of conflict-of-interest scandals that rocked Canada's politics, the Canadian parliament began debating a new ethics in government law.[15] It was like ours in some respects. It also contained provisions that sounded as if they had been penned by another species. For instance, the Canadian law was to be administered by a government commission, which could waive postemployment lobbying laws "in situations in which the public interest in ensuring reasonable employment for former ministers . . . outweighs the public interest" in prohibiting contacts between the ex-minister and the government.[16] The idea that there could conceivably be such a thing as a public interest in "ensuring reasonable employment for former ministers" would be unintelligible to an American reformer.

In the legislation, moreover, the commission was given the power to decide whether an officeholder's financial data should be made public. Violations of the code were not made criminal. Financial data not public? Worse, code violations not criminal? In this country, you cannot even take a seat at the enforcement table unless you are talking felonies and treble damages.

In the end, the Canadians chose not to enact even these restraints, leaving modern-day America clearly unique in the degree to which we have elevated motives and the potential for transgression to a primary place in our politics.

The world that is now reshaping itself around us will give American goods, services, and ideas a lot of new competition. We may have to worry considerably more than in the past about how well our politics and government perform when compared with everyone else's. This probability is reason enough for us to stop letting anxieties bred by scandal dominate our public choices and force even those federal policymakers who are honest to spend so much of their time, energy, and intellect trying not to look like crooks.

Our system is now able, perhaps for the first time, to produce scandals at will, in steady and unending supply. This means that we must, also for the first time, make some decisions about just how many we want. None of us would want a system that offered blanket protection for crooks, but we must start to think about what sorts of people—in what positions, with what interests and what values—should be given the power to decide on our behalf who is a crook and who is not. We sometimes hear that the present scandal system will endure because Americans' appetite for it is insatiable. Sometimes the same argument appears in a more high-minded version: The system will last because the populace thinks that politicians are crooks and deserve even harsher treatment than what they get now. But there is a difference between people's tastes as scandal consumers and their judgments as citizens. In the spring of 1991 author Kitty Kelley published a much-ballyhooed, and highly critical biography of Nancy Reagan. It was, like much 1980s political journalism, filled with unnamed sources and highly personal details—all justified, said Kelley, as an exploration of the now-familiar character issue. People bought many copies of the book. But 62 percent also knew enough to say, when asked by pollsters, that it was "trashy." Only 17 percent labeled it "accurate."[17] As for the alleged bloodthirstiness of the public, we should remember that today's scandal practices did not simply spring up in response to public demand; they were elaborately crafted by a political elite that has the freedom to correct its course.

There are specific changes of various sorts that would make our system less scandal prone without returning us to the depths of public criminality. For instance, those who care about good government should concentrate more of their intelligence and energy on getting and keeping talented people for the government and on helping government make its decisions effectively. We have spent enough time closing every loophole that might permit a Defense Department manager to go to work for a defense contracting firm after he retires from government. Now it is time to worry in the opposite direction, and start devising ways to make it possible for defense industry managers to serve in government after they retire. We have devoted enough ingenuity to building checks and counterchecks into our procurement and grant processes. It is time to start analyzing the rules with a view to getting these decisions made expeditiously and permitting government managers to use their experience and judgment to do the job.

We have had two decades of explosive growth in the government's investigative staffs, both in the executive branch and on the Hill. At present we do not need any more. Indeed, it is time for congressional leaders, especially in the House, to take some control of Congress's investigative function by trying to make the size of the investigative staffs of the various committees and subcommittees correspond to something vaguely resembling a reasonable allocation of Congress's investigative expenditures. In the executive branch, it is time to start focusing on the improvement of skills, prudence, and professionalism among all the new investigators who have come on board in the past decade, and to revise the reimbursement rules to give officials confidence that they will not be financially ruined, even if not guilty, by the financial costs of scandal.

The office of the independent counsel, that jewel in the post-Watergate crown, has become more trouble, more expense, and more danger than it is worth. It has done a good job of investigating a number of cases that would also have been investigated well, and occasionally better, by ordinary prosecutors. And in a test like Iran-contra, it has proved incapable of reasonable self-discipline or maintaining a sense of proportion. The office has a vast capacity for making big scandals out of smaller ones, and this is something we no longer need.

As for regular federal prosecutors, they will continue to be, thank goodness, prosecutors. But we have had 20 years of the criminalization of politics, and it is time for a strong presumption against creating any more new crimes in the field. We also need a demystification of the cult of the prosecutor and more healthy skepticism from journalists and others about the information that prosecutors dispense publicly and privately. As for the press, it, too, will remain pretty much what it is today. The balance of forces will change for the better, though, if more political people yell publicly not just about inaccuracies in the media but about the instances in which personal interests blind journalists to the difference between the pursuit of a story and pursuit of the truth. The complaints will usually not bring short-term action, but they will have their cumulative effect.

Some of the changes that would be good for us are more far-fetched. For instance, generations of reformers may well be right in having suggested that our civil servants should have more general training, more of a sense of themselves as a party-neutral class of public managers, and more of the jobs in the upper reaches of American government. But if American politics were capable of engineering such a feat, it would be hardly recognizable as American politics. It would be yet another good thing to have a sensible campaign finance reform that would not simply limit PAC contributions but give more encouragement to small contributions and raise the ceiling for individual contributors. Current campaign finance proposals, though, seem to be moving in the opposite direction.

More important, none of the specific changes that might be made is of much importance without a broader change in attitudes. Abolishing the independent counsel does not accomplish much if regular prosecutors in U.S. attorneys' offices are even more bloodthirsty. Devising a better mix of funding sources for our political campaigns will not make our system look any better to us as long as journalists treat every sizable contribution as a corrupt claim on a politician.

Most important, we will stay mired in our current scandal trap until more people start saying that contempt for ordinary politics, an attitude we see underlying many of our current scandals, is a corruption even more dangerous than stealing money from the public till, and that a prosecutorial class with no sympathy for human frailties can be a much greater danger to a democracy than the simple peddling of influence.

Finally, we need to start applying some elementary rules when we judge our political scandals. Scandals in government are good if they expose abuses, lead to correction, and thus increase citizens' confidence in public authority. If, on the other hand, they expose behavior that is not really an abuse of public trust, they are not justified. If they expose abuse that is trivial, they are worth no more than trivial attention.

If scandal making proceeds at full tilt for years without making government work better, it is not practical or wise or even ethical. Such activity may satisfy partisanship or personal ambition or the need for moral certainties, but it is not the road to virtue in government and should not be paid the respect that we give to morally mature actions.

If we judge scandals and ideas about ethics in government by these tougher and more honest standards, we may be able to start bringing political scandal back to its perennial, venerated, and distinctly secondary place in American public life.

N   O   T   E   S

Introduction

1. *The New York Times*, May 24, 1990, p. A-25.
2. Our politics has become obsessed with the exhumation of misdeeds, real and alleged. We are still mesmerized by each new theory or fragment of information related to Watergate. Major media and congressional attention goes to charges about plots to rig the presidential election of 1980, more than a decade ago.

    For a report on the recent growth of feelings of alienation in the electorate see Donald S. Kellerman, Andrew Kohut, and Carol Bowman, *The People, the Press and Politics 1990: A Times Mirror Political Typology* (Washington: Times Mirror Center for the People and the Press, 1990), pp. 2, 12–13, 22.
3. *The New York Times*, June 1, 1990, p. D-2.
4. In the executive branch, my list does not go below the level of deputy assistant secretary or the equivalent. For Congress the list extends down to senior aides. With the federal judiciary, I included only the judges themselves. Except at the presidential level, I did not include charges that lived and died within the boundaries of an election campaign.
5. Elder Witt, "Is Government Full of Crooks, or Are We Just Better at Finding Them?" *Governing*, September 1989, p. 33; *Report to Congress on the Activities and Operations of the Public Integrity Section*, 1988, p. 30; *ibid.*, 1985, p. 40.
6. This argument is from James Q. Wilson, "The Newer Deal," *The New Republic*, July 2, 1990, p. 33.
7. Alan S. Ehrenhalt, *The United States of Ambition* (New York: Times Books/Random House, 1991) makes this argument.

1. In the Great Tradition

1. An account of these scandals is given in Mark W. Summers, *The Plundering Generation: Corruption and the Crisis of the Union, 1849–1861* (New York: Oxford University Press, 1987).
2. Ted Morgan, *FDR:* (New York: Simon and Schuster, 1985), pp. 134–145.
3. John T. Noonan, Jr., *Bribes* (New York: Macmillan, 1984), pp. 565–567.
4. W. A. Swanberg, *Sickles the Incredible* (New York: Charles Scribner's Sons, 1956), p. 61.
5. *Id.* Also *Frank Leslie's*, March 12, 1859.
6. Swanberg, *op. cit.*, p. 67. See also *Harper's Weekly*, "Domestic Intelligence," May 14, 1859.
7. Edward Pessen, "Corruption and the Politics of Pragmatism: Reflections on the Jacksonian Era," in *Before Watergate: Problems of Corruption in American Society*, A. S. Eisenstadt, A. Hoogeboom, and H. L. Trefousse, eds., Brooklyn College Studies in Society in Change, no. 4 (Brooklyn, N.Y.: Brooklyn College Press, 1978), p. 80.

8. *Congressional Quarterly Almanac*, vol. 18, 1962 (Washington: Congressional Quarterly Service, 1962), p. 992.
9. *Ibid.*, vol. 20, 1964 (1965), p. 949.
10. *Ibid.*, p. 959.
11. Margaret Susan Thomas, *The Spider Web: Congress and Lobbying in the Age of Grant* (Ithaca, N.Y.: Cornell University Press, 1985), p. 53.
12. Alexander B. Callow, Jr., *The Tweed Ring* (New York: Oxford University Press, 1966).
13. Maury Klein, *The Life and Legend of Jay Gould* (Baltimore, Md.: Johns Hopkins University Press, 1986), p. 496.
14. Morton Keller, *Regulating a New Economy: Public Policy and Economic Change in America, 1900–1933* (Cambridge, Mass.: Harvard University Press, 1990), pp. 4–5.
15. For an account of the political mood of the time see Maurice Isserman, *If I Had a Hammer . . . : The Death of the Old Left and the Birth of the New Left* (New York: Basic Books, 1987). See especially pp. xv–xviii.
16. Rachel Carson, *Silent Spring* (New York: Houghton Mifflin, 1962).
17. Ralph Nader, *Unsafe at Any Speed* (New York: Grossman Publishers, 1965).
18. A broader discussion of this change will be found in E. J. Dionne, *Why Americans Hate Politics* (New York: Simon and Schuster, 1991).
19. *Newsweek*, August 1, 1966, p. 22.
20. Lyndon B. Johnson, "62nd Press Conference, April 22," *1966 Presidential Papers*, vol. 188 (Washington: U.S. Government Printing Office, 1967), p. 446.
21. *Time*, March 24, 1967, pp. 16–17.
22. *The New York Times*, April 29, 1967, p. 36.
23. *Ibid.*, May 1, 1966, p. 70.
24. Associated Press, April 28, 1987.

2. An Honest President

1. The book was Len Colodny and Robert Gettlin, *Silent Coup: The Removal of a President* (New York: St. Martin's Press, 1991).
2. J. Anthony Lukas, *Nightmare: The Underside of the Nixon Years* (New York: Viking Penguin, 1988), pp. 302–306.
3. *Newsweek*, July 26, 1976, p. 23. Quoted in Paul F. Boller, Jr., *Presidential Campaigns* (New York: Oxford University Press, 1984), p. 345.
4. Associated Press, July 15, 1977.
5. *The Washington Post*, July 26, 1977, p. A-1.
6. Associated Press, August 18, 1977.
7. David S. Broder, *Behind the Front Page* (New York: Simon and Schuster, 1987), pp. 104–105.
8. *The Washington Post*, December 18, 1977, p. G-1.
9. Rudy Maxa, "Carter Aide's Manners Are No Laughing Matter," *The Washington Post Magazine*, February 19, 1978, p. 5.
10. Arthur H. Christy, *Report of the Special Prosecutor on Alleged Possession of Cocaine by Hamilton Jordan*, New York, May 28, 1980, pp. 15–18.
11. Associated Press, June 29, 1986.

3. The Responsible Media

1. Richard M. Clurman, *Beyond Malice: The Media's Years of Reckoning* (New York: New American Library, 1990), p. 27.
2. *The Wall Street Journal*, October 28, 1980, p. 1.
3. *The Boston Globe*, July 22, 1981, p. 1.
4. United Press International, November 13, 1981.
5. *The Washington Post*, November 14, 1981, p. A-1.
6. *Ibid.*, November 15, 1981, p. A-1.
7. Reuters, November 14, 1981.
8. *The New York Times*, November 22, 1981, p. D-4.
9. *Newsweek*, December 7, 1981, p. 32.
10. United Press International, January 1, 1982.
11. *Ibid.*, November 29, 1981.
12. *Ibid.*, November 13, 1981.
13. *Ibid.*, November 20, 1981.
14. *The Wall Street Journal*, July 27, 1982, p. 1.
15. Joseph A. Califano, Jr., Special Counsel, "Report on the Investigation Pursuant to House Resolution 12 Concerning Alleged Illicit Use or Distribution of Drugs by Members, Officers or Employees of the House," *Report of the Committee on Standards of Official Conduct*, House Calendar no. 142, report 98–559 (Washington: U.S. Government Printing Office, 1983), p. 129.
16. *Ibid.*, p. 34.
17. *Ibid.*, pp. 220–221.
18. Martin Mayer, *Making News* (Garden City, N.Y.: Doubleday and Company, 1987), pp. 157–162.
19. Martin Schram. *The Great American Video Game: Presidential Politics in the Television Age* (New York: William Morrow, 1987), p.57.
20. Charles McCarry, *Citizen Nader* (New York: Saturday Review Press, 1972), p. 110.
21. Bob Woodward, *The Commanders* (New York: Simon and Schuster, 1991).
22. Lincoln Steffens, *Autobiography of Lincoln Steffens* (New York: Harcourt Brace and Company, 1931), p. 504.
23. David Graham Phillips, *The Treason of the Senate*, 2nd ed. (Chicago: Quadrangle Books, 1964), p. 59.
24. *Ibid.*, p. 67.
25. *IRE Journal*, Summer 1986, p. 6.
26. *Ibid.*, July–August 1979, p. 1.
27. *Ibid.*, Summer 1984, p. 13.
28. *The Wall Street Journal*, October 6, 1977, p. 20
29. *Id.*
30. *Id.*
31. "Jerry Landauer," March 29, 1981, p. 16.
32. *The Washington Post*, June 1, 1989, p. C-2.

4. The Ethics Apparat: Independent Counsels

1. *The New York Times*, October 24, 1973, p. 31.
2. Charlotte Low Allen, "Caught in a Web of Politics, Power," *Insight*, June 5, 1989, pp. 8–16.

3. An account of the law's provisions and amendments can be found in Terry Eastland, *Ethics, Politics and the Independent Counsel: Executive Power, Executive Vice, 1789–1989* (Washington: National Legal Center for the Public Interest, 1989).
4. *Congressional Quarterly Almanac*, vol. 40 (1984), p. 249.
5. *The New York Times*, March 29, 1984, p. A-24.
6. Letter from Leonard Garment and Peter W. Morgan to Senator Strom Thurmond, chairman, Senate Committee on the Judiciary, April 7, 1984.
7. Jacob A. Stein, *Report of Independent Counsel Concerning Edwin Meese III* (Washington: U.S. Court of Appeals for the District of Columbia Circuit, September 20, 1984), p. 3.
8. *The Washington Post*, September 22, 1984, p. A-1.
9. Reuters, January 27, 1981.
10. United Press International, January 29, 1981.
11. *The Washington Post*, December 18, 1981, p. A-1.
12. Leon Silverman, *Report of the Special Prosecutor [on the Investigation of Raymond Donovan]* (Washington: U.S. Court of Appeals for the District of Columbia Circuit, no. 81–2, June 25, 1982), p. 8.
13. Leon Silverman, *Supplemental Report of the Special Prosecutor* (Washington: U.S. Court of Appeals for the District of Columbia Circuit, no. 81–2, September 10, 1982), p. 1.
14. Associated Press, October 2, 1984.
15. *Legal Times*, September 29, 1986, p. 4.
16. United Press International, May 25, 1987.
17. Leon Silverman, *Report of the Independent Counsel in re Raymond Donovan*, no. 85–1 (Washington: U.S. Court of Appeals for the District of Columbia Circuit, October 22, 1987), p. 61.
18. *The New York Times*, October 10, 1983, p. 1.
19. Alexia Morrison, *Report of the Independent Counsel in re Theodore Olson and Robert M. Perry* (Washington: U.S. Court of Appeals for the District of Columbia Circuit, December 27, 1989), pp. 106–108.
20. *Ibid.*, p. 7. From interview of Alan Parker, former general counsel, House Judicial Committee, July 24, 1986.
21. *Ibid.*, p. 17.
22. *Morrison* v. *Olson*, 487 U.S. 654, 108 S. Ct. 2597 (1988).
23. *Ibid.*, Dissent, p. 6.
24. *Ibid.*, Dissent, p. 7.
25. *Ibid.*, Dissent, p. 10.

5. The Ethics Apparat: A Cast of Thousands

1. Alexander Toland Bok, "The Prosecutorial Discretion of the United States Attorney," B.A. Thesis, Department of Government, Harvard University, March 1981, p. 22. Update, by telephone, Patty Garrett, Planning Office, U.S. Bureau of Prisons, June 17, 1991.
2. *Budget of the United States Government, Fiscal Year 1991* (Washington: U.S. Government Printing Office, 1990), actual obligations, Department of Labor, p. 889, and Department of Transportation, p. A-953; *ibid., Fiscal Year 1981* (1980), Department of Labor, p. 660, and Department of Transportation, p. 740.

3. Thomas H. Henderson, Jr., "The Expanding Role of Federal Prosecutors in Combatting State and Local Political Corruption," *Cumberland Law Review*, vol. 8 (1977), p. 385.

4. *Report to the Congress on the Actions and Operations of the Public Integrity Section for 1986* (Washington: Criminal Division, U.S. Department of Justice, June 1987), p. 44, *ibid., 1988* (July 1989), p. 30.

5. Bok, *op. cit.*, pp. 20–24. Also telephone conversation with Gary Patchett, Statistical Office, Executive Office of U.S. Attorneys, August 1990.

6. Arthur Maass, "U.S. Prosecution of State and Local Officials for Political Corruption: Is the Bureaucracy Out of Control in a High-Stakes Operation Involving the Constitutional System?" *Publius: The Journal of Federalism*, vol. 17, Summer 1987, p. 204.

7. Stuart Taylor, Jr., "Wallach's Appeal from Rampant Rudyism," *Legal Times*, November 5, 1990, p. 31.

8. *USA Today*, January 9, 1989, p. 6-B.

9. *The New York Times*, July 19, 1988, p. A-1.

10. *The Washington Post*, July 19, 1988, p. A-1.

11. James C. McKay, *Report of the Independent Counsel in re Edwin Meese III* (Washington: United States Court of Appeals for the District of Columbia Circuit, no. 87–1, July 5, 1988), p. 75.

12. *Ibid.*, p. 99.

13. *United States* v. *Wallach et al.*, Indictment 587 Cr. 985 (RO), Southern District of New York, December 22, 1987.

14. "The Lynching of Bob Wallach," *The American Lawyer*, June 1988.

15. *Ibid.*, p. 114.

16. *Id.*

17. *The New York Times*, June 1, 1991, p. A-1

18. *Ibid.*, June 23, 1987, p. D-30.

19. *The Washington Post*, November 6, 1989, p. A-11.

20. Joseph J. Trento, *Prescription for Disaster: From the Glory of Apollo to the Betrayal of the Shuttle* (New York: Crown Publishing, 1987), p. 184.

21. *Ibid.*, p. 286.

22. Malcolm McConnell, "The Ordeal by Indictment of James Beggs," *Reader's Digest*, March 1988, pp. 169–175.

23. *The Washington Post*, November 6, 1989, p. A-11.

24. Fred Strasser, "Defending Contractors Against the Pentagon," *National Law Journal*, March 3, 1986, p. 1.

25. "On the Docket," *Forbes*, April 6, 1987, p. 84.

26. *The Washington Post*, March 19, 1988, p. D-11.

27. *Ibid.*, June 21, 1988, p. A-11.

28. *Ibid.*, December 27, 1988, p. A-1.

29. *Id.*

30. For an account of this phenomenon, see Steven Kelman, *Procurement and Public Management: The Fear of Discretion and the Quality of Government Performance* (Washington: AEI Press, 1990).

6. Prosecutors on the Hill

1. Norman J. Ornstein, Thomas E. Mann, and Michael J. Malbin, eds., *Vital Statistics on Congress, 1989–1990* (Washington: Congressonal Quarterly, Inc., 1990), p. 136, Table 5–5.

2. John Melcher letter to Clarence Thomas, August 25, 1987.
3. Clarence Thomas letter to John Melcher, February 1, 1988.
4. Equal Employment Opportunity Commission chronology prepared for Senate Special Committee on Aging, undated.
5. *St. Louis Post-Dispatch*, January 10, 1988, p. 5-D.
6. *EEOC's Reprisal against District Director for Testimony before Congress on Age Discrimination Charges, Hearings before the Employment and Housing Subcommittee of the Committee on Government Operations, H.R. March 20, 1989* (Washington: U.S. Government Printing Office, 1989), p. 40.
7. *The Washington Post*, July 28, 1989, p. A-23.
8. *The New York Times*, February 10, 1990, p. A-9.
9. See, e.g., Forrest McDonald, *Insull* (Chicago: University of Chicago Press, 1962), pp. 264–268.
10. *The Wall Street Journal*, May 7, 1985, p. 1.
11. *Ibid.*, May 14, 1985, p. 14.
12. *Id.*
13. Suzanne Garment, "Capital Chronicle," *The Wall Street Journal*, November 8, 1985, p. 32.
14. *Id.*
15. *Id.*
16. *Id.*
17. *Id.*
18. *The Wall Street Journal*, May 27, 1986, p. 62.
19. *Ibid.*, May 16, 1986, p. 2.
20. *Ibid.*, May 27, 1986, p. 62.
21. Andrew Stark discusses the distinctiveness of this modern American idea in his paper "Conflict of Interest in American Public Life," undated.
22. Justin D. Simon, "Make Congress Play by the Rules," *Criminal Justice*, Spring 1989, p. 10.
23. *Congressional Quarterly Weekly Report*, July 11, 1987, p. 1507.
24. *Ibid.*, June 10, 1989, p. 1409.
25. *The New York Times*, November 15, 1989, p. A-23.
26. *The Washington Post*, August 3, 1990, p. A-6.
27. *The New York Times*, October 24, 1976, p. D-14.
28. *Ibid.*, April 5, 1976, p. A-23.
29. *Ibid.*, May 5, 1989, p. A-13.
30. *Ibid.*, April 1, 1991, p. A-10.
31. *Science*, February 1, 1991, p. 508.
32. *Ibid.*, p. 510.
33. *The New York Times*, May 3, 1991, p. B-11.

7. Sex

1. Rita Jenrette with Kathleen Maxa, "Diary of a Mad Congresswife," *The Washington Post Magazine*, December 7, 1980, p. 8.
2. United Press International, March 13, 1981.
3. Associated Press, May 7, 1981.
4. "The Ear," *The Washington Post*, May 23, 1982, p. K-1.
5. *The New York Times*, September 28, 1987, p. C-15.
6. Marion Clark and Rudy Maxa, *Public Trust, Private Lust* (New York: William Morrow and Company, 1977), p. 75.

7. *Ibid.*, p. 121.
8. *Ibid.*, pp. 135–136.
9. *The New York Times*, September 28, 1987, p. C-15.
10. *Newsweek*, March 16, 1981, p. 26.
11. "Beauty and Bureaucracy," *Playboy*, November 1980, p. 128.
12. Associated Press, March 10, 1981.
13. *The Washington Post*, August 18, 1988, p. C-2.
14. Rudy Maxa, "Women of Washington," *Playboy*, November 1988, p. 87.
15. United Press International, December 8, 1988.
16. Rudy Maxa, "Dancing with Danny," *Washingtonian*, October 18, 1988, p. 202.
17. *Late Night with David Letterman*, May 4, 1987. Reported in *The Washington Post*, May 6, 1987, p. B-1.
18. *Life*, July 1987, pp. 82–88.
19. *U.S. News & World Report*, June 8, 1987, p. 16.
20. *The Washington Post*, June 8, 1987, p. C-3.
21. United Press International, June 9, 1987.
22. Associated Press, June 17, 1987.
23. *Ibid.*, June 18, 1987.
24. *The Washington Post*, August 4, 1987, p. D-6.
25. Associated Press, September 9, 1987.
26. United Press International, February 12, 1988.
27. *People*, December 21, 1987, p. 29.
28. *The Washington Times*, January 3, 1990, p. E-1.
29. *The Washington Post*, May 5, 1987, p. D-1.
30. Daniel J. Boorstin, *Image: A Guide to Pseudo-Events in America* (Magnolia, Mass.: Peter Smith Publishers, 1984). *See 184*
31. *The Washington Post*, May 7, 1987, p. C-1.
32. *The Wall Street Journal*, February 25, 1985, p. 1.
33. Charlotte Fedders and Laura Elliott, *Shattered Dreams* (New York: Harper and Row, 1988).
34. *The Washington Post*, June 12, 1989, p. A-20.
35. *Ibid.*, July 19, 1989, p. A-1.
36. *Ibid.*, July 20, 1989, p. A-6.
37. *The New York Times*, October 19, 1989, p. A-24.
38. *The Washington Post*, October 19, 1989, p. A-5.
39. *Ibid.*, September 29, 1988, p. A-12.
40. *Ibid.*, September 28, 1988, p. A-12.
41. *Ibid.*, September 29, 1988, p. A-12.
42. *Ibid.*, September 28, 1988, p. A-12.
43. *Ibid.*, June 5, 1989, p. A-7.
44. *Ibid.*, September 28, 1988, p. A-12.
45. Rudy Maxa, "The Senator and the Girl," *Washingtonian*, November 1988, p. 114.
46. *Ibid.*, March 3, 1989, p. A-1.
47. *The Boston Globe*, May 30, 1987, p. 1.
48. *Congressional Quarterly Weekly Report*, June 6, 1987, p. 1186.
49. American Psychiatric Association Committee on Nomenclature and Statistics, *Diagnostic and Statistical Manual of Psychiatric Disorders*, 2nd ed. (Washington: American Psychiatric Association, 1968).
50. *The Washington Post*, May 1, 1988, p. A-1.
51. *The Washington Times*, May 10, 1988, p. F-1.
52. *The Washington Post*, May 2, 1988, p. A-1.
53. *Ibid.*, p. B-1.

54. *Ibid.*, May 3, 1988, p. A-1.
55. *The Washington Times*, August 25, 1989, p. A-1.
56. *Ibid.*, August 25, 1989, pp. A-1, A-7.
57. *Ibid.*, August 30, 1989, p. A-1.
58. *Ibid.*, September 7, 1989, p. A-1.
59. *The Washington Post*, September 19, 1989, p. A-4.

8. The Scandal Olympics: Iran-Contra

1. *Report of the Congressional Committees Investigating the Iran-Contra Affair*, H. Report No. 100–433, S. Report No. 100–216 (Washington: U.S. Government Printing Office, 1987), pp. 33, 396.
2. *Ibid.*, p. 398.
3. *Ibid.*, p. 59.
4. *Ibid.*, p. 271.
5. *Ibid.*, p. 314.
6. For an account of the Ervin hearings see Stanley I. Kutler, *The Wars of Watergate* (New York: Alfred A. Knopf, 1990), pp. 340–382.
7. Theodore Draper, "Revelations of the North Trial," *The New York Review*, August 17, 1989.
8. *Testimony of Robert C. McFarlane, Gaston J. Sigur, Jr., and Robert W. Owen, May 11, 12, 13, 14, and 19, 1987,* Joint Hearings before the House Select Committee to Investigate Covert Arms Transactions with Iran and Senate Select Committee on Secret Military Assistance to Iran and the Nicaraguan Opposition (Washington: U.S. Government Printing Office, 1987), p. 546.
9. Oliver L. North to Robert C. McFarlane, December 4, 1984.
10. *Ibid.*, February 6, 1985.
11. *Ibid.*, March 5, 1985.
12. *Ibid.*, March 16, 1985.
13. *Ibid.*, April 11, 1985.
14. *Ibid.*, May 31, 1985.
15. Jeffrey Toobin, *Opening Arguments: A Young Lawyer's First Case: United States* v. *Oliver North* (New York: Viking, 1991), pp. 171–173.
16. *The Washington Times*, May 4, 1989, p. A-3.
17. *The New York Times*, May 5, 1989, p. A-19.
18. *The Wall Street Journal*, May 30, 1990, p. A-13.
19. Gordon Crovitz, "Lawrence Walsh, Drug Cases and the Costs of Selective Prosecution," *The Wall Street Journal*, May 30, 1990, p. A-13.

9. Congress in the Dock

1. Frederick M. Kaiser, "Executive Investigations: A Comparison of Abscam and the Land-Fraud Schemes," *Police Studies: The International Review of Police Development*, vol. 13, no. 1 (Spring 1990), p. 16.
2. *The New York Times*, June 21, 1989, p. A-25.
3. The best history of this critique is in Michael J. Malbin, "Looking Back at the Future of Campaign Finance Reform: Interest Groups and American Elections," in Michael J. Malbin, ed., *Politics and Money in the United*

States: Financing Elections in the 1980s (Chatham, N.J.: Chatham House Publishers, 1984).
4. *Common Cause News*, March 26, 1991, House Chart II.
5. Norman J. Ornstein, Thomas E. Mann, and Michael J. Malbin, *Vital Statistics on Congress, 1989–1990* (Washington: Congressional Quarterly, Inc., 1990), p. 144.
6. Alan S. Ehrenhalt, *The United States of Ambition* (New York: Times Books/Random House 1991), p. 235.
7. Ornstein et al., *op. cit.*, p. 144.
8. Jim Wright, *Reflections of a Public Man* (Ft. Worth, Tex.: Madison Publishing Company, 1984).
9. *The Wall Street Journal*, May 2, 1989, p. A-20.
10. *Atlanta Business Chronicle*, July 24, 1989, p. 1-A.
11. *The Washington Post*, May 4, 1989, p. B-1.
12. *The New York Times*, May 23, 1989, p. A-28.
13. *Id.*
14. *Ibid.*, May 24, 1989, p. A-1.
15. *Ibid.*, p. A-26.
16. *Ibid.*, June 1, 1989, p. D-22.
17. *Ibid.*, June 27, 1989, p. A-14.
18. Brooks Jackson, *Honest Graft: Big Money and the American Political Process* (New York: Alfred A. Knopf, 1988).
19. *The Washington Post*, April 13, 1989, p. A-1.
20. *The New York Times*, May 18, 1989, p. B-6.
21. *The Los Angeles Times*, May 25, 1989, p. 1.
22. *The Washington Times*, May 22, 1989, p. A-4.
23. *The National Journal*, April 28, 1990, p. 1018.
24. *The New York Times*, June 7, 1989, p. A-25.
25. Associated Press, June 12, 1989.
26. *The Washington Post*, May 31, 1989, p. A-1.
27. *Ibid.*, June 29, 1989, p. A-1.
28. *Congressional Quarterly*, May 19, 1990, p. 1530. *Roll Call*, June 10, 1991, p. 3.
29. *The New York Times*, April 8, 1991, p. B-2.
30. *Lincoln Savings and Loan Association* v. *M. Danny Wall, Director, Office of Thrift Supervision* and *American Continental Corporation* v. *M. Danny Wall, Director, Office of Thrift Supervision*, Consolidated Civil Action nos. 89–1318 and 89–1323, Memorandum Opinion, August 22, 1990, p. 9.
31. *Statement of Richard T. Pratt before the U.S. House of Representatives Committee on Banking, Finance and Urban Affairs*, October 1, 1990, pp. 46–47.
32. A related argument is made in Ronald C. Moe, "Traditional Organizational Principles and the Managerial Presidency: From Phoenix to Ashes," *Public Administration Review*, vol. 50 (March–April 1990), pp. 129–140.
33. *Statement of Richard T. Pratt*, p. 53.
34. David Pryor to Edwin J. Gray, October 3, 1986.
35. James Ring Adams, *The Big Fix: Inside the S&L Scandal* (New York: John Wiley and Sons, 1990), p. 245.
36. *Ibid.*
37. *The Wall Street Journal*, November 5, 1990, pp. A-1, A-6.
38. *Dayton Daily News*, May 21, 1989, p. A-1.
39. Martin Mayer, *The Greatest-Ever Bank Robbery: The Collapse of the Savings and Loan Industry* (New York: Charles Scribner's Sons, 1990), p. 168.

40. *The New York Times*, November 17, 1990, p. A-11; *ibid.*, November 20, 1991, p. B-8.
41. John R. Cranford, "Keating Five Ask Exoneration as Panel's Hearings End," *Congressional Quarterly*, January 19, 1991, pp. 169–170.

10. Personal Effects

1. Charlotte Low Allen, "Caught in a Web of Politics, Power," *Insight*, June 5, 1989, p. 12.
2. Larry J. Sabato, *Feeding Frenzy* (New York: Free Press, 1991), p. 53.
3. *The New York Times*, July 18, 1984, p. A-20.
4. *Ibid.*, August 13, 1984, p. A-16.
5. *The Washington Post*, August 16, 1984, p. A-2.
6. *The New York Times*, September 2, 1984, p. A-1.
7. *New York* magazine, August 27, 1984, p. 7.
8. *The Washington Post*, January 8, 1985, p. A-7.
9. *The Wall Street Journal*, September 13, 1984, p. 28.
10. *The Washington Post*, September 22, 1984, p. A-3.
11. *Ibid.*, October 23, 1984, p. A-1.
12. *The New York Times*, April 30, 1985, p. B-4.
13. *The Washington Post*, March 25, 1986, p. C-3.
14. *The New York Times*, October 7, 1987, p. B-1.
15. *Ibid.*, October 15, 1987, p. B-8.
16. Associated Press, August 19, 1988.
17. Murray Kempton, "A Ritual of Class Vengeance," *Newsday*, August 3, 1989, p. 8.

11. A Culture of Mistrust

1. The National Commission on the Public Service, *Leadership for America* (Washington: U.S. Government Printing Office, 1989), p. 17.
2. Allan J. Lichtman, "Tommy the Cork: The Secret World of Washington's First Modern Lobbyist," *The Washington Monthly*, February 1987, pp. 41–49.
3. *Congressional Quarterly Almanac*, vol. 18, 1962 (Washington: Congressional Quarterly Service, 1962), p. 992. See also Aaron Wildavsky, "If Institutions Have Consequences, Why Don't We Hear About Them from Moral Philosophers?" *American Political Science Review*, vol. 83, no. 4 (December 1989), pp. 1343–1351.
4. *St. Louis Post-Dispatch*, April 6, 1988, p. 1.
5. United Press International, April 6, 1988.
6. *St. Louis Post-Dispatch*, April 7, 1988, p. 1.
7. *New York Daily News*, April 8, 1988, p. 1.
8. *St. Louis Post-Dispatch*, April 10, 1988, p. 1.
9. *Id.*
10. Associated Press, April 18, 1988.
11. *St. Louis Post-Dispatch*, April 30, 1988, p. 1.
12. *The Washington Post*, November 17, 1989, p. A-14.

13. *The New York Times,* December 4, 1990, p. A-24.
14. *The Los Angeles Times,* July 20, 1990, p. A-1.
15. Andrew Stark, "Public Sector Conflict of Interest in Canada and the U.S.: Differences in Understandings and Approach," The 1989 Neil Staebler Conference, "Ethics: Cornerstone of the Public Trust," Institute of Public Policy Studies, University of Michigan, February 17, 1989.
16. Members of the Senate and House of Commons, "Conflict of Interest Act," House of Commons of Canada, Bill C-114, 2nd Session, 33rd Parliament, 1986–87–88, First reading February 24, 1988, p. 12, sect. 13(1).
17. Yankelovich Clancy Shulman, *Time/*CNN poll, April 10–11, 1991.

I N D E X

ABC Entertainment, 182–83
ABC News, 53, 64, 81
ABC-TV, 172, 182–83
Abscam, 111–12, 171, 225–26, 282
Acheson, Dean, 286
Acquired Immune Deficiency Syndrome (AIDS) research, 161–67
Adams, Brock, 188–89, 190
Adams, Henry, 25, 35
Adams, James Ring, 313n
Adams, Paul A., 142
Agency for International Development, 297
Agnew, Spiro T., 37, 79
Agriculture, Department of, 22
alcoholism, 47, 176, 271
Allen, Charlotte Low, 307n, 314n
Allen, Richard V., 58, 60–66, 72–74, 83, 93
    financial charges against, 60–64, 72
    media stakeout of, 62, 64–65
    as national security adviser, 60, 63, 73–74

press relations of, 73–74
resignation of, 58, 62, 63
vindication of, 58, 63–64
American Association of Retired Persons (AARP), 145
American Bar Association (ABA), 157–58, 159, 161, 289
    Congressional Investigations Subcommittee of, 157
American Civil Liberties Union, 8
American Enterprise Institute for Public Policy Research, vii, 316
American Lawyer, 123
American Psychiatric Association, 192
American Scholar, 89
Americans for Democratic Action, 49
Anchor Gasoline Corporation, 153, 154, 157
Anderson, Jack, 32, 68, 265, 293, 294
Animal House, 43, 50

Anthony, Susan B., 20
anticommunism, 31, 33, 152, 200
antiwar activism, 7, 9, 30–31,
    37, 57–58, 71, 174–75
Apollo program, 131
Armed Services Committee,
    Senate, 136
Armitage, Richard L., 293–94
Asner, Ed, 174
Associated Press (AP), 178, 187,
    252
Atlanta Business Chronicle, 236
automotive industry, 29
Aviation Consumer Action
    Project, 71

Bacon, Kenneth H., 79
Baird, Bruce A., 117–18
Baker, Bobby, 23–25, 33
Baker, James A., 62
Baltimore, David, 144, 161–64,
    166–68
Barnes, Michael D., 213, 218
Barry, Marion S., Jr., 112, 119
Bartley, Robert L., vii-viii
Bates, Jim, 188
Bates, Jim, 188
Battistella, Anabella, *see* Foxe,
    Fanne
Baucus, Max S., 229
Bauman, Robert E., 191, 192
Beggs, James M., 110, 127–28,
    130–34, 135, 283
Bennett, Robert S., 134–35, 253,
    256
Berlin Wall, 138
Bethesda Naval Hospital, 213
Biaggi, Mario, 120
Biddle, Francis, 98–99
Billygate, 47–50
blackmail, 17–18, 189
Blaine, James G., 16
Bok, Alexander Toland, 308n,
    309n
Boland, Edward P., 201

Boland amendment, 201, 203–4,
    212, 213, 214–15, 216, 217
Boller, Paul F., Jr., 306n
Bolshevik revolution, 231
Bookin, Stephen, 94–95
Boorstin, Daniel J., 184, 311n
Boston Globe, 60, 191, 192
Bourne, Peter G., 51, 282
Bowman, Carol, 305n
Boyd, Gordon D., 21
Bradley, Thomas, 242
Brand, Stanley M., 158, 224,
    225
Breckenridge, William, 20
break-ins, 15, 36, 37, 38
bribery, 3, 6, 16, 27, 37, 79, 92,
    115, 119, 187, 279
Bright Hope Baptist Church,
    243–44
Brill, Steven, 123–24
Broder, David, 48–49, 306n
Brown, James, 126–27
Bruner, Lynn, 147–49, 150–51
Buchanan, James, 13, 16
Budget and Impoundment Act,
    39
Budget Committee, House, 46
Buffalo News, 231–32
Burch, Dean, 191
Burford, Anne, 101, 102, 282–
    83
Bush, George, 158, 180, 221,
    286, 290, 293, 294
Byron, Beverly B., 229

Cable News Network (CNN),
    69, 70, 181, 254
Caldwell, Evelyn B., vii
Califano, Joseph A., 67–69,
    307n
Callow, Alexander B., Jr., 26–
    27, 306n
Cambodia, 39
    secret bombing of, 31
Canada, 300

Capone, Al, 274–75
Carson, Rachel, 29, 306n
Carter, James E. "Jimmy," Jr.,
42–44, 59
Democratic enmity toward,
42–43
ethical standards promised by,
42, 43, 47, 56
Playboy interview with,
173–74
political defeat of, 36, 56
Carter, Sybil, 49
Carter, William A. "Billy," III,
47–50
Libyan connection of, 48–49
Carter administration, 41–56
oil price control program of,
153
foreign policy of, 200
rumors of drug use in, 51–55
scandals in, 10, 41–56
social relations of, 43, 50–52,
55
car thefts, 111
cartoons, political, 231–32
CBS Evening News, 67, 68, 242
CBS-TV, 182
Cell, 162–64
Center for Concerned Engineer-
ing, 71
Central Intelligence Agency
(CIA), 6, 31, 37, 201, 214
Challenger disaster, 131–33
Chappaquiddick scandal, 16,
185
Cheney, Richard B., 293, 294
Chevrolet Corvair, 29
Chicago Tribune, 187
Chile, 162
Christic Institute, 293–94
Christy, Arthur H., 53–54, 86, 89
Civiletti, Benjamin R., 53
civil rights movement, 28, 29, 38
Civil Service Commission, 40
Civil War, U.S., 36

political climate after, 13,
25–27
Clark, Marion, 176–78, 310n
Clark, William P., 63
Clean Water Action Project, 71
Cleveland, Grover, 16, 20
Cleveland *Plain Dealer,* 78
Clifford, Clark, 118, 190
Clurman, Richard M., 57, 307n
cocaine, 52–53, 67–68, 112,
279
Coelho, Anthony L. "Tony,"
237, 240–41, 242
Cohen, Jeffrey N., 119
Collins, Tai, 176
Colodny, Len, 306n
Commanders, The (Woodward),
75
Committee on Labor and Human Resources, Senate,
91–92
Committee to Re-Elect the President (CREEP), 37, 71
Common Cause, 40, 45, 71–72,
234
compensating balances, 44, 46
conflict-of-interest cases, 155–
56, 272, 276
Conglomerate (Jenrette), 172
Congress, U.S., 85, 100
Abscam scandal and, 111–12,
171, 225–26, 282
censure by, 32–35, 39, 256
ethical oversight and investigation in, 4, 5, 9, 11, 15,
18, 24–25, 39, 142–68,
223–24
Iran-contra scandal and, 158,
198–99, 206–13
prosecutorial power of, 105–8,
109, 238
see also congressmen; House
of Representatives, U.S.;
legislation; Senate, U.S.;
specific committees

Congressional Record, 236
congressmen:
   incumbency power of, 231
   financial contributions to, 22,
     23, 32, 33, 80, 249–50
   financial limitations on, 15,
     71, 224
   pay raise vs. honoraria for, 71
   reelection rate of, 231
   in scandals, 11, 15, 23, 24,
     31–35, 66–69, 80, 171–97,
     223–58
   sex and drug charges against,
     66–69, 171–97
Conservative Opportunity Society (COS), 232
Constitution, U.S., 38, 155, 198
see also Fifth Amendment
Continental Army, 112
Continental Congress, 112
Contract Dispute Act, 134
contras, 198–202
   congressional policy toward,
     201–4, 212–17, 221
   U.S. covert support of, 201,
     204, 205, 212, 214–15, 217,
     220
   see also Iran-contra scandal
Conyers, John, Jr., 292
Corcoran, Thomas G. "Tommy
   the Cork," 286
Corporate Accountability Research Group, 71
corruption:
   actuality vs. perception of, 4–7
   changing standards on, 6, 14–
     15, 17, 34–35, 47, 187–88,
     190–91
   fundamental change in federal
     investigation of, 109–10
   methods of fighting, 8–11
   new breed of crusaders
     against, 8–11, 47, 59–60
   political and social critics of,
     25–27, 34–35

   reform efforts against, 4–11, 13
   relationship of scandal to, 4–7,
     13, 14
   stepped-up prosecution of, 5,
     7
Costello, Frank, 53
Cox, Archibald, 84
Crane, Daniel B., 69, 191
Crane, Philip M., 180
Cranford, John R., 314*n*
Cranston, Alan, 249–50, 254,
   255–56
Crovitz, Gordon, 312*n*
Credit Mobilier scandal, 3, 16,
   25
Current Affair, 70

dairy industry, 79
Dallas, 182
D'Amato, Alfonse M., 127, 278–
   79, 280
Dart, Justin S., 59
Dean, Deborah Gore, 159–60
Deaver, Carolyn, 299
Deaver, Michael K., 62, 74, 90,
   107, 160, 262, 271, 282,
   299
DeConcini, Dennis W., 249–50,
   254, 255–56
Defense Contract Audit Agency
   (DCAA), 126–29, 133–34
Defense Department, U.S., 133–
   41, 201, 224, 264, 293, 302
Defense Intelligence Agency,
   294
defense procurement, 110,
   126–41
Del Monte corporation, 79
Democratic Congressional Cam-
   paign Committee, 240, 241
Democratic House and Senate
   Council, 228–29
Democratic party, 10, 12, 22–24,
   42–43, 228–29, 230–31
Democratic-Republican party, 18

Democratic Steering and Policy Committee, House, 237
Dempsey, Charles L., 113, 142
Depew, Chauncey, 76
Depression, Great, 17, 152
Detroit News, 178
Diagnostic and Statistical Manual of Psychiatric Disorders, 192
"Diary of a Mad Congresswife" (Jenrette and Maxa), 171
Dies, Martin, Jr., 152
Dingell, John D., Jr., 87, 102, 107, 162–64, 166, 167
Dionne, E. J., 306n
Dinkins, Carole E., 104
direct mail, computerized, 229–30
District of Columbia Bar Association, 89
Division Air Defense (DIVAD), 128–29
Dixon, Don Ray, 235
Dixon, Julian C., 238, 242
documents:
    free access to, 40
    investigative journalism and, 77
    stealing of, 32, 34
Dodd, Thomas J., Jr., 31–35, 253
    censure of, 32–33, 34–35, 39, 256
    misappropriation of funds by, 32–33
    personal and office documents of, 32, 34
Dole, Robert, 45, 293
Donna Rice Story, The, 182–83
Donovan, Raymond J., 91–98, 107, 253
Dornan, Robert K., 67, 68
double billing, 32
Draper, Theodore, 312n
Drexel Burnham Lambert, 241
Durenberger, David F., 213, 236
Dyson, Roy P., 191, 192–93

Eagleton, Thomas F., 154–55, 157
Eastland, Terry, 308n
Eaton, Peggy, 18, 20
Edgartown District Court, 185
Education and Labor Committee, House, 145
Ehrenhalt, Alan S., 231, 305n, 313n
Eisenhower, Dwight D., 16, 296
elections:
    of 1964, 24, 190–91
    of 1968, 36
    of 1972, 60, 71, 224–25
    of 1976, 36, 42
    of 1980, 36, 54, 58, 60, 200, 286
    of 1984, 201, 203
    of 1988, 180
Elliott, Laura, 311n
Ellsberg, Daniel, 37
Employment and Housing Subcommittee, House, 148
Energy and Commerce Committee, House, 87
    Oversight and Investigation Subcommittee of, 153, 162–64
Energy Department, U.S. (DOE), 153, 154, 282
Entertainment Tonight, 70
entrapment, 112
entrepreneurs, 25, 27
environmental movement, 8, 29, 100–101
Environmental Protection Agency (EPA), 40, 100–102
    scandal of, 100–107, 109, 142, 150, 272, 282–83
Equal Employment Opportunity Commission (EEOC), 143–51
Ervin, Samuel J., 38, 206, 207, 208

Estes, Billy Sol, 21–23, 31, 33, 251
  federal subsidy programs exploited by, 21–22
  indictment and conviction of, 22, 28
Ethics in Government Act, 40–41, 42, 52, 53, 61, 72, 85, 107, 120
  amendments to, 96, 99–100, 105
Evans, Thomas B., Jr., 20, 179–80
executive branch:
  abuse of power in, 31, 36, 37, 39
  conflict of interest restrictions on, 40–41, 42
  corruption fighters in, 5, 11, 109–10, 112–14
  deception and lying in, 31
  federal investigators in, 109–10, 112–14
  legislative limitations on, 39, 40–41
executive privilege, 102–3

Fall, Albert B., 3, 16–17
Fedders, Charlotte, 186, 311n
Fedders, John M., 186
Feder, Ned, 162–63, 167
Federal Bureau of Investigation (FBI), 31, 37, 52, 92, 153, 156, 180, 190, 242–43, 263, 282, 290, 291
  Allen investigated by, 61, 62–63, 66, 72
  change and expansion of, 110–12
  Hoover's direction of, 110–11
  undercover operations of, 111–12, 171, 226
federal deposit insurance, 245, 246, 248–49

Federal Election Commission (FEC), 45, 46, 243–44, 264, 276
federal government:
  accountability of officials in, 4–5, 39–41, 42, 82
  growth of, 3, 6, 26
  public cynicism about, 2, 4, 7, 8–10, 25, 28, 29–31, 41, 57, 74
  restrictions on former officials of, 4, 40, 107
Federal Home Loan Bank Board, 235, 248
Federalist party, 18
Federal Reserve Board, 43
Ferraro, Geraldine, 275–81
Ferrugia, John, 67, 68
Field, Stephen J., 20
Fielding, Fred F., 186
Fifth Amendment, 152, 158, 159, 160, 212, 215
financial scandals, 3, 11, 21–27, 31–35, 79–80, 224–32
  amounts involved in, 3, 21, 24, 32, 60–61, 79, 80, 177, 225, 226, 290
  blackmail and, 17–18, 189
  bribery and, 3, 6, 16, 27, 37, 79, 92, 115, 119, 187, 279
  embezzlement and, 21, 289–90
  kickbacks and, 21–22, 24
  personal vs. political expenses and, 32–33, 39
  press coverage of, 61–62, 64, 80, 120, 236–37, 243
Fisher, Elizabeth W., vii
flag burning, 2, 4
Flake, Floyd H., 244
Fleming, Peter E., Jr., 116
Foreign Affairs Committee, House, 213
Foreign Agents Registration Act, 48

Foreign Intelligence Advisory Board, 299
Foreign Relations Committee, Senate, 269
Fortas, Abe, 190
Foundation for Public Affairs, 72
Foxe, Fanne, 20, 176, 177, 184
France, 33
Frank, Barney, 191–92, 193–96, 228
Frankel, Benjamin, vii
Freedom of Information Act, 40, 78, 129–30
Freedom of Information Clearinghouse, 71
Freeman, Orville, 22–23, 287
Fried, Charles, 295–96
Friedman, Milton, 162, 165
fundamentalism, religious, 38

Galbraith, Peter W., 269
Gallo, Robert C., 167
Gambino crime syndicate, 277
Garcia, Robert, 120
Gardner, Colleen, 178
Garfield, James A., 16
Garment, Leonard, 12, 308n
Garment, Suzanne, 12, 310n, 316
Garrett, Patty, 308n
gay-bashing, 193
Gellman, Kenneth, viii
General Accounting Office, 107
General Dynamics Corporation (GD), 127–30, 132
General Motors (GM), 29
General Services Administration (GSA), 42, 112, 297
General Telephone and Electronics (GTE), 135–37
Genovese, Vito, 53
Georgia Mafia, 43
Geraldo, 70, 181
Gergen, David R., 62
Gesell, Gerhard A., 218

Gettlin, Robert, 306n
Geyer, Georgie Anne, 193
Giaimo, Robert, 46
Gilded Age, 25
Gingrich, Newt, 232–34, 236
Ginsburg, Douglas H., 263, 282
Girl's Guide to Chaos, A, 172
Giuliani, Rudolph W., 117–18, 119, 121, 124
glasnost, 231–32
Glenn, John H., Jr., 44, 249–50, 253
Gobie, Stephen L., 194–95
gold market, 27
Gore, Albert, Jr., 154, 157
Gorsuch, Anne, see Burford, Anne
Gould, Jay, 27
Government Accountability Project, 148
Government Accounting Office, 145
Governmental Affairs Committee, House, 153–55
Government in the Sunshine Act, 40
Government Operations Committee, House, 148
Government Operations Committee, Senate, 43–44, 45, 46, 152
Graham, William R., 130–31
Grant, Ulysses S., 16, 25, 26
Grassley, Charles E., 127, 135–36
Gray, Edwin J., 12, 248–50, 252, 313n
Gray, William H., III, 242–44
Great Barbecue, 25
Great Hunting Lodge Caper, 224
Great Society, 144
Guatemala, 79, 214
Gulf of Tonkin resolution, 31
Gulf Oil scandal, 225, 255

Hamilton, Alexander, 17–18
Hamilton, Lee H., 213
Hanna, Richard T., 225
Harriman, Pamela, 229
Harris, Wiley P., 21
Hart, Gary, 15, 20, 181–83, 282
Harvard Law School, 38, 154
Hatch, Orrin G., 92
Hatfield, Mark O., 265–66, 282
Hawkins, Augustus F., 145
Hays, Wayne L., 20, 176–77,
  178
Heflin, Howell T., 253
Hefner, Hugh, 174–75
Helms, Jesse, 294
Henderson, Thomas H., Jr., 309n
highway safety, 29
Hill, Ralph, 23–24
Hobbs Act, 115
Holmes, Oliver Wendell, 239
homosexuality, 190–96
  admission of, 191–92
  changing standards on,
    192–93
  FDR's efforts to expose, 16
  page scandal and, 66–69, 191
  prostitution and, 67–69, 191,
    194–96
  taboo on discussion of,
    190–91
Honest Graft (Jackson), 240
Hoover, J. Edgar, 31, 110–11
Horner, Charles E., 296
House of Representatives, U.S.,
  39, 102
  ethics committee of, 15, 67–
    69, 187, 188, 195–96, 225,
    234–36, 238–39, 242, 276
  page scandal in, 66–69, 191
  Republican vs. Democratic
    status in, 230–31, 232, 234
  see also specific committees
Housing and Urban Development Department, U.S.
  (HUD), 107

scandal of, 113, 142, 158–61,
  285
Howe, Allan T., 178
Hubbard, Michael, 68
Hume, Ellen, 1
Hunt, Albert R., 285
Hustler, 173

Imanishi-Kari, Thereza, 162–67
impeachment, 206, 209
Imperial Presidency, 39, 83
impoundment, 39
independent counsels, 11, 87–
  91, 96–108, 120–21
  EPA scandal and, 103–7
  Iran-contra hearings, use of,
    198–99, 205–6, 210–14,
    220, 222
  see also special prosecutors
inflation, 244–45
influence peddling, 23, 24, 32,
  60, 80, 113, 159
Ink, Dwight A., 296–97
Inside Edition, 70
Inspector General Act, 40
inspectors general (IGs), 40,
  112–13
Institute for Policy Studies, 81
Interior Department, U.S., 100–
  101
Internal Revenue Service (IRS),
  45, 46, 195, 264
  scandal of, 3, 16
International Telephone and
  Telegraph, 24
investigative journalism, 77–82,
  275–76
  adversarial stance of, 77, 79,
    81–82
  dangers of, 80–81, 82
  definition of, 77
  fairness and accuracy issues
    in, 80–81
  proliferation of, 78
  techniques of, 78–80

Investigative Reporters and Editors, Inc. (IRE), 77–78
Iran:
American hostages in, 48, 54
U.S. arms shipments to, 204–5, 212, 217, 219
Iran-contra scandal, 11, 86, 90, 119, 198–222, 263–64, 270, 282
background and causes of, 199–201, 221
congressional investigation and hearings on, 158, 198–99, 206–13
coverup of, 210, 217
criticism of probe on, 86, 90, 209–10, 211
immunity issue and, 211
North testimony on, 158, 205, 208–9, 211, 213
Reagan and, 198, 199, 202–5, 206, 207, 209, 215, 217, 219, 220
trials stemming from, 211, 213–22
use of independent counsels and, 198–99, 205–6, 210–14, 220, 222
Watergate comparisons with, 198, 206–7, 208, 209
Iraq, 222, 270
see also Operation Desert Storm
Isserman, Maurice, 306n
Israel, 125

Jackson, Andrew, 18, 21
Jackson, Brooks, 185–86, 240, 313n
Jackson, Rachel, 18
James, E. Pendleton, 1
Japan, 60–61, 66, 294
Jaworski, Leon, 80
Jefferson, Thomas, 18
Jenkins, Walter, 24, 190–91

Jenrette, John, 171, 176, 225
Jenrette, Rita, 170–74, 176, 178, 225, 310n
John Houseman Theater Studio, 170
Johnny C, 53
Johnson, Lyndon B., 22, 190–91, 276, 306n
Bobby Baker scandal and, 23–25
Dodd scandal and, 32
political career of, 23–24, 30–31
Vietnam war and, 7, 30–31
Jo-Pel, 95
Jordan, Benjamin Everett, 24
Jordan, Hamilton, 50–55, 56, 89
drug allegations against, 52–53, 55
investigation and exoneration of, 53–55, 86, 99
reputation for crassness of, 50–51, 55
Judeo-Christian moral tradition, 14–15
Judiciary Committee, House, 150
Judiciary Committee, Senate, 107, 135, 290
Junior Chamber of Commerce, U.S., 14
junk bonds, 240–41
Justice Department, U.S., 31, 48, 49, 52, 85, 99–105, 109, 113–15, 210, 260, 272
Antitrust Division of, 263
Criminal Division of, 114, 129, 250
Defense Procurement Fraud Unit of, 129–30, 133, 134, 135–36
investigations by, 41, 45, 48, 53, 61–64, 72–73, 80, 99–100, 155, 156, 180, 241, 251, 263–66, 276, 278–79

Justice Department, U.S. (*cont'd*)
  Office of Legal Counsel in, 102
  organized crime strike force of, 111–12, 115–16
  Public Integrity Section of, 114–15

Kaiser, Frederick M., 312*n*
Kampelman, Max M., 118
Kassebaum, Nancy Landon, 63
Kaufman, Hugh, 101–2
Keating, Charles H., Jr., 249–56, 289
Keating Five scandal, 70, 249–57
Keker, John W., 218
Keller, Morton, 306*n*
Kellerman, Donald S., 305*n*
Kelley, Kitty, 301
Kelly, Richard, 226
Kelman, Steven, 309*n*
Kemp, Jack F., 158–59
Kempton, Murray, 281, 314*n*
Kennedy, Edward M., 16, 86, 88, 92, 185
Kennedy, John F., 7, 22–23, 173
  assassination of, 29–30
  on corruption, 287–88
  popularity and charisma of, 29, 30
  press protection of, 15
Kennedy administration, 7, 28, 30, 116
Kennedy Space Center, 131–32
Kenny, John V., 115
Kerner, Otto, Jr., 115
Kerr, Robert S., 23, 24
Key, Phillip Barton, 19
Keyworth, George C., 130
Khashoggi, Adnan, 182
Khomeini, Ayatollah Ruhollah, 205
kickbacks, 21–22, 24
King, Larry, 181

Kissinger, Henry, 212
Klein, Maury, 27, 306*n*
Kohut, Andrew, 305*n*
Kopechne, Mary Jo, 185
Koreagate scandal, 80, 225
Kotz, Nick, 78
Kraft, Joseph, 73–74
Kraft, Tim, 54
KTBC, 276
Kutler, Stanley I., 312*n*
Kwitny, Jonathan, 277

Labor Department, U.S., 113, 148–49
Lance, T. Bertram, 43–47, 50, 56
  bank fraud indictment and acquittal of, 45–46
  financial investigation of, 43–44, 46
  resignation of, 45
Landau, Barry, 52
Landauer, Jerry, 78–81
Landesman, Avrom, 154–55
Lantos, Thomas P., 148
Lardner, George, Jr., 92
Larry King Live, 181
Last Picnic, The, 172
Lavelle, Rita, 109, 272, 282
Lebanon, U.S. hostages in, 204–5, 212
Lederer, Raymond F., 226
Lee, Susan, vii-viii
Leggett, Robert L., 178
legislation:
  civil rights, 38
  covert activity, 39
  ethics, 38–42, 109–10
  federal campaign, 39, 71
  federal spending, 39
  inspectors general, 112–13
  political reform, 38–42
  special prosecutor, 53–54
  supplemental appropriations, 39
  troop commitment, 39

whistle-blower, 40
see also specific legislation
Letterman, David, 182, 311n
Levin, Carl M., 155
Levitas, Elliott H., 102
libel suits, 64, 65
Libya, 48–49
Lichtman, Allan J., 314n
lie detector tests, 53
Life, 182
Liman, Arthur L., 209
Lincoln, Abraham, 16
Lincoln Savings and Loan Association, 249–50, 252
Little Caesar, 115
lobbying, 4, 26, 178–79
    ex-government officials restricted on, 4, 40, 90, 107, 120
Long, Russell B., 33, 34, 256
Los Angeles International Airport, 242
Louisiana Territory, 33
Lukas, J. Anthony, 306n
Lukens, Donald E. "Buz," 186–87, 257

Maass, Arthur, 309n
MacBird (Garson), 30
McCain, John S., III, 249–50, 253, 256
McCarry, Charles, 307n
McCarthy, Eugene J., vii-viii
McCarthy, Joseph R., 33, 152, 160
McConnell, Malcolm, 309n
McDonald, Forrest, 310n
McFarlane, Robert C., 12, 203, 211–16, 217–18, 219, 282, 312n
McGrory, Mary, 277
McHugh, Matthew F., 195
Mack, John P., 237, 239, 282
McKay, James C., 90, 120–21, 261, 309n

Madison Hotel, 79
Madison Square Garden, 173
Making News (Mayer), 69
Malbin, Michael J., 309n, 312n–13n
Mallick, George A., 235, 238–39
Mann, Thomas E., 309n, 313n
Mansfield, Stephanie, 183–84
Marble Collegiate Church, 172
marijuana, 51, 282
Marshall, Thurgood, 144
Massachusetts Institute of Technology (MIT), 162
Masselli, Nathan, 93
Masselli, Pelligrino William "Billy the Butcher," 93
Maxa, Kathleen, 171–72, 310n
Maxa, Rudy, 51, 170–72, 176–78, 181, 182, 310n, 311n
Mayer, Martin, 69, 307n, 313n
media, 57–82
    competitive pressure within, 49–50, 69–70, 78, 80
    emotional impact of, 55–56, 69–70
    limitation of campaign spending on, 39
    newsgathering methods of, 15, 62, 64–66, 68, 69–70, 77–82, 266–68
    old vs. new standards of morality in, 15, 25, 34
    stakeouts by, 15, 62, 64–65, 181, 266
    see also investigative journalism; press; television; *specific media*
Meese, Edwin, III, 104–7, 283, 289–90
    Allen scandal and, 61, 63, 66, 72
    as Attorney General, 104–7, 118–19, 121, 124, 217
    confirmation hearing of, 12, 86–89

Meese, Edwin, III (cont'd)
  financial investigation of, 12,
    65, 120–21
  resignation of, 121
  Wallach and, 110, 118–21,
    124, 126
Melcher, John, 145–49, 310n
Merola, Mario, 94–95
Metzenbaum, Howard M.,
  87–88
Meyers, Roy C., 86–87
Miami Herald, 15, 78, 181, 184
Middlebury College, 279
Milken, Michael, 241
Miller, James C., III, 155
Miller, Richard R., 264
Mills, Wilbur D., 20, 176
Milton, John, 17
Mintz, Morton, 78
Missouri, University of, 77–78
Mitterrand, François, 15
Moe, Ronald C., 313n
Mondale, Walter, 275, 277,
  278
money-market funds, 245
Monimbo, 214
Monroe, Marilyn, 173, 175
Montuoro, Mario, 92, 93
Moon, Sun Myung, 194
Moore, Jesse, 132
Morgan, Peter W., 308n
Morgan, Ted, 305n
Morgenthau, Robert M., 116–17
Morrison, Alexia, 90, 100,
  104–5, 107, 261, 306n
mortgages, 245
Moynihan, Daniel P., 29
muckrakers, 25–26, 76
Myers, Michael J. "Ozzie," 226,
  282

Nader, Ralph, 8, 29, 70–72
National Aeronautics and Space
  Administration (NASA), 40,
  127, 130–33

National Association of Minority
  Contractors, 95
National Bank of Georgia, 43
National Cotton Advisory Com-
  mittee, 22
National Democratic Club, 229
National Institutes of Health
  (NIH), 162–67, 292
National Science Foundation,
  113
National Security Council
  (NSC), 63, 74, 202–4, 213,
  214, 263
Naval Investigative Service, 114,
  136
NBC News, 69
NBC-TV, 92, 181–82
New Deal, 152
newsletters, 78
Newsweek, 63
New York, N.Y., 26–27, 275–76
New York, 277
New York Blasters, Drillers and
  Miners Union, 92, 93
New York City Transit Author-
  ity, 95
New York Daily News, 290
New York Times, 34, 76, 120,
  160, 172, 178, 242, 275,
  276
NEXIS, 180
Nicaragua, 199–203, 233
Nields, John W., Jr., 209
Nixon, Richard M., 31, 36–39,
  60, 84, 233, 234, 297
  illegal campaign contributions
    to, 224–25
  political comeback of, 37–38,
    299
  political opposition to, 36–37,
    83, 206
  resignation of, 37, 43
  writing and personal appear-
    ances of, 37, 299
  see also Watergate scandal

Nobel Prizes, 161, 162
No Excuses jeans, 183
Nofziger, Franklyn C. "Lyn,"
   120, 121, 262–63, 267, 272
Noonan, John T., Jr., 305n
North, Oliver L., 204, 213–19,
   312n
   Iran-contra testimony of, 158,
      205, 208–9, 211, 213
   memos and diaries of, 214–17
   trial of, 211, 215, 217–19,
      220, 264, 289
North Carolina, Agricultural and
   Technical College of, 28
Northrop Corporation, 224
Nuremberg trials, 31

Obey, David, 238
Office of Government Ethics,
   155
Office of Management and Bud-
   get (OMB), 43, 44, 45, 144,
   153, 155, 247–48
Office of the Comptroller of the
   Currency, 44–45, 46
Olson, Theodore B., 90, 100,
   102–7, 109, 150, 257, 260–
   62, 265, 283
O'Neill, Thomas P. "Tip," Jr.,
   42, 158, 233
Operation Desert Storm, 65, 70,
   139, 270
Operation Ill Wind, 136–37,
   139, 140, 168, 292
Operation Uncover, 136, 139
organized crime, 92–94, 111–12,
   115–16, 277
Ornstein, Norman J., 143, 309n,
   313n
Ortega, Daniel, 233
Osnos, Peter, viii
Oswald, Lee Harvey, 30
O'Toole, Margot, 162, 164–67
Owen, Richard, 125
Oxford English Dictionary, 14

page scandal, 66–69, 191
Panama Canal, 54
Pappas, Tom M., 192–93
Parker, Alan, 308n
Parkinson, Paula, 20, 78,
   178–81
Park Police, U.S., 176
Patchett, Gary, 309n
Peale, Norman Vincent, 172
Pearson, Drew, 32
Pell, Claiborne H., Jr., 269
Pentagon Papers, 31
Penthouse, 173, 179
People, 174, 181
Percy, Charles, 45
Permanent Select Committee
   on Intelligence, House,
   201
Perot, H. Ross, 294
Perry, Robert M., 308n
Persian Gulf, 70, 270
Pessen, Edward, 305n
Phelan, Richard J., 234–35, 238,
   239
Philadelphia Inquirer, 275
Philadelphia Story, The (Barry),
   172
Philippines, 294
Phillips, David Graham, 76,
   307n
Picardo, Ralph, 92
Pickelle, Paul W., 279
Pierce, Samuel R., Jr., 107,
   159–60
Playboy, 170–74, 177, 179, 180,
   184
Playboy Clubs, 174
plumbers, 37
Podhoretz, Norman, vii–viii
Poindexter, John M., 205, 211,
   212, 218–20
police, 29, 67, 176
political action committees
   (PACs), 39, 227–31, 240,
   254–55, 303

political campaigns:
  disclosure and limitation of
    funding for, 4, 6, 39, 227,
    251
  fund-raising for, 228–31, 240
  illegal contributions to,
    224–25
  improper use of funds for, 33,
    60
  rising costs of, 5, 228–30, 255
  television and, 229–30
political parties:
  communications systems of,
    75
  contributions to, 22, 23, 24
  decline in influence of, 7–8,
    58, 228
  effects of scandal on, 10, 13
  see also specific political parties
political reform movements,
    25–27
  legislation stemming from,
    38–42
  post-Watergate, 35–42
politicians:
  disclosure requirements of, 39,
    40–41, 278, 300
  press relations of, 34
  private vs. public lives of,
    9–10, 15, 19, 196–97,
    266–68
Postal Service, U.S., 113
Powell, Jody, 48, 51
POW/MIA issue, 293–94
Pratt, Richard T., 248
press:
  anonymous sources in, 19–20,
    55, 63, 74–75, 79
  criticism of, 58, 64, 65, 181
  defensiveness of, 65
  dependence on sources by,
    74–75
  growth in power of, 7, 34, 57–
    58, 75, 82
  ideological bias of, 75, 81–82

  hostility to authority in, 75–
    77, 82
  inaccuracy in, 27, 63–64, 65
  innuendo and suggestion in,
    66
  leaks to, 18, 19–20, 52, 62,
    63, 74–75
  legal threats to, 64, 65
  moralism in, 34
  nonofficial sources for, 70–72
  publicizing of official malfea-
    sance in, 4, 5, 9, 15, 19–20,
    22, 25–26, 32, 34, 44–46,
    60–67
  sensationalism and, 2, 19–20,
    55–56, 66, 70
  see also investigative journal-
    ism; media; specific media
press releases, 59
Pritikin, Nathan, 118
pro bono work, 118
Profaci, Joseph, 277
Progressive Era, 13
prostitution, 67–69, 186, 191,
    194–96
Provenzano, Anthony "Tony
    Pro," 92, 93
Proxmire, William, 45, 46
Pryor, David H., 147, 148, 249,
    313n
pseudo-events, 184
public relations firms, 59
Puccio, Thomas P., 111–12
Puritanism, 47

Qaddafi, Muammar al, 48
Quaaludes, 51
Quayle, J. Danforth "Dan," 179,
    180
Quinn, Sally, 50, 51

Racketeering Influenced and
    Corrupt Organization Act
    (RICO), 115–16, 120–24,
    134

railroads, 27
Railsback, Thomas F., 179
rape, 186
Ray, Elizabeth, 20, 176–78, 195
Reader's Digest, 132
Reagan, Nancy, 58–63, 301
  political influence of, 63
  extravagant tastes of, 59
  Japanese interview with, 58,
    61–62
Reagan, Ronald W., 107, 179,
    186, 239, 296
  criticism of, 58, 60, 208, 285
  elections of, 36, 56, 58, 60,
    200, 203, 286
  Iran-contra scandal and, 198,
    199, 202–5, 206, 207, 209,
    215, 217, 219, 220
  staff relations with, 60, 62, 63,
    74, 91, 94, 120
  Supreme Court appointments
    of, 105–6, 108
Reagan administration, 1, 10–
    12, 118, 130, 261
  corruption and scandal in, 6,
    56, 58–66, 119, 137–38,
    159, 198–222, 270
  environmental policy of, 100–
    103
  foreign policy of, 203–4, 206,
    220
  low ethical standards seen in,
    5, 6, 56, 58, 59–60, 219,
    223, 285
  money and power flaunted in,
    58–59, 229
recreational drugs, 8, 41, 51,
    52–53, 55, 67–68, 112, 279,
    282
Reflections of a Public Man
    (Wright), 235
Regan, Donald T., 203, 206, 248
Rehnquist, William H., 106
Republican National Committee,
    170

Republican party, 10, 11–12, 22,
    230, 232
Reynolds, James, 17–18
Reynolds, Maria, 17–18
Ribicoff, Abraham, 45
Rice, Donna, 20, 78, 181–84,
    282
Richardson, Elliot L., 84
Riegle, Donald W., 178, 249–50
Rivera, Geraldo, 181
Rivers, Joan, 183
Robb, Charles S. "Chuck," 176
robber barons, 25, 27
Robinson, Edward G., 115
Rockefeller, John D., 25
Rodino, Peter W., 103–4
Rodriguez, Paul, 194
Rogovin, Mitchell, 52
Roosevelt, Franklin D., 16, 98,
    152, 285, 286
Roosevelt, Theodore, 76
Rose, Charles G. "Charlie," III,
    228
Roth, William V., Jr., 127
Roybal, Edward R., 225
Rubell, Steve, 52, 55
Russert, Timothy J., 69–70

Sabato, Larry J., 314*n*
Safire, William, 48
Saigon, fall of, 212
St. Germain, Fernand, 45, 46
St. Louis Post-Dispatch, 148,
    289–90
St. Paul Pioneer Press Dispatch,
    78
Sandinistas, 199–200, 214, 233
San José Mercury News, 78
Saudi Arabia, 212
Savage, Gus, 187, 195, 257
savings and loan institutions
    (S&Ls), 24, 235, 244–52
  losses of, 247–48, 252
  regulation of, 245–47, 249
  of Texas, 235, 249

savings and loan scandal, 5, 11, 223, 244, 250–57
background and causes of, 244–48, 289
congressional hearings on, 253–54, 256
cost to taxpayers of, 1, 3, 244, 251, 257
press coverage of, 1–2, 4, 78, 252–54
Savonarola, Girolamo, 14
Scalia, Antonin, 106–8
scandal:
components of, 14
consequences of, 4, 11, 13, 15–16, 18–19, 20, 259–84
coverup efforts and, 16, 30, 37, 210, 217, 273
definition of, 14
dismissals resulting from, 3, 23
financial dimensions of, 1, 3, 21, 24, 244, 251, 257
highly placed vs. low-level officials in, 3–4, 23, 25
historical overview of, 2–5, 10–11, 13–35
indictments and convictions resulting from, 3, 5, 16–17, 24, 38, 187
momentum of, 65–66, 70
morale and efficiency compromised by, 4, 168
moralism inherent in, 4, 6, 8–10, 14–15
numbers of officials involved in, 3–4
personal costs of, 259–84
political survival of, 16, 18, 20, 24, 185, 187, 191, 299
public taste for, 2, 4, 17, 55–56
purported causes of, 4–5, 6, 13, 57
recurring elements in, 17, 21

relationship of corruption to, 4–7, 13, 14
reputations damaged by, 55, 95, 157–58, 180
rise in incidence of, 2–6, 9–10
see also financial scandals; sex scandals; specific scandals
Scheuer, James H., 229
Schiavone Construction Company, 91–92, 94–95, 96
Schmults, Edward C., 103–4
Schrager, Ian, 52
Schram, Martin, 69, 307n
Science, 167
scientific fraud, 161–67
Scott, Hugh D., Jr., 225
Secord, Richard V., 204
Secret Service, 163–66, 257
Securities and Exchange Commission (SEC), 6, 45, 46, 87, 186, 225
Select Committee on Standards and Conduct, Senate, 25
Dodd case and, 32–33
Select Committee on Presidential Campaign Activities, Senate, 38
Senate, U.S., 23–25
causes and frequency of censure in, 33
ethical oversight and investigation in, 24–25, 32–33, 38, 39, 134, 225, 249, 253, 257
moral criticism of, 34, 76
physical violence on floor of, 33
unwritten ethical standards of, 35, 43
Senior Executive Service's Performance Review Board, 147
sex scandals, 11, 15, 17–21, 67–69, 169–97
press coverage of, 176–78, 182–84, 187, 190, 192–93

see also blackmail; homosexuality; prostitution
sexual coercion, 188–90, 192–93
sexual harassment, 186, 188–89
sexual revolution, 173, 174–75
Seymour, Whitney North, Jr., 90
Sharansky, Avital, 124–25
Sharansky, Natan, 124–25
Sharon, William, 20
Shepherd, John C., 289–90
Shultz, George P., 203
Sickles, Daniel E., 19–20
Sickles, Teresa, 19
Sierra Club, 101
Silent Spring (Carson), 29
Silveira, Milton, 131–32
Silverman, Leon, 91, 93, 94, 95–96, 308n
Silver Slipper Club, 176
Simon, Justin D., 310n
Sinner, Denise, 289–90
Sirica, John J., 38
sit-ins, 28
Small, Pamela, 236–37
Small Business Administration, 87
Smith, William French, 63, 72–73, 83, 92–93, 180
Somoza, Anastasio, 200
South Korea, 80, 87, 225
South Vietnam, 30, 212
Soviet Union, 200, 204, 231–32
space program, 127, 130–33
Speakes, Larry, 61, 62
special interest groups, 58, 70–72
  ideologically based corruption fighting by, 7–10, 70–72
  indebtedness of congressmen to, 5, 6
  see also lobbying; political action committees
special prosecutors, 41, 52–54, 61, 62, 83–86, 93–96, 99, 210

see also independent counsels
Spider Web, The (Thomas), 26
Sporkin, Stanley, 6, 244
spying, 37
stakeouts, 15, 62, 64–65, 181, 266
Stark, Andrew, 310n, 315n
Stark, Fortney H. "Pete," 151
"Star Spangled Banner, The," 19
State Department, U.S., 264, 286, 295, 296, 299
Steffens, Lincoln, 76, 307n
Stein, Jacob A., 87–89, 308n
Stern, Larry, 78
Stevens, Theodore F. "Ted," 154
Stewart, Walter W., 162–63, 167
sting operations, 112
stock market crash of 1929, 17
Strasser, Fred, 309n
Strauss, Robert, 118
street demonstrations, 7, 8, 28, 29
Studds, Gerry E., 69, 191
Studio 54, 51–53
Sullivan, Brendan V., Jr., 158
Summers, Mark W., 305n
Sununu, John, 286–87, 299
Superfund, 101–2, 109, 272
Supreme Court, U.S., 144, 220, 263
  Reagan appointees in, 105–6, 108
Susman, Stephen D., 238–39
Swanberg, W.A., 305n

Tammany Hall, 26–27
tape recordings, 187, 297
tariff legislation, 33
Taulbee, William P., 20
Tax Reform Research Group, 71
Taylor, Stuart H., Jr., 309n
Teapot Dome scandal, 3, 16–17
Teicher, Howard R., 263, 270

telecommunications industry, 27
telegraph, 27
television, 28, 57, 271
  competition among networks
    of, 69–70
  Iran-contra hearings on,
    208–9
  political campaigns and,
    229–30
  S&L hearings on, 253–54
  Watergate hearings on, 38,
    198, 206–7, 209
Texas:
  annexation of, 33
  S&Ls of, 235, 249
Texas, University of, 170
Third World, 30
Thomas, Clarence, 144–48,
  310n
Thomas, Margaret Susan, 26,
  306n
Thurmond, Strom, 308n
Tidal Basin incident, 176
Time, 32, 270
Time-Life News Service, 57
Today, 92
Tolchin, Martin, 76–77
Toles, 231
Toobin, Jeffrey, 312n
Torrijos, Omar, 54
Tower, John G., 189–90, 205,
  213, 299
Tower Commission, 205, 213, 263
Towey, James, 266
trade associations, 33
Transportation Department,
  U.S., 113
Treason of the Senate, The
  (Phillips), 76
Treasury Department, U.S., 44,
  248
Trento, Joseph J., 132, 309n
Truman, Harry S., 16
Tsakos, Basil, 265–66, 282
Tucker, Katie, 193

Tufts University, 162
Tupper, Kari, 188–89
Turner, Ted, 69
Tuttle, Holmes, 59
Twain, Mark, 25, 35
Tweed, William Marcy, 26–27
Tweed Ring, 26–27
20/20, 53, 182

Un-American Activities Commit-
  tee, House (HUAC), 28, 29
  Investigations Subcommittee
    of, 152
undercover operations, 111–12,
  171, 226
Unification Church, 194
United Nations Human Rights
  Commission, 118
United Press International
  (UPI), 60, 190
United States Information
  Agency (USIA), 264, 296
Unsafe at Any Speed (Nader), 29
Unsoeld, Jolene, 229
Untermeyer, Charles G., 290–91
U.S. News & World Report, 182

Valentine, Itimous T. "Tim," Jr.,
  229
Vanderbilt, Cornelius, 25
vending machines, 23–24
Vesco, Robert, 60
Vietnam war, 10, 212, 244–45,
  293
  opposition to, 7, 9, 30–31, 37,
    57–58, 71, 174–75
  political climate after, 39,
    57–58
  treated as scandal, 31
Village Gate, 30

Waggoner, Joseph D. "Joe," 178
Wall, M. Danny, 313n
Wallach, E. Robert, 110, 118–
  19, 121–26, 233, 257

Wall Street Journal, 1, 60, 64, 67, 78–80, 116, 153, 155, 185–86, 236, 240, 275, 285

Walsh, Lawrence E., 86, 90, 206, 211, 213, 215, 217, 220

Walters, Barbara, 182

Warner, John W., 136

War Powers Resolution, 39

Warren Commission, 30

Washington, George, 112

Washington Blade, 194

Washingtonian, 186, 189

Washington Post, 48–49, 75, 78, 92, 132, 194, 240, 266, 275
   financial scandal stories in, 61–62, 64, 80, 120, 236–37, 243
   sex scandal stories in, 176–78, 182, 183–84, 187, 190, 192–93
   style section of, 50, 236–37

Washington Post Magazine, 51, 171

Washington Times, 194–95

Watergate scandal, 71, 297, 299
   coverup attempts and, 37, 269
   Democratic headquarters break-in and, 36, 38
   foreign response to, 14–15
   ideological and partisan roots of, 38
   Iran-contra comparisons with, 198, 206–7, 208, 209
   political climate after, 2–7, 9–12, 35, 36, 38–41, 47, 50, 56, 69, 72, 83, 111, 112, 126, 198, 208, 210
   revisionism on, 37–38
   televised hearings on, 38, 198, 206–7, 209

Watt, James G., 100–101, 159

Ways and Means Committee, House, 176

Webster, William H., 61, 62–63, 72

Wedtech Corporation, 119–24, 267

Weinberger, Caspar W., 203

Weiss, Baruch, 125

Weld, William F., 130

Wertheim Schroeder, 241

Western Hemisphere Affairs Subcommittee, House, 213

Whiskey Ring scandal, 3, 25

whistle-blowers, 40, 68

white-collar crimes, 111, 116–18

Whitehead Institute for Biomedical Research, 162

wife-battering, 185–86

Williams, Edward Bennett, 158

Williams, Harrison A. "Pete," Jr., 225–26

Williams, John J., 24

Wilmington *News-Journal,* 78, 179–80

Wilson, James Q., vii–viii, 305n

wiretaps, 15

Witt, Elder, 305n

women's movement, 175

Woodward, Bob, 75, 307n

Wooten, James T., 81

Wright, James C. "Jim," Jr., 232–42, 282, 299, 313n
   charges against, 234–36
   press coverage of, 81, 236, 240
   resignation of, 239–40, 241, 242

Wright, Joseph R., Jr., 144, 153–57, 208, 282

Yarborough, Ralph W., 22

Young, John A., 178

Young Americans for Freedom, 94

Young Men's Christian Association (YMCA), 190

Zaccaro, John A., 276–80

Zaccaro, John A., Jr., 279–80

Zaire, 187

Zombie Island Massacre, 172

ABOUT THE AUTHOR

Suzanne Garment is a resident scholar at the American Enterprise Institute for Policy Research in Washington, D.C. She has taught political science at Harvard and Yale, written on American antitrust policy, and served as special assistant to the U.S. Permanent Representative to the United Nations. For six years, her column, "Capital Chronicle," appeared in *The Wall Street Journal.* She lives in Washington with her husband and daughter.